Romanticism and the Vocation of Childhood

William Wordsworth in the Lake District, at cross-purposes.

Romanticism and the Vocation of Childhood

Judith Plotz

palgrave

ROMANTICISM AND THE VOCATION OF CHILDHOOD
© Judith Plotz, 2001

All rights reserved. No part of this book may be used or reproduced in any manner whatsoever without written permission except in the case of brief quotations embodied in critical articles or reviews.

First published 2001 by
PALGRAVE
175 Fifth Avenue, New York, N.Y. 10010 and
Houndmills, Basingstoke, Hampshire RG21 6XS.
Companies and representatives throughout the world

PALGRAVE is the new global publishing imprint of St. Martin's Press LLC Scholarly and Reference Division and Palgrave Publishers Ltd (formerly Macmillan Press Ltd).

ISBN 0-312-22735-3 hardback

Library of Congress Cataloging-in-Publication Data

Plotz, Judith A. (Judith Ann), 1938–
  Romanticism and the vocation of childhood / by Judith Plotz.
    p. cm.
  Includes bibliographical references and index.
  ISBN 0-312-22735-3
  1. English literature—19th century—History and criticism. 2. Children in literature. 3. Wordsworth, William, 1770-1850—Criticism and interpretation. 4. Lamb, Charles, 1775-1834—Criticism and interpretation. 5. De Quincey, Thomas, 1785-1859—Criticism and interpretation. 6. Coleridge, Hartley, 1796-1849—Criticism and interpretation. 7. Romanticism—Great Britain. I. Title.

PR468.C5 P57 2001
820.9'352054—dc21   00-066876

A catalogue record for this book is available from the British Library.

Design by Westchester Book Composition.

First edition: July, 2001
10 9 8 7 6 5 4 3 2 1

Printed in the United States of America.

This book is for Paul Plotz, a grown-up.
Where the heart lies, let the brain lie also.

Contents

Acknowledgments ix

Permissions xi

Preface   The Romantic Fixation   xii

Chapter One   "One Shape, One Feature, and One Size": Romanticism and The Quintessential Child   1

Chapter Two   More Clouds Than Glories: Wordsworth and The Sequestered Child   41

Chapter Three   Charles Lamb and The Child Within   87

Chapter Four   Little Mr. De Quincey and The Affliction of Childhood   129

Chapter Five   The Case of Hartley Coleridge: The Designated Genius   191

Notes   253
Works Cited   275
Index   295

Acknowledgments

This little book has been a long time in the making and is indebted for inspiration, critique, and reinforcement to many who may by now have forgotten all about it. But I have not forgotten—it would be to forget myself—the essential early discussions of this project with Gill Cook, Barbara Finkelstein, Richard Flynn, Peggy Garrett, David Perkins, Barbara Rosen, Fran Stephens, and Rajeswari Sunder Rajan. Nor can I ever forget the generous help of Grevel Lindop, Anne Scott MacLeod, and Anya Taylor. I am grateful to the students in my graduate seminars in Romanticism and Childhood—especially to Supriya Goswami, Joetta Harty, Karen O'Connor-Floman, Michael Slevin, and Catherine Smith—for lively and profitable discussions. Above all, I am grateful beyond words to Marilyn Gaull, the most generous, encouraging, and sagacious of editors.

I am deeply indebted to my never-to-be-adequately-thanked chair at George Washington University, Faye Moskowitz, for her magical gift to me of a term of reduced teaching. To other colleagues at George Washington, I also owe serious debts of gratitude: to research librarians Scott Stebelman of the Gelman Library and Daphne Pierre of the Himmelfarb Library of Medicine, for their swift and indispensable help in a series of difficult searches; to Ann Romines, scholar of American childhood culture, for her collegiality; to Chris Sten for his long support, as chair and as friend; to Bob Ganz and Jon Quitslund for their years of friendly opposition; to You-me Park and Raji Sunder Rajan for their oppositional friendship; to Judith Harris for her Romantic faith; to Cynthia Leenerts and Honey Nashman for their indefatigable support; to Rod French and Robert Kenny for their administrative humanity; and to Miriam Dow for her relentless generosity.

I am grateful too to Dr. Martha Denckla, Dr. Marius Valsamis, and Dr. John Zinner for fielding various pediatric and psychiatric questions and sending me in quest of fruitful answers. Thanks for their lively Romantic questionings and valuable answerings to the late Jack Frey, Gerd El-Naggar, Richard Flynn, Tim Fulford, Judith Harris, Angela Leonard, Becky Martin, Thomas McFarland, James McGavran, Meenakshi Mukherjee, David Perkins, Pam Presser, and Harish Trivedi. To my son and fellow scholar John M. G. Plotz, I have a special debt of gratitude for his support in general and his Wordsworthian suggestions in particular. This project also owes much to the stimulating interrogatories of many colleagues in the Children's Literature Association—Gillian Adams, Elizabeth Goodenough, Meena Khorana, Valery Krips, Claudia Nelson, Marilynn Olson, Jean Perrot. Mary Galbraith's wonderful paper on attachment theory at the 1999 Children's Literature Association Conference spoke to my condition at a crucial moment. I wish to express my thanks to the Harry Ransom Humanities Research Center of the University of Texas for access to the Hartley Coleridge Papers, part of their extensive holdings of Coleridge Family Papers. To Mrs. Joan Coleridge and the Coleridge Estate, I am deeply grateful for permission to quote from previously unpublished Hartley Coleridge materials. Portions of chapter four appeared in three articles in *The Wordsworth Circle*; very small portions of chapter five appeared in articles in *Children's Literature* and in *Studies in Romanticism*. I am most grateful to the kindness and encouragement of the editors of these publications.

Last and most, I thank my family. If my own childhood still remains largely golden in memory, it is because of the labors of my indomitable, great-hearted mother, Helen Abrams, the companionship of my brother, Zachary, and to the never-forgotten voice of my late father, Harold Abrams, reciting poetry to me. I am also grateful to my much-missed mother-in-law, Helen Plotz, a gifted children's anthologist, who stimulated and heartened me through many years. To my sons, John and David, and the joy their vivid childhood inspired, I attribute the genesis of this book. But it is the competently and lovingly grown-up John and Lisa and David and Hanna who encouraged and supported me in the last sticky days of its completion. My beautiful, beloved, and brand-new granddaughter Noa, a true child of joy, has renewed my fervor for this study. But deepest thanks, now as always, go to Paul.

Permissions

For permission to use Max Beerbohm's "Wordsworth in the Lake District, at cross-purposes," acknowledgment is made to the Estate of Max Beerbohm, by permission of London Management. Copyright © by the Estate of Max Beerbohm, by permission of London Management.

Excerpt from *The Letters of William and Dorothy Wordsworth: The Middle Years. Part I,* edited by Ernest de Selincourt, 2nd ed., revised by Mary Moorman (1969), p. 286 appears in chapter 2. Copyright © 1969 by Oxford University Press. Reprinted by permission.

Excerpts from the Hartley Coleridge Papers appear throughout chapter 5. Acknowledgment is made to Mrs. Joan Coleridge and to the Harry Ransom Humanities Research Center, The University of Texas at Austin. Reprinted by permission.

Preface

The Romantic Fixation

My aim in *Romanticism and the Vocation of Childhood* is to investigate the fixation on childhood by a group of Romantic writers. This fixation applies both to the figure of the child who is "fixed" and reified as *The* Child and to the figure of the adult writer who is self-defined and given a vocation—a meaningful work and a meaningful life—by a commitment to childhood. Fixation implies intense preoccupation that is a virtual collector's passion for children; a developmental arrest manifest both in the child who is written and the adult who writes; and the representational violence that, in the language of the OED definition, reduces "a volatile spirit or essence to a permanent bodily form." Such a fixation secures the vastly amorphous category of childhood in a single ideal form of an uncannily beautiful child—Wordsworth's "little mountaineer" of "We are Seven," for example: "She had a rustic woodland air, / And she was wildly clad: / Her eyes were fair, and very fair" (*PW* 73).[1]

Others have pursued this track before me but none more sardonically than Max Beerbohm.[2] His famous 1904 caricature from *The Poet's Corner*, "William Wordsworth in the Lake District, at cross-purposes" raises some of the questions that also trouble me in this book. In his caricature of interrogating adult and stupefied child, tall poet and small girl, an inspired revision of "We are Seven,"[3] Beerbohm sketches a dolorous lakeside scene. The background consists of medium-size black pyramidical mountains and gigantic gray pyramidical mountains with bulbous clouds veiling the dim glories of a setting sun. The middle ground is a gray lake. In the foreground on the olive-drab turf are two dour figures. A vertical rain washes over everything and, in the one touch of warm color, slightly reddens the poet's beaky nose. The child, scrawny and short, is an unexpressive figure in an unbecoming white smock and huge poke-bonnet. Her mouth is open (she is perhaps a mouth-breather); her snub nose points upward toward her interlocutor. She does not seem at all quick on the uptake: all marks of intellect are obscured by her hat and there is a hint of goiterous rural idiocy in her receding chin and gaping mouth. But her face turns up toward the adult's; perhaps she has been hypnotized by the blank lenses of his spectacles. Almost twice the height of the child, Wordsworth dominates the picture. His enormous feet (evidence of pedestrian prowess) are planted firmly on the ground. One of his large heavy hands grasps a cane; the other points or pokes at the child about at the level of her jugular vein. It is evident from his sour expression (his mouth turns down at an angle of forty-five degrees) that the child is not giving satisfaction. "A crabbed and morose old gentleman" (Thompson qtd. in Riewald 42), he is not the twenty-eight-year old radical who wrote "We are Seven" but a top-hatted Victorian Wordsworth, a figure of canonical and clerical authority, black-clad even to the gaiters. He is white-haired, wrinkled, hollow-cheeked, gaunt, flat-footed, and short-sighted. His spectacles are large, round, and blank; his eyes cannot be seen behind the lenses. His jaws are so lank that he may be toothless; his spectacles are so useless that he may be blind. Certainly Beerbohm's poet is clueless, "at cross-purposes," puzzled and distressed by the stupid child before him. This is not a radiant wise child with "eyes . . . fair, and very fair," but a dim and unappealing little peasant made uneasy by a peculiar adult fixation. The Beerbohm caricature raises a whole series of questions about how and why aging writers might look fixedly at little girls and little boys. Why is this Romantic scene so doleful, featuring more clouds than glories? Why is this Romantic child eyeless and speechless? Why is this Romantic poet heavy-handed, flatfooted, and myopic? Why are there only the two of them present? Why is there no human society? Doesn't the child have playmates? Doesn't the adult have a family? Why are they standing around in the rain instead of going home? What does age want from youth? Why that firmly grasping forefinger? Why won't he let her go? Why, in other words, the focus on isolated children in an evacuated rural space?

Beerbohm's comic creepiness defamiliarizes the familiar phenomenon Geoffrey Hartman has elegantly called "eudaemonia" and James Kincaid has more ironically labeled "child-loving,"[4] that is, the fixation on a child as the embodiment of eternal youth and fullness of being. Such relentless focus on an unchanging child forever fixed in childhood is an important Romantic trope: the trope of the Erl King's grasp. In Goethe's 1782 poem, well known to English readers through both Walter Scott's and Monk

Lewis' translations of 1791 and 1798, the uncanny Alder King of the woods carries off a beautiful boy to certain death and an uncertain realm of perpetual play. He snatches the boy away from his father who is purposively and progressively traveling with his son through the woods toward the productive world of getting, spending, and growing up. The Erl King's grasp is a violence committed in the name of beauty: ("Ich liebe dich, mich reizt deine schöne Gestalt / Und bist du nicht willig, so brauch ich Gewalt": "I love you, your lovely form; / If you don't come with me willingly, I'll use force"). The Erl King arrests, eternalizes, and destroys the living child for any productive human purpose.

Such uncanny fixity on arrested beauty fascinates the writers treated in this book. Wordsworth, for example, represents a beautiful toddler at play in a London theater as forever fair:

> He hath since
> Appeared to me ofttimes as if embalmed
> By Nature—through some special privilege
> Stopped at the growth he had—destined to live,
> To be, to have been, come and go, a child
> And nothing more . . . (1805 *Prelude* 7: 388-405)

Lamb invents a "Child Angel" whose "portion was, and is, to be a child forever . . . to keep perpetual childhood." To remain fixed in childhood is the admonition of Hartley Coleridge to the young: "Stay where thou art / Thou canst not better be." Leigh Hunt (himself cruelly mocked by Dickens for his "boy-man" demeanor as the manipulatively childlike Harold Skimpole of *Bleak House*) glosses early childhood death as an aesthetic preservative: "The other children grow up to manhood and womanhood and suffer all the changes of mortality. This one alone is rendered an immortal child." Thomas De Quincey treats the recursion to childhood, constructed as the grounding self, as the profoundest act of self-discovery and self-assertion: "In some potent convulsion of the system, all wheels back into its earliest elementary stage. . . . The romance has perished that the young man adored, the legend has gone that deluded the boy; but the deep, deep tragedies of infancy . . . these remain lurking below all, and these lurk to the last."

This is a book that fixes on this Romantic fixation of "the eternal child," the "immortal child," "the child forever," the "child / And nothing more." This fixation is especially (though not exclusively) apparent in the four male Romantic writers who are the subject of this book, four writers who found a life-defining vocational interest in arresting and invoking childhood as a permanent state to provide both subject matter for the work and meaning for the life—thus "the vocation of childhood." This book is therefore not a survey of all texts touching childhood written during the Romantic period but the study of a particular modality.

The omission of any extended discussion of William Blake or of the important children's writers of the period is a function of their generally developmental and integrated view of childhood. Neither Blake nor such Romantic children's writers as Anna Letitia Barbauld, Mary Wollstonecraft, Maria Edgeworth, and Barbara Hofland, reify childhood as a state of being or represent the Child as different in kind from the adult. Though it is hard to overstate the importance of Blake's *Songs of Innocence and Experience* to such Victorian and Edwardian cultists of childhood as Algernon Swinburne, Alice Meynell, and Kate Greenaway, his vocabulary of Innocence and Experience and his nostalgic pastoral imagery is co-opted principally by those who ignore Blake's critique of Innocence. Blake's Innocence is a dialectical contrary, existing as a way station to something larger, freer, and more empowered. Similarly the children's writers of the Romantic era— in particular Barbauld, Edgeworth, Wollstonecraft, and Hofland—see childhood as continuous with rather than distinct from adulthood. Largely uninterested in staging "The Child" in a decontextualized state of being, these women writers—unlike the four male Romantics who reify the Child—focus on multiple states of social and ethical becoming rather than on unitary states of being. Their stories stage interactions among members of a family or other small communities in which children learn the life lessons that help them to function as self-regulated adults. Jean Piaget has argued that what has often been praised by Romantics as a childlike sense of wonder has more to do with an authoritarian social structure than with the intuitions of the child's nature. It is the habit of cooperating and negotiating among equals that makes one who is a child chronologically an adult psychologically. In such an egalitarian spirit, the largely progressive children's writers—Barbauld, Edgeworth, Wollstonecraft, Hofland—model such self-legislating behavior for children. Their world thus features the interassimilation of adulthood and childhood

I see the extreme hostility displayed by Lamb, Coleridge, and De Quincey toward Barbauld and Edgeworth—they are mocked as preachy bare-and-bald ladies suffering from a lack of imagination as an innate sexual disability—as a defensive maneuver against their very different model of childhood.[5] With the exception of Blake, the male Romantics produce children not as integrated into the social realm but as a race apart. This difference is inscribed in the Erl King maneuver. The male Romantics practice a kind of forcible repatriation of childhood, a patriarchal kidnapping that wrests children away from the female sphere, so powerfully patrolled by important women writers, and sequesters them in a paternally circumscribed realm of permanent difference.[6]

This book investigates this realm of difference by focusing on the work of four male Romantic writers from three different generations whose work was produced between the 1790s and the 1850s—Wordsworth and Lamb born in 1770 and 1775, respectively; De Quincey born in 1785; and Hartley Coleridge, born in 1796. De Quincey and Hartley Coleridge, in fact, belong as much to Victorian as to Romantic culture. The work of these four writers urgently and centrally represents and produces childhood as a separate sphere of being that offers the adult a professional and personal vocation: a profession devoted to exploring, describing, circumscribing, worshipping, preserving childhood; and an inner life invigorated by a connection to the taproot.

The embrace of absolute child is both a creative and destructive force in these four Romantics. I began this study almost ten years ago out of a quite simple enchantment at the beauty and power of their Romantic depictions of childhood. But the more closely I considered the textual representations of childhood, the darker they seemed and the less tenable generalizations seemed about Romantic childhood joy and idyllic innocence. Hugh Cunningham and others have already written cogently on Romantic omissions, that is, on the ways in which the Romantic discourse of childhood has worked ideologically to obscure the actual lives of the children of the poor, those I call in chapter one "the children of history." My emphasis, however, is less on what these Romantic writers omit than the ways in which they multiply illuminate what De Quincey calls "the affliction of childhood." It is for that reason that the book concludes with an extended treatment of Hartley Coleridge who more than any other Romantic figure embodies and judges the Romantic vocation of childhood.

Chapter One

"One Shape, One Feature, and One Size": Romanticism and The Quintessential Child

> *He insisted upon speaking of The Child as a sort of abstract metaphorical figure—one of those Virtues or Graces represented in stone on public monuments . . . full of Needs that are in danger of being "unmet" and of Creative Potential that must be "developed" . . . [She] yawns angrily. There is no Child, she wants to shout . . . there are only children.*
> —Alison Lurie, Foreign Affairs *(1984)*

Colonizing the New Continent

Horace Elisha Scudder, editor of *The Atlantic Monthly* during the last decade of the nineteenth century, was a man who loved both children and large cultural generalizations about them.[1] When with magisterial authority Scudder looked back on his century from 1885, he declared it an age of exploration with Wordsworth the principal explorer. Through the agency of the Romantics, the nineteenth century had "discovered, as no one had done before" "childhood as a distinct, individual element of human life" (473, 474). Scudder declared that

> The discovery of this new continent of childhood by such explorers of the spiritual world marks the age as distinctly as does the discovery of new lands and explorations in the earlier renaissance. It was indeed one of the great signs of the period ushered in by the French Revolution and the establishment of the American republic, that the bounds of the spiritual world were extended. ("Childhood in English Literature" 477)

2   *Romanticism and the Vocation of Childhood*

This Victorian claim of a Romantic discovery of childhood was widespread.[2] De Quincey, writing in 1851, paid Wordsworth the tribute due to the great explorer. It was Wordsworth's revelation that "'*The Child is father of the man*'" that called "into conscious notice the fact, else faintly or not at all perceived, that whatever is seen in the maturest adult and bearing fruit, must have preexisted by way of germ in the infant" (*CW* 1: 121). Regarding childhood as *terra incognita,* De Quincey noted "that mighty silence which infancy is privileged by nature and position to enjoy . . . *which Wordsworth was also the first person to notice*" (*CW* 1: 122, italics mine).

By the late nineteenth century, such claims to childhood as a domain for exploration and to Wordsworth and his contemporaries as its explorers had become commonplace. In "The Legend of Childhood" (1887), a sequence of eighteen poems designed to repair the omissions of centuries, poet and essayist William Canton categorized children as hitherto "Unnoticed by philosopher or sage," but now "These bright-eyed chicks" are acknowledged as what they have always been "in every age / The one supreme majority . . ." (*A Lost Epic* 134). In this age of discovery, this "supreme majority," the important resource, can no longer remain unknown. By 1892, anthologist Wilfred Meynell could claim that "the nineteenth century has almost discovered the Child" (*The Child Set in the Midst* ii).

Throughout the great nineteenth-century age of geographic colonization, "this new continent of childhood" is also named, mapped, explored, and colonized. Increasingly throughout the nineteenth century, British childhood—like the East, like the Empire—becomes a career. The new continent of childhood—as a domestic colony, a remembered internal realm, an accessible otherness—opens up creative space for a number of writers, notably Romantic conservatives like Wordsworth, De Quincey, and Lamb. No longer the humble sphere of flogging schoolmasters and shadowy governesses, childhood becomes a profession, a vocation, even a habitat for scientists, anthropologists, philosophers, novelists, and poets.

The metaphor of discovery produces strangeness and wonder where there had been familiarity. The differentness of children and the separateness of the child world come to the fore. For some writers the discontinuity is so extreme as to mark children as a different species, "'these small school-going people of the dawn' . . . The pigmy people," as William Canton frames it (*IP* 31). For Walter Savage Landor the species difference is no mere metaphor: "Children are not men and women, they are almost as different creatures, in many respects, as if they were never to be one or the other; they are as unlike as birds are unlike to flowers and almost as blossoms are unlike birds" (Meynell 153). For Lamb the difference is principally moral: "From what have I not fallen if that child I remember was indeed myself" ("New Year's Eve," *Works* 2: 28).

Every child is an island—at any rate a peninsula, separate from the adult world and from its own adult self. De Quincey characteristically represents childhood as a world elsewhere:

> Infancy . . . is to be viewed, not only as part of a larger world that waits for its final complement in old age, but also as a separate world of itself; part of a continent, but also a distinct peninsula. Most of what he has the grown-up man inherits from his infant self; but it does not follow that he always enters upon the whole of his natural inheritance. (*CW* 1: 121)

In the many imaginary island kingdoms invented by and for nineteenth-century children—De Quincey's dreadful Gombroon, mathematical Thomas Malkin's orderly Allestone, Hartley Coleridge's oratorical Ejuxria, the Brontes' treacherous Gondal and Gaaldine, James Barrie's eclectic Never-Never Land—the children or their surrogates are emphatically enisled and separated off from the adult world as if the inhabitants belonged to a different species from adults. Thomas De Quincey's people, the Gombroonians, are in fact sub-humans with tails, somewhat like chimpanzees. Indeed, the sub-genre of children's fantasy and the island narrative both sustain nineteenth-century assumptions of childhood as a world, or at least a treasure island apart.

Childhood, in fact, operates both as an adult imaginary kingdom and as an adult research institute. As imaginary kingdom, it is almost always figured as a lost garden paradise presided over by a child-redeemer or child-idol: "Infancy is the perpetual Messiah which comes into the arms of fallen men, and pleads with them to return to paradise" (Emerson, "Nature" 54). "What little of Paradise we see still upon earth is due," essayist Amiel wrote, to the presence of childhood. "Without fatherhood, without motherhood I think that love itself would not be enough to prevent men from devouring each other . . ." (Ivor-Parry 30). "Childhood hath saved me!" Bronson Alcott claimed (Strickland 43); childhood can save us all, William Canton urged: "Oh, you who are sad at heart, or weary of thought, irritable with physical pain, coax, beg, borrow, or steal a four- or five-year-old and betake you to blowing bubbles in the sunshine of your recluse garden" (*IP* 61). And Wilfred Meynell enjoined "that the worship of the Child should be fostered" (xxii) (meaning not the Christ Child but Everychild).[3] Even as an object of knowledge rather than of worship, the *differentness* of children, or rather the Child, becomes a major area for nineteenth-century study, both scientific and literary. Even before Freud and the Freudians, the psychology of childhood is the object of study by Johann Heinrich Pestalozzi, Friedrich Froebel, and their followers: for example, Baroness Bertha von Marenholtz-Bulow's *The Child and Child-Nature* (1868); William Hailmann's *Law of Childhood* (1889). The anthropology of childhood is obsessively documented in such works as *The Child and Childhood* (1898) by Alexander Chamberlain, *Child Culture in the Home* (1898) by Marsha Mosher, *Child Lore* (1879) by Clara Bates, and even *Childhood and Ponyhood Blended* (1909) by Oscar White. The sociology of childhood is treated as well in, for example, *The Children of the Future* (1898) by Nora Smith, *The Century of the Child* (1898) by Ellen Key. So too a trove of largely forgotten literature of the late nineteenth century centered on the separate world of childhood, delivering to its adult readers reports from this alien realm. Thus Adelaide Smith's *Child Dialect Verse* (1908) treats the language of the tribe; anthologies such as *Child Life in Literature* (1900) and *Child Life in Tale and Fable* (1899) by Etta Austin McDonald recount its exotic lore. John Greenleaf Whittier produced two volumes of child study: *Child Life: A Collection of Poems* (1871) and *Child Life in Prose* (1874); James Whitcomb Riley *A Child-World* (1896).

As the late-nineteenth-century idiom of Child Study, Child Life, Child Dialect, Child World, Child Lore indicates, Victorian writers assume and produce a being who is no longer seen, in Scudder's words, as in the BW ("Before Wordsworth") era "as one of a group, as part of a family" but as "a distinct, individual element" (474), a quintessential Child. This Quintessential Child is the product of a Romantic Discourse of Childhood that is drawn from a few Romantic writers, notably Wordsworth, the Coleridges, Lamb, and De Quincey. It is not *the* defining discourse of Romanticism—there is no such thing—but *a* discourse that is intelligible, self-consistent, and effective at producing a Quintessential Child who figures powerfully in Golden Age children's literature, especially male-authored fantasy literature, and in high Victorian and Edwardian Anglo-American fiction and poetry as well. I am reluctant to label this Quintessential Child—largely the product of limited readings of Wordsworth, De Quincey, and Lamb—as "the" defining Romantic Child, although others (and I too) have done so before. The diverse representation of childhood in Romantic novels, Romantic children's literature, and in the mass of Romantic period poetry makes nonsense of a single Romantic type of child.[4] But it is from Romantic texts, notably those of Wordsworth, Lamb, Coleridge, De Quincey and their epigones that Victorian writers were able to piece together a new Discourse of Childhood that produced and naturalized "The Child," as both the normative human being and also the fetishized "sublime object" that deploys multiple cultural fantasies, to use Slavoj Zizek's useful term (Rose xv). This discourse made it easy, unavoidable almost, to assume the living reality and splendor of such an essential being as *The* Child, who is unmarked by time, place, class, or gender but is represented as in all places and all times the same. This discourse makes it desirable and possible and attractive for adults to make a career by colonizing and inhabiting childhood.

The Singular Discourse of the Essential Child

Romantic Discourse produces the Child, a timeless figure of essential childhood. This representative being is "father of the man" and "the evolutionary being of our species" (Chamberlain); it "always *finds* and never seeks" (Coleridge, "Christabel"). This being is frequently heralded by the definite article and honored by capitalizations, "The Babe leaps up on his mother's arm," "Blest the infant Babe," "behold the Child" (Wordsworth). Within the singular discourse, the chief difference between children and adults is that there are many adults but only one child. Adults differ from one another and within themselves; they are divided by multiple individual differences of history, profession, circumstance. But children do not differ from each other. To Hartley Coleridge, for example, the essential child is fungible and archetypal because instinct with the life force: "all babies are so much alike / 'Twere easier far to single out a spike, / The fairest spike in all a field of barley," than to distinguish one baby from another. This uniformity augurs the final redemption "at the last day" when all the saved, all in the form of Baby Jesus

>Shall spring from earth and meet the promised skies,
>All in one shape, one feature, and one size . . .
>Alike all blessed, and alike all fair,
>And only God remember who they were ("To Dear Little Katy Hill,"
> *CPW* 191)

The often ungendered representation of "the Child" noted by James Kincaid (64-65) derives from an identification of the child, that "breathing image of the life of Nature," with the undifferentiated life force.

This essential timeless figure is principally produced by two initiatives: the identification of childhood with Nature—both as Law and as the green world—and the attribution to children of an autonomous, unitary consciousness.

As Nature, the child is "the evolutionary being of our species," embodying what is best in the physical endowment of humanity and also a link to mute insensate things. In an age dominated by vitalist biological ideas, children are regularly depicted as the indigenes of nature: at once *originary* models of ideal nature, unselfconscious and self-sufficient models of natural beauty, and irrepressible engines of vital power. It is axiomatic for Friedrich Froebel, nineteenth-century founder of the kindergarten movement, and for Gertrude Jekyll, the great Edwardian authority on British gardening, that children and gardens go together.[5] The figure of the child in the garden is for both the emblem of true developmental education. "Child-nature" has an affinity with green growing things, an affinity explored in Jekyll's famous *Children and Gardens* (1908). Equally important, children mentally resemble the most valuable and most "natural" kind of adult, the creative genius, master of genial and generative growth: "Every child is, to a certain extent, a genius, and every genius is, to a certain extent, a child" (Schopenhauer qtd. in Chamberlain, *The Child and Childhood in Folk-Thought* (379). As Immanuel Kant's *Critique of Judgment* argues, the kind of creative consciousness known as "genius" is a principle of growth by which "nature gives the rule to art" (156). Although Kant does not himself identify genius and childhood, his emphases encourage such a link. As a spontaneous faculty inexplicable by its possessor, genius does not require education; for it is "not a mere aptitude for what can be learned by a rule" (150) but a force of nature. Everychild can be seen in important ways already as a creative genius, a solitary idealist fashioning a visionary world of its own.

The equation of childhood with the ancient and abiding realm of nature universalizes and essentializes the child as a figure of nature rather than culture who is therefore the guardian of human nature. This equation is powerfully established in Friedrich von Schiller's great essay *On Naive and Sentimental Poetry* (1795). Here Schiller defines modernity (the "sentimental") in terms of self-consciousness estrangement from nature, and antiquity (the "naive") in terms of harmony with nature. Modernity is self-consciousness, antiquity nature. Schiller assumes nature to be the sole form of pastness that cannot be voided by modernity; it is timelessly available. Writing in 1795, in full consciousness of the French Revolution and of the Terror, Schiller balances the serenely conservative world of nature against the troubled modern realm associated with radical self-consciousness. If the carnage of the Revolution was, as Schiller implies, the work of idea-driven self-conscious men emancipated "from moral compulsion" (189), then the realm of nature stands as counterpoise and stabilizer with children as the unquestioned indigenes of its timeless realm:

> There are moments in our lives when we dedicate a kind of love and tender respect to nature in plants, minerals, animals, and landscape, as well as to human nature in children . . . not because it gratifies our understanding or taste . . . rather, simply *because it is nature* . . . Nature, considered in this wise is for us nothing but the voluntary presence, the subsistence of things on their own, their existence in according with their own immutable laws. . . . Particularly powerfully and most universally this sensitivity to nature is given expression at the instance of such objects as stand in close connection with us, affording us a retrospective view of ourselves, and revealing more closely the unnatural in us, as, for example, in children and childlike folk. (83-86)

Schiller's nature is defined by the unconflicted, unself-conscious, spontaneous "subsistence of things on their own, their existence according with their own immutable laws." Of all human beings, children in their early years most seem to exist "in according with their own immutable laws." As supremely adequate expressions of the life of nature, children are obedient to the deepest natural law that rolls through all things. Thus to submit to childhood's law rather than to break the child's will is the Romantic note. Emerson delighted in the baby's lawless law-unto-itself: "Infancy conforms to nobody; all conform to it, so that one babe commonly makes four or five of the adults who prattle and play to it" ("Self-Reliance" 148). Alice Meynell describes a child as unpredictable yet as deeply lawful as a songbird: "You cannot anticipate him, Blackbirds, overheard year by year, do not compose the same phrases; never two leit-motifs alike. Not the tone but the tune alters. With the unconvenanted ways of a child, you keep no tryst"; you are "fellow traveller with a bird" (*The Children* 9). Absolute as nature is absolute, the child keeps his own season, Meynell claims: "Flowerlike," the child blooms in winter. "He overcomes both heat and cold by another climate, which is the climate of life . . ." (*The Children* 121-22). As a being, in Coleridge's words, "that always finds, and never seeks" ("Christabel" 235), the child in nineteenth-century poetry is regularly depicted as a figure of plenitude, absolute in himself: "Dare not bless him!" Elizabeth Barrett Browning enjoins presumptuous parents, "but be blessed by his peace" ("A Child Asleep," 257).

The identification with natural law means that children can be figured in both fixed and in dynamic terms, as likely to be figures of abiding being as figures of surging vitality. Children take on the conservative authority of nature in various ways. Before acquiring a differentiated national language, the infant's comfortably monotonous "brook-like gurglings . . . the catholic speech of infancy" expresses the unebbing resource of nature:

> But well for us that there is something yet,
> Which change cannot efface, nor time forget,
> The patient smile of passive babyhood . . .
> Let mutability, then, work its will,
> The child shall be the same sweet creature still ("To K.H.I." *CPW* 181-82)

By living among children and wandering in such texts as *In the Gardens of Childhood,* adults can be stabilized:

> All the good and wholesome feeling which is intertwined with childhood and the cradle is one of the secrets of the providential government of the world. Blessed be Childhood for the good it does, and for the good is brings about carelessly and unconsciously, by simply making us love it and letting itself be loved. What little of Paradise we see still upon this earth is due to its presence among us. Without fatherhood, without motherhood, I think that love itself would not be enough to prevent men from devouring each other. (Amiel, in Ivor-Parry 30)

Because children are deemed free of the imprint of their culture, they often are framed as figures of extreme antiquity, the original human model. William Canton's "Legend of Childhood" (1902) features a philosopher who muses: "To think these mites . . . / Should be as ancient as the Miocene, / That ages back beneath a palm-tree's shade / These rosy little quadrupeds have played . . ." ("A Philosopher," *The Legend of Childhood* #4, *The Comrades*). Hartley Coleridge opposes the archaic culture of childhood to the individuality, mechanism, and institutional rationality of his own age:

> the literature of the nursery has every mark of extreme antiquity; an antiquity far beyond the reach of chronology, or written records. Oral tradition, a musical accompaniment, a quaint simplicity of phrase, a number of allusions to forgotten circumstances; a variety of readings . . . a prevalence of the supernatural . . . above all, the utter uncertainty—nay, the absence of so much as a rumor, as to the author of these truly popular compositions—these are the characteristics that can meet only in productions of the remotest era; such as our lullabies, nurses songs and fondling ditties . . . So intimately intertwined are these madrigals with the fibres of the brain, that it is not without effort we remember that they must alas have been made at

sometime by somebody.—We rather deem them like the song of the birds, "a natural product of the air" . . . They were originally derived from an age anterior to letters; and they still pertain to the unlettered part of human life.

Hartley goes on to fantasize a nightmare vision of modern mechanized child rearing—"A single engine will put in motion as many cradles as spindles; and official nurses, appointed by the committee, will sing 'Songs of Reason' to the grinding of a steam apollicon":

> . . . there is still, thank heaven, in the kind, sensible hearts of English mothers, a genial feeling of old times about a nursery. When I see a numerous small family at play, my mind sinks back, through dream and vision, to the world's infancy. In the life, the innocence, the simple bliss before me, I hail a something that is not changed. The furniture of a well-littered play-room reminds me of Chaldea, Egypt, Etruria, and the Druids . . . ("A Nursery Lecture by an Old Bachelor," *Essays and Marginalia* 1: 305)

Like nature in its seeming immunity to contemporary culture, the child is thus an "old fashioned" stabilizing figure.

If the nature analogy sometimes implies the distantly archaic, it can also imply a contemporary dynamism and an authority linked to science. The habitual metaphorical identification of children with vitalistic life processes of movement (represented by air, breeze, wind) or of growth (represented by gradual plant growth) ties them into natural law. The movement is usually airy, elemental, planetary; the growth botanical—thus Longfellow's claim that "a boy's will is the wind's will"; and Wordsworth's garden girl: "Three years she grew in sun and shower . . ." In a telling botanical metaphor, Coleridge depicts children as the life-sustaining plants whose function is the "keeping up the stock of *Hope* in the great organized Body of the whole Human Race, in all men considered as the component Atoms of MAN, as young Leaves are the organs of supplying vital air to the atmosphere" (*NB* 2: 2549). Coleridge in particular habitually likens his children to spirits of elemental air. Little "doted-on Hartley—he moves, he lives, he finds impulses from within & from without—he is the darling of the Sun and of the Breeze! Nature seems to bless him as a thing of her own! He looks at the clouds, at the mountains, the living Beings of the Earth, & vaults & jubilates!" (*CCL* 1: 625). He is "indefatigable in Joy—a spirit of Joy dancing on an Aspen Leaf. From morning to night, he whirls about, whisks, whirls, and eddies, like a blossom in a May-Breeze" (*CCL* 2: 668). Using "the air and the Breezes as skipping Ropes," (*CL* 2: 746), Baby Hartley seemed to his father "a perpetual Nitrous Oxyde" (*CL* 1: 612), that exhilarating (and dangerous) laughing gas Coleridge had whiffed in Humphrey Davy's Bristol laboratory. Just as nitrous oxide was revealed in all its exhilarating force by modern chemists of genius, Joseph Priestley and Davy, so childhood was an equally buoyant, exhilarating natural force being opened to the world. Coleridge habitually depicts children as figures of elemental natural energy. In one brilliant description he underlines the analogue between the two frisking Coleridge boys and the wild-swept trees beneath which they play:

> It is in very truth a sunny, misty, cloudy, dazzling, howling, omniform Day / & I have been looking at as pretty a sight as a Father's eyes could well see—Hartley & little Derwent running in the Green, where the Gusts blow most madly—both with their Hair floating & tossing, a miniature of the agitated Trees below which they were playing / inebriate both with the pleasure—Hartley whirling round for joy—Derwent eddying half willingly, half by the force of the Gust—driven backward, struggling forward, & shouting his little hymn of Joy. (*CCL* 2: 871-72)

A similar identification of childhood with global movement and power is asserted in "An Unknown Child-Poem" (1887), William Canton's strange tour-de-force in the manner of Thomas Carlyle's *Sartor Resartus*. The poem is winkingly attributed to a German poet, "Altegans," the "Old Goose," an appropriate alter ego for the dotingly paternal Canton, author of latter-day nursery rhymes as a Victorian Father Goose. The "child poem," "Erster Schulgang" ("The First Day of School"), attributes to the world's children the vivid energy, the diversity, the "Natural Supernaturalism" that Carlyle had imputed to the miraculous natural universe (*Sartor Resartus* 254-67):

> The poem opens with a wonderful vision of children; delightful as it is unexpected: as romantic in presentment as it is commonplace in fact. All over the world—and all under it too, when their time comes—the children are trooping to school. The great globe swings round out of the dark into the sun; there is always morning somewhere; and for ever in this shifting region of morning-light the good Altegans sees the little ones afoot—shining companies and groups, couples and bright solitary figures; for they all seem to have a soft heavenly light about them! . . . The morning side of the planet is alive with them; one hears their pattering footsteps everywhere. And as the vast continents sweep "eastering out of the high shadow which reaches beyond the moon" . . . and as new nations, with *their* cities and villages, their fields, woods, mountains and seashores, rise up into the morning-side, lo! fresh troops, and still fresh troops, and yet again fresh troops of "these

small school-going people of the dawn" ... What are weather and season to this incessant panorama of childhood? The pigmy people trudge through the snow on moor and hillside; wade down flooded roads; are not to be daunted by wind or rain, frost or the white smother of "millers and bakers at fisticuffs." Most beautiful picture of all, he sees them travelling schoolwards by that late moonlight which now and again in the winter months precedes the tardy dawn. (*IP* 31-32)

Childhood energy and gusto mimic the dynamism of the great turning globe itself. In one popular nineteenth-century anthology piece, Charles Tennyson Turner's "Letty's Globe," little Letty, a three-year-old Britannia, plays in "her world-wide bliss" with "a colour'd sphere / Of the wide earth" so that "old empires peep'd / Between her baby fingers" until finding England on the map, she bends: "And, while she hid all England with a kiss, / Bright over Europe fell her golden hair" (Miles 57). The girl's natural exuberance serves to gloss and legitimate as natural law the process by which the lucky Letty (Letty=Letitia=fortunate) and the fortunate British empire command the globe.

As these tropes signify, childhood is charged with the surging energies of natural processes. For some nineteenth-century commentators, therefore, children are *the evolutionary representatives* of the human species. There is but a single step between admiration for the process of vitality embodied in the child and the embrace of continuing potentiality—perpetual childlikeness—as the proper destiny of the human species. Indeed D. G. Brinton, an American anthropologist, citing Havelock Ellis, argued that the goal of evolution was the *immaturing of the human species.* The goal of evolution was toward childlikeness:

> The child, the infant in fact, alone possesses in their fullness "the chief distinctive characteristics of humanity. The highest human types, as represented in men of genius, present a striking approximation of the child-type. In man, from about the third year onward, further growth is to some extent growth in degeneration and senility." Hence the true tendency of the progressive evolution of the race is to become childlike ... (qtd. in Chamberlain, *Child and Childhood in Folk-Thought* 2)

In a remarkable work published in 1900, *The Child: A Study in the Evolution of Man,* Alexander Francis Chamberlain, professor of Anthropology at Clark University, argued that human growth must in its inevitable evolution and should in its willed progress toward improvement be a movement into greater and greater childlikeness. More and more, he considered, it would be wise and necessary to learn to interassimilate children's traits with those of adults. Coleridge had commented on "the wisdom & graciousness of God in the infancy of the human species" in providentially shaping "its beauty, its long continuance" into the means of creating the greatest of all human institutions, the family (*NB* 330). Chamberlain too finds in protracted human childhood the providential wisdom of evolution. Protracted youth is what makes humanity sapient—and the longer the childhood, the wiser the species:

> In many respects this lengthening of the period of growth or adolescence in man is one of the most remarkable phenomena of his existence—intrauterine life, infancy, childhood, youth, seem all to have increased in duration, for the shaping of the human being, and the complicated environment accompanying modern civilization tends to lengthen more and more the period of immaturity. In a sense, then, the child is really "father of the man," for the modern man is becoming more and more of a child, or rather the modern child is losing less and less of childhood in the process of becoming a man. (8-9)

Echoing the theologian Friedrich Schleiermacher's hope that "being a child must not hinder becoming a man; becoming a man must not hinder being a child" (9), Chamberlain predicts that future evolution will make it possible for human beings for the first time in history to fulfill the promise of their childhood and fully tap child's play as the source of ever-progressive creativity. Genius, defined as a type of "prolonged infancy," will become the normal rather than the exceptional human condition:

> It is in large part through the preservation and further development of the resemblances to the young that the highest human likeness and affinities are secured. Rather the parent strives to be like the babe than the babe to be like the parent. The things often foreshadowed in the child seem to be those which will one day be the most valuable possession of the race. (445)

Chamberlain reads the child as the biological prophet of the human species:

> The child, in the helpless infancy of his first year, in his later activity of play, in his *naivete* and genius, in his repetitions and recapitulations of the race's history, in his wonderful variety and manifoldness, in his atavism and his prophecies, in his brutish and his divine characteristics, in the evolutionary being of our species, he in whom the useless past tends to be suppressed, and the beneficial future to be foretold. In a sense he is all. (464)

As "the evolutionary being of our species," the carrier of change, the child is both goal and source of human nature.

The essentializing Romantic discourse attributes the authority of Nature to this child who is a figure of natural law, of archaic being from time immemorial ("rosy little quadrupeds"), and of lawful evolutionary development. As an unthreatening figure of safe change, the child brings together law-driven spontaneity, abiding permanence, and dynamic movement and development. But as Chamberlain's vocabulary of brutish-divine paradox indicates, childhood is not construed simply as the sphere of unselfconscious spontaneous energy and blind growth. It is not simply as the most natural of human beings—natural and unconscious like "a *bee,* or a *dog,* or a *field of corn*" (Coleridge, *Biographia* 2: 140)—that the child is of interest to the Romantics. It is by reason of children's mental powers as well. "Nothing," Bronson Alcott once adjured his skeptical wife, "is too metaphysical for the mind of a child" (Strickland 43).[6]

The mental qualities imputed to childhood are those befitting a solitary creative genius who in isolation from human society is able to form unitary visions of a world instinct with meaning. Within the Romantic discourse of essential childhood, the mind of the child is set up as a sanctuary or bank vault of valuable but socially-endangered psychological powers: idealism, holism, vision, animism, faith, and isolated self-sufficiency. From these powers is derived the spiritual authority that made Wordsworth speak of the child as a "seer blest" and De Quincey praise the child's "special power of listening for the tones of truth" (*CW* 1: 122). It is through these powers of consciousness, that the solitary child becomes, especially in the writings of Wordsworth and Coleridge, both the symbolic representative of the creative mind and the repository of creative power to be reclaimed by the retrospecting adult self.

This Romantic discourse supplies a cluster of cognitive qualities among which childhood idealism is primary. Children are innate Berkeleyans for whom the Idea, whether defined as the thoughts of their own minds ("The indomitableness of the spirit within me," in Wordsworth's formulation), or more grandly as their intimations of the spiritual force that sustains the world, is more real than mere physical reality: "I was often unable to think of external things as having external existence, and I communed with all that I saw as something not apart from, but inherent in, my own immaterial nature. Many times while going to school have I grasped at a wall or tree to recall myself from this abyss of idealism to the reality . . ." (Wordsworth, *Prose* 3: 194).

This "abyss of idealism" is the *ordinary habitat* of the normal child who is not imprisoned and deformed in a noxious environment. The idealist imposition of an intuited form on the material world is the ordinary work of childhood: "To that dream-like vividness and splendor which invest objects of sight in childhood, everyone, I believe, if he would look back, could bear testimony . . ." (*Prose* 3: 194-95)." This propensity to subject the thing to the thought, Coleridge also takes as the norm of the human mind. In his own childhood, Coleridge notes, "I never regarded my senses as in any way the criteria of my belief. I regulated all my creeds by my conceptions, not my *sight*." (*CL* 478-79). His usual boyhood habit was "to *abstract* and as it were unrealize whatever or more than common interest my eyes dwelt on; and then by a sort of transfusion and transmission of my consciousness to identify myself with the Objects" *The Friend* 1: 521n).

Coleridge was pleased to note and to stimulate the same idealism in his first-born child as validating his view of idealism as the normal childhood mode of thought—normal and exemplary like normal vision. Hartley Coleridge's youthful idealism, his father's boast (and to a great degree his father's creation), early became part of the folklore of Romanticism. Of baby Hartley, aged one "Mr Poole . . . used to remark as a curious fact—that the little fellow never shewed [*sic*] any excitement at the *thing,* whatever it was, but afterwards, often when it had been removed, smiled or capered on the arm as at the *thought* of it" (*CCL* 5: 113). By the age of four, the boy, at his father's urging, could "abstract" and "unrealize" himself enough to note "that there might be five Hartleys, Real Hartley, Shadow Hartley, Picture Hartley, Looking Glass Hartley, and Echo Hartley" (*CCL* 2: 673). In his self-abstraction, Hartley as a child was reported to be indifferent to such treats as a long-anticipated wheelbarrow ride that he daydreamed through, later apologizing: "The pity is, the pity is that I'se-[*sic*]-always thinking my thoughts" (Southey 1: 241). At four, Hartley was reported to have said, "speaking of some Tale & wild fancy of his Brain—'It is not yet, but it will be—for it *is* and it cannot always stay *in* here' (*pressing one hand on his forehead and the other on his occiput*)—'and then *it will be*—because it is not nothing'" (Coleridge, *NB* 3: 3547). And at seven Hartley treated his uncle Southey to "a history of the Kings of England, who are to be," defending his prediction on the grounds that "it must be something or it would not be in my head" (Southey 1: 240). Of Hartley's childhood distinction among his multiple physical and mental selves, Crabb Robinson noted that the boy "must have been drawn to reflect on what Kant calls the great and inexplicable mystery, viz. that man should be both his own subject and object, and that these should yet be one" (1: 44). Whether this assessment of the toddler's mental powers was accurate is less interesting than Crabb Robinson's casual willingness to take idealism as the native cast of childhood thought.

The child idealist is a stock hero or heroine in Romantic literature. The child of Wordsworth's "We are Seven" denies death any dominion over her resolutely intact family. In like manner, Blake's innocent chimney sweeper sees no contradiction between the physical shearing of little Tom Dacre ("who cried when his head / That curl'd like a lamb's back was shav'd") and the continued existence of his curls in the mind's eyes ("Hush, Tom! never mind it, for when your head's bare / You know that the soot cannot spoil your white hair"). Even Dickens' crippled Jenny Wren, the doll's dressmaker of *Our Mutual Friend,* though prematurely shrewish and worldly, can reclaim childhood in her reverie of flowers:

> I wonder how it happens that when I am work, work, working here, all alone in the summer-time, I smell flowers . . . [This] is not a flowery neighborhood. It's anything but that. And yet as I sit at work, I smell miles of flowers. I smell roses, till I think I see rose-leaves lying in heaps, bushels, on the floor. I smell fallen leaves, till I put down my hand—so—and expect to make them rustle. I smell the white and the pink May in the hedges, and all sorts of flowers that I never was among. For I have seen very few flowers indeed, in my life. (226-27)

Such idealism is not conceived as a neutral quality; it is intensely prized. In the Intimations Ode, Wordsworth explicitly links access to the "abyss of idealism" both with the power of poetry and the very will to life. Idealism, the power to impute meaning and value of the material universe, belongs in infancy to all human beings and in adulthood only to the chosen:

> Such, verily, is the first
> Poetic spirit of our human life,
> By uniform control of after years,
> In most, abated or suppressed; in some,
> Through every change of growth and of decay,
> Pre-eminent till death (*Prelude* 2: 260-65)

Along with idealism, the Romantic discourse of childhood privileges holism and imaginative synthesis, what Kate Douglas Wiggin called "the heaven-born imaginative faculty [that] is the heritage of every child" (Ivor-Parry 177). Thinking synthetically rather than analytically, habitually intuiting a whole overarching pattern or informing emotion before attending to particular parts, children are unifiers. This unitary empathetic knowledge is selfless in the sense that it is unreflective, unselfconscious, and fully absorbing. Children are unitary thinkers first, Coleridge intensely believed, and only later learn to think analytically. Whether speaking of "a boy, sucking an Icicle with what affectionate Remembrance of a Lollipop" (*NB* 1: 1805) or of Babies who "touch *by taste* at first—then about 5 months old they go from the Palate to the hand—& are fond of feeling what they have tasted" (*NB* 1: 924), or of "A child scolding a flower in the words in which he had himself been scolded & whipt" (*NB* 1: 789), his constant theme is the unitary power of the child's intellect:

> In the child's mind there is nothing fragmentary; its numeration table is truly Pythagorean. The numbers are each and all, units and integers and slowly and difficultly does it exchange this its first awakened arithmetic for that of aggregation, apposition, in one word, of result. (*Coleridge on Logic and Learning* 127)
> I saw in early youth, as in a dream, the birth of the planets; and my eyes beheld as *one* what the understanding later divided into (1) the origin of the masses, (2) the origin of their motions, and (3) the site or position of their circles or ellipses. (*Anima Poetae* 77)

The assumption that children naturally move from the whole to the part is deep-rooted in Romantic thought. Affective-sensuous unitary knowledge is prior to all else: "Hart.[ley] seemed to learn to talk by touching his mother," Coleridge noted (*NB* 1: 838) and counseled: "In the education of children, love is first to be instilled, and out of love obedience is to be educed. The impulse and power should be given to the intellect and the end of a moral being exhibited" (*Miscellaneous Criticism* 194). In consequence of this unitary assumption, Wordsworth and Coleridge emphatically deride analysis and comparison as an educational tactic:

> We should address ourselves to those faculties in a child's mind, which are first awakened by nature, and consequently first admit of cultivation, that is to say, the memory and the imagination. The comparing power, the judgement, is not at that age active, and ought not to be forcibly excited, as is too frequently and mistakenly done in the modern systems of education, which can only lead to selfish views, debtor and creditor principles of virtue, and an inflated sense of merit (Coleridge, *Lectures* 2: 192-93).

Because the unitary modes of intellectual activity—memorization and imagination—are natural and appropriate in early childhood, they come spontaneously and are not an object of self-consciousness to the child. But the dissociative, analytic modes of thought are against the grain and cannot, so Wordsworth and Coleridge maintain, be carried out spontaneously. An education that inculcates the habit of comparison and requires a child to set herself against any other child is pernicious:

> Nothing should be more impressed on parents and tutors than to make children forget themselves; and books which only told how Master Billy and Miss Ann spoke and acted, were not only ridiculous but extremely hurtful; much better give them "Jack the Giant-killer" or the seven Champions, or anything which, being beyond their own sphere of action, should not feed this self-pride. (Coleridge, *Lectures* 1: 587)

Rather than immersion in "their own sphere of action" and regular competitive comparison with other children, children do best when permitted to follow their own solitary imaginative bent. At the very least, analysis and comparison will breed childhood self-conceit or self-contempt, at worst an arrested development that locks a child into a premature social role. Wordsworth's contempt for premature self-consciousness is notoriously violent. In Book 5 of *The Prelude*, he derides the "specimen . . . model of a child," the crammed child prodigy so adept at "nice" satire, at weighing, at measuring, at judging, that he is trapped "within the pinfold of his own conceit" (1850 *Prelude* 5: 336). His mockery of foolish adults demanding measured answers from the children of "Anecdote for Fathers" and "We are Seven" is linked to his sense that comparative analytic thinking violates the natural development of a young mind and is both psychologically and morally damaging. But imaginative romantic tales speak to the whole of the child's desire:

> Oh! give us once again the wishing cap
> Of Fortunatus, and the invisible coat
> Of Jack the Giant-Killer, Robin Hood,
> And Sabra in the forest with St. George!
> The child whose love is here, at least, doth reap
> One precious gain, that he forgets himself (*Prelude* 5: 341-46)

The temporary loss of the self, or absorption of the self, into a grand tale or an imagined world is an exercise in possibility.

Such childhood ability to engage deeply with multiple modes of being seems to Coleridge to *teach a lesson* about the proper nature of the true human self, a self at once imaginatively empathetic and capacious, the self of an imaginative and moral being. So unitary a habit of mind means that children are confident, creative, and self-forgetful *non-specialists* whether they are prodigious polymaths such as Thomas Malkin and Marjory Fleming or ordinary "little children from 3 to 6 years old," who, Coleridge says, in their imitative play empathetically "exist in the form of others," but always return from their copycat "little plan or chart," their "dream of human life," to play roles as Tinker, Tailor, Soldier, or Sailor to their core selves that are more capacious than any mere social role:

> The first lesson, that innocent Childhood affords me, is—that it is an instinct of my Nature to pass out of myself, and to exist in the form of others. The second is—not to suffer any one form to pass into *me*—and to become a usurping *Self* in the disguise that the German Pathologists call a *fixed Idea*. (*Inquiring Spirit* 68-69)

Coleridge assumes that childhood reveals the genuine being, the deep real self, that merely plays at multiple social identities. In such a reading of human nature most pursuits and professions, unless pursued merely provisionally as in child's play, seem limiting and dehumanizing. If the human wholeness discernable during childhood is to be preserved into adulthood, the only professional life compatible with the Coleridgean *me* is that of a protean creator or imaginative unifier, that is, a person like the myriad-minded Shakespeare who can "exist in the form of others" or like the imaginative Wordsworth who is able to bring "the whole soul of man into activity." For the Romantic poet, as constructed by Wordsworth and Coleridge, is the representative unified and unifying non-specialist whose paradoxical specialty is the imaginative creation of wholenesses. The Wordsworthian description of the poet as "a man speaking to men" sets him out as the representative human being, the one who is fully what other people are only in part, a person with "a more comprehensive soul," and whose knowledge is "a necessary part of our existence, our natural and unalienable heritage" ("Preface to *Lyrical Ballads*," *WWLC* 77). In this Romantic discourse, the role of Poet and Child are mutually supportive. Just as the model of childhood wholeness works to valorize poetry as the sole human profession, so the Romantic assumption of poetic primacy carries with it the privileging of childhood.

The holism and idealism that are crucial to the essentializing discourse of childhood consciousness are sometimes tied into *animism,* the child's perception of the universe as instinct with life that is an analogue of his own life. The imputation of animism, "the tendency to regard objects as living and endowed with will," to children in general is Piaget's (*CCW* 194). The tendency, however, is deeply Wordsworthian. The most habitual animist among all nineteenth-century writers, Wordsworth repeatedly ascribes a unitary "Presence" to nature. Sometimes the life is clearly an emanation of the child's own power of feeling

> For him, in one dear Presence, there exists
> A virtue which irradiates and exalts
> Objects through widest intercourse of sense (*Prelude* 2: 238-40)

Often however, the child is merely the object of the enveloping "sentiment of Being," which spreads

> O'er all that moves and all that seemeth still;
> O'er all that, lost beyond the reach of thought
> And human knowledge, to the human eye
> Invisible, yet liveth to the heart;
> O'er all that leaps and runs, and shouts and sings,
> Or beats the gladsome air; o'er all that glides
> Beneath the wave, yea, in the wave itself
> And mighty depth of waters (*Prelude* 2: 402-9)

Whether benevolent (as in the "unutterable love" in the "silent faces of the clouds" in Wordsworth's *Excursion*) or threatening (as in the "low breathings coming after me" [*Prelude* 1: 323]), inanimate nature is perceived by every properly childlike child as instinct with a life that is an analogue of her own: "And the little ones leaped & shouted & laugh'd / And all the hills echoed" (Blake 15). Animism is at once a psychologically harmonizing and a socially isolating perception. The plenitude of the life-to-life relationship leaves no room for other life in the universe: Presence and Child are the only inhabitants.

In nineteenth-century representations of childhood, a visionary faculty often "finds / Its full maturity in youth, / Its antitype in infant minds" (Barton, "On the Death of a Child of Extraordinary Endowments and Piety," *Poems* 334):

> For no divine
> Intelligence, or art, or fire, or wine,
> Is high-delirious as that rising lark—
> The child's soul and its daybreak in the dark
> (Meynell, "Two Boyhoods," *Poems* 102)

Intuition beyond language is routinely imputed to young children. Marie Corelli, for example, assigns to the four-year-old "Boy" the Wordsworthian "intuition of some truer life than those around him dreamed of,—the halo of divine things was still about him" (*Boy* 17). Swinburne's "Birth Song" for the speechless baby, Olivia Rossetti assigns to her "dumb lips divine" and "bright mute speech" the same visionary authority Shelley had given his skylark:

> If thou couldst tell, or we
> Ask, and be heard of thee,
> For love's undying sake,
> From thy dumb lips divine and bright mute speech
> Such news might touch our ear
> That then would burn to hear
> Too high a message now for man's to reach (589)

Children's vision is usually represented as a grand, often animist, perception, holistically meaningful in excess of the elements that compound it. In representative moments such as Wordsworth's boat-stealing episode and skating party or the six-year-old De Quincey's rapt trance at the bedside of his dead sister ("flight of the solitary child to the solitary God—flight from the ruined corpses to the throne that could not be ruined!" ["The Affliction of Childhood," L 106]),[7] a lone child is the silent center of the moral and physical universe. In this vastness of strange solitary forms, the wheeling landscape, and the throne of God withdrawing into the infinite void, the child perceives a meaningful but not rationally paraphrasable universe. Neither Wordsworth nor De Quincey is retrospectively disposed to explain away these charged moments, but rather to affirm, as in De Quincey's blank verse interjection into his prose memoir, "how rich thou wert in truth for after years" (L 106).

Even the childhood credulity that cannot survive childhood—the belief in magic, in fairies, in magicians, in monsters—is honored. In express opposition to the Edgeworths and Barbauld, who favored realism and moral role models, Wordsworth and Coleridge frequently praise childhood credulity, praising fairy tales and wonder books because they encourage the native childhood tendency toward faith in the meaningfulness of the world. Such works build up the capacity to hold to a grand idea of humanity, a grand idea of the world, a grand idea of the Deity, ideas in excess of the observed actuality but conforming to one's own spiritual reach. It is right Coleridge insists that "children be permitted to read Romances &

relations of Giants and Magicians & Genii," for "I know no other way of giving the mind the love of 'the Great' & 'the Whole'"(*CCL* 1: 478). It is right, Wordsworth insists, that children read magical claptrap that is a visionary antidote to "reconcilement with our stinted powers / . . . this state of meagre vassalage" in ordinary life:

>   Ye dreamers, then,
> Forgers of daring tales! we bless you then,
> Imposters, drivellers, dotards, as the ape
> Philosophy will call you; *then* we feel
> With what, and how great might ye are in league,
> Who make our wish, our power, our thought a deed,
> An empire, a possession,—ye whom time
> And seasons serve; all Faculties; to whom
> Earth crouches, the elements are potters' clay,
> Space like a heaven filled up with northern lights,
> Here, nowhere, there, and everywhere at once (*Prelude* 5: 523-33)

Such credulity is the very prerequisite to intellectual and moral progress, for it is out of trust in the possibility of meaning that all childhood learning proceeds:

> Have you children or have you lived among children, and do you not know, that in all things, in food, in medicine, in all their doings and abstainings they must believe in order to acquire a reason for their belief? (Coleridge *Aids to Reflection* 1: 144)

What others may call childhood ignorance, Wordsworth labels a faith essential to growth. Speaking of the shepherds he admired in childhood, ordinary men only accidentally glorified by their intersection with sunlight, fog, and mountain scenery, Wordsworth insists both on the value of the visionary accidents and on the childhood isolation that makes such accidents possible:

>   Call ye these appearances—
> Which I beheld in shepherds in my youth,
> This sanctity of Nature given to man—
> A shadow, a delusion, ye who pore
> On the dead letter, miss the shape of things;
> Whose truth is not a motion or a shape
> Instinct with vital functions, but a block
> Or waxen image which yourselves have made,

> And ye adore! But blessed be the God
> Of Nature and of Man that this was so;
> That men before my inexperienced eyes
> Did first present themselves thus purified,
> Removed, and to a distance that was fit:
> And so we all of us in some degree
> Are led to knowledge, whencesoever led,
> And howsoever; were it otherwise,
> And we found evil fast as we find good
> In our first years, or think that it is found,
> How could the innocent heart bear up and live! (*Prelude* 8: 293-311)

Wordsworth considers this childhood "removal," this fit distance from human society, essential to his development. The mental faculties credited to the Romantic child are those that grow in solitude. Idealism, holism, animism, vision are all unitary perceptions that comparative analysis diminishes. Comparative common sense deflates "the dream-like vividness and splendor" of the individual's chosen object; comparative rationality makes the bereaved child recognize that her family of seven is diminished by two. Social experience teaches that different people have different motives and desires; so the unified world becomes multifarious. But in solitude, unity is easier and it is solitude that marks childhood consciousness. Self-sufficient isolation and mental solitude virtually define what a child is.

The insistent claim for isolated autonomy is original with Romantic writers and is closely connected to the redefining of imaginative creativity. Wordsworth habitually focuses on solitary children assimilated to a landscape—Lucy, the Idiot Boy, Ruth, the Highland Boy, the Norman Boy, the Boy of Winander, the Danish Boy—all elemental beings who in their singleness can mediate between the unitary landscape and the unitary human mind. A Hartley Coleridge poem celebrates a six-week-old baby's "mute simplicity of passive being" for manifesting the same paradoxical presence-in-seeming-absence as does nature itself ("To Jeannette, Six Weeks Old" 185). The most unstinting rhapsodist of romantic childhood, Hartley Coleridge favors childhood vacuity, blankness, singleness: "Some say, sweet babe, thy mind is but a blank, / As white and vacant as the level field / Or Unsunn'd snow . . ." ("To an Infant" 178). Fascinated with children doubly and triply isolated by geography or class or disability—children such as Wordsworth's "Blind Highland Boy" and "Idiot Boy"—Hartley finds an exemplary self-sufficient solitary in a "Deaf and Dumb Little Girl":

> Like a loose island on the wide expanse,
> Unconscious floating on the fickle sea,
> Herself her all, she lives in privacy;
> Her waking life as lovely as a trance ...
> ... all her little being
> Concentred in her solitary seeing. (179)

By preference, Romantic discussions of childhood tend to focus on single figures called "the child," "the boy," "infancy," "childhood," each, like Hartley's mute girl, "herself her all" with "all her little being / Concentred in her solitary seeing." Solitude is assumed by De Quincey to be the norm condition and privilege of childhood life: "that mighty silence which infancy is ... privileged by nature and position to enjoy." This "mighty silence" enjoyed by the solitary child is a precondition for adult achievement: "No man will ever unfold the capacities of his own intellect who does not at least checker his life with solitude. *So much solitude, so much power*" (*CW* 1: 121-22). Solitude is the natural landscape of childhood, De Quincey holds:

> God speaks to children also in dreams, and by the oracles that lurk in darkness. But in solitude, above all things ... God holds "communion undisturbed" with children. Solitude, though silent as light, is, like light, the mightiest of agencies: for solitude is essential to man. ... Oh burthen of solitude that cleavest to man through every stage of his being. ... Deep is the solitude in life of millions upon millions. ... But deeper than the deepest of these solitudes is that which broods over childhood. (L 114-15)

This "mighty silence" De Quincey identifies with Wordsworth is the speaking silence of nature that children, the child, enters in moments of wordless communion with his own mind. In Wordsworth's account of the Boy of Winander "who would stand alone" hooting at the owls, the emphasis falls on the boy's sudden reception in his own stilled being of the resonant stillness of nature. Thus in the stilled silence of the natural world and in the seemingly idle child "who is gazing on the stream, or laying upon the earth; the basis of all moral character may then be forming" (Coleridge, *Lectures* 1: 586). The solitary child in the empty landscape has access to "all the *elementary* feelings of human life":

> My opinion is, that where circumstances favour, where the heart is deep, where humility and tenderness exist in strength, whether the situation is

favourable as to solitude and as to genial feelings, children have a specific power of contemplating the truth, which departs as they enter the world. (De Quincey, L 127)

Such all-sufficing solitude is glossed not as desolation or abandonment but as the analogue of childhood and as the protective environment in which intellectual power grows. In such solitude the child may engender a seagirt solitary imaginary kingdom—as Hartley Coleridge imagined Ejuxria and Thomas Malkin Allestone—or create a sustaining idea of human life. Because such isolation sequesters the child from time and change, the Romantic child can become an emblem of fixity rather than of growth and development. In its rural isolation childhood is timeless and stable.

The Romantic discourse of the quintessential child is at once *honorific* and *decontextualizing*. It honors and glorifies a single being in terms of Nature and Autonomous Consciousness. As the emanation of Nature, the child is set against the limitations of culture; as the possessor of an autonomous consciousness, the child is set against the social sphere of dialectical exchange, compromise, and modification. This essential Romantic child is a project of what Jerome McGann calls the Romantic Ideology, that is, the assumption of the autonomy of the mind, an autonomy implicit in such privileged terms as *imagination, creativity, nature,* and *spirit*. The Romantic Ideology means assuming the creative independence of imagination from the vicissitudes of history; it means assuming a timeless nature spirit rolling through and validating all things. But it should be plain from the association of childhood with spirit and mind, that *childhood* operates along with *imagination* and *nature* within romantic discourse as the third autonomous power immune to the pressures of history. If ideology may be thought of as an orphan idea that does not know its own mother, that fails to acknowledge the material conditions from which it springs, then it is no surprise that the Romantic discourse managed to produce a glorified solitary essential child at the same time that it relegated most actual historical children to obscurity.

Both the equation with nature and the attribution of mental qualities serves to produce a solitary essential Romantic child, "single in the field," without social moorings. To identify childhood with nature means that children are conceived as existing free of the social net. Like flowers and breezes, like birds and stones, children exist outside of the context of cultural institutions—of schools, of the state, and especially of their families. Analogously, the attribution to children of holistic idealism assigns them a kind of mental process that thrives in isolation and perishes in the kind of social exchange satirized in Wordsworth's "We are Seven." Such idealism (Piaget's "a-dualism") is necessarily unitary in its totalized individual world-view and solitary in its practice, since the admission of other consciousnesses would require compromise and adjustment.

The essential child, unitary as nature, unitary in vision, is *honored and exalted* by the new Romantic discourse that figures as strengths real and/or postulated childhood qualities that others had and would treat as weaknesses. There is a systematic transvaluation—by redefinition or omission—both of children's inadequacies (ignorance and naivete are promoted) *and* competencies (precocity and work skills are demoted).

It is hardly necessary to emphasize that the equation of childhood and nature, childhood and idealism are honorific. The authority of the term Nature in Western thought at least from the Stoics through the Enlightenment has been amply documented. A talismanic term so powerful that (in George Orwell's phrase) everyone wanted to steal it, "Nature" in the political debates of the late eighteenth century was claimed as a source of political authority by conservatives such as Edmund Burke and radicals such as Thomas Paine. Furthermore, the dominant power of biological evolutionary thinking in the nineteenth century[8] means that "Nature" and its laws attached particularly to living beings, especially in "the evolutionary being of the human species."

Not only is Nature honorific in its association with children but it is *insulating and consolatory*. For the child to be linked to nature is to be linked to power. In a dynamically evolutionary universe, the link to nature makes for a paradoxical and consolatory association of childhood with power, a way of ignoring actual social powerlessness. Nineteenth-century painting in particular bears witness to the child as the figure of force and power: Philipp Otto Runge's burly child daimons burst like giants out of their frames, all worship William Orchardson's "Master Baby"; all traffic gives way to the masterful toddler in the roadway in Arthur Drummond's "His Majesty the Baby," (Rosenblum 23, Garland 34). The high mortality and social powerlessness of nineteenth-century children—their widespread exploitation in mines, mills, and chimneys; their vulnerability to a raft of childhood illness—are masked under the vocabulary of childhood authority. Coleridge defies the power of institutional religion; he will not baptize his child who is already blessed by nature:

> . . . he is the Darling of the Sun and of the Breeze! Nature seems to bless him as a thing of her own! He looks at the clouds, the mountains, the living Beings of the Earth, & vaults & jubilates! Solemn Looks & solemn Words

have been hitherto connected in his mind with great & magnificent objects only—with lightning, with thunder, with the waterfall blazing in the Sunset- / -then I say, Shall I suffer the Toad of Priesthood to spurt out his foul juice in this Babe's Face. (*CCL* 1: 625)

John Keble's sleeping innocents have the power to thwart evil:

> A little child's soft sleeping face
> The murderer's knife ere now hath staid.
> The adulterous eye, so foul and base,
> Is of a little child afraid ("Carved Angels" 268)

In a telling passage, Francis Kilvert attributes devastating erotic and emotional authority to little Gipsy Lizzie, a power he links to the innocence he sees and desires in her:

> How is the indescribable beauty of that most lovely face to be described—the dark soft curls parting back from the pure white transparent brow, the exquisite little mouth and pearly tiny teeth, the pure straight delicate features, the long dark fringes and white eyelids that droop over and curtain her eyes, when they are cast down or bent upon her book and seem to rest upon the soft clear cheek, and when the eyes are raised, that clear unfathomable blue depth of wide wonder and enquiry and unsullied and unsuspecting innocence. O child, child, if you did but know your own power. Oh Gipsy, if you only grow up as good as you are fair. Oh that you might grow up good. May all God's angels guard you, sweet. The Lord bless thee and keep thee. The Lord make His Face to shine upon thee and be gracious unto thee. The Lord lift up his countenance upon thee and give thee peace both now and evermore. Amen. (1: 168)

This astonishing tribute to a little girl's "power" is clearly a self-serving justification of Kilvert's prohibited desire. This is a transparent example of the way in which the claim of the child's *power* answers the adult's wish for self-justification or comfort.

Along with natural vitality, childhood idealism, holism, animism, and solitary consciousness are consistently described and honored. Though there is no necessary connection between a description of childhood idealism and adulation of it, the contextual vocabulary of Romanticism is emphatically honorific, placing these mental qualities as supreme strengths rather than defects or lunacies.

In this context, it is enlightening to note the work of Swiss psychologist, Jean Piaget. In thirty-nine books, published between 1923 (*The Lan-*

guage and Thought of the Child) and 1976 (*Behavior and Evolution*), Piaget established himself as the preeminent twentieth-century student of childhood cognition. Although much debated, Piaget's theories of children's intellectual development have been the most powerfully comprehensive twentieth-century explanatory paradigm. To a remarkable degree, his findings confirm more impressionistic Romantic claims as to how children perceive the world. He brings empirical confirmation to Romantic claims for childhood idealism ("a-dualism" is Piaget's term), holism, animism, credulity, and solitary consciousness ("solipsism" is his preferred term). But his deflationary positivist judgment on these qualities throws the prior Romantic inflation into relief.

Piaget confirms that children begin in what he calls "realism" or "a-dualism," that is, an idealist subjugation of the senses to mental conceptions. Realism is defined by Piaget as "ignoring the existence of the self." It issues in regarding one's own perspective as immediately objective and absolute and leads to the "anthropocentric illusion" by which young children value "the entire content of consciousness on a single plane in which ostensible reality and the unconscious interventions of the self are inextricably mixed" (*CCW* 46). The young child, Piaget argues, subjugates all external reality to the patterns of his own mind in the idealist manner without knowing that he is doing so. Feeling no distinction between the self and the world, "the child always begins by regarding his own point of view as absolute" (*CCW* 152). Whatever he feels, the world feels; whatever he desires, the world desires; whatever motivates him, activates the world. Piaget regards this "being knowing nothing of the distinction between mind and body" as a defective adult. "Such a being would be aware of his desires and feelings, but his notion of self would undoubtedly be much less clear than ours" (*CCW* 49). Unlike Wordsworth who emphasizes the intense regret felt by *all* adults for the "first / Poetic spirit of our human life" (*Prelude* 2: 260-61) ("I have deplored, as we all have reason to so," a subjugation to common sense materialism [*Prose* 3: 194]), Piaget stresses the ignorance and confusion of the child, clearly the adult's inferior: "Compared with us, he would experience much less the sensation of the thinking self within him, the feeling of a being independent of the external world" (49).

Piaget agrees with the Romantic assumption that children are "syncretists" who think synthetically rather than analytically. In learning to read, for example, children tend to grasp the "schema or the *gestaltqualitat*" of words, or even of a whole page. Children "not only perceive by means of general schemas, but these actually supplant the perception of detail. Thus they correspond to a sort of confused perception, different from and prior to that which in us is the perception of complexity or of forms" (*LTC* 144). But Piaget shows little enthusiasm for this "confused" state. Wordsworth and Coleridge had attributed virtually all intellectual, moral, and creative virtues to unitary childhood thought, holding it to underpin all constructive thinking. By framing energizing conceptions of "the Great" and "the Whole" (Coleridge, *CL* 1: 479), childhood holism is ethically enlarging and imaginatively exemplary. Piaget, however, emphasizes the mental muddle generated by the child's insistence on factitious synthesis: "Everything is connected with everything else, nothing happens by chance" (*LTC* 156). Indeed, he cites philosopher Henri Bergson to authorize his view that real thinking owes little to the drive toward unification; association is the enemy of thought. "Association is not the fundamental fact; it is by *dissociation* that we begin, and the tendency of every memory to gather others round it can be explained by a natural [and, in childhood, dominant] return of the mind to the undivided unity of perception" (*LTC* 145). Piaget bears witness to an observed childhood drive to interconnect all experience: "the idea of chance is absent from the mentality of the child" who tends to "connect everything with everything else" (156). But whereas the Romantics valorize such interconnectedness as in Coleridge's ecstatic intimation of "one life within us and abroad" or De Quincey's initiate pride in decoding the *latentis semita vitae* ("the hidden pathway of life"), Piaget treats it as an obsessional paranoia. He likens such childhood unifications to those he labels "interpretational maniacs" who need "justification at all costs" (*TLC* 159, 158).

Overall, Piaget labels as defects the very attributes the Romantics cite as excellences. The childhood propensity for animist thought, glossed and exalted as that "one life within us and abroad" and grounding so much nineteenth-century poetry and home-made faith, is for Piaget nothing but a form of mental backwardness that, happily, disappears with "the growth of the consciousness of the self" (*CCW* 270). Piaget argues that the less self-consciousness a child has, the younger and more backward he is, the more likely he is to diffuse his consciousness across the landscape and to perceive all objects as motivated by his own motives. The less self-consciousness a child has, the more likely he is to impute living energies to the natural world. As children grow up, they become less animistic.[9]

Piaget is dismissive of the kind of childhood credulity Wordsworth and Coleridge credit with formative experience of grandeur. If holistic/animist/unitary seeing links the Romantic child to the poet and the Piagetian child to the paranoid interpretational lunatic, so childhood credulity links the Romantic child to the creative genius and the Piagetian child to the obediently conforming subject of a backward patriarchy. Both the credulity and the paranoic connectedness of childhood thought are linked by Piaget to the young child's isolation from corrective social exchange in the society of his or her equals.

Piaget acknowledges a childhood capacity for wonder and credulity but links it to the experience of "unilateral respect." The deference felt by children toward seemingly omniscient adults leads to a habit of belief in authority, a habit of imputing quasi-divine authority to all rule systems they encounter (*MJC* 57). Subjected to an adult world of external order (the sunrise, the moonshine, other regularities of nature; the walk, the bath, the school and other regularities of Swiss nurture), the child develops an habitual *credulity*. This, for Piaget, evinces more the passivity of a child's situation than the insight of his nature. Such faith recedes as the child moves into the society of his equals in which mutuality rather than unilateral respect is the norm. Much in the spirit of his intellectual ancestor Jean Jacques Rousseau, Piaget draws a parallel between psychological and political structures. A childlike consciousness is one appropriate "in the strictly conformity and gerontocratic societies designated as primitive," where an adult consciousness properly belongs to the more advanced society of egalitarian democracy. To "cooperate with his equals" makes one who is a child chronologically, an adult psychologically. An adult consciousness, in Piaget's reading, belongs in an egalitarian, progressive society; to remain childlike implies an acquiescence in a hierarchical, patriarchal, and unchangeable world.

Confirming the Romantic association of childhood and solitude, Piaget classes all children under seven as solipsists who cannot understand that their consciousness is not identical to the consciousness of others. Only gradually do children recognize that natural objects and other human beings are motivated differently from themselves and have different centers of consciousness. The failure to distinguish their own selves from the selves of others means that each child is the center of its own universe. In a sense, he is the only inhabitant. No matter how objectively populous the child's world, it is a psychological solitude. "[The] adult thinks socially even when he is alone . . . the child under seven thinks egocentrically even in the society of others" (*LTC* 40). To Piaget, such a state is defective; movement into social intercourse is movement into social usefulness.

Piaget's muted, even hostile, descriptions of childhood perception coincide with the more impressionistic and exalted claims of the Romantics. All agree that the child is an idealist, a syncretist, a visionary, an animist, a believer, a solitary, but Piaget's skeptical rationalism throws into relief the Romantic glorification of these childhood traits. The Romantics regularly set forth the superiority of childhood to adulthood, while Piaget asserts that the difference between those he habitually calls "us" and "them" is entirely to the advantage of the adult. For Piaget, the residual child within means trouble and the sooner the solipsistic child can become a group-minded adult, the better. For the Romantics, however, the existence of residual childlike qualities within an adult—"filiation between their former and their latter"—is entirely salutary (H. Coleridge, *HCP* "On Pride / In Continuation"). Indeed, "prolonged infancy" is the source of adult creative and intellectual force (Chamberlain, *The Child* 445).

For the Romantics, children possess such remarkable gifts of consciousness that there can be little psychological or emotional advantage in relinquishing childhood feelings and perceptions—though there may be certain intellectual and political advantages. The desire to hold on to childhood excellence involves a new ideal of human excellence: willed reconstitution of the adult self as child-man lest one "exist in fragments" cut off from "the whole of his natural inheritance."[10]

The Children Who Are Not Children

If the quintessential child is both source and goal of humanity, this essentialized being can play that role only when set apart from humanity. The definitional child, whether Romantic and Piagetian, is inevitably seen in isolation. Indeed, Piaget treats socialized children, those who as playmates set the rules of their own games, as functional adults. Adulthood is cognate with negotiated mutuality. The Romantic emphasis, however, is on the perceptual, ethical, and aesthetic gains to be exacted from refusing the negotiations that make up society, history, calculation, and self-limitation.

In its honorific use, however, the Romantic discourse not only elevates solitary and imaginative essential Children, but it also declassifies and erases certain kinds of merely literal children by stripping them of that honorific label. These children/not children—Richardson's "ethnographic" children (11-12), Cunningham's "Children of the Poor"—are the children of circumstance, embedded in a thick social context from which they cannot be extricated. Because their lives are so clearly shaped and deformed by their environments, these young persons cease even to be seen as real children at all. Especially blocked from view are those children whose identity emerges from congested institutions and social contexts, notably child prodigies and urban laboring children.

Youthful prodigies of learning, adept at assimilating the transmitted lessons of their cultures cease in the nineteenth century to be exemplary and become instead bizarre or pitiful deviants from the true nature of childhood. Increasingly, precocity is regarded either with pity or distaste. Thus Alice Meynell in 1897 incredulously notes the pride of seventeenth-century diarist John Evelyn in his learned son who, at two-and-a-half spoke and read English, Latin, and French. By the age of five, shortly before his death,

> He got by heart almost the entire vocabulary of Latin and French primitives(?) and words, could make congruous syntax, turn English into Latin, and *vice versa,* construe and prove what he read, and did the government and use of relative verbs, substantives, ellipses, and many figures and tropes, and made a considerable progress in Comenius's "Janua" and had a strong passion for Greek. (*The Children* 30)

Meynell rebukes Evelyn and his age for prizing such intellectual precocity: "They thought their little boy hopeful because he was so quick on his way to be something else. . . . It is difficult to imagine what childhood must have been when nobody looking on, saw any fun in it; when everything that was proper to five years old was defect" (30-31).

In so far as education is conceived as a matter of cultural transmission rather than as the development of mental faculties, it is increasingly conceived the enemy of childhood. Romanticism uncouples the link between schooling and childhood; the more schooling, the less childhood: "These prodigies of learning commence their career at three, become expert linguists at four, profound philosophers at five, read the fathers at six, and die of old age at seven" (Malkin 4). "I never was a boy," John Stuart Mill reflected of his prodigious and effective education, "I never played at cricket. It is better to let nature have its way." The formulaic lament for an intellectually surfeited child like John Stuart Mill is that he is *no child* : "'tis a child, no child, / But a dwarf man; in knowledge, virtue, skill, / In what he is not, and in what he is, / The noontide shadow of a man complete" (Wordsworth, *The Prelude* 1805, 5: 294-97). This boy wonder is in all things the creature and prisoner of society, "a worshipper of worldly seemliness" (5: 298), a sharp social satirist skilled in mocking "the broad follies of the licensed world" (5: 311) in language "Massy and ponderous as a prison door" (5: 321). His knowledge—"in books / He is a prodigy" (2: 319-20)— is all instrumental:

> The ensigns of the empire which he holds—
> The globe and sceptre of his royalties—

> Are telescopes, and crucibles, and maps.
> Ships he can guide across the pathless sea,
> And tell you all their cunning; he can read
> The inside of the earth, and spell the stars;
> He knows the politics of foreign lands,
> Can string you names of districts, cities, towns,
> The whole world over, tight as beads of dew
> Upon a gossamer thread. He sifts, he weighs,
> Takes nothing upon trust (1805, 5: 328-38)

Normal childishness muscles out extraordinary and premature erudition, piety, and competence as praiseworthy. William Canton's express intention in *WV Her Book* (1896) is to describe a child who is wonderful precisely because she is *not* a *wunderkind*. She is no prodigy but merely "this commonplace little body . . . merely the average" child making her father "joyously content with the small mercies which came to him in the beaten way of nature" (*WV Her Book, IP* 60).

An acceptable Romantic prodigy must succeed in being prodigiously childlike as well as prodigiously learned. The reputation of Marjory Fleming—"Pet Marjorie," "The Wonder Child"—is a case in point.[11] To her Romantic and Victorian admirers, Marjory Fleming was a child-genius whose achievement was at once prodigious and natural. Leslie Stephen had deplored John Stuart Mill's education of cram ("I cannot help thinking, with the so-called 'Philistine,' that a little cricket would have been an excellent substitute for half the ancient literature instilled into a lad who was not prepared really to appreciate either the thought or the literary charm" [*EU* 9]) but found Marjory Fleming the very type of childhood accomplishment: "no more fascinating infantile author has ever appeared"(*DNB* 19: 28). All praise Marjory Fleming's capacity to be both genius and normal girl. Sir Walter Scott allegedly declared the child "the most extraordinary character I ever met with" (Brown 90) and Mark Twain labeled her the most quintessentially childlike child: "she was the world's child, she was the human race it little" (358). Arundell Esdaile, editor of the Fleming manuscripts in the National Library of Scotland, ranked her with the great diarists of literary history—Pepys, Boswell, Dorothy Osborne (xix)—while Twain considered that "Nothing was entirely beyond her literary jurisdiction: if it had occurred to her that the laws of Rome needed codifying she would have taken a chance at it" (371). But these Victorian patriarchs emphasize her *extraordinary* powers only in order to insist on how *ordinary* and childish she was. Thus Edinburgh essayist John Brown draws a portrait that shows her "fearless and full of love, passionate, wild, wilful, fancy's child" (91). He adds: "How childish and yet how strong and free is her use of words!" (101). L. MacBean, her turn-of-the-century biographer, echoes Stephens' praise of this "charming character" and emphasizes that the girl is childlike in being a "loving and charming child genius" (3). Esdaile too insists on her normality as a child, bracketing the very qualities that make her a writer. With "no trace of the morbid tendencies too often associated with infant prodigies" (Stephen 28), Esdaile finds her normal "in everything except her intensity and her gift of expression" (xv).

Marjory escapes the disapproval reserved for culture-crammed children because each of her cultural acquisitions is crossed with a valorized childlike quality. On the one hand, she is a voluminous and hard-working writer, author of four journal volumes full of moral reflections, social commentary, handwriting exercises, and eighteen poems including two long historical poems on the monarchs of Scotland. On the other hand, she is an egregiously original speller: she will "jump with filisity"; she "is a Pisplikan just now and a Presbeteren at Kercaldy"; she learns "to make Simecoloings, notes of interriogations, peorids and commoes; she is a "loveress" of Mr. Craigie and beloved of a "marrade man" named Balfour; love is "papithatick"; her new collar is "amoniable"; and she poetically "longs to leave the bustel of the nosey town behind." If she is an assiduous reader (History, the Bible, *Tom Jones,* the Newgate Calendar), she is also a rebellious student: "I am now going to tell you about the horrible and wretched plaege that my multiplication gives me you cant conceive it—the most Devilish thing is 8 times 8 & 7 times it is what nature itself cant endure" (54). Her literary ambitions are conventionally learned (elegies, historical essays, birthday tributes to the monarch) but wildly indecorous observations keep breaking in. In her lament for the death of several turkey chicks, she pities the grieving mother turkey:

> A direful death indeed they had
> that would put any parent mad
> But she was more than usual calm
> she did not give a single dam (81)

She piously strives for moral rectitude ("I think the price of a pine-apple is very dear for There is a whole bright goulden geinei that might have sustained a poor family for a whole week and more perhaps" [32]) but is also exuberantly tactless:

> Miss Potune, a lady of my acquantance, praises me dreadfully. I repeated something out of Deen Swift and she said I was fit for the stage. . . . This

horrid fat Simpliton says that my Aunt is beautifull which is intirely impossible for that is not in her nature. . . . Miss Potune is very fat she pretends to be very learned. (25, 27)

Marjory seemed to her admirers a very special kind of genius—less a child prodigy than a prodigious child: a genius at being a child. Without being heroically learned (at least not at spelling and "plaege"-ridden mathematics), without being notably good ("I stamped with my feet and threw my new hat which [Isabella] made on the ground and was sulky" [MacBean 52-53]), Marjory possessed extraordinary verbal power to articulate the freshness, enthusiasm, and affection other children could only embody. Her childlikeness redeems her prodigious gifts. But for most prodigies, their gifts swallowed up their childlikeness and made them unworthy of the name.

Even more athwart the true nature of childhood because more socially embedded were the children of the poor—especially the urban young, "Scurf and mildew of the city," as Elizabeth Barrett Browning's "Song for the Ragged Schools of London" calls them (530).[12] It is rare to find "the Child" among the packs of homeless, impoverished and scrofulous children, "the sad products of our nineteenth century civilization" (Barnardo, "A City Waif" 1). Lord Shaftesbury, indefatigably active on behalf of impoverished nineteenth-century children, both working children and homeless children, described the dehumanized offspring of London's East End, as the teeming, thronging, swarming, barbarian inhabitants of a vast pullulation:

> Everyone who walks the streets of the metropolis must daily observe several members of the tribe, bold, pert, and dirty as London sparrows, but pale, feeble, and sadly inferior to them in plumpness of outline. . . . Many are spanning the gutters with their legs and dabbling with earnestness in the latest accumulation of nastiness; while others, in squalid and half-naked groups, squat about at the entrance of the narrow, foetid courts and alleys that lie concealed behind the deceptive frontages of our larger thoroughfares. Whitechapel and Spitelfields teem with them like an ant's nest; but it is in Lambeth and Westminster that we find the most flagrant traces of their swarming activity. There the foul and dismal passages are thronged with children of both sexes, and from the age of three to thirteen. Through want and hazard, they are singularly vivacious and engaged in every sort of occupation but that which would be beneficial to themselves and creditable to the neighborhood. The matted hair, the disgusting filth that renders necessary a closer inspection before flesh can be discerned between the rags which hang about them, and the barbarian freedom from all superintendence and restraint, fill the mind of a novice these things with perplexity and dismay. (qtd. in Barnardo, *Memoirs* 65)

Stationed here as a walker in the city, Shaftesbury looks around for the children of the city and sees none—nothing recognizable as a Child. His gaze produces no radiant singular child but rather a dehumanized mass of barbarian others in the heart of the English metropolis: "members of the tribe, bold, pert, and dirty as London sparrows" "spanning the gutters with their leg and dabbling . . . in . . . nastiness"; "squalid and half-naked groups, squat about . . . foetid courts"; they "teem" as in "an ant's nest"; the city shows "traces of their swarming activity"; they are "children of both sexes" with "matted hair" and "disgusting filth" who live in "barbarian freedom."

These "teeming," "swarming" street children of nineteenth-century London, these children of history, acutely troubled the conscience and the eyes of those who looked at them, partly because they contradicted the culture's noblest thoughts of what a true child was supposed to be. These swarming "tribes" of the young, these "street arabs," these "gamins," these "mudlarks," these "gutter-snipes" and "gutter-slushes" engendered a kind of cognitive dissonance in those for whom the essentializing discourse of childhood was strong—virtually every literate Briton. There is a studious avoidance of the word "child" in descriptions of street children. Even to call these beings children produced discomfort. Thus Charles Lamb's explicit refusal to assign to the progeny of the poor the honorific name of child:

> The careless little darling of the wealthier nursery, in their hovel, is transformed into a premature reflecting person. . . . It was dragged up, to live or to die as it happened. It had no young dreams. It broke at once into the iron realities of life. A child exists not for the very poor as any object of dalliance; it is only another mouth to be fed, a pair of little hands to be betimes inured to labour. It is the rival, till it can be the co-operator for food with the parent. . . . It makes the very heart to bleed to overhear the casual street-talk between a poor woman and her little girl. . . . It is not of toys, of nursery books, of summer holidays . . . of the promised sight, or play; of praised sufficiency at school. It is of mangling and clear-starching, of the price of coals, or of potatoes. The questions of the child, that should be the very outpourings of curiosity in idleness, are marked with forecast and melancholy providence. It has come to be a woman before it was a child. It has learned to go to market; it chaffers, it haggles, it envies, it murmurs; it is knowing, acute, sharpened; it never prattles. ("That Home is Home Though It is Never So Homely" 2: 264-65)

This competent urban operator cannot retain the name of child. The essential child is young, playful, spontaneous, invulnerably "embalmed / By nature," in Wordsworth's phrase. But the multitudinous children, the swarms of the street, are old and wizened with cares. Thus Hesba Stretton's ten-year-old heroine in *Little Meg's Children* (1869) is an old woman:

> A small, spare, stunted girl of London growth . . . with the shrewd anxious air of a woman upon her face, with deep lines wrinkling her forehead and puckering about her eyes. Her hands were hard with work and her step was slow and silent, less like that of a child than of a woman, who was already weary with much labor. (10-11)

Her youngest brother is "a wan sickly baby with an old face" (30) as is the doomed baby in Arthur Morrison's *A Child of the Jago* (1895), "[its] eyes . . . large and bright, its tiny face . . . piteously flea-bitten and strangely old" (49). In *Froggy's Little Brother* (1875) by the pseudonymous "Brenda," the toddler "little Deb" can only recover her youth by dying: "How calm and peaceful little Deb looked!—all the suffering gone out of her old woman's face. All her cries hushed, and all the wrinkles smoothed away" (103). Dr. Barnardo describes "My First Arab," a child "sadly over-wise" in similar aged terms: "he was only ten years of age, though his face was not that of a child. It had a careworn, old-mannish look, which was only relieved by the bright glances of his small sharp eyes (8-9).

Unlike the decontextualized and solitary Romantic child, these children of the city are firmly set into "a seething mass of human misery" (Barnardo in Wagner 183). A subhuman or savage mass, "[they] swarm, do these children of suffering; and easy-going people have no idea of the density of savagery amid which such scions of our noble English race are reared" ("Waifs and Strays," Runciman 176). These swarms inhabited pullulant "rookeries," as the noxious urban tenements were called, living "almost like dogs upon garbage, picking up means of subsistence where creatures less sharp and vigilant must perish and herding at night in dens of vice and crime" (Barnardo, "A City Waif" 27). An East End social worker, James Runciman, depicts the urban children as "predatory animals" and noxious parasites. He fantasizes about this mass elimination in metaphors that make such execution thinkable, even attractive. However socially convenient it might be, he notes somewhat wistfully, "We cannot put the benighted starvelings into a lethal chamber, and dispose of their brief lives in that fashion" (78). Neither would it be acceptable Victorian practice to

> take Chinese methods of lessening the pressure of population, and we must at once decide on the wisest way of dealing with our waifs and strays; if we do not, then the chances are that they will deal unpleasantly with us. The locust, the lemming, the phyloxera are all very insignificant creatures; but,

when they act together in numbers, they can very soon devastate a district. (183)

Nowhere is the degradation of city youth from the privileged status of the essential child clearer than in varied terms that emerge in the 1840s in relation to the children of London's East End: waifs and strays, arabs, pariahs, gamins, guttersnipes, gutterslushes, mudlarks.[13]

"Waifs and Strays" is a term incorporated in the name of Barnardo's Homes ("Society for Waifs and Strays") and in its publication, *The National Waif Magazine*. Both "waif" and "stray" refer to non-human property alienated from its rightful owners. A waif is a category of goods, a stray a category of animal. Waifs are goods that are ownerless; strays are animals that have wandered away from their flock and become ownerless. As George Needham, an American social activist, notes, the term "waif" is a legal one. In English law, it means "goods found of which the owner is not known. They were originally such goods as a thief, when pursued, threw away to prevent being apprehended. A *waif* then, being something ownerless and unclaimed, the terms easily became applicable to children deserted [or badly neglected] by their parents" (Needham 24). These "Nobody's Children," these "pariah children" (common contemporary synonyms for Waifs and Strays) were perceived as the effluvium of their degraded environment and thus "guttersnipes," "gutterslushes," "mudlarks." Even more marked by estrangement is the pervasive term "Street Arab." The use of "Arab" to mean a child of the street is attributed by the OED to Lord Shaftesbury whose speeches of the 1840s repeatedly speak of "City Arabs . . . like tribes of lawless freebooters bound by no obligations, and utterly ignorant or utterly regardless of social duties" (*OED*). Barnardo too habitually uses the term to denote homeless children: thus "an arab of the street, a gutter child . . . who lived *on* the streets and *by* the streets" (*Saved from a Crime* 8) and thus his pamphlets "Labours of Love among our East End Arabs" (1871), "Nobody's Children: A Brief Account of what is being done to save the Arab Children of our Great City" (nd), and "My First Arab" (1893). These urban "Ishmaels" are characteristically "sharp and sly" (Needham 115). They wander through a waste desert of the city, each "a very Bedouin in the midst of the thronging city multitude," with the restlessness of "real sons of Ishmael" (21). Sometimes the term "pariah children" (Barnardo, "Seeds of the Righteous" 1) serves as synonym for "Arab." This conflation of two kinds of dark other—one Arab, one Indian—demonstrates the domestic orientalism that blocked empathetic understanding of the street children. Helped by the appellation "street arabs," Needham and others find it plausible to believe that these children enjoy and thrive in their urban desert; that these arabs prefer wandering in poverty to static comfort since they have ample scope for their "warlike and predatory" natures (21); they despise government and trust none but their own brotherhood, their "emirs, sheiks" who bind them to be "uncertain, vindictive, selfish" (22). They are the enemy of civil life.

The discourse of these children of history, children inescapably defined by their environment, is antithetical to Romantic discourse. By a kind of domestic orientalism, the homeless masses—waifs, strays, Nobody's Children, mudlarks, guttersnipes, pariahs, and arabs—are represented as an alien element within western civilization. Non-western, non-Christian, uncivilized, outcast, these children are more a source of fear than of either love or pity. Such children are regularly likened to threatening primitive people or even to lower organisms: "We cannot call such beings barbarians, because 'barbarian' implies something wild, strong, and even noble; yet, to our shame we must call them savages, and we must own that they are born and bred within easy gunshot distance of our centres of culture, enlightenment, and luxury" (Runciman 175). In their unfitness for modern civilization, "these same infants resemble the black fellows of Western Australia or the Troglodytes of Africa in general intelligence" (Runciman 176). These are an uncivilized lower pariah people who inhabit the alien heart of darkness in "the wide wilderness of London" ("The Seed of the Righteous" 8). Their haunt in "darkest London" is sometimes characterized as a desert, sometimes as a trackless waste, sometimes as a maze inhabited by carrion birds ("rookery") and vermin (lemmings, lice). Their "Ishmael-like love of liberty" (*A Jubilee Message from Dr. Barnardo's Homes* 22) disqualifies them from civil society. They represent a political problem or a sanitary problem or a military problem. They need not, however, be perceived as children.

The glorification of the quintessential child through the essentializing Romantic discourse is fraught with paradox, for it did not mean effective social reform on behalf of children. As C. J. Sommerville has noted, in the nineteenth century "the greatest exploitation of children coincided with the greatest glorification of childhood" (160). "The Child" was a cherished object of contemplation to many—Wordsworth, Lamb, Coleridge, for example—who were indifferent to the contemporary humanitarian child relief movement. Indeed, the very category childhood as a valorized *state*, a new continent, a separate world, tends to discourage social intervention.

What explains the emergence of the Essential Child? What explains the nineteenth-century idolatry toward the "Child set in the midst," an idolatry that is demonstrated in the nineteenth-century proliferation of books for and about children, especially in the triumphant efflorescence of children's literature. What explains the will toward exploring and colonizing the new continent of childhood, a will clearly evident both in writing for adults and in the new and gloriously successful genre of nineteenth-century children's literature? Even the explanatory Jungian archetype of the *puer aeternus* is itself a nineteenth-century artifact emerging from a Romantic context

Historians of childhood and the family, notably Phillipe Aries, John Demos, Lawrence Stone, and C. J. Sommerville have traced the steady rise throughout the early modern period of companionate nuclear family centered on child-rearing. With the developing emphasis on the horizontal family rather than the vertical "line," the raison d'être of family relationships become overtly affective rather than economic. *Feelings about children* are increasingly seen as the foundational center of the family rather than its ornamental superstructure. Thus the "child set in the midst" defines the shape of the circle.

The shift in family structure is only a partial explanation. What is most striking about the new embrace of childhood is the de-contextualizing of the child. It is as a being outside of the social and familial net that this Romantic child is prized. Childhood is a valorized state, associated with timeless immutability rather than change and history. As an embodiment of abiding Nature and as a possessor of autonomous consciousness, the Romantic Child became available to fill the symbolic gap left both by "the disappearance of God" (in Hillis Miller's phrase) and the waning of historical utopianism that followed both the French Revolution and failed revolutions of 1848. Preoccupation with childhood, or rather with a single child self, becomes in the nineteenth century a non-threatening means of commitment to social hope without the need of a political and social transformation. The Romantic child, like the Romantic imagination, is placed beyond the shocks of history. Sometimes produced through retrospective reclamation of the self embalmed within, sometimes constructed as a sequestered pastoral solitary, the Romantic child serves as a buffer against the vicissitudes of the public sphere. By *growing down*, the adult can insulate himself as a child self from the shocks of history and also ally himself in fellowship with true timeless childhood, thus blotting out the actual contemporary ugliness of child exploitation.

The chapters that follow explore four ways of privileging and using childhood, four ways of acquiring authority or safety through recapturing and reconstructing childhood identity. In each chapter, the quest is to discover and explain "the vocation of childhood." Wordsworth creates and glamorizes an autonomous child, divorced, "sequestered," "destitute," daemonic, isolated, and exemplary. Lamb creates a fragile lambkin child sheltered in various archaic and dilapidated institutions. De Quincey reenacts the afflictions and satisfactions of childhood through masochistic bodily identification. Hartley Coleridge elevates docile filial child's play to a lifelong life-evading vocation. For each writer, childhood offers thematic resources, a constructed identity, and a justification for both the life and the career.

Chapter Two

More Clouds Than Glories: Wordsworth and The Sequestered Child

"Dear old Wordsworth" and the Received Narrative

May 1870. The Reverend Robert Francis Kilvert, twenty-nine years old and the curate of Clyro, attends a village supper party. Recently back from London and a visit to the Royal Academy, fresh from the melting sight of "The Good Shepherd," Murillo's smooth-limbed boy among his lambs ("The child's eyes are uplifted and in them and over his whole face there is a marvellous beauty . . . [an] indescribable look of heavenly light and purity" [1: 23]), Kilvert is a devout admirer of childhood beauty. He soon sees a shy child notable for her "tiny slight form, the little delicate head, the pure severe features and the quick, bright, full eye as quick and bright and full as the eye of a bird, so watchful and grave, but so sweet" (1.131). His journal entry describes their encounter as an episode in the received narrative of Wordsworthian childspotting. He quickly gloms on to her:

> I devoted myself almost entirely to my bewitching little friend, stood behind her chair and took care of her, brought her as quickly as possible the best wing of the best chicken I could find to carve at the sideboard and saw that she had plenty of jelly and wine afterwards, so that she might not feel strange or lonely or think herself neglected for people who might be thought by some to be of higher rank or greater consequence. I believe she saw I was trying to be kind to her and keep her from feeling uncomfortable among people she did not know, and, poor child, she looked at me so gratefully.
>
> I've heard of hearts unkind, kind deeds
> With coldness still returning.

> Alas, the *gratitude* of men
> Has oftener left *me* mourning.
> Dear old Wordsworth! (Kilvert 1: 132)

The elements in this encounter play out the Victorian Child Romance featuring a country child who is at once uncannily beautiful ("bewitching") and pathetically vulnerable ("tiny light," "little delicate," "poor child"); a world that ignores her ("people she did not know"); a tender-hearted delicate-minded adult who intervenes to rescue her ("stood behind her chair and took care of her"); and "Dear Old Wordsworth" who presides. The elements are deployed in a verbal medium of clammy emotion: *devoted, bewitching, feeling strange or lonely, neglected, kind, feeling uncomfortable, gratefully, hearts unkind, kind deeds, gratitude, mourning.* An isolated and vulnerable girl, this "little friend" is Kilvert's object of desire both for her pure loveliness and for her distress, persecuted and humiliated by a society of enemies who prize adult stature ("higher rank . . . greater consequence") above such delicate little people; she is rescued from this hierarchical social world by a solitary introverted quixotic knight who has been trained by a venerable and celebrated counselor, "Dear old Wordsworth!" In rescuing the child, the knight is himself rescued from his lonely self-consciousness. The romance with the child is wordless; the speechless child must be represented, served, and interpreted by Kilvert who alone can understand her ("I believe she saw I was trying . . ." "she looked at me so gratefully") because he has learned to read her through the medium of Wordsworth.

Wordsworth also bodes over Elizabeth Bowen's darkly comic subversion of the Victorian Child Romance.[1] Writing some seventy years after Kilvert's supper party, Bowen also sets her "The Easter Egg Party" (1941) in the same kind of country village, all "gladey and glittering with the first greens of spring" (529). The formidable Evers sisters, single women in their fifties and powers in their Glocestershire village of West Wallows, invite the little daughter of a shopworn schoolmate (grown up to become a divorced actress) to visit over the Easter holidays. According to a veiled newspaper account, something dreadful has happened to the child, a rape perhaps: "The case was given in outline, with unusual reticence. When they saw what had either happened or nearly happened—they were not quite clear which—to the little girl of a friend they had known as a little girl" (529), the sisters resolve on reparations: "Their object was to restore her childhood to her." Like Kilvert's, their understanding of childhood is mediated through a 'Wordsworth', who is both the genius loci of their neighborhood ("and in the garden and in the strip of orchard the other side of the brook daffodils blew their trumpets" [531]) and the master-text of all their being: Eunice and Isabelle Evers "still received intimations of immortality" (530). When tough, brisk Hermione arrives, she turns out not to be anything the Evers sisters can recognize as a child but rather a thoroughly modern city girl, indeed a proleptic Valley Girl, urban rather than rural, social rather than solitary. She is no damaged flower but a self-contained person with an urban sensibility; a seductive sense of playing to an audience; and a sophisticated wardrobe. She loves to shop—especially for anything plastic; she has a stony indifference to the rural landscape and the kittens, ponies, sheep, birds, trees, and flowers that populate it. In this reversal of the Victorian Child Romance, it is the two superannuated old Evers girls, forever young, who embody nature-loving "child-like" simplicity and vulnerability under the sign of Wordsworth; while it is young Hermione who embodies acquisitive worldliness. The failed Easter Egg Party for Hermione and the neighborhood children is Bowen's comic denouement. Instead of a harmonious spring rite of the innocents or a good-natured game of playfellows, it becomes a battle. Here the sisters' Wordsworthian imperium breaks down: Hermione and the local children loathe each other on sight. Hermione especially detests Harriet, her antithesis, and the village's most successful child—successful both at playing the game of Easter Egg Hunt and also the game of being a gladsome country girl. Hermione sabotages the occasion by stealing the candy eggs found by Harriet and hides them in the orchard where, days after Hermione has been shipped home, the sisters discover not merely the "trampled daffodils" (536) but the dissolved candy eggs: "the chocolate under the paper had gone to a pulp, and the gold and colours of the paper had run" (538).

Bowen's project is the pulping and discoloring of Wordsworthian childhood, which in her reading becomes nothing but a sugary confection contrived by regressive adults for their own comfort. In the role reversal enacted in Bowen's astringent fable, it is the adults who need children to perform a charade of happy childhood for their benefit. But a girl who does not play by Gloucestershire rules is defined as damaged goods and better off invisible or dead. "The sisters seldom speak of her even between themselves; she has left a sort of scar, like a flattened grave, in their hearts" (538).

Though these two Wordsworthian rescue narratives differ, one operating in the doleful love/loss register of romance and the other in the dissolving medium of satire and farce, they both utilize the masterplot, the received narrative, that almost two hundred years of Wordsworth criticism has made canonical. As in Max Beerbohm's cartoon of the bespectacled poet and the eyeless girl, the characters are always a scrutinizing Adult and a scrutinized Child. The triple plot involves discovery, intervention, and rescue. Guided by Wordsworth, the master child-spotter, the adult *discovers* a child instinct with power. The adult then *intervenes and interpellates* an exemplary child subject by asking the right questions or by supportively serving the right delicate viands or by providing the right "gladey and glittering" environment. Finally, the adult carries out a rescue of the child and him/herself by comforting *and/or internalizing* that child as a source of emotional or moral authority. There is inevitably an unresolved ambiguity, covert in idealized versions like Kilvert's but overt in satiric versions like Bowen's, as to who really needs and who really gets the comfort—the adult's child self or the accosted child. Thus Kilvert hones in on the "bewitching" girl who is isolated in the midst of a large group of people; by means of his assiduous service of invalid fare (the chicken wing, the jelly, the wine), he interpellates her as a delicate and introverted and sensitive child. He carries away a psychological love token, an inner assurance of this delicate child's delicate gratitude. Bowen's subversion features the adults' random discovery in the newspaper of a mysteriously damaged child. They intervene and attempt to call into being a child of nature; but Hermione has fallen too far into self-consciousness. She is a resistant subject whose own firmly articulated self-conception of herself blocks theirs: "You keep on making me take an interest in things, and you never take the slightest interest in me" (537). Their failure with Hermione is a failure of imagination—they cannot enter into her otherness—and it is internalized as a death of the heart, theirs not hers. Kilvert uses the Wordsworthian narrative as a source of uplift and reaffirmation while Bowen critiques it as a sentimentalism destructive to adults and children alike.

The Kilvert and Bowen positions represent two extremes of the long consensus on Wordsworth's representation of childhood as the site of discovery, intervention/interpellation, and rescue/comfort. Whether the narrative is affirmed as visionary and/or psychologically profound or deconstructed as puerile and/or pernicious (the former is the principal Victorian and Modern response; the latter belongs more to Wordsworth's contemporaries and our own),[2] the plot line is the same. The retelling of this one story and one story only keeps intact a single, partial, and sentimentalized version of Wordsworth who is sometimes praised and sometimes reviled as discoverer, expositor, and profiteer of visionary childhood.

Even since De Quincey (in the role of Stanley) fingered Wordsworth as the Livingston of the great undiscovered continent of childhood—Wordsworth, he alleges, "was the first person to notice" that childhood has a privileged state on its "distinct peninsula," the first to notice that childhood "is endowed with a special power of listening for the tones of truth" (*CW* 1: 122)—Wordsworth has been seen as the poet of origin, as the father of the child who is father of the man.[3] Even in the most skeptical contemporary demystifications of golden childhood, for example, art historian Marina Warner's *Six Myths of Our Time* (1995), use a kind of ideational shorthand that casts Wordsworth as begetter or at least the first cultivator of "the present cult of the child . . . grown in the ground of Romanticism: for Wordsworth, heaven lay about us in our infancy and the child was father to the man"(49). Two recent collections edited by James H. McGavran, both focused on Romanticism and Childhood, bear witness to Wordsworth's predominance. Wordsworth figures as presider in *Romanticism and Children's Literature in Nineteenth-Century England* (1991) as the main subject of four of the eleven essays and with one hundred sixteen index citations, vastly more than any other writer. In McGavran's more recent volume, *Literature and the Child: Romantic Continuations, Postmodern Contestations* (1999), Wordsworth is a more equivocal but still powerful presence as tarnished but mighty prophet of a narrow masculinist canon and a discredited "Romantic Child." He remains the most frequently cited writer in the volume.[4] This is simply to make the obvious point that Wordsworth remains the touchstone and origin figure in discussion of Romantic childhood. If as Mitzi Myers suggests, with good reason, to scholars of Romanticism "the Romantic child is our foundational fiction," Wordsworth is the founding father of that fiction and that child ("Reading Children" 45).

If there is consensus on Wordsworth for good or ill as the exemplary Romantic childspotter, there is also agreement on the qualities Wordsworth spots or imputes.[5] Paradoxical, like all heavily laden symbols, the Wordsworthian child ("A simple Child") is a compound figure signifying the compensatory simplicity of what the adult is not. The Wordsworthian child ("that creature of fire and dew, that child of genius" [in Knoepflmacher 393]; "Blest, and powerful" ["Personal Talk" *PW* 347]) is a "quiescent" (Douglas' term [122]) border figure moving lightly, unselfconsciously, and ahistorically between Nature and Spirit. The culturally recurring Wordsworthian child that has been teased out of the Intimations Ode is a superior being at once associated with Joy ("The Babe leaps up on his mother's arm"), with transcendence, with power, but also with loss. This child's charge is to patrol the border between the finite and the infinite (witness the seashore image source of numerous sub-Wordsworthian Victorian redactions).[6]

Finally, there is consensus on the uses of childhood. The Wordsworthian child is both beautiful and useful, an agent of adult pedagogy and self-improvement. Wordsworth emphatically did not write *for* children but *about* children for the benefit of adult. He was "much surprised and more hurt" to find his "Pet Lamb" "in a children's school book" (Garlitz, "Baby's Debut" 89). Nor did nineteenth-century children generally much like Wordsworth's poetry: "we considered it all bosh" (Ward 407). John Keble's heavily Wordsworthian *Lyra Innocentium* (1846), a work with an epigraph out of "Anecdote for Fathers," is intended not for children but for teachers learning how to manage them. George Eliot's deeply Wordsworthian *Silas Marner* (1861) points an adult lesson in her epigraph from "Michael" on the therapeutic uses of childhood: "A child, more than all other gifts / That earth can offer to declining man, / Brings hope with it, and forward-looking thoughts." The power—indeed the duty—of children to awake feeling in a torpid adult soul, to bring the dead to life, is a lachrymose trope in Victorian and Edwardian children's fiction, most notably in *Little Lord Fauntleroy* (1886).[7] (It is also a deadly trope in adult literature, since the more exalted the genre, however, the more adult-inflected, the higher the likelihood that the child's dutiful service will mean the sacrifice of the child's life.[8] In the Alcott-Emerson iteration of the Wordsworthian child, the function is higher still, not merely morale-building but redemption: "Infancy is the perpetual Messiah, which comes into the arms of fallen men, and pleads with them to return to paradise" (Emerson 53).[9]

In excoriating the "adultist" writing not *for* but *about* children "characteristic of masculine Romanticism" (Myers, "Here's Looking" 162, 161), notably Wordsworth, Myers notes that Wordsworth and, still more, writers of "that peculiarly decadent Romantic moment that produced so much writing about and depiction of childhood at the end of the nineteenth century" (159) produce a child either as a "transcendental or nostalgic object" (161). In such a painful example (painful in evocation of parental grief and painful as an instance of the perversion of reason) as Leigh Hunt's essay on the "Deaths of Little Children," it is plain that the transcendentalizing of a child as a idol dehumanizes that child:

> If there were *no childhood deaths* . . . we would regard every little child as a man or woman secured, and it will easily be conceived what a world of endearing cares and hopes this security would endanger. The very idea of infancy would lose its continuity with us. Girls and boys would be future men and women, not present children. . . . On the other hand, those who have lost an infant, are never, as it were, without an infant child. . . . The

other children grow up to manhood and womanhood and suffer all the changes of mortality. This one alone is rendered an immortal child. (6)[10]

Thus objectified, the immortal child is also the alienated child—alienated from the adult who depends on its difference and alienated from its own subjectivity. Such a child is stripped of agency and of life itself. It is this Wordsworthian pacification that provokes Myers' judgment on Wordsworth as "peerless poet for adults" but a "poisonous influence on literature for children" and on modern conceptions of childhood (162).

But this familiar account of ideal childhood needs amplification. Wordsworth's representation of childhood is much more complex, tough-minded, and dreadful than is conceded by the pervasive crushing cliches of Wordsworth's visions of "idyllic childhood innocence" (Nodelman 31) that generally feature the "Wordsworthian child of Nature" (Knoepflmacher), the "healing . . . *puer aeternus*, the divine child" (Woodman 72), and "the innocent child arrived here from a pre-natal existence" (Ward 423). As Marilyn Gaull has recently argued, the cultural dominance of the Wordsworth/innocent child equation has blocked consideration of his difficult even "savage" childhood and his association of childhood with traumatic events and brutal folkloric traditions.[11] McGavran too has suggested that the hero of *The Prelude* is a Wordsworthian rambling boy who is more problem than ideal, more threat than comfort.[12] But so powerful and so familiar is the transcendent child trailing clouds of glory and the developmental child fathering forth mighty manhood that it is necessary to turn now to the Wordsworth of clouds rather than glories. If Wordsworthian childhood is indeed the font of Romantic childhood then that childhood is a much darker and more complicated entity than is generally acknowledged.

On Beyond Idyll

Wordsworth is an unlikely source of sentimentality about childhood joy and innocence. Wordsworth's overt flatfooted autobiographical memorandum of himself when young delivers a child who is neither good, innocent, nor adorable. Indeed, he takes pains to represent himself as prickly, difficult, and intermittently wretched. A less cute child would be hard to find. He was orphaned early, left "destitute" (*Prelude* 1805 2: 259): the death of his mother when he was seven effectively deprived him of both parents since his abstracted, overworked father sank into depression when his wife died and "never recovered his usual cheerfulness of mind" (*Prose* 3: 219) in the few remaining years of his life.

Wordsworth's specific references to his parents are fraught with anxiety: those to his father are scant, those to his mother few and anxious. The single memory, articulated late in his life, of unambiguous maternal tenderness—"pinning a nosegay to my breast when I was going to say the catechism in Church, as was customary before Easter" (*Prose* 3: 219-20) generates the 1821 Ecclesiastical Sonnet, "Catechising," which proclaims so emotionally labile and fragile a recollection that it suggests a tremulous swoop into unassuaged grief. The poem recalls the "trembling, earnest Company" of communicants, their "low soft murmur, like a distant bee," the atmosphere of "thought-perplexing fears," and maternal anxiety:

> Belovèd Mother! Thou whose happy hand
> Had bound the flowers I wore, with faithful tie:
> Sweet flowers! At whose inaudible command
> Her countenance, phantom-like, doth re-appear:
> O lost too early for the frequent tear,
> And ill-requited by this heartfelt sigh! (*PW* 629)

The mother's identity is intertwined with something "inaudible" and "phantom-like" but also exclamatory and minatory (three exclamation marks in six lines) in its insatiable emotional demands ("too early for the frequent tear," "ill requited").

Wordsworth describes himself in boyhood as "of a stiff, moody, and violent temper" (Prose 3: 372). This idiom has nothing in common with the Victorian child discourse of original innocence but rather locates the boy Wordsworth in a tragic universe that his two remembered anecdotes illustrate. Wordsworth the boy is dangerous, vengeful, capable of violence, even of suicide:

> I remember going once into the attics of my grandfather's house at Penrith upon some indignity having been put upon me with an intention of destroying myself with one of the foils which I knew was kept there. I took the foil in hand, but my heart failed. Upon another occasion, while I was at my grandfather's house in Penrith, along with my oldest brother Richard, we were whipping tops together in the large drawing-room, on which the carpet was only laid down upon particular occasions. The walls were hung round with family pictures, and I said to my brother, "Dare you strike your whip through that old lady's petticoat?" He replied, "No, I won't." "Then," said I, "here goes" and I struck my lash through her hooped petticoat, for which no doubt, though I have forgotten it, I was properly punished. But possibly, from some want of judgment in punishments inflicted, I had

become perverse and obstinate in defying chastisement, and rather proud of it than otherwise. (*Prose* 3: 372)

In this autobiographical recollection, Wordsworth situates himself proudly, obstinately, perversely among the swords and portraits of his ancestral attic. Both memories are sharply specific. The suicide attempt is so circumstantially situated as to betoken serious premeditation. The whipping scene is detailed as well, an assault on the principle of authority. In both recollections—Wordsworth with fencing foil, Wordsworth with whip—the boy is figured not as an androgynous Child, but as an angry scourge like the Avenger in a Jacobean tragedy, hypermasculine and full of rage. This is the portrait of the artist as a young tragic hero, part Hamlet, part Satan. He is a furious and suicidal boy Hamlet torn between annihilating himself or turning his rage against his family. Although it is Byron who was habitually mocked as a Satanic poet, it is Wordsworth here and later who shows the proud indifference to punishment ("perverse and obstinate in defying chastisement and rather proud of it") and "the resolve to find in itself alone the one absolute motive for action," which Coleridge defined as Satanic (Perkins 503). If Wordsworth omits these vivid recollections from *The Prelude,* it cannot be because of the child's perilous poise on the brink of annihilation in the one or the surrender to violent impulse in the other are irrelevant to the growth of the mind. Indeed the dizzying apprehension of annihilation is key to many of the spots of time (notably the panic at the execution site and the Boat Stealing) as is the unleashing of a violent impulses (notably in transgressive assaults on a feminized nature in Nutting and Birds' Nesting). But the intimate domestic specificity of it may give too much away.

Even in his most sanitized passages, most purged of his feints with nothingness and violence, it is the intensity and seriousness of childhood passion and feeling that Wordsworth most emphasizes. Goodness and innocence are downplayed in Wordsworth's tributes to that "race of real children, not too wise, / Too learned or too good" (*Prelude* 5: 436-37). But he is insistent about "wild appetites and blind desires / Motions of savage instinct" ("Home at Grasmere" 913-14). Indeed as Gaull notes shrewdly, despite *The Prelude*'s emphasis on the pleasures of boyhood and the childhood "bond of union between life and joy" (1: 558), of love "there seems to be very little in his boyhood" (13) and of tenderness even less. The traumatic experiences in the spots of time are transgressive moments of fear, later construed as disciplinary, enacted on a morally serious being defiantly insisting on being in both physical and moral jeopardy:

> — Nothing at that time
> So welcome, no temptation half so dear
> As that which [urged] me to a daring feat.
> Deep pools, tall trees, black chasms, and dizzying crags—
> I loved to look at them, to stand and read
> Their looks forbidding, read and disobeyed,
> Sometimes in act, and evermore in thought ("Home at Grasmere" 915-21)

The nine-year-old's bird stealing is construed as a psychomachia in which "a strong desire / O'erpowered my better reason"(*Prelude* 1: 318-19); his self-styled plundering of birds' nests takes him into danger on "the perilous ridge" (1: 336). Though there are moments of ecstatic animist stepping out of the conscious self in a great merge

> when with bliss ineffable
> I felt the sentiment of Being spread
> O'er all that moves and all the seemeth still. (2: 400-402)

Such a loss of the self in Being, such an ec/static stepping out of the boundaries of the self can be a deeply destabilizing descent into an abyss of idealism in which the sole self dissolves into the landscape. Indeed, Michael Friedman reads such moments as a terrifying descent into solipsism in which only the self exists in the empty universe, "a self devoid of relation to anything outside the self" (22).[13] Just such a commentary on the terrors of *The Prelude* occurs in A. S. Byatt's *The Virgin in the Garden* (1978) where Marcus Potter, a late-born Wordsworthian child, is driven to the brink of madness by "being spread" across the landscape in a kind of "falling, vanishing" from normal consciousness.[14] Marcus' Wordsworthian lineage is established on his entry into the novel. Walking upon the playing fields that "lay about him in his infancy" and bending like the leech-gatherer over a leech-filled Bilge Pond "stirring with a long stick," he lapses compulsively into the game he called "spreading himself":

> This began with a deliberate extension of his field of vision, until by some sleight of perception he was looking out at once from the four field-corners. . . . It was not any sense of containing the things he saw. Rather he surveyed them, from no vantage point or all at once. . . . Sometimes, for immeasurable instants, he lost any sense of where he really was, of where the spread mind had its origin. He had to teach himself to find his body by fixing the mind to precise things, by shrinking the attention until it was momentarily located in one solid object. . . . He could in some spyglass way

search out the crouching cold body, and with luck leap the mind across to it. (27)

After "being spread," Marcus, like Wordsworth, needs to grasp "at a wall or a tree to recall myself from this abyss of idealism to the reality." Byatt's revisionist account of this nearly psychotic Wordsworthian child who also receives light "photisms," suggests that Wordsworth's childhood experiences as represented in *The Prelude* can as readily be glossed as occasions of terror as of insight. Such terror, as Marcus' case makes plain, cannot be easily resolved to the convenient category of the sublime because, to cite Boris Pasternak's *Dr. Zhivago,* "the figurative has become literal, children are children and the terrors are terrible" (463).[15] In staking a claim for his "race of real children," Wordsworth also claims real dangers and real terrors.

If Wordsworth did not attribute ideal serenity and innocence to his own childhood, neither was he much inclined to idealize any of the children within his ken. He was never an ostentatious child-lover. Indeed, Wordsworth's more critical neighbors compared the middle-aged poet unfavorably to another local poet of childhood, young and engaging Hartley Coleridge. Unlike Wordsworth, Hartley Coleridge had been a wise, good, happy, and much doted upon boy, a *wunderkind.* Hartley had loved being a child and he loved children—at least all babies, most girls, and a few small boys. But Wordsworth seemed to his neighbors much inferior to Hartley in inventiveness, readability, affability, and kindness to the young. As one neighbor recalled:

> But as fur Mr. Wudsworth, he'd pass you, same as if ya was nobbut but a Stoan. He niver cared for children, however; ya may be certain of that, for didn't I have to pass him four time in t'week up to the door w' the meat? And he never oncst said owt. Ye're well aware if he'd been fond of children he'ud spoke. (Rawnsley 86)

Even though the influence of Wordsworth on nineteenth-century activists such as Barnardo and Lord Shaftesbury was notable,[16] Wordsworth himself did not notably participate in contemporary public efforts for the relief of childhood distress. He returned a courteous refusal to James Montgomery's request for a poetic contribution to an anthology on chimney sweepers: "I feel much for their unhappy situation and should be glad to see the custom . . . abolished. But at no period of my life have I been able to write verses that do not spring from an inward impulse . . ." (*WLLY* 2: 136). Though *The Excursion* famously deplored the plight of child factory laborers and urged the institution of national education, he was nonetheless opposed to philanthropic schemes to enlarge educational opportunities for working-class children, employing an argument that promoted familial and social concord over unique childhood potential: "Human learning, so far as it tends to breed pride and self-estimate . . . is against the spirit of the Gospel. . . . Can it, in a *general* view, be good that an infant should learn much which its *parents do not know?*" (*WLLY* 2: 21). His argument makes plain that for Wordsworth, childhood as a category was emphatically trumped by class.

As a parent and guardian, he was anxiously, and even intrusively involved with childrearing. He was intelligent, kind, unsentimental, and unempathetic. To little Basil Montagu, their ward at Alfoxden, he and Dorothy were thoughtfully but not dotingly attentive. Part of their program for "unspoiling Basil Montagu" (Johnston's phrase 537) whose habitual lying they took quite seriously, was a salutary *inattention:* ample time and space for running free in the countryside combined with a "negative" discipline that punished misbehavior by sequestering rather than lecturing or spanking the malefactor. To Caroline, Annette Vallon's daughter, he was honorably correct but necessarily and self-preservingly distant and self-justifyingly uninterested. To his and Mary's children, he was, to adapt psychologist D. W. Winnicott's phrase, a "good-enough" father, conscientious, moderately attentive, enabling appropriate growth into maturity. He broke no norms, however; he never doted on, gloated over, boasted about, nor conversed with his children in the hyper-empathetic manner of Coleridge or Southey. He was a responsible father, concerned for their welfare, financial, physical, and educational. According to John Beer, one reason Wordsworth never published the great poem of his own life was to "preserve its copyright for his children" (247). He was earnestly concerned about finding a place in the world for his boys; he worried painfully about his grown daughter's increasingly fragile health and was almost broken by her death in her early forties. But he was no great noticer of his children's early development, differing in this from Coleridge who delighted in sharing—indeed appropriating—little David Hartley's dreams and from Thomas De Quincey who shared in the games of the Wordsworth children. De Quincey, for example, knew precisely what toy ("*His Artillery*") to bring back to Johnny Wordsworth from London even though neither William or Mary Wordsworth nor Johnny himself could think of anything better for this halting reader than a wretched "book, poor fellow, little use books are to him" (*Love Letters* 96). The quality of Wordsworth's attention to his own children did not approach the delicacy and brilliance of his attention to his own constructed childhood. Like any ordinary patriarch he worried about his children's academic progress and was particularly vexed at the academic incapacity of John, whom he considered to be "lamentably slow. This is to me a mortification as I promised myself of much pleasure in rubbing up my Greek with him" (*WLMY* pt. 2, 3: 8). The empathetic De Quincey watched Johnny's habits closely and came up with a brilliant "multisensory" method used even today by special educators instructing dyslexic children (Huston).[17] De Quincey quickly realized that John was physically adroit but lexically inept and suggested bringing a commercial printing press to Grasmere so that the child could learn to read by setting type (Jordan 126-27). But Wordsworth responded to John's learning difficulties with a mounting irritation that led the boy to fear and shun his father. Though Wordsworth as student had been the most recalcitrant and indocile of young men (Johnston, chaps. 5-7), Wordsworth as father quashed the impractical and romantic military ambition of both his surviving sons and steered them instead into professions for which they had neither taste nor talent—the Church and the Stamp Office. It is evident from Wordsworth's firm management of his boys' careers that he had ordinary ambitions for them and used ordinary patriarchal methods: he never assumed that nature would guide them aright to a choice of life. His poignant sonnet of 1833, "In Sight of the Town of Cockermouth," addressed to his grown-up children, suggests that he eventually doubted his own guidance too: "If e'er, through fault of mine, in mutual pain / We breathed together . . . / The wrong, by love provoked, let love arraign" (*PW* 707).

Despite Wordsworth's evident devotion, however, there is no doubt that he was sometimes a distracted and preoccupied parent. Though the deaths of three-year-old Catherine and six-year-old Thomas in 1812 drove Mary to a near breakdown, Wordsworth himself seemed to some observers at the time cushioned from the loss by his constant preoccupation with his writing. (He may have seemed so to himself judging from the anguished apology for a forgetfulness that is itself characterized as "the worst pang that sorrow every bore" in the beautiful elegy, "Surprised by Joy" written three years later.)

Wordsworth's distanced parental stance may have been calculation as much as preoccupation. In some passages, Wordsworth reveals something like a fear of the Evil Eye, an almost superstitious dread of attending too much to a child. However calculated, for example, young Basil Montagu's education, Dorothy and William earnestly eschewed the elaborate forms of surveillance recommended by eighteenth-century pedagogical theory, especially Locke's and Rousseau's (Richardson 49), condemning those busybody helpers "ever on the watch" to manipulate all childhood experience (*Prelude* 1805, 5: 356). To be the center of a little universe "fretted by sallies of his mother's kisses," to move in the "light upon him from his father's eyes," to be one over whom inescapably "Immortality / Broods like the Day, a Master o'er a Slave," courts disaster. Too much adult presence—even that of guilt-inspiring Immortality here, as Mark Edmundson has noted—is "perhaps even sadistic and intimidating" (745), and is a mixed blessing.

In an extraordinary letter to an unknown correspondent written in 1804,[18] Wordsworth agonizes over the problem of educating a gifted child. Although Wordsworth's inflamed eyes made letter writing a misery to him, the theme of parental intervention evidently troubled him enough to spur an elaborate response. Though the formal content of Wordsworth's recommended education program is predictable (teachers should deracinate egotism by encouraging the child to read fairy tales to liberate her imagination and to study natural history to stabilize her reason), his analysis of the perils of her situation is surprising. This is a child endangered by the prospect of a happy childhood in a loving family:

> It appears then to me that *all the permanent evils which you have to apprehend for your Daughter, supposing you live to educate her yourself, may be referred to this principle: an undue prominence of present objects over absent ones,* which, as she will surely be distinguished by an extreme love of those about her, will produce a certain restlessness of mind, calling perpetually for proofs of ever-living regard and affection: she must be loved as much and in the same way as she loves, or she will not be satisfied. Hence, quickness in taking offence, petty jealousies and apprehensions lest she is neglected and loses ground in people's love, a want of a calm and ready sense of her own merits to secure her from these fits of imagined slights; for, in the first place, she will . . . be in general deficient in this just estimate of her own worth, and will further be apt to forget everything of that kind in the present sense of supposed injury. She will (all of which is referable to the same cause) in the company of others have too constant a craving for sympathy up to a height beyond what her companions are capable of bestowing; this will often be mortifying to herself and burdensome to others; and should circumstances be untoward, and her mind be not sufficiently furnished with ideas and knowledge, this craving would be most pernicious to herself, preying upon mind and body: She will be too easily pleased, apt to overrate the merits of new acquaintances, subject to fits of overlove and overjoy, in the absence of those she loves full of fears and apprehensions, &c., injurious to health; her passions for the most part will be happy and good, but she will be too little mistress of them. The distinctions which her intellect will make will be apt, able, and just, but in

conversation she will be prone to overshoot herself, and commit [?illogical] blunders through eagerness. In fine her manners will be frank and ardent, but they will want dignity, and a want of dignity will be the general defect of her character. (*WLMY* 1: 286, italics mine)

This analysis centers on the child's adult character as an excessively social being; she will turn out to be too volatile, "too easily pleased," too affectionate, too undignified, subject to "fits" of "overlove and overjoy." Her probable "want of dignity" includes a want of proper pride in her own worth, a puppyish willingness to please, a common friendliness rather than a general benevolence, an easily kindled affection toward others, and—above all—a need to love and be loved. These evils—and they are represented as evils—are linked to the fact that the child is beloved and *not an orphan*. Her parents are neither dead nor absent nor neglectful. All "the permanent evils which you have to apprehend for your Daughter" are tied up with Wordsworth's supposition that the parents "may live to educate her yourselves." It is this continuing presence of loving parents that will lead the child into what Wordsworth identifies as the root evil: "an undue prominence of present objects over absent ones." From the girl's habitual expectation of loving parents, Wordsworth infers a lifetime's debilitating dependence on other people for love and responsiveness. Departing from the modern commonplace that emotional security in childhood is a foundation for adult autonomy, Wordsworth assumes that a doted-upon child will become so addicted to love that in adulthood she will be unable to create her own pleasures, her own world. Never forced back on her own solitary resources in an unresponsive atmosphere, never having to stand on her own without the aid of props, she will never know herself, never come to the magisterial mind's ability, the ability Wordsworth ascribed to the poet, to "rejoice more than other [women] in the spirit of life that is in [her]; delighting to contemplate similar volitions and passions as manifested in the goings-on of the Universe, and habitually impelled to create them where [she] does not find them" ("Preface to *Lyrical Ballads*," *PW* 794). Through sheer excess of responsive parental presence, she will be robbed of the opportunity to develop that key quality of the creative soul: ". . . a disposition to be affected more than other [women] by absent things as if they were present" (794).

From the standpoint of creativity, the letter suggests it is better for children to be orphans, to be thrown back upon themselves, to be cut off from secure anchorage in the bosom of loving parents. In *The Prelude,* Wordsworth notes that the feeling initially called forth in a baby by its "mute dialogues with my mother's breast" soon returns upon the self. Once the feelings are generated, the external "props of my affection"—as Wordsworth calls parents—are no longer necessary to sustain the edifice of the self. To live continuously in a world of literal parental presence is to spill the essential self promiscuously over the whole affectional world. To live in a world from which parents are absent, however, is to deepen, concentrate, and enlarge the inner self so that it becomes capable of parthenogenetically recreating the lost world and the lost relationship, a better world and a better relationship. An orphan self, torn from the contaminating middle marches of the social environment, thrown back on its own self-originating creative power is the creative self who can see the old world afresh. As Alan Liu points out, Wordsworth is the great poet of "defamiliarization": "in the poetry of Wordsworth's self, we might say, all the familiar world will now be felt to be as fresh and new—and also as frightening—as the world seen through an orphan's eye" (300). It is clear that Wordsworth's focus in the letter in particular and in childhood poems in general is much less on childhood happiness than childhood strength at whatever cost.

If Wordsworth is not especially focused on childhood happiness and the love of children, neither is he the prophet of the "idyllic childhood innocence" so often associated with him (Nodelman 31). "Innocence" as a category is much less interesting to Wordsworth than to the Wordsworthians. The word and concept appear relatively infrequently in the poetry. Of the thirty-seven instances of "innocence" and the ninety-two of "innocent" reported in the Lane Cooper *Concordance,* the majority (seventy-three of one hundred twenty-nine) refer to adult legal and moral innocence like the French Revolution's "innocent victims sinking under fear" (*Prelude* 10: 404). When the word is used for children, the usage is generally traditional. The "innocent child" dead in "Vandracour and Julia" and Ellen's wasted "innocent babe" in *The Excursion* (6.811) are blameless unformed victims like "my innocent child and me" in Shakespeare's *Much Ado About Nothing* (5.1) or the "innocent babe truly begot" in *A Winter's Tale* (3.2). All are *privatively* defined by the qualities they lack: harmless, they are undeserving of harm. Innocence, because privative, is characterized by Wordsworth as presocial, a lack of self-conscious knowledge that is compatible to all kinds of potentially dangerous desires: "While yet an innocent . . . / I breathed . . . / Among wild appetites and blind desires / Motions of savage instinct" ("Home at Grasmere" 910, 912-14). Wordsworth's admirer John Keble was consistent with his master in including in his *Lyra Innocentium* a "cradle song" on the infancy of Judas. Even Judas was once an innocent baby on a mother's innocent breast: "Where Judas lay, a harmless Child, / By gold as yet unbought"; even "The Antichrist, they write, will be, / From as soft bosom duly fed, / Rock'd on a loving knee" ("Judas's Infancy" 67, 68). The technical blamelessness of this child is chronological only and not authoritative.

At most, innocence is a crucial precondition to healthy adulthood, something like mother's milk and clean air. Although the shepherds of Wordsworth's youth may actually have presented a spectacle of "vice and folly, wretchedness and fear" (1805, 8: 426), the innocent eye needs to be protected: "were it otherwise / And we found evil fast as we find good / In our first years, or think that it is found, / How could the innocent heart bear up and live" (8: 444-46). Innocence is here a medium of development not an end or a power in itself. Indeed Wordsworth's most emphatic use of the term is mocking. Citing the prodigy as the exemplary innocent, he suggests that the term is already cant: "Yet innocent himself withal, though shrewd / And can read lectures upon innocence" (5: 313-14).

But fatuous lectures on innocence are much less to Wordsworth's point than lectures on the fraught experience of being a parent burdened with a child or a child burdened with a parent. Indeed, parenthood is represented as a dangerous and largely doomed institution. Though adults in single solitude—the Peddler, the Leech Gatherer—are frequently sources of authority, adults represented in the company of child, in charge of children, are usually at their worst—helpless, useless, sometimes stupid, and even if well-meaning, ineffectual. The infantile Vandracour's insistence on caring for his infant son is a death warrant for the baby. Indeed Jacobus speculates on the infanticidal will veiled by the language of blunder (201):

> It consoled him here
> To attend upon the orphan and perform
> The office of a nurse to his young child,
> Which, after a short time, by some mistake
> Or indiscretion of the father, died (1805 *Prelude* 9: 904-8)

The similarly ineffectual and broken-hearted mother is a recurrent figure. The homeless Female Beggar of "An Evening Walk," whose children freeze to death—"Thy breast their death-bed, coffined in thine arms" (*PW* 7)—is the prototype of a series of mothers unable to protect their children: neither Margaret, nor Ellen the wet-nurse, nor the crazed protagonist of "Her Eyes are Wild" can do much for their children. On the contrary, it is their silent children who maintain their parents: "Suck, little babe, oh suck again! It cools my blood; it cools my brain!" (*PW* 79). It is the night magic of the woods that protects Betty Foy's Idiot Boy, not the flapping and bustle of his mother.

In counterpoise to the mad mothers, some wise fathers cultivate nonattachment. In the pattern noted by Gayatri Spivak in the latter books of *The Prelude,* which she reads as "textual signs of a rejection of paternity" (47); fathers and marks of paternal responsibility get rubbed away. Matthew, for example, venerable schoolmaster and child lover, is lovable as a former father who has outlived his children, who refuses to be anybody's father's figure. In "Two April Mornings," he recalls his dead daughter Emma with great tenderness; then seeing another child, "A blooming Girl, whose hair was wet / With points of morning dew." The girl "so very fair" is a figure of "pure delight" and yet, "I looked at her and looked again / And did not wish her mine" (*PW* 116). In the companion poem, "The Fountain," the young narrator offers to be Matthew's substitute child:

"And Matthew, for your children dead
I'll be a son to thee!"
At this he grasped my hand, and said,
"Alas, this cannot be" (*PW* 117)

Instead of accepting a new daughter or son, Matthew leads the young man on a walk in which the old man demonstrates that he who is already "Nature's favorite child," has become his own child and needs no other ("Matthew" *PW* 115). Playfully "frolic," he chants his giddy "witty rhymes / About the crazy old church clock / And the bewildering chimes." Matthew is too busy being his own child to take on any adoptees. He can thus hang on forever, fixed in an eternal moment with that "bough of wilding in his hand" (116). Wilding, wild crab apple, needs no tending.

Even the Intimations Ode, so often cited for its influence on nineteenth-century child rearing,[19] is a counsel of despair or at least of unemployment for parents. Childhood triumphalism becomes cognate with parental superfluity as Gerard Manley Hopkins' bemused interrogation suggests. "'The child is father to the man' / How can he be? The words are wild . . . / No; what the poet did write ran, / 'The man is father to the child,' / 'The child is father to the man!' / How *can* he be? The words are wild" (248). Some read the epigraph as Wordsworth's "desire to be a self-begetter" (Carnochan 31) or a "writing Daddy out of the script" (Easthope 44). Easthope even urges a new title: "Memories of Primary Narcissism and Imaginary Plenitude taken as Guarantees that the I is Self-Sufficient and Not Constituted in Relation to the Other" (86). The self-origination implied in the epigraph is consistent with the demotion of parents throughout the poem. In projecting a child whose divine destiny in "that imperial palace whence he came" is consistently thwarted by step-parental warders, the Intimations Ode as a Family Romance dissolves all actually existing families. From infinite imperial space, the outdoor child falls into enclosure—hence "shades of the prison house" for the "Inmate Man" where he is pent up in this enclosure, diminished and degraded with the best of institutional intentions and turned into a shrunken grotesque version of what he might have been: "A six-years' Darling of a pigmy size!" Basking in artificial light "from his father's eyes" and "Fretted by sallies of his mother's kisses," he is initiated, "fretted," into culture through an erosion of the self. To be "fretted" (in the derivation from the Anglo-Latin *frectatus,* ornamented . . . embroidered with gold) suggests being elaborately decorated and adorned. To be fretted in a second sense (from Middle Dutch *vreten,* to eat) is to be gnawed, consumed, corroded, or irritated. The fretful, fretting maternal "sallies," these sudden starts, impetuous attacks, transports of emotion, these "fits of overlove and overjoy" (*MLMY* 1: 286), are simply normal acculturation. The beloved child is at once adorned and devoured by the volatile intellectual and emotional demands of the parents, becoming both cute and irritable, both learned and empty. Emotional assault and intellectual badgering in a small space are the Ode's dark version of family love.

Even in Wordsworth's greatest poem of family love, fatherhood fails. "Michael" dramatizes the impossibility of fatherhood by making foiled Abrahamic claims for Michael, the old patriarch.[20] The identification with Abraham is emphatic. Michael is judaized by receiving the name of the powerful archangel who is the patron of the Jews (Daniel 12.1). He is expressly Abrahamic as the old father of a single male heir by an aging wife; a master of flocks; a maker of a covenant; an agonized but consenting sacrificer of his son. Further, Michael is pulled out of historic time to inhabit an Abrahamic time warp. Although Wordsworth's letter to Fox clearly locates Michael as a "statesman" of contemporary Cumbria, within the poem the Biblical penumbra and the close knit nuclear household excluding all larger structures create the sense of Michael's household as timelessly self-sustaining. Michael, aided by Luke, tends the flocks out of doors; Isabel within spins wool and flax. Indeed timeless fixity in legend is associated with the family. The household is "a proverb in the vale / For endless industry" (*PW* ll. 94-5), their cottage is known as "THE EVENING STAR" (l. 139), and their shearing spot as "The CLIPPING TREE" (l. 169). Though Michael's family is necessarily dependent on economic forces beyond the immediate community, the reference to the debt, the note, the brother's son, and Michael's early struggles shockingly "bursts through" (Collings' phrase [162]) a text that has studiously constructed a patriarchal pastoral idyll.[21]

Within the seeming stasis, Michael's Fatherhood is total: Father is All; he defines the family. As critic John Bushnell remarks, Michael is an "Adam before Eve . . . successfully effacing his wife and child in his attempt to assert a pure, absolute relationship to the land" (l. 252). He contains the identities of both wife and son. Isabel barely exists. Until line 226 (midway through the poem of 482 lines), Luke's mother is denominated only "his Helpmate" (ll. 79, 142) and "the Housewife" (ll. 107, 114, 126). She becomes "Isabel" only at line 226 when Michael (who has a name throughout) addresses her: "'Isabel,' said he." The address signals the incursion of weakness: disastrous financial news has arrived and Michael's "heart failed him" (l. 226). Until then Isabel has been undefined, swallowed up in Michael's androgyny. Michael has been both father and mother to the child and "done him female service," "rocked / His cradle, with a woman's gentle hand" (l. 154, ll. 157-58). Michael is so powerful a figure of ascendancy that he can encompass both masculine and feminine roles that render the female principle superfluous. In his double role of Father/Mother, Michael heads a family that is also double: the family as line defined by law that is also the family as circle of concern, defined by love. Michael's family is represented as both a synchronic small nuclear family bound by affective ties and a diachronic family line existing over many generations bound by a common property. The arrangement fulfills what social theorist Talcott Parsons calls both the expressive and instrumental functions (Poster xiii).

Neither Isabel nor Luke has a voice in this patriarchal household. Isabel is all but silent, speaking only twice to no avail: once vainly to urge Luke to stay, once fatuously to praise "The prettiest letters that were ever seen" (l. 435) sent by feckless Luke. Luke is both speechless and disappointing. Luke is permitted no direct speech at all, merely the indirect reports of his "jocund voice" toward his mother and of tears to his father's affectionate farewell benediction: "Luke had a manly heart; but at these words, / He sobbed aloud" (ll. 357-58). As Reeve Parker has indicated, Luke is definitionally a disappointment, an object of "fond correction and reproof" (l. 173) who is "from conception, always already dissolute" (58) and a disappointment to his father, a boy whose playfulness is described in an excised line as responsible for "Forgetfulness through the Father's thoughts" (Parker 62). By deleting this line, as Parker emphasizes, Wordsworth blocks any exchange of qualities between father and son and maintains the sharp distinction between the father's words, law to the boy, and the excess, play, and childishness of the unstable silent son. The primacy of Michael demands the silencing and disappearance of Luke, who is by definition unworthy. In a poem shadowed by Old Testament echoes of unworthy sons contending for paternal blessings (Isaac and Ishmael, Jacob and Esau), Luke proves the most unworthy vessel. His legacy is usurped by his unseen cousin,[22] the Brother's son who commandeers Luke's inheritance as the poet commandeers the story of Michael, which Luke was never able to utter. Michael's authority as father depends on the dwarfing and disappearance of the son.

Some of Wordsworth's most powerful poems enact liberation from parenthood, nowhere more effectively than in "It is a Beauteous Evening, Calm and Free." The sonnet was written during William and Dorothy's 1802 visit to Calais to meet Annette Vallon and his nine-year-old French daughter Caroline, the "Dear Child! Dear Girl! That walkest with me here." Wordsworth wished to make a financial settlement with Annette that would provide for her and Caroline and would clear the way for his marriage with Mary Hutchinson. Thus Wordsworth needed to mark and acknowledge his paternity but also definitely to put it behind him. Stephen Gill suggests that the meeting with Caroline was not altogether a success. The nine-year-old Caroline, seeing her English father for the first time, "a 32-year-old foreigner, an enemy of her country who spoke rusty French" (207), probably did not warm to him. At its most obvious level, the sonnet is at once a tribute and a not very veiled rebuke to the evidently unresponsive girl: "If thou appear untouched by solemn thought / Thy nature is not therefore less divine." The simple surface of the poem is a tissue of paradoxes fixing the girl to nature in such a way as to render the child invulnerable and the adult father unnecessary.

The moment of articulation is antithetically depicted to cushion the girl from normal transience. It is characterized in terms of *instantaneity* and of *eternity*. "The holy time is quiet as a Nun" now at this charged instant; the sun, at this very moment, "is sinking down"; the imperative "Listen!" exhorts attention to a sound just heard. But the sound is from "an eternal motion" made "everlastingly." The landscape also encodes *life* and *death, virginity* and *maternity:* it is "breathless" and "sinking down in its tranquility" but it is also "free" and wakeful: the "mighty Being is awake." Virgin chastity ("quiet as a nun") and maternal comfort ("gentleness . . . broods o'er the sea") are equally available. Available within the landscape is a depth of parental care that makes human intervention otiose and legitimizes paternal decathexis. The female protector is present in the gentle nun and the brooding gentleness, the male in Father Zeus the thunderer and in Abraham whose very name means father.

The pattern of antithesis suggests that the sonnet is a field for resolving contraries and conflicts: the momentary impulse that begets a child and the permanent responsibility that cares for her; bachelor independence and parental responsibility; Mary/William and Annette/Caroline; blood tie and freedom. Although the party on the beach at Calais included Annette, Caroline, Dorothy, and William, the human figures in the sonnet are reduced to two with the effect of deepening the play of antitheses. The antithetical pattern has the effect of making the child a timeless icon who is fully protected by surrogate parents in nature while the earthly protectors are obliterated. She is under religious protection: like the nun she is chaste and "untouched" but she is also fertile like the Virgin Mary ("God being with thee"). Further she is represented as simultaneously here and there, transient and eternal; at this moment she "walkest with me here" but she also somewhere else "liest in Abraham's bosom all the year."

But *Abraham's bosom* is a highly charged shelter. The locution drives from a passage in *Luke* (16: 19-31). After boil-covered beggar Lazarus starves outside the rich man's gates, "the beggar died and was carried by angels into Abraham's bosom" (16: 22) while the rich man burned miserably in Hell. Although "Abraham's bosom" was a proverbial synonym for death from the sixteenth century, eighteenth- and nineteenth-century use of the phrase was most frequently ironic, drawn from Shakespeare's version in *Richard III*.[23] Richard receives the report of the "tyrannous and bloody act"—the strangling of his nephews, the Little Princes, in the Tower of London—with the coolly comfortable observation that "The sons of Edward sleep in Abraham's bosom" (iv 3: 38). These "sons of Edward," smothered on their uncle's orders, are the rightful heirs to the throne of England. The children's rightful inheritance must be set aside, their voices must be stilled "in Abraham's bosom" so that the adult Richard can get on with his proper grown-up business of commanding the kingdom. The smothered princes in the Tower, an obsessive subject in nineteenth-century painting and even of Madame Tussaud's waxworks, were the very epitome of childhood's usurped rights.[24] Their background presence in this context of Caroline's displacement is as unsettling as the juxtaposition of "Abraham" with "the Temple's inner shrine." Although Abraham is the type of the good father of all the children of Israel, he is also the sacrificing father prepared to slay his son on Mount Moriah, later the Temple Mount in Jerusalem, the site of the Holy of Holies. Thus "the Temple's inner shrine" where Caroline rather ominously dwells is the site of the sacrifice of Isaac by Abraham. In this scarcely veiled place of sacrifice, parent and child are legitimately severed from each other. Caroline is given into the care of some more-or-less maternal nature or some more-or-less paternal patron or some androgynous synthesis in the bosom of Abraham. And her father is free to go.

A Child / And Nothing More

This separation of adult from child defines the Wordsworthian child. It is not innocent radiance or joy but an aesthetically embalmed apartheid that constitutes Wordsworth's major contribution to the nineteenth-century literature of childhood. Wordsworth's poetry regularly erases social context, intersubjective communion, and sequesters an iconically framed child in emptiness from which superfluous companions, social landmarks, and psychological and physiological faculties have been whittled away. Whether the child self figures the extreme of total plenitude by oceanically encompassing all Being within the self or is the extreme of utter evacuation, whether the child cipher is 1/0 or 0/1, the self is always *disjunct*.

Wordsworth's focus on the unaccomodated child, particularly in the balladic lyrics of 1798 to 1805,[25] is overdetermined. In these representations, the Georgian painter's topos of the child in a landscape, the Enlightenment experimental child, the strange isolated child-changeling of ballad tradition dovetail with Wordsworth's own experience of bereavement.

As is made clear in James Christen Steward's recent monograph *The New Child: British Art and the Origins of Modern Childhood, 1730–1830,* the single portrait of a child alone was one of several modes available for depiction of Georgian childhood even though family group portraits, moments of warm mother-child interaction, interior genres scenes of children at play, exterior genres scenes of children's toys, games, and romps were more usual representational modes. But the works of artists who focused on single figures in a landscape were well received largely because the *comfortable* quality of domestic painting envelops the isolated images of children. The contemporary praise of such paintings as Joshua Reynolds' much lauded "Lady Caroline Scott as Winter" (c. 1777), his "Master Hare" (1788), and Thomas Gainsborough's "Cottage Girl with Dog and Pitcher" (1785) indicates the ready appeal of such representations—both of upper-class children for comfort or lower-class children for pathos. Though Reynolds' depiction of Lady Caroline as a tiny girl bundled up against the cold may indeed, as Steward suggests, gesture at "an icon of vulnerability in a wintery landscape" (20), the representation is a kind of game: Lady Caroline is perfectly safe, radiantly healthy, richly dressed, and has no need for the easily provoked/easily forgotten sympathy of the viewer. The utterly adorable Lady Caroline, bright-eyed, rosy-cheeked with cold—by a trick of perspective made huge and tiny at the same time (the scale is given by her companion robin and toy terrier, both of which look much larger than life-size)—is lavishly muffed and cloaked and bonneted in fine fabrics. She is relatively much larger and much more important than the landscape she inhabits and not threatened by it at all.

Folklore and ballads, so important to Wordsworth, as Duncan Wu and Marilyn Gaull have indicated,[26] provide an additional source of the topos of the single child, lost or questing, and fronting his or suffering her destiny. Such folkloric children, both the uncanny (revenants, changelings, ghosts, grateful/ungrateful dead) and the homey (the Jacks of the British Jack tales like "Jack the Giant Killer" [*Prelude* 368] and the lucky Arabian Nights heroes) stand behind Wordsworth's empowered isolates. Among Percy's *Reliques of Ancient English Poetry,* a book that was Wordsworth's constant resource from the 1780s on (Wu), is "Sir Aldingar," the tale of Queen Elinore slandered by a false knight and in need of a courtly champion. In the woods a simple child springs out of nowhere, "a tinye boye":

A tinye boye she mette, Got wot,
All clad in mantle of golde;
He seemed noe more in man's likenèsse,
Than a childe of four yeere olde. (Percy 2.58 ll. 120-24)

No champion will stand forth for the Queen, until "When riding upon a little white steed, / The tinye boy they see" (2: 60, ll. 163-64); he smites the false knight, vindicates the queen, rights all wrongs, and miraculously vanishes. In a more ribald version, "The Boy and the Mantle," another wise child makes an incursion out of nowhere into Arthur's court and administers the test of chastity: a mantle that adorns only faithful wives but shows the unfaithful as naked, ugly, tattered (Sargent and Kittredge 46-49). This power child, enforcer of the true and the good, is less prominent in the ballads, however, than the brutalized child whose voice—like that of Wordsworth's balladic Danish Boy and Lucy Gray—arises mysteriously from beneath the earth or sea where the murderous mother had stowed it. Buried children shriek from the ground (variant of "Leesome Brand" 27); they return as revenants to beguile and torment her: "O look not sae sweet, my bonnie babe, / Gin ye smyle so, ye'll smyle me dead" ("The Cruel

Mother" 38); transformed children—"the laily worm" and "the macherel of the sea"—curse their betraying stepmother ("The Laily Worm and the Macherel of the Sea" 63). And lone boy heroes such as Jack the Giant killer whom Wordsworth cites and the intrepid picaresque boy protagonists of *The Arabian Nights,* which Wordsworth so loved, enact a pilgrimage of the single small being against the world.[27]

The focus on the isolated child extending as far as educational experiments in pedagogic isolation is also a period interest (Bewell 51-20, Richardson 48-64) that Wordsworth shares. "He had, in fact, almost a scientific or experimental attitude towards children which was very characteristic of his generation" (Moorman 34). By the mid-eighteenth century feral children had become intellectually interesting. In his *Wolf Children and the Problem of Human Nature,* Lucien Malson cites fourteen instances of feral children who were found and studied in seventeenth- and eighteenth-century Europe (80-81) including the famous Victor, "The Savage Boy of Aveyron" whom Coleridge fingered as potentially valuable for "William's great poem" (Coleridge, *NB* 3: 3538), noting especially Victor's "restless joy & blind conjunction . . . with natural Scenery," his swift and powerful gait, his feral survival skills, his persisting mutism in society, his aversion to other children, and his intense responsiveness to nature. The isolation of what was assumed to have been Victor's early life was analogous to the isolation sought in the visionary pedagogies of Rousseau, Richard Edgeworth, Thomas Day, and Thomas Wedgwood—though the experimentalists posited not merely rural isolation but isolation mediated through an omniscient rational tutor. Indeed Wedgwood's scheme for rearing a child genius required a sequestration so extreme that "the child must never go out of his own apartment" (Moorman 334).

The importance of the experimentally isolated child is implicit in the fact that from the publication of Rousseau's *Emile* (1760) until late in the Victorian period, Daniel Defoe's *Robinson Crusoe,* the classic abandonment/ self-reliance text became a normative children's text. Though Rousseau forbade his Emile all fictions and discouraged early reading altogether, *Robinson Crusoe* was exceptional and enjoined: "This is the first book Emile will read; for a long time it will form his whole library" (147). Rousseau and his disciple Thomas Day constructed educational schemes designed for permanently shipwrecked individuals who could thereby acquire immunity to the social world they perforce inhabit: "Emile is no savage to be banished to the desert; he is a savage who has to live in town." (167). Robinson Crusoe could serve as model of an autonomous self-sufficient being whether on a desert island or in the desert of the modern city.

Although Rousseau brings up his Emile in recognition of his eventual movement into society, and although Day's Harry Sandford and Tommy Merton must live in a class-ridden, wealth-corrupted Britain, both authors counterpoise social exposure with subnarrative of isolation (Rousseau with *Robinson Crusoe,* Day with inset tales of Russian sailors shipwrecked in the arctic, Laplanders in frozen isolation, Greenlanders eking out subsistence living, Swiss peasants buried under an avalanche), and they situate their experimental children—as Wordsworth situates his—safely within the isolated countryside under Rousseau's panoptic or "Sequester'd in some secret glade" (Day, "Written During a Tour of the West of England" 24).

Above all, Wordsworth was an ordinary orphan in a period of ordinary orphanhood. Losing his mother when he was seven years old, his father when he was thirteen; brought up partly under the frosty care of his Cookson grandparents of Penrith and later under the indifferent eyes of his uncles, Wordsworth—along with his siblings—seems to have lost all tender care when he lost his mother, "she who was the heart / And hinge of all our learnings and our loves; / She left us destitute, and as we might / Trooping together" (*Prelude* 1805, 5: 257-60). "Destitution," a word that crops up obsessively, here connotes not total want (though with their father's death, the homeless children became financially beholden to their grudging grandparents and uncles) but the now obsolete sense of abandonment and desertion. From *destituere* (to set down or place away from), "destitution" suggests the disheartened and unhinged state of an Ishmael or a Robinson Crusoe or any ordinary bereaved child.

There is nothing extraordinary about Wordsworth's orphan state. As Alan Liu has emphasized, the phenomenon of nineteenth-century orphanhood was commonplace, an entirely "ordinary sorrow of man's life" (*PW* 419). Any reader who attempts to link the fact of childhood loss to the literary output of such orphaned writers as Wordsworth, Keats, Byron, Coleridge, and De Quincey needs to confront the *normality* of such loss. Liu cites Lawrence Stone's finding that a high percentage of Wordsworth's contemporaries grew up lacking one or both parents:

> As Stone's stress on the typical death of a parent suggests, every family was its own mutability canto . . . Even as late as the early nineteenth century, Stone points out, adults 25 to 40 years of age still stood a 1 percent chance of dying each year, meaning that 2 percent of all marriages ended annually in the death of one of the spouses. As a result, roughly 30 percent of all marriages ended within fifteen years. (Liu 246-47)

With so many marriages ending relatively early, multitudes of minors were orphaned. According to Liu's figures, approximately 21 percent of all children from 1600 were bereft of at least one parent; about 13-17 percent of all children of the 1790s were orphans (247). Though Liu argues that a properly historicized reading would see loss as cushioned—as was Wordsworth's—by fostering within "complex family ensembles" (238) a complex kinship network. But recent scholarship confirms historian Peter Laslett's finding of four centuries of relatively stable family size (Poster x) and suggests that the British family from the seventeenth century to the present can be defined as the conjugal unit plus a small number (two to four) of children. As Liu emphasizes (249-50), Wordsworth himself writes as if the tight family of affective individualism were the norm, as if it is an unnatural and sorry thing for children to be brought up outside the charmed domestic circle. The assumed norm is companionate. Every baby leaps up on the arm of his mother, not his wet nurse's or his nanny's. Every mother breast-feeds her own child (*Prelude* 1799, 267-310; 1805, 2: 238-80; 1850, 2: 232-64; "Michael" *PW* 242). Every mother away from home pines for her own child ("The Emigrant Mother," *Excursion* 6: 787-92). Mothers adore their children to the point of frenzy ("The Affliction of Margaret," "The Idiot Boy"). As Liu has noted, the departure from home even of a grown child like Michael's Luke is profoundly unsettling. Each child is unique and irreplaceable ("Two April Mornings"). Himself the center of a tight domestic circle and the chief idol of what Kurt Heinzelman calls a "cult of domesticity," Wordsworth habitually treats the tight domestic circle of the companionate family as a norm whose shattering transforms consciousness. Wordsworth's own ordinary orphanhood provides a partial explanation both for his intense, preternatural consideration of the isolated child but also for the sensitivity of the reading public to Wordsworth's spectacle of loss in widest commonality spread.

The great twentieth-century student of such loss is John Bowlby. So marked is Wordsworth's poetry by destitution that it can be glossed by John Bowlby's great twentieth-century trilogy *Attachment and Loss* (1969-72).[28] The great expositor of how the ways in which we lose our lives become our lives, Bowlby made his reputation in the years following World War II with a series of studies of children who had been separated from their parents permanently or for long periods by war, sickness, or death. Bowlby concluded that early prolonged separation from parents was devastating, often irrevocably so, to young children. Without the return of lost parents or any emotionally cushioned period of mourning, bereaved children were more likely than others to grow up as "psychiatric casualties" (*Loss* 195).[29] The originality of Bowlby's research was his focus on the profundity and importance of childhood loss, the "long duration of grief, and the difficulties of recovering from its effects, and the adverse consequences for personality that loss often brings" (8). The conditions that cushion mourning are described by Bowlby:

> The child should have enjoyed a reasonably secure relationship with his parents prior to the loss; the child should have been given prompt and accurate information about the death and be allowed to ask questions and participate in the grieving; and the child should have the comforting presence of a surviving parent or trusted substitute. (320)

But the Wordsworth children were not so fortunate. The children were sent away from home during their mother's final illness that was later blamed on the so-called London friend with the icy so-called best bedroom (*Prose* 3: 219). Rather than comforting his children, John Wordsworth withdrew further from them and "never recovered his usual cheerfulness of mind" (3: 219). In effect, the children were doubly bereaved since their father's depression and/or withdrawal into work and business anxiety made him almost as inaccessible as their dead mother. Nor were the chilly Cooksons disposed to comfort the children.

Bowlby has argued that the failure of mourning may lead children into the pathological lifetime obsession with loss. There have been historical periods, in the multiple separations of the war years, for example, but also during whole centuries of heavy parental mortality when the pathological may become the commonplace and "normal." Just because a behavior is commonplace, as is a bereaved unassuaged child's obsession with loss, does not mean it is not pathological; just because it is pathological does not mean it is not commonplace. Indeed its very pervasiveness may account for the appeal of the varied and expressive poetry of loss found not just in Wordsworth but in many other nineteenth-century elegiac poets such as Tennyson, Arnold, Hardy, and Housman.

Almost all the pathologies of loss described by Bowlby mark Wordsworth's poetry of childhood. Indeed the Wordsworth corpus stands as a virtual anatomy of childhood loss and thwarted mourning. In *Loss,* Bowlby sets out the common patterns among children who have not been able to find comfort and support after the loss of a parent. Chief among the patterns he notes are ways either to magically restore the lost object (notably through wandering to find the lost object or through death to join the lost object), or to protest again the loss of the object by fear or rage (fear of further loss, blame of the surviving parent), or to insulate against the loss (compulsive self-reliance or care-giving, euphoria and/or depersonalization).[30] These are the patterns that govern Wordsworth's poetry of childhood, all modes of transforming loss to triumph.

With a compound lineage in art, in folklore, in experimental pedagogy, and above all in ordinary orphanhood, the sequestered child is a dominant presence in Wordsworth's poetry. The tactics of segregation are manifold and all work to characterize childhood as a world adequate unto itself. The banishments are worked by multiple means—by stylistic technique, by spatial position, by iconic framing, by reductive subtraction, by severed communication, and by triumphal self-sufficiency.

Children are sequestered as objects of poetic representation by manipulations of the conventions of spelling, syntax, and prosody. Sequestration by fixity habitually *denaturalizes* children, often marking their peculiar status by some mechanical convention such as capitalization or prosody.

An intermittent tactic is selective capitalization that singles out and centers children: "Blest the infant **Babe**" of *The Prelude* (2: 232);[31] "a simple **Child** / That lightly draws its breath" in "We are Seven"[32]; in "Alice Fell" "And there a little **Girl** I found;" the stunning conclusion of "The Danish Boy," "Like a dead **Boy** he is serene"; the chosenness of the afflicted blind Highland child, "For God took pity on the **Boy** / and was his friend" (*PW* 304); "There was a **Boy**; ye knew him well, ye cliff / And islands of Winander" (*Prelude* 5: 364);[33] Matthew's "blooming **Girl** whose hair was wet" (*PW* 116); "Behold the **Child**" of the Intimations Ode "among his new-born blisses." But from the scorned prodigy of *Prelude* 5 (1805) capitalization and honor are both withheld: "tis a child, no child / But a dwarf man" (294-95).[34]

Prosodic manipulation will center a key word. "We are Seven" opens two feet short to represent unaccommodated "A simple Child." The placement of the caesura in "Alice Fell" deepens the perception of the girl's isolation: "And there a little Girl I found / Sitting behind the chaise // alone" (*PW* 274). Similarly the caesura and syntax help construct the intensely concentrated solitary being of the Boy of Winander: "There was a Boy; // ye knew him well, ye cliffs / And islands of Winander" (*Prelude* 5: 364-65). On one side of the caesura is the single essential child with his verb of being ("There was a Boy"); on the other is the multiplicity of the environment ("Ye cliffs / And islands"). The solitude of the reaper is also enforced by metrical means:

> Behóld | hér, sín | glé in | thé field,
> Yón sóllitáry Híghland Láss!
> Reáping| and sínging bý| hersélf;
> Stóp hére, or géntlý páss!
> Alóne she cúts and bínds | the gráin . . . (*PW* 298)

In the opening lines of this iambic tetrameter poem, the girl's singleness inhabits every possible foot position: in line one, she is *single* at feet two and three; in line two *solitary* in feet one and two and three; in line three *herself* in foot four; and in line five *alone* in foot one. Further, the characterizing solitudizing words *single solitary, herself alone* themselves make up a resonant pentameter line of three trochaic "falling" feet answered by two assertive "rising" iambic feet: Síngle, sólitáry, hersélf alóne—her solitude is multitudinous, filling every space.

Isolation is further enforced by the Wordsworthian child's spots in space, the "child set in the midst." Wordsworth habitually sets up solitary single children who are the human center of a vast emptiness—mostly rural, occasionally urban. They are literally and metaphorically out of touch— among "untrodden ways," "untouched by human fears," "untouched by solemn thought." Thus the solitary hero of "The Norman Boy" exists alone in a King Lear landscape evacuated of both the natural and the human:

> High on a broad unfertile tract of forest-skirted Down,
> Nor kept by Nature for herself, nor made by man his own,
> From home and company remote and every playful joy,
> Served, tending a few sheep and goats, a ragged Norman boy . . .
> There *was* he . . . (*PW* 771)

This "poor ragged Thing" (as described in the sequel, "The Poet's Dream" [*PW* 771-72]) is placed in a region that is sterile, rejected by nature and by human beings, even poets: "Him never saw I" (771). He is a figure of pure being at the tag end of existence—"There *was* he" (771, italics Wordsworth's)—who constructs out of his nothingness a shelter in the "houseless waste": "A tiny tenement forsooth, and frail, as needs must be / A thing of such materials framed, by a builder such as he."

Children are regularly positioned as centers of a circumambient nature, at the hub of the great wheeling spectacle of the subservient natural world. Thus Wordsworth the skater "reclining back upon my heels, / Stopped short—yet still the solitary cliffs / Wheeled by me, even as if the earth had rolled / With visible motion her diurnal round" (1805 *Prelude* 1: 483-86). As Liu has noted (210-12), Wordsworth's "spots of time" tend, as here, to be panoramic, organized around a central point from which a totality of vision is possible. And at the center of the Wordsworthian panopticon there typically stands a child. In the autobiographical texts the child is the subject seer, elsewhere the child is the cynosure and object. The silent nine-year-old of "It is a Beauteous Evening, Calm and Free" is a slight figure surrounded by and ministered to by vast principalities and powers—the docile sun "sinking down" in homage, the brooding nurturant "gentleness of heaven" waiting upon her needs, the watchful "mighty Being," even Father Abraham. Similarly, the stationary Boy of Winander is single and fixed ("a Boy . . . would . . . stand alone") amongst the vast pluralities of nature—the cliffs, islands, hills, and stars ranged accountably before him and for him. Even in packed urban setting, a chosen child is the single center of a multitude—the theater child elevated, celebrated "on a board" "environed with a ring / Of chance spectators" (1805 *Prelude* 7: 386-87) or a sickly infant "eyed . . . with unutterable love" (8: 859) by his father, represented as the "one man" "Sitting in an open square" in crowded London.

This fixative centering often produces a collector's child, a rarity among Rarees, a child as aesthetic object seen and desired by all.[35] The toddler of *Prelude* 7, placed appropriately in "the vast theatre" (1850 7: 358) is the most elaborate and exemplary instance of childhood fixity manifoldly framed. The theater child is central because he is systematically differentiated from his surroundings. He is radically other, "a sort of alien scattered from the clouds" (7: 378). He is vital, pretty, "rosy" "lusty," unlike Mary's silent dead baby. He is "cottage-child" in the whorish Babylon of "the falsely gay" (1805 7: 381). The truth and loveliness of "the lovely Boy" (1850, 7: 367) are antithetical to the "dissolute men / And shameless women" around him (386-87). In his "rosy" bloom of health, he is the antithesis of his raddled mother: "on the mother's cheek the tints were false / A painted bloom" (7: 373-74), to Mary Jacobus an echo of Milton's Sin (212). He is a chosen being like the martyrs who defied Nebuchadnezzar in Babylon and "walked with hair unsigned / Amid the fiery furnace" (400). The intensely vital child enacts an allegory of human mutability ("Ate, drank, and with the fruit and glasses played" [363]); he is centered, "environed with a ring" of gazing adults (1805 7: 386), "Upon a board . . . had this child been placed / *His* little stage in the vast theatre / And there he sat surrounded with a throng / Of chance spectators..." (1850, 7: 355-56). The child's iconic significance is heightened by the cutting away of all that is not child. Jacobus argues persuasively that the mother is repressed (the speaker insistently denies remembering her), "cast out—in Kristevan terms... 'abjected'" (213). With the mother cast out and the child centrally fixed in his sight, the retro-spectator moves to snatch/kidnap the child through the language of arrest and seizure that demands he be "embalmed / By Nature" (1805, 7: 400-401), "Stopped at the growth he had" (402), "checked" and "detained" in childhood forever (1850 7: 374, 376). Like Goethe's Erl-King,[36] beguiled by "deine shōne Gestalt," the poet pulls the beautiful boy out of mutability to arrest him in a state of eudaemonic plenitude (Hartman 195).[37] In this realm of aesthetic fixity, the child will remain on the boards as a stage star just like his alter ego William Betty, the thirteen-year-old "Young Roscius" who was playing the lead in Hamlet to great acclaim in London during the very months in 1804 in which Wordsworth was composing Book 7.[38] Just as the theater child appears among the "dissolute... and... shameless... and falsely gay" (7: 386-87), so in Dorothy's mind's eye, as she wrote in a letter of November 1804, she sees "with melancholy feeling" the "wonderful Boy," young Betty, "among the Crowd of his admirers *unsullied* by praise." "My Brother vows that if the Boy grow up as he has begun he will write a play on purpose for him.... Indeed what good effects that the Child may produce on the English Theatre cannot be calculated " (*WLEY* 520). The theater child, doubled with Young Roscius in the theater of the mind, acts and re-enacts the Wordsworth script in a boy's version of Hamlet, his favorite tragedy of introversion, isolation, and parental destruction: "To be, to have been... a child / And nothing more" (1805, 7: 403-4).

To be "nothing more" or less than a child can involve an exigent subtraction or an omnipotent addition. To pare down to the core or to supervene upon otherness are equally means to set a child apart as an essential entity. Wordsworthian children are sequestered not only by fixity in plenitude of being but by defects, lacks, fallings, vanishings that leave them single and unsupported in the field of consciousness. When in his "Address to my infant Daughter," Wordsworth prays "that Heaven support / Thy feeble motions and cheer thy *loneliness,*" he normalizes a conception of childhood as isolation (italics Moorman's 69-70). Distanced, apart, estranged, disconnected, not quite there, many of Wordsworth's minors are human minus signs: the "Orphan Quire" (a phrase from "Address to the Scholars of the Village School of __" [*PW* 114]) of children minus parents (both the "Pet Lamb" and the beautiful child who feeds it are motherless like

Ruth); children minus vision ("The Blind Highland Boy"); children minus decipherable speech ("The Idiot Boy," "The Danish Boy"); children minus companionship ("Ruth," "Lucy Gray"); spectral children minus bodies ("The Thorn," "Lucy Gray"); parish children minus everything except their bare bodies ("Alice Fell"). In "Alice Fell; or Poverty" Wordsworth treats an embodied nothing, a child who has nothing and from whom even that nothing is taken away. Her name is dire: *Fell,* a northern word befitting a daughter of the north ("I to Durham, sir, belong" [*PW* 275]), betokens not just the high waste moors of the north but also "a knockdown blow" and also horrible cruelty and "intensely painful and destructive" suffering (*OED*). Alice chimes with Alas, A loss, A less. Her existence is truncation: "Sitting behind the chaise, alone," she is "fatherless and motherless." Her defining possession, "a weather-beaten rag," "[a] miserable rag," is just a used-up remnant, a worthless tatter but it is all she has to act as her symbolic interface with the world. As Carlyle's *Sartor Resartus* so emphatically insists, clothing mediates between the naked needy self and the outside world; clothing is every child's myth, her supreme fiction. In Alice's case her cloak is also Winnicott's "transitional object," an object that stands in for the mother or nurturer and acts as "an intermediate area of *experiencing* to which inner reality and external life both contribute." (Winnicott 5). Though a transitional object—a blanket, a stuffed animal, any object that has been suffused with the mother's comforting presence—is an external object from the adult's point of view it is not so from the omnipotent infant's point of view. But neither is the object an hallucination (5). By losing her rag of memory, Alice has lost connection with whatever nurturing she has received and also her connection to the social world to which she now becomes indecipherable.[39] The well-meaning narrator can only guess at her feelings: "*as if* her innocent heart would break" (l. 23), "*as if* her grief / Could never, never have an end" (ll. 49-50), *as if* the thought would choke / Her very heart" (ll. 46-47), "*As if* she'd lost her only friend"(l. 51). Alice vanishes from the poem into a hypothetical happy ending celebrating the efficacy of charity. But the focus of the text is on the girl as exemplary spectacle of human creativity. If Coleridge in "Frost at Midnight" in a more exalted vein turns a mere flake of soot "which flutters on the grate" into an agent of mind, so Alice's intense fixation on the meanest rag is like the author's fixation on the child pauper herself. Her power to make everything out of nothing, in her utter destitution, makes evident the irreducible and horrible power of formative imagination at the heart of loss.

If loss is the trigger of self-creation, it is not surprising to see that a rejection of the parent is in Wordsworth often cognate with creativity. In

"Beggars" and "Sequel to the Beggars," two children insistently and blithely proclaim the death of their mother: "She has been dead, Sir, many a day" (*PW* 276). These lying boys are wreathed like poets; one indeed wears laurel: "a rimless crown / With leaves of laurel stuck about." They inspire the poet-narrator productively "in a *genial* hour" ("Sequel" 583). Associated with the chosen children of Israel who walked "through fire with unsinged hair" (as the theater boy was similarly likened to those "with hair unsinged / Amid the fiery furnace"), the boys, like the theater child, become emblems of power by being cut free of a dubious mother [40] who is a dehumanized "weed of glorious feature." At once foreign with "skin ... of Egyptian brown"; a liar ("on our English land / Such woes, I knew, could never be"); equivocally gendered with her "tall man's height or more ... fit person for a Queen / To lead those ancient Amazonian files / Or ruling Bandit's wife among the Grecian isles" *(PW* 275). It is the boys' lie of pronouncing their mother dead that makes these "joyous vagrants" (276) types of the creative spirit.

Alienation from adults is pervasive. Wordsworthian children are often incapable of human speech or speaking. Mutual incomprehension is the norm between children and adults. Wordsworth represents children as resistantly incommunicado, verbal but not comprehensible in "prattle" (a favorite word), in "words of a forgotten tongue" ("Danish Boy" *PW* 118), "a mock apparel ("H.C., Six Years Old" *PW* 290). Adults fail to connect with children ("'Twas throwing words away" ["We Are Seven"]) and children use language to block such a connection. It is especially doted-on children like the Blind Highland Boy and the Idiot Boy, objects of intense maternal attention ("above her other children him did love." "Him who she loves her Idiot Boy") whose language is resistant. The Blind Highland Boy cries out to his would-be rescuers the Gaelic word Wordsworth had begged from Scott, the foreignness of the word enforcing the willed estrangement of the boy:

> "*Lei-gha—Lei-gha*" he then cried out,
> "*Lei-gha—Lei-gha*"—with eager shout;
> Thus did he cry, and thus did pray,
> And what he meant was, "Keep away,
> And leave me to myself!" (*PW* 306)

In the mutual incomprehension of parent and child what is agony to his doting mother is to him "the triumph of his joy"; what is the ecstasy of the mother's relief at the boy's rescue ("She was too happy far") is for the boy the reverse: "heartfelt cross / To him, a heavy, bitter loss, / As he had ever known."

If motherly love is resisted, so is paternal pedagogy. "Anecdote for Fathers," Wordsworth's extended catechetical tragic-comedy of misunderstanding, not only reveals, as McGavran has shown, Wordsworth's ironic mockery of "the traditional catechetical relationship of teacher and student" [66]), but opens a vein of separation, marking differences, "contrariety of modes" (Wolfson 48) just where the parent-child bond might be deemed closest. "Anecdote for Fathers" is unusual for its extended but eventually thwarted interaction between a father and a son. (Edward is, of course, not a Wordsworth son—there are *no* poems dedicated to Wordsworth's own boys [Moorman 117]—but Basil Montagu). There is a lot of interchange framed by the father's insistently explanatory glosses: the authoritative father speaks four times for eleven of sixty lines and receives ten lines of response (four spoken, six gestural) (*PW* 73-4). It is the possessive and confident father ("I *have* a boy") who six times interrogates "my boy" (so labeled three times). It is the father who controls the child's movement (" I . . . took him by the arm" "still I held him by the arm"). Most of all, it is the father who claims the superior emotional position of being loved: "And dearly he loves me."

The interaction is doggedly pedagogic and catechetical with insistent emphasis on lessons taught, lessons learned, proper/improper questions, and proper/improper answers. The father's Q and A makes the spontaneous outing into a dreary learning experience, a "dry walk." Even though the father's relentless questions ("And three times to the child I said / Why, Edward, tell me why?") drive the boy to burst out with an evidently absurd answer suggesting a fraudulent rationalization ("no weather-cock"), the father, ever educationally on the alert learns "how the art of lying may be taught" and, according to Steven Marcus, the child learns, satisfactorily, how to "rationalize" and to give explanations of what is incommunicably intuitive. Edward thus becomes able to communicate with other people on a neutral rational level. "In this poem we see the autonomy of the child being violated"; but it is violated in the interests of achieving "a new phase of cognitive development as well" (Marcus 10).

That such a success is brutal the poem makes clear. Though the lambs are bounding free, Edward is held in an iron grim of reason: "I . . . took him by the arm" and "still I held him by the arm . . . And three times to the child I said / Why, Edmund, tell me why?" The child hangs his head, blushes, is generally abashed and uncomfortable about his interrogations as he is "being violated," forced into a mode of thinking, the mode of measured comparison that Coleridge certainly regarded as damaging to the prepubescent child: "The comparing power, the judgement, is not at that age active, and ought not to be forcibly excited" (Coleridge, *Lectures* 2: 192-93).

Apart from the intellectual forcing—not rape perhaps, just tough love—associated with a triumphal parent-child nexus, however, is Edward's nonsense answer—Kilve for its lack of weather-cocks—that acts as ideological resistance to the father's intelligible will. As John Williams has suggested, the Kilve-Liswyn question is a real one, with "a thinly veiled reference to the dilemma of having to choose between an active political life and one of contemplative retirement" (92). Liswyn, as the home of radical Thelwall, belongs to the active world, Kilve and five-year-old Edward to the world of stasis.

Such a reading is strengthened by Wordsworth's head note, political rather than pedagogic, which links the poem to the famous radical John Thelwall[41] but inexplicably omits Thelwall's link to Llyswen, his home after the Gagging Acts had made his political activism dangerous. Wordsworth's note merely identifies Liswyn as "a beautiful spot on the Wye" (*PW* 74). In the same note, Wordsworth comments on Thelwall's susceptibility "[t]hough brought up in the City on a tailor's board" to natural beauty and gives a version of his praise of Alfoxden, near Kilve:

> I remember once, when *Coleridge,* he and I were seated together upon the turf on the brink of a stream in the most beautiful part of the most beautiful glen of Alfoxden, Coleridge exclaimed: "This is a place to reconcile one to all the jarrings and conflicts of the wide world."—
> "Nay," said Thelwall, "to make one forget them altogether." (*PW* 74)

As Kenneth Johnston has noted, Wordsworth's memory of Thelwall's visit works at "universalizing, *un*specifying" the exchange that Coleridge had recalled as much more explicitly political (524). Coleridge recollected praising the glen to Thelwall in political terms: "Citizen John, this is a fine place to talk treason in!" But Thelwall, thoroughly exhausted by government persecution, differed: "'Nay! Citizen Samuel,' he replied, 'it is a place to make a man forget that there is any necessity for treason'" (*Table Talk* 1: 180-81). Despite differences in emphasis, both recollections represent Alfoxden-Kilve as a realm of forgetfulness. Liswyn-Llyswen, however, had become by Summer 1798 the home ground of Thelwall who "a long, long year before" had visited the Wordsworths at Kilve-Alfoxden, where a man could "forget" the world and the need for political action. Liswyn's "broad and gilded vane," like any weathercock, is an index of change. No one in Wordsworth's circle was more dedicated to change than Thelwall, no one more a weatherman who knew which way the wind blew. In his recoil from such radicalism, Wordsworth later associated wind vanes with the Terror likening the Jacobin desire for blood ("If light desires of innocent little ones / May with such heinous appetites be matched" [1805 *Prelude* 10: 338-39]) to a child's exhilaration with a toy wind vane:

> Having a toy, a windmill, though the air
> Do of itself blow fresh and makes the vane
> Spin in his eyesight, he is not content,
> But with the plaything at arm's length he sets
> His front against the blast, and runs amain
> To make it whirl the faster (340-45)[42]

But Kilve, "a place to forget there is any necessity for treason," is a place where vain changes need not be registered by brilliant, gilded vanes. The adult interlocutor rooting out unexamined prejudice with his relentless inquisition of unexamined opinion is the very type of the radical intelligence that took "the knife in hand / And stopping not at parts less sensitive, / Endeavored with my best of skill to probe / The living body of society / Even to the heart" (1805 *Prelude* 10: 872-76). As a parodic figure of inquisitorial radicalism, conscious of the changing times, the father puts the past "long, long year" behind him for his current weathercock life of unsteady change. Edward, however, with his kingly Saxon name, opts spontaneously for the old and familiar and unexamined. Childhood as the unexamined unhistoricized life, opts for Kilve the place of forgetting. It is less that Edward is, in Alan Richardson's formulation, an "ideology-proof organic sensibility . . . unsocialized and frozen in a state of eternal innocence" (72) than proof against all argument and as such the anchor of a conservative ideology.

This resistance to process and development is of a piece with Wordsworth's persistent depiction of childhood self-sufficiency. Beyond mere resistance to process and development, childhood is represented as euphoric self-sufficiency, a floating lightness of being beyond loss. Against all obvious historical and medical sense, in defiance of everything nineteenth-century parents knew about mortality rates, the textual child is jury-rigged to be a quaint device that cannot be hurt, cannot be affected by any outside force. Like the egg in the eleventh-grade physics class eggdrop competition, the Wordsworthian child is bizarrely insulated against impending threat.

Selfhood is reified in a vocabulary of copulatives and self-validating neologisms, enforcing a syntax in which dissonance cannot exist, from which antitheses are banished.[43] Such self-sufficient equilibrium is generated by Wordsworth's habitual use of the copulative that makes the children embodiments of unadorned Being: "There was a Boy"; "there was he" (the Norman Boy; "A simple Child"). These children do not have to act to explicate their lives. By merely existing they are adequately complete. "The Infant M__ M__," "Characteristics of a Child Three Years Old," and "Personal Talk" all represent children as "self-sufficing" or "all sufficient" or "blest and powerful," joyfully self-dependent because rejoicing (in Dorothy Wordsworth's phrase) in "the mere life that is in him" (*EY* 222). In such poems as "The Kitten and the Falling Leaves," "Three Years She Grew in Sun and Shower," "To H.C., Six Years Old," and "Characteristics of a Child Three Years Old," the child possesses a joyous self-sufficiency, a creative energy "unthought of, unexpected," which requires no social support. Wordsworth depicts this autonomy in images of unselfconscious self-generating activity and in a vocabulary of newly-coined self-reflexive works—mostly incorporating "self" as prefix or suffix connected to another term connoting completeness or energy. Thus three-year-old Catherine:

> And, as a faggot sparkles on the hearth,
> No less if unattended and alone
> Than when both young and old sit gathered round
> And take delight in its activity;
> Even so this happy Creature of herself
> Is all-sufficient; solitude to her
> Is blithe society, who fills the air
> With gladness and involuntary songs (*PW* 392)

As in Coleridge's "Frost at Midnight," a father contemplates his child as an image of "involuntary" motion: the child, the sleeping infant Hartley, is associated by Coleridge with a moving flake of ash on the grate, while the whirling Catherine is associated by Wordsworth with a faggot sparkling on the hearth. In Coleridge's construction, the flake takes on meaning as a "companionable form" but only through the initiating companion spectator: the ash is nothing in itself without the watcher's mediation, just as, by implication, the baby too is in need of the adult for nurture and education. Wordsworth, in contrast, emphasizes the flame's independence of spectators and thus the little girl's indifference to, independence from, and lack of any need of adult intervention. Similarly, Nature's darling girl in "Three

Years She Grew" is indifferent to all human company, possessing instead Nature as "law and impulse."

Such equivocal but triumphal lightness of being, such mobility and emotional vagrancy is connected to an inner emptiness, a destitution. This combination of lightness and loss is evident in the uncannily euphoric child music makers of 1798-99. The power and discomfort of such poems as "The Danish Boy," "Lucy Gray," and "Ruth" lies in the uncanny juxtaposition of seeming happiness and inner emptiness. Though Ruth is half-crazed and Lucy Gray and the Danish Boy are revenants, they are also figures of self-reliant independence and serenity. All three poems take as their donee the disappearance of a protecting adult society replaced by a bare, threatening landscape inhabited by serene affectless music-making children. All poems set up adult betrayal or parental ineptitude as a norm. Such dereliction, however is the fortunate fall, the precondition of a life in poetry that makes possible Lucy's "solitary song," the Danish Boy's "songs of war . . . like songs of love," and Ruth's flute music. Each of the three children makes a music associated at once with violence or terror (Lucy's death in the snow, Ruth's triple desertion, the Danish Boy's murder) and with the numinous and liminal (Lucy's solitary song in the wind, Ruth's hemlock songs in the twilight hills, the Dane's harp music in the deserted dell). Each child produces a music that suggests the healing of contradictions: Ruth's natural but potentially lethal hemlock music melds with the concluding "Christian hymn"; Lucy's song beguiles rough and smooth; the Danish boy's music reconciles war with love and life and death. In all three instances it is childhood loss that generates the music of self-sufficiency, so that the damaged poet becomes the type of the poem.

In each poem, the condition of music is a normalized adult betrayal. The Danish prince, a boy Hamlet like Betty, turns nature poet because of his murder (elided) by those who should have sheltered him. Lucy Gray also makes natural music out of parental dereliction. Instead of being herself guided, Lucy Grey is dispatched by her father to find and guide her missing mother. Lucy's disappearance turns her into a ghostly genius loci who is now invulnerable because she had accepted the magical condition of *never looking behind,* a condition imposed on those such as Orpheus or Lot who would escape the normal constraints of human mortality. Those who yield to retrospect are, like Lot's wife, petrified to a stony salt tear, but Lucy who will not look back creates haunting music beyond pain and pleasure, beyond rough and smooth, out of her loss-won immunity to concern.

Ruth's double losses produce a double music, first pastoral, then elegiac.

Left "half-desolate" by her mother's death (though the word mother is repressed in the poem), her father's marriage when she is six leaves her a destitute "slighted child" whose loss gets figured as independence. She is free to go "wandering over dale and hill / In thoughtless freedom bold." Without a protecting family, Ruth becomes a mini-Crusoe in her play hut, "a bower upon the green"; this "infant of the woods," makes her first spontaneous natural music: "And she had made a pipe of straw / And music from that pipe could draw / Like sounds of winds and flood" (*PW* 119). Like Rousseau's Emile, Ruth is prepared for the worst; she lives within human society like one who is independent of society, "a savage who has to live in the town" (Rousseau 167). She conforms to the model of Bowlby's mourning child who has no avenue for her mourning except "to banish so far as she could all hopes and desires for love and support and to develop instead a premature and assertive self-reliance" (*Loss* 343):

> Beneath her father's roof, alone
> She seemed to live; her thoughts her own;
> Herself her own delight;
> Pleased with herself, nor sad, nor gay;
> And passing thus the live-long day
> She grew to woman's height (119)

Within the "woman's height" remains the vulnerable child's heart despite her seeming invulnerability to parental abandonment (mother dead, father neglectful). But, as Steven Marcus has noted, once the Georgia Youth, another wild child, enters her life and awakens her to human hopes, fears, and connectedness, her tranced invulnerability dissolves: "The wakeful Ruth at midnight shed / A solitary tear" (120). The enchanting young American has the disenchanting power to turn Ruth the nature spirit into a human girl who can shed real tears.[44] (The inability to cry is a traditional fairy mark, shared by Undine and Peter Pan, of magical invulnerability and perpetual youth.) The "Youth from Georgia's shore," is himself an adept of sensibility, subject to the "fits of overlove and overjoy" Wordsworth had warned against (*WLMY* 1: 286), responsive to all that is mutable and shifting in the New World, the "plants that hourly change / Their blossom" and he opens a similar vein of responsiveness in Ruth. Awakened by the volatile young man to human need, Ruth for the first time since erecting her childhood defenses again becomes dependent on that fatal "predominance of present objects over absent ones." Thus she fails to weather her latter losses so well as her earliest ones. The lover, so tempting to a neglected daughter, who woos her with talk "about a father's love," "[deserts] his poor Bride." Destitute and abandoned, Ruth reverts to the pursuits of her earliest childhood, dabbling in water, "setting her little water mills." In her regression, Ruth returns to her earliest pursuits—playing with water, playing with blades of grass, a "hemlock stalk" from which she makes nature's music. Both the early and the later loss educe music, in childhood from the "oaten flute," later from "a hemlock stalk." These pastoral instruments, flute and pipe, are the musical equivalents of the solitary Ruth herself: both are instruments made of a single stalk plucked from a country field, knotted at one end and cut with a slit near the knot for a musical reed (Brewer 772). So Ruth too, the solitary child is cut off from a grounding family and pierced by a loss from which she makes music. The early loss enables a limited aesthetic success producing Ruth as a pastoral poet playing "sounds of winds and floods" on an "oaten flute" in the tradition of the poet shepherd of *Lycidas*: "Meanwhile the rural ditties were not mute / Temper'd to the oaten flute." But the later loss and the later music are absolute. Ruth's uncannily comforting night music is drawn from a poisonous instrument (ordinary field hemlock is a poisonous herb, *conium maculatum* [45]) in the euphoria of self-destruction.

The most radical and effective form of self-sufficiency is becoming one's own source and origin. By both emptying and filling the universe, the Wordsworthian self-as-child becomes himself by usurping the paternal and incorporating the maternal.[46] In the "Blest the infant Babe" passage in *Prelude* 2, especially in the 1850 version, Wordsworth emphatically links the secure interfusion of child with world to the interfusion of the nursing couple, noting especially the baby's immersion in a liquid or liquefying medium that is his mother. The baby is "Nursed in his Mother's arms" (2: 235); he "sinks" into sleep "Rocked on his Mother's breast" (2: 235-36); and "Drinks in the feelings of his Mother's eye" (2: 237). Thus the liquid circulating through her system has become the liquid circulating through his. To "sink" into or "rock upon" the oceanic maternal breast—source of the very life within the self, kin to the oceanic source of all life—is to belong to a world in which inside and outside, self and other, even death and life have no meaning. In the Body of the Mother, "For him, in one dear Presence, there exists / A virtue which irradiates and exalts / Objects through widest intercourse of sense" (2: 238-40). The "one dear Presence," "the beloved presence"—the nurturing mother who is outside and inside enables the child's connection to and power in the world: "For feeling has to him imparted power" (2: 255), notably what Winnicott calls the "capacity to be alone," a power that comes "from a successful internalization of his mother's presence" (Friedman 11). As Hopkins suggests, Wordsworth anticipates Winnicott's discovery that the capacity to be alone is "being alone in the presence of someone . . . [who] continues to be available even after being forgotten" (Winnicott 48), so that the more solitude, the more Presence.[47]

In the Boy of Winander passage, Wordsworth describes the child's internalization of the deep silence of nature—the lake, the reflected heaven, the birds, the hills. Just as the lake receives within itself the reflection of the scene, so does the child receive it within the lake of his mind and body. The complex imagery of lines 405-13 suggests infinite depths within both the boy and the landscape. Just as the "uncertain heaven" is received into the "bosom of the steady lake," so is the visible scene received into the boy's mind that has so far internalized his mother as no longer to need her. As Rehder has noted, throughout *The Prelude,* Wordsworth draws on a pattern in which a male figure bending over water is likened to a baby hanging from his mother's breast. The Boy of Winander drinking in landscape is analogous to the youth in Book 2 moving "upon the breast of a still water." When "the calm / And dead still water lay upon my mind" (2: 170-71) "and the sky, / . . . sank down / into my heart" (2: 172-74) the child has successfully incorporated all he still needs from the lost mother. To hang over the lake is to possess the tranquil oceanic wholeness of the nursing couple; it is to appropriate for the sole self the calm, stillness and depth of maternal stability. The child who "hung / Listening" by the owl-haunted lake, the child who "hangs" upon the breast of nature just as he hung upon his mother's breast is now the container for the thing contained. The bosom that received him now is received within him, so that the mother can disappear further into the child.

If the mother is parthenogenetically embodied as the living circulatory system that can overflow into power, the more threatening oedipal father is usurped and banished. Critic Antony Easthope argues that virtually every traumatic spot of time in *The Prelude* can be glossed as a triumphant usurpation, a confounding of the Law of the Father and a recapitulation of an internalized, oceanic mother/infant bond in an anaesthetizing "sense of dyadic unity [that] replaces any pain or loss engendered by the loss" (65).

No scene in Shakespeare affected Wordsworth more powerfully than the encounter of Hamlet with his father's ghost, "in particular, Hamlet's wild language after the ghost has disappeared" (*WLEY* 1: 587). Throughout his life, Wordsworth donned what Greenberg has called his "Hamlet vocation" and recapitulated the father-son encounter/separation especially in contexts in which the son's usurpation of paternal power is problematized.

Among the nuclear passages of the 1799 *Prelude,* the two that define "spots of time" are both those in which father is overmastered by son. The Defiance of James and the Waiting for Horses episodes operate under the shadows of Hamlet and Oedipus. In the first passage, the five-year-old is separated from his father's surrogate, "honest James . . . my encourager and guide" (1799, 302-3), identified in the later version as "an ancient servant of my father's house" (1850, 12: 229) and evidently the same James Dorothy described in bitter terms after her father's death:

> Each day do we receive fresh insults . . . of the most mortifying kind: the insults of servants. . . . James has even gone so far as to tell us that we had nobody to depend upon but my Grandfr, for that our fortunes were but very small, and my Brothers cannot even get a pair of shoes cleaned without James's telling them they require as much waiting upon as any *Gentleman.* (*WLEY* 3-4)

This tyrannical James—and, indeed, the still more tyrannical Sir James Lowther, also associated, as its owner, with "my father's house"—needs to be mastered. Separated from this fatherly guide, the child blunders into a scene of patriarchal aggression, a "bottom," where "in former time / A man, the murderer of this wife, was hung" (1799 1: 308-9). This "rough and stony"(306) scene of male violence is associated with the authority of the law (the gibbet where "a murderer had been hung in iron chains" [1805 11: 289]) and of history ("monumental writing . . . engraved / In times long past" [12: 295-96]). The crime is inscribed on the landscape: "the bones / And iron case were gone, but on the turf / Hard by, soon after that fell deed was wrought, / Some unknown hand had carved the murderer's name" (11: 190-93). Frightened by such aggression, potentially his own, the child flees into a landscape presided over by a female figure (first noted as "A girl who bore a pitcher on her head" [1: 317] but also as "the woman and her garments vexed and tossed" [1: 326]) and associated with a bare pool of water and a very distant beacon. This is a movement from recognition of aggressive male identity to return to a unity of self and landscape. In the traumatic isolation of this nodal scene, the child masters both the fate of James and the father as wife murderer. He marks this mastery with the affirmation that the mind is its own lord and master, and that "outward sense / Is but the obedient servant of her will" (1805, 11: 271-72). The move demotes James to his lower servile status and restores the isolated orphan to his proper ascendancy.

This mastery is reiterated in the Waiting for Horses episode. As the thirteen-year-old Wordsworth and his brother await the horses that will bring them back home, back to the house where their father will soon die, they look out upon two misty roads and are struck by "the mist / That on the line of each of these two roads / Advanced in such indisputable shapes" (1799, 1: 365-67). The allusion is to Hamlet's address to his father's ghost— "Thou comest in such a questionable shape" (1.4.43)—an address at once fearful, resentful, and curious. That resentment is underlined by the very crossroad setting at "the meeting-point / Of two highways" (1799, 1: 336-37) itself alluding, as Spivak has noted, to "the setting of Oedipus' crime," the murder of his father (52). In the earliest draft of this passage, the recollection of the advance and disappearance of the ghostly father gives way immediately to a feminized landscape figured as udder from which he "would drink / As at a fountain" (1799, 1: 369-70). The ghostly mist, moreover, that cloaks the dead father recurs in another pivotal memory, Crossing the Alps. Here too the moment of self-possession, of self-appropriation, is the moment of losing an external guide and usurping his power. Separated from the guide, Wordsworth has unknowingly crossed the Alps where:

> That awful Power rose from the mind's abyss
> Like an unfathered vapour that enwraps,
> At once some lonely traveller. I was lost. . . .
> But to my conscious soul I now can say—
> "I recognize thy glory": in such strength
> Of usurpation . . . doth greatness make abode (1850, 6: 594-602)

The being empowered by such "strength of usurpation" has a mighty androgyny of soul: "Strong in herself and in beatitude / That hides her, like the mighty flood of Nile / Poured from his fount of Abyssinian clouds / To fertilise the whole Egyptian plain" (613-16). Here the "unfathered vapour" of the imagination becomes the beclouded "fount" that is the source of Father Nile. Classically figured as the great autonomous paternal river, the Nile, its tributaries picayune and its source unknown until the mid-nineteenth century, was not fully charted until the mid-twentieth century. The poet-as-Nile gives birth to himself out of darkness, as an "unfathered vapour" from an obscure "fount of Abyssinian clouds." Mystifying and nullifying his origin, he is a son who is his own father.

The vanquishing of loss by constructing a child who is his own father, his own mother, who is sequestered in actively, energetic, and sometimes exuberant autonomous self-hood explains much that is uncanny, something that is influential, and a little that is glad about the Wordsworthian child. The great fact about the Wordsworthian childhood is neither goodness nor small frailty[48]; it is segregation in a realm of difference.

It is the efficacy of Wordsworth's realm of childhood as difference that has made possible the cultural use and abuse of the Romantic Child. Despite the textual presence of Wordsworth's "race of real children," his elaborate modes of marking the conceptual space between the grown-ups and the young, creates a blank mystification where childhood might be. Hypothesized as different in kind from adults, the Wordsworthian child stands in the blank place of desire, a projection of adult desire. To careless readers in full textual abandon that child may be decoded in the easy shorthand of "idyllic innocence"; to the more careful readers, that child may seem so much an adult projection as not to be there at all. As Alan Liu remarks: "it may be said there are no children in Wordsworth's poetry" (605n). In all readings, however, it is Wordsworth's emphatic attention to the marks of difference that opens up childhood as a space to be possessed.

The emphatic sequestration produces childhood as a space of freedom, emphatically for adults, but very questionably for children. It is a ticket of release for parents, granting them *freedom from* parental responsibility. When children are safely lodged "in Abraham's bosom all the year" a parent is free to bring himself up as his only child. The segregation also produces the conscience-salving appearance of *free children,* represented as invulnerably oblivious to loss and time and hurt, who need never look behind into history or time. Indeed, in the eternal youth enforced by sequestration, children solve the adult problem of historical process: as the very type of hope, the fixed child can be both the source and the end of reform, a utopian symbol of "resistance to oppressive social forms" (Edmundson 751) that abides in the fixed space of retrospect. "At Kilve there was no weather cock; and that's the reason why."

Chapter Three

Charles Lamb and
The Child Within

> *Mrs. K., after expressing her love for her young children, added tenderly, "And how do you like babies, Mr. Lamb?" His answer, immediate, almost precipitate, was "Boi-boi-boiled, ma'am."*
>
> —(Lamb, Bon-Mots)

The Boy-Man

Like the "Immortal Boy," Leigh Hunt (Blainey 178) and "Li'le Hartley" Coleridge, Charles Lamb seemed to his contemporaries not quite an adult. Rather, like his own "Child-Angel," he was an "Amphibium," part adult, part child ("The Child Angel: A Dream" 2: 245).[1] As "Gentle-hearted Charles," as "Agnus . . . in wit a man, in heart a child," as a "child of impulse" bearing the "desolation of the very childless," Lamb seemed to exemplify (so Crabb Robinson thought) Friedrich von Schiller's observation that "all great men have a childlikeness in their nature."[2] Victorian novelist William Makepeace Thackeray apostrophized him as "Saint Charles!" (*Letters* 2: 448n) after seeing Lamb's minute and playful postscript to a letter sent to a child.[3] Though Lamb on occasion kicked against these attributions of childishness—"For God's sake," he wrote Coleridge, "don't make me ridiculous any more by terming me gentle-hearted in print . . . I hope my *virtues* have done *sucking*" [Marrs 1: 217-18]—he chose as his most durable literary persona one who was "too much of the boy-man. The *toga virilis* never sate gracefully on his shoulders. The impressions of infancy had burnt into him, and he resented the impertinence of manhood" ("Preface, by a Friend of the Late Elia," 2: 153). Through Elia the boy-man, Lamb writes habitually of childhood and childlike people and perceptions. Though Elia is not identical and coextensive with Lamb,[4] the creation of a persona who is a superannuated boy made expressly marginal by his untimely childishness and his unwearied retrospection, indicates a preoccupation with both the meaning and the literary uses of childhood.[5]

Lamb's choice of childhood as a literary subject is all the more interesting because he was never a man who loved children in general. With Elia in "A Bachelor's Complaint of the Behaviour of Married People," he showed no great interest in admiring children in bulk, and scorned loving "a whole family, perhaps, eight, nine, or ten indiscriminately" (2: 129). He was mildly fond of the odd child here and there. He took to little Derwent Coleridge, a round rosy infant, "little *Pi-Pos* (or flying Opossum) the only child . . . I had ever an inclination to steal from its parents" (Marrs 2: 66), though not to his elder brother, the brilliant "young Philosopher" Hartley (Marrs 1: 221). Fond of Thornton Hunt, "my favourite child" ("To T. L. H." 5: 36), Leigh Hunt's eldest child, he expressed little concern for Hunt's other "young fry" even when he knew them to be destitute in Italy (*Letters* 2: 233). With heavy irony, Lamb mocked the intellectual dullness of the nine-year-old Willy Wordsworth, "a well-mannered child . . . though no great student," by exaggerating the banality of the boy's offhand remarks: "Being taken over Waterloo Bridge, he remarked that if we had no mountains, we had a fine river at least; which was a Touch of the Comparative, but then he added, in a strain which augured less for his future abilities as a Political Economist, that he supposed they must take at least a pound a week Toll" (*Letters* 2: 265-66). Emma Isola, adopted in her early teens by the Lambs, was a favorite walking companion "whose mirthful spirits were the 'youth of our house'"(*Letters* 3: 371) but whose presence hardly intrudes on the essays. With these exceptions, Lamb maintained an astringent, briskly anti-sentimental view of children, once interrupting the noise of an obstreperous children's party with a toast to the "m-much ca-ca-calumniated g-g-*good* King Herod" (*Bon-Mots* 58). He even cheerfully chided the lugubrious Quaker poet Bernard Barton: "It seems as if you were for ever losing friends' children by death, and reminding parents of the Resurrection. Do children die so often, and so good, in your parts?"(*Letters* 3: 10) After hearing a friend's account of a darling baby, a "pretty baby," a "yeanling" who was the child of a sheep-stealer, Lamb wrote, "The Gipsy's Malison," a sonnet predicting that the babe now hanging from his mother's neck would eventually hang from the gallows. Should any mother see this poem, Lamb wrote a friend, "I shall be Orpheusized, scattered into Hebrus" (*Letters* 3: 207-8).

Nor was Lamb especially interested in the educational process. Though Lamb collaborated with Mary on a series of children's tales and a collection of poems, he treated them as hack work exhibiting no sustained interest in how children learn though considerable insight into how Charles Lamb himself grew up.

Lamb's interest in childhood was entirely personal. It was his own childhood between the ages of six and fourteen that he reconstructed and reimagined in such as essays as "Christ's Hospital Five and Thirty Years Ago," "New Year's Eve," and "Witches, and Other Night-Fears." His tenderness and empathy are reserved for himself when young rather than for other youngsters. He is paternal toward his own child self, tenderly remembering "the child Elia—that 'other me'," crying "over its patient smallpox at five" and nursing "its poor fevered head" ("New Year's Eve" 2: 28), but to the visiting sick child in the adult Lamb household he is indifferent: "We have had a sick child, who, sleeping or not sleeping, next to me, with a cardboard partition between, killed my sleep. The little bastard is gone" (Schorsch 11). In the Elian essays of his own childhood, Lamb attempts to set up a kind of protected "neutral ground" a "sanctuary and quiet Alsatia" ("On the Artificial Comedy of the Last Century" 2: 142), a "little Goshen" ("The Old Benchers of the Inner Temple" 2: 90) in which a version of his childhood self, a pre-pubertal boy of six or seven, that "other me" ("New Year's Eve" 2: 28) can co-exist with his adult self.

Though the "other me" of the essays occupies a fictional family space largely cleared of intimates, the historical Lamb had no shortage of family. Born in 1775, Charles was the youngest of the three surviving children of John and Elizabeth Lamb. Charles was raised in a household of elders: his parents were middle-aged (John was fifty years older than his youngest child), his doting aunt Hetty (Sarah Lamb) was over sixty at his birth, his brother John was twelve years his senior, his sister Mary, ten. Charles Lamb was raised in London's Inner Temple, a walled enclave within the City of London, a *rus in urbe*, with "its church, its halls, its gardens, its fountain, its river" ("The Old Benchers of the Inner Temple" [2: 82]), where his father was servant to Samuel Salt, a Bencher of the Inner Temple and a Member of Parliament. From age seven until fourteen he was educated within the cloisters of Christ's Hospital, the venerable foundation of "that godly and royal child, King Edward the Sixth . . . the boy-patron of boys—the serious and holy child" ("Recollections of Christ's Hospital" [1: 149]). He passed some of his school holidays with his grandmother at Blakesware, an old manor house, "my Eden" (2: 155), of which she was housekeeper. Removed from school at fourteen, Lamb was set to work as a clerk, eventually in 1791 finding permanent employment in the accountant general's department of the East India House where he remained until his retirement in 1825. Disappointed of a university career, consigned to a monotonous and empty trade, disappointed in love, galled by the demands of a nearly paralyzed mother and a senile father, Lamb at twenty had a breakdown and in December 1795 and in January 1796 was briefly committed to an asylum. Shortly after his recovery, when Lamb was twenty-one, Mary Lamb became violently psychotic and on September 22, 1796, the "day of horrors"(*Letters* 1: 43), stabbed her mother to death and wounded her father. Soon after his mother's death came the deaths of Lamb's invalid aunt and senile father. Lamb then obtained Mary's release from the asylum into his custody. Until his death in 1834, Charles and Mary Lamb lived together as "marked" beings (Marrs 1: 202), fearing the recurrences (and they were many) of Mary's disease and recoiling from any sustained explicit recollection of their parents, especially of their murdered mother. Indeed the first of Mary's many relapses occurred about a year after her first release; it was precipitated by the death of their long-time servant Hetty who had been a surrogate mother to Mary for many years. As Mary grew older her periods of insanity—sometimes manifested as violence, sometimes as incoherence on a general ground of depression—lengthened from weeks to months. In 1833, shortly before his death, Lamb wrote: "half her life she is dead to me, and the other half is made anxious with fears and lookings forward to the next shock" (*Letters* 3: 371). The relationship with Mary made marriage impossible and thus blocked Lamb's posterity even as it made too searching a retrospection dangerous.

However binding the intimacies of Lamb's historical existence, Elia's family strictures are comfortably loose. An only child ("Brother, or sister, I never had any—to know them"), Elia has only a pair of cousins to anchor him in his generation. Though Elia has clearly been young and is perpetually middle-aged within the essays, his parentage is muddied. No identifiable father enters the essays though father-images abound. School supplies "a care scarce less tender than the paternal" (1: 140) and the protective walls of the Inner Temple furnish worthily patriarchal figures—some fearsome (Coventry "who made a solitude of children wherever he came" like "an Elisha Bear," Pierson who poisoned the sparrows, "'old men covered with a mantle'" [2: 85, 90]), some benign (forgetful old Salt, old Lovel in second childhood). The mother, as Fred Randel has observed (115), is even less visible with only an occasional and ambiguous "maternal lap" (My First Play [2: 98]) or "gentle posture of maternal tenderness" ("New Year's Eve" [2: 28]) to hint her existence. The "aunt or . . . maid" ("Witches, and Other

Night Fears" [2: 67]), "maid or aunt" ("Christ's Hospital Five and Thirty Years Ago" [2: 13]), rendered unimportant by the non-specificity of her identity, preempts from the unnamed mother the maternal roles of food provider and of bedtime companion (Randel 115-16). None of these figures, however, is permitted to come very close to the child Elia whose memories set him apart in solitude—wandering in Blakesmoor in H____shire, set apart from classmates at Christ's Hospital. Childhood in Lamb does not emerge from a context of family relationship. It sits apart and is set apart iconically to be contemplated and revered. Such an instance of the protective isolation of childhood occurs strikingly in Lamb's treatment of child chimney-sweepers.

Lamb and the Chimney Sweepers

On January 1, 1824, the humanitarian poet, James Montgomery of Sheffield dispatched a letter to British writers recruiting contributions to a propagandistic anthology aimed at abolishing child labor in chimney sweeping. Lamb and Wordsworth were solicited, as were Walter Scott, Samuel Rogers, William Bowles, Thomas Moore, and Joanna Baillie. The anthology, *The Chimney Sweeper's Friend and Climbing Boy's Album* (1824) is the principal Romantic period literary anthology addressing the exploitation of the child sweeps. Though child labor in the mills and mines of industrialized Britain was a fact of nineteenth-century life, the details of this slaughter of the innocents were not systematically reported until the publication of Chadwick's *Report on Sanitary Conditions of the Labouring Population of Great Britain* in 1842. But the little laboring chimney sweepers were everywhere visible and their scandalous abuse was flagrant and well-publicized by early in the century.

Though chimney-sweeping was an ancient traditional trade throughout northern Europe, eighteenth-century building practices in England, particularly in London, had transformed the trade and made it much more dependent than in earlier centuries on the labor of child apprentices, the so-called climbing-boys. The buildings constructed after the Great Fire of London and throughout the Georgian era were taller and narrower than earlier houses. Instead of having large central fireplaces with single straight chimneys, houses were built with multiple narrow fireplaces, each with a narrow flue. By the end of the eighteenth century, the average flue in a London building was nine inches by fourteen. Many were only eight or nine inches square; some were as tiny as six inches square (Phillips 1). To conserve heat, architects zigzagged the flues through the walls of buildings;

in large public buildings especially—in the House of Lords, for example—flues covered long distances with "as many as eleven changes in direction, *including downwards*" (Strange 3). By the eighteenth century, English householders burned coal that produced a more adhesive deposit than wood, especially around the angling turns of the zigzagging flues. These changes in construction and in fuel made more frequent cleaning of chimneys necessary and required smaller chimney sweepers to do the work. Georgian chimneys were too narrow for adult sweeps and too zigzagging for the traditional long broom. Thus adult master sweepers increased the number of these "climbing boys" (who were sometimes girls) whom they apprenticed to the trade. Only quite small children could get up into the narrow flues to scrape them out, so master sweeps sought the youngest and smallest apprentices allowed by law or suffered by the law's indifference. The law permitted eight-year-olds to be apprenticed, but it was common to start children at six or five. Four-year-olds were sometimes bound as apprentices and at least one case of a three-year-old sweeper has been recorded (Strong 14, 21). The trade was brutal. In the words of Samuel Roberts, a Sheffield philanthropist, the climbing boys' lives were a succession of being

> scarfed, bruised, flogged and crippled—of their having their nails torn off—their eyes inflamed—their growth stunted, and their limbs distorted—of their suffering and death from their cureless cancers—of their being suffocated, burnt, and scalded to death—of their being dashed to pieces in pots falling from the tops of the highest chimneys. ("An Address to British Females," *Improving the Lot* . . . 13-14)

At first terrified of entering the narrow chimneys, new sweeps were routinely beaten or burned to force them up. To harden them, as one master sweep testified, the children would be rubbed "chiefly on the elbows and knees with the strongest brine, as that got from a pork shop, close by a hot fire. . . . At first they will come back from their work with their arms and knees streaming with blood, and the knees looking as if the caps had been pulled off. Then they must be rubbed with brine again, and perhaps go off at once to another chimney" (Strange 14). Sometimes the children became wedged in narrow flues where they charred or smothered before they could be rescued. The annals of the Society for Superseding the Necessity of Climbing Boys founded in 1803 are full of cases such as that of a boy "forced up a chimney, *on fire,*" or of another "sent up a chimney *on fire;* the upper part being stopped, he was . . . suffocated"; or of a third "stuck in a turn of the flue [with] most barbarous means used to drag him down, but it was found impracticable. After seven hours he was dug out, but quite dead"; of a fourth "smothered by falling soot" (Montgomery 328-29).

The little sweepers were dehumanized and deformed in many ways. Moving through the chimneys minimally clothed—usually they wore caps to protect their eyes and shirts but no trousers—they became soot-covered from head to toe. Indeed, they lived in soot, since part of their job was to collect the loose soot scraped from chimneys, gather it into sacks (which weighed thirty to sixty pounds when full) and carry it back to their masters' houses to be sold for fertilizer. Most sweeps were expected to use their empty soot-sacks as blankets at night. Because this coating of black soot was held to "harden" the children against bruises, the masters seldom encouraged bathing. It was usual for sweeps to go a month or more between baths; one former sweep, Richard Stansfield of Manchester, told a Parliamentary commission that "I have been fifteen months without being washed except by the rain; why I have been almost walking away with vermin" (Strange 16); while the labor historians J. L. and Barbara Hammond even report another Parliamentary witness who "in 1788 stated that he had known many boys serve four or five years without being once washed" (Hammond & Hammond 156). The filthy sweeps suffered a high incidence of diseases, especially severe eye inflammations leading to damaged vision and, more deadly, from "soot wart" or chimney-sweeper's disease, cancer of the scrotum. Many of the younger children simply died of fatigue under the labor—"they go off," said a master sweep, "just as quietly as you might fall asleep in the chair, by the fire there" (Strange 15). Many more were deformed and stunted. The damages to the cartilage of the knees from tearing against the sides and angles of flues and the damage to young bones from bearing heavy weights of soot long distances combined with the poor diet intended to keep them small meant that the children who survived their apprenticeships and reached the liberating age of sixteen were hardly fit to work. As David Porter, a master sweep, noted in his "Considerations on the Present State of Chimney Sweepers" (1801), the superannuated climbing boys had mostly learned "a trade they cannot work at," since their growth disqualified them for the one thing they have learned and their years of labor have made them too weak and "too little for anything else" (*Improving the Lot* . . . 39). Some philanthropists noted sadly that the climbing skills of grown-up sweeps combined with their ignorance of any other trade made them very adept thieves. Though the young sweeps were technically apprentices, they were not in fact prepared for a trade they could practice when adults.

Because few parents would choose such a lot for their children, most sweeps were either orphans, sold like Dickens' Oliver Twist by the parish into servitude, or else children of the utterly destitute or the utterly heartless.

Ironically the cruelties of the trade were largely unnecessary. As a succession of philanthropists working through the Society for Superseding the Employment of Climbing Boys made plain, other nations had devised equally effective ways for cleaning chimneys, ways that did not require the mutilation of children. European chimneys were larger and straighter. Germany chimney sweeps, much like American sweeps today, for example, were all adults who used a variety of brushes and other gadgets to clean chimneys. Though North American householders still employed some children to supplement machine cleaning of chimneys, the practice was much less widespread than in England and chimneys were generally larger. Between 1803 when George Smart invented his chimney-cleaning machine and 1828 when John Glass marketed his machine, which was approved by all the leading fire insurance companies of Britain, a whole series of mechanical substitutes for the "human brushes" (Hammond and Hammond 154) was devised. Yet most master sweeps, as Phillips notes (34n), preferred boys to equally efficient machines, since the boys were cheaper to acquire, use, and replace. Obtaining and maintaining machines was expensive and time-consuming; obtaining and maintaining children was cheap and easy. A virtually inexhaustible supply of pauper children was available from almshouses, no questions asked. These children hardly needed to be fed since they could beg their food or be fed on scraps; the less they ate, in fact, the smaller and more useful they would remain. Whereas the machines were expensive to buy and required careful tending to minimize wear and tear, a damaged or dead child could be replaced by another just as good. Perishability was a drawback in a machine but handy in a growing child liable to get too big to use. Moreover, a machine had to be operated by two full-grown men, whereas a child sweep could work alone on his master's behalf.

Unlike the many children who labored out of sight underground in mines or sequestered in factories, the climbing boys were highly visible. They cried their trade ("Sweep! Sweep!") through the morning streets of every city in England. (An 1834 Act of Parliament, however, prohibited the cry though not the trade [Phillips 38].) They entered the houses of almost every family in urban England. Knowledge of their mistreatment could hardly be evaded. Despite the manifest cruelty of the practice, it took 102 years to abolish child labor in chimney sweeping. The campaign to abolish child labor in chimney sweeping, begun in 1773 with the publication of

Jonas Hanway's *State of Chimney Sweepers' Young Apprentices,* fully succeeded in the total and effective prohibition of the employment of persons under twenty-one in chimney sweeping only in 1875 with the passage of an effective licensing act.

In the early decades of the nineteenth century the drive to abolish child labor in chimney sweeping was fervid. From this campaign, the child-centered Romantics (with the exception of political Blake) were largely absent. Lamb, however, participated ambiguously. His curious involvement with this campaign may throw some light on the general Romantic recoil from the actual child of history, and some light on the co-existence throughout the nineteenth century of an intense literary idealization of childhood and calm resignation to widespread institutional abuse of real children.

As the first extended literary response to child labor, Montgomery's anthology is of considerable interest. *The Chimney Sweeper's Friend and Climbing Boy's Album* (1824), consists in part of documentary accounts of the sufferings of sweeps and in part of poems and stories dramatizing their plight and enlisting public concern. The documentary section, *The Chimney Sweeper's Friend,* contains extracts from a series of pamphlets urging abolition, a list of "instances of oppression and cruelty," a physician's testimony on chimney-sweeper's cancer, testimony of master sweeps, and accounts of mechanical substitutes. The "album" or literary component, consists of poems by James Montgomery himself, by Bernard Barton, Allen Cunningham, William Blake, William Lisle Bowles, and others. There are several short stories as well: Ann Gilbert's "The Stolen Child bound to the trade" and "Frank and Will" by Barbara Hofland, a widely-read children's writer.

As a philanthropic work of literary activism, the volume has three clear themes. The first is slavery and the call to abolition. Because they are black-skinned like the black slaves of the West Indies (whose victimization the contributors also deplore), and because they are driven, abused, mutilated, and robbed of joy and life, these children are slaves. Almost every contributor deplores what Montgomery calls "this home slave trade in little children" (xiv) and calls for the liberation of "these little oppressed ENGLISH SLAVES" (2n). Bernard Barton protests this "HOME-BRED Slavery" (252), while John Holland's "Appeal to the Fair Sex" begs that the campaign against negro slavery in the West Indies be extended to the "slaves at home" (279), those M.S. (an otherwise unidentified contributor) calls "the little negroes of England" (395). J. C. Hudson's "Letter to the Mistresses of Families" suggests that the child sweep suffers, like the black slave, from crude color prejudice and that adults assent to his slavery because the sweep looks different: "He partakes in some degree of the fate of the negro: we lose, in his sooty complexion, all sympathy with him as a fellow-creature; forgetting that he was ever one of ourselves, or that a single plunge into a bath would restore the relationship" (76-77).

The second theme is the pathos of innocence betrayed and abused. As S. R. (probably Samuel Roberts) develops the comparison between climbing boys and West Indian slaves, he underlines the children's greater vulnerability: "The poor African negro is kidnapped and sold, but it is by strangers or by foes. These children are kidnapped and sold, and that by their own countrymen, and by their own parents. The negroes are selected for their strength and consequent power of bearing hardship; these poor children are chosen for their youth, small stature, and consequent inability to sustain labor" (12). The principle of contrast of their littleness and innocence with the degradation of their plight is everywhere. Both Blake's "The Chimney Sweeper" and Montgomery's "The Dream" turn on a set of poignant contrasts between the child as lamb and the master as "a butcher" (405), between the filth and dark constraint and exhaustion of the child's life and his free dream of light and freedom:

> . . . I became another child,
> And not the climbing lad:
>
> A child as fair as you may see,
> Whom soot hath never soil'd;
> As rosy-cheek'd as I might be,
> If I had not been spoil'd ("The Dream" 413)

Montgomery's poem is frankly modeled on Blake's "The Chimney Sweeper" with his *unspoiled* white hair. In another poem, "Easter Monday at Sheffield," Montgomery's sweep, an experienced, hardened worker, soliloquizes on his sight of two new children:

> Two toddling five-year-olds were there,
> Twins, that had just begun to climb,
> With cherry-cheeks and curly hair
> And skins not yet engrained with grime.
>
> I wish'd, I did, that they might die,
> Like "Babes i' the Wood," the little slaves,
> And "Robin Redbreast" painfully
> Hide them "with leaves" for want of graves.

—Rather than live like me, and weep
To think that ever they were born;
Toil the long day, and from short sleep
Wake to fresh miseries every morn. (423-24)

Even the lists of misadventures befalling "an apprentice not eight years old in a most emaciated state . . . forced up a chimney *on fire,*" the "boy, nine years old, sent up a chimney *on fire,*" the "child five years old" who worked for a sweep, the boy "wedged in a narrow flue" who was extricated but "died through exhaustion" (38-39) juxtapose the horror of their fate with their little lives.

The third theme is activism: the need and duty to take action and the possibility of change. The whole volume is a tribute to and a call upon freedom of the will. Human beings have the power to change the world. All they need do is act. Both technology and humanity can reform the world. Action is explicitly solicited by the documentation of efficacious machines for cleaning. Essay after essay offers testimony—by master sweeps, by parliamentary committees—to the wisdom of replacing human with mechanical labor. Detailed diagrams impress the possibility of change on the reader. Implicitly, *The Chimney Sweeper's Friend* calls to action through hortatory rhetoric that makes the reader party to the sweepers' plight. Virtually every poem is constructed as an address to the reader: "your chimneys I sweep," notes Blake's sweep. Bernard Barton's contribution is a series of confrontational pleas to "Gentle Reader!" to "FATHERS! unto you we speak; / MOTHERS! your support we seek"; to " BRITONS!"; and to "CHRISTIANS!" William Lisle Bowles' "The Little Sweep" is subtitled "To British Senators!" and is cast as a plea to the Lords and Commons. The poems have a palpable design on the reader, seeking to move a powerful response and to enact change.

Neither of the giants of the contemporary literary scene, neither Wordsworth nor Scott, offered Montgomery a contribution for this volume. Both expressed mild sympathy for the chimney sweeps, but felt unable to write to order. Lamb, however, sent a contribution strikingly different in kind from those of the literary philanthropists. Indeed, Lamb had already indicated his literary interest in chimney-sweepers: a poem, "Choosing a Profession" (probably by Mary) had appeared in Charles and Mary Lamb's *Poetry for Children* (1809); a humorous sketch involving a sweep, "A Sylvan Surprise" appeared in *The Examiner* in 1813; and "The Praise of Chimney-Sweepers" appeared in the *London Magazine* for May 1822 shortly before its inclusion in *Essays of Elia* (1823). Though he "batter'd my brains . . . for a few verses" (*Letters* 2: 425), Lamb felt unable to come up with another composition for the anthology. Instead Montgomery received "Communicated by Mr. Charles Lamb, from a Very Rare and Curious Little Work" (Montgomery 343), a copy of the innocent chimney sweeper's song from Blake's *Songs of Innocence and Experience*.

Lamb regarded Blake's lyric as "the flower" of Montgomery's collection (*Letters* 2: 426). Though Lamb knew and admired some of Blake's graphic works, it is uncertain how many of Blake's poems he knew. (He mentions hearing some read, but does not specify any except "The Tyger" [*Letters* 2: 425]). It would be interesting to know if Lamb had heard and then rejected for inclusion in the anthology Blake's two other chimney-sweep poems—"The Chimney Sweeper" of the *Songs of Experience* and "London"—but both his choice of the lyric of Innocence and the change he introduces into its text indicate that Lamb's mode of viewing the abused child is very different from the philanthropic mode of Montgomery and most of his collaborators.

Lamb indicates his emphasis in the single change he introduces by which Blake's "little Tom Dacre" becomes in Lamb's version "Little Tom Toddy." A bitter name gives way to a sweet one. "Dacre" carries the bitter implications of "acrid" and "darker" and the associated ideas of the bitter taste of soot, the bitter lot of the child, the darkness of the night in which the sweeps rise, the darkness of their filthy skins, and the darkness of their fate. The alliterating "Tom Toddy" suggests the comfort of a hot drink (like the hot sassafras tea, the "Saloop" rhapsodized in "The Praise of Chimney-Sweepers" [2: 110]) and, especially, the charm of a toddler. According to Eric Partridge's *A Dictionary of Slang and Unconventional English* (892) "Toddy" is a mid-nineteenth-century colloquialism cognate with "toddy" (or little) and "toddles" (a toddling child). (Dickens' often down but never out Tommy Traddles bears the same kind of comfortable name.) From all accounts, however, young sweeps did not toddle; rather they staggered and shuffled because of the weight of their soot bags and the deformities of their knees. "Dacre" is a name suggesting the environmental conditions; "Toddles" is a name attaching to the child in and of himself. The changed name indicates that Lamb prefers to contemplate the untouched ideal atemporal essence of the child rather than concentrating on determining circumstances.

Lamb's choice for Montgomery's anthology is a poem of innocence that his change has made even more innocent. The innocent lyric is entirely a first person narrative mediated through the consciousness of the sweeper who is innocent in the root sense of being in/nocens, not harming, both harmless and unharmed. He is harmless because so very young "my tongue / Could scarcely cry "weep! 'weep! 'weep!,'" because he is like a lamb among other lambs (Tom has hair "that curl'd like a lamb's back" and all the children sport by the river), because he is sometimes locked up and sometimes liberated by authorities whom he obeys, because he submits to his burdens. Yet he is also unharmed spiritually because of the supremacy of his consciousness. Every detail of the threatening environment is transformed: the coffin-chimneys to open doors, the soot-bags to clouds, the death-dealing masters to the angel of liberation, the external cold to the internal warmth of faith, the betraying father to a loving God. The poem is a first-person narrative of a child, an urban Lamb, who interprets all his dreadful experiences—the death of the mother, desertion of the father, labor, physical disfigurement, death-in-life—as subject to the overmastering idea of a loving God and a loving environment. There is neither judgment of nor protest at these conditions; the flat childish conjunctions—"*So* your chimneys I sweep" "*And so* he was quiet," "*And* by came an angel . . . *and* he opened," "*And so* Tom awoke," "*So* if all do their duty"—indicate total acquiescence in the way of the world. But the claims for the reality of Tom's hair, still existing white as the fleece of the lamb of God, in idea, and the claims for the realm of dream vision with its compensatory clean river bathing, make the child impervious in his innocence. The sweep of Innocence perceives all things, suffuses all reality with his own qualities of love and harmlessness. He holds it possible—for so the last line implies—to change the world by persisting in his power of love. The sweep of Innocence, vulnerable and abused as he is, meets Schiller's criterion of the moral grandeur of the child as living representative of ideal humanity. Despite the most hellish environmental conditions, the child continues to experience the world as if he were free. He refuses to be determined. Compared to this child, adults, in Schiller's words, "*look upward* from the *limitation* of our condition, which is inseparable from the *determination* which we have attained, to the pure unlimited *determinacy* of the child. . . . The child is . . . a lively representation to us of the ideal, not indeed as it is fulfilled, but as it is enjoined; hence we are in no sense moved by the notion of its poverty and limitation, but rather by the opposite: the notion of its pure and free strength, its integrity, its eternality" (Schiller 87). The sweep of Innocence, though his situation shames the adult reader, is in a sense impervious to harm because his human heart is intact. He functions as a human being should function *despite circumstance*. Though "The Chimney Sweeper" of Innocence is susceptible to many readings (including a reading that could stress the child's manipulated consciousness), Lamb seems to have read the poem triumphantly, as a victory of pure-heartedness over circumstance, as the resistance of another shorn Lamb by imaginative reconstruction of the world.

"The Chimney Sweeper" of *Songs of Innocence* asserts the supremacy of mind over environment. This poem is thus dissonant with the others in Montgomery's anthology because it suggests that *no essential harm* can befall the essentially innocent child. But Samuel Roberts had maintained, on the contrary, that by abuse and cruelty chimney sweepers might be damned for eternity: "It is a fact that the *Child* is in a great measure the father of the *Man.* Reflect, then, that as you form the child from seven to fourteen years of age, you form the man through life, and in all probability the *immortal being* after death" ("An Address to British Females . . ." *Improving the Lot . . .* 15-16). In not submitting Blake's other "The Chimney Sweeper," that from *Songs of Experience,* however, Lamb withholds (perhaps deliberately) a poem more consistent with the activism of Montgomery's collection. For the lyric of Experience treats its sweeper as a child of history and circumstance, a degraded angry creature of his degrading maddening situation. "The Chimney Sweeper" of *Songs of Experience* is a poem of determinism. That sweep is depicted partly in the third person, partly in the first, as an It, "A little black thing among the snow," who is conscious of having been manipulated by *them.* "*They* clothed me in the clothes of death, / And taught me to sing the notes of woe." This child's existence is defined *against* the existences of others because his situation has been determined and exploited by his keepers, his parents and their collaborators, "God & his Priest & King / Who make up a heaven of our misery." For this child who feels himself a thing, "heaven" is nothing but a *made-up* illusion meant to keep him quiet and also the material wealth alienated from the insulted and the injured ("our misery") on which the lords of this world batten. Whereas the chimney sweeper of Innocence lives imperviously in the world of timeless eternal love and of all-powerful consciousness, the chimney sweeper of Experience lives vulnerably and angrily in history. This child feels the contrast between subjective moments of cheerfulness and his objective constraint: "And because I am happy and dance and sing, / They think they have done me no injury." The philanthropist Robert Stevens picked up the same antithesis between the allegedly innate childish cheerfulness of the sweepers and their plight:

> And yet these children are said to be the merriest little fellows in the world. "Go where you will, Chimney-sweepers are to be seen showing their white teeth in high glee!" The impugners of this awful traffic have never dreamt of proving that their tears are always flowing. That would be to deny the

infinite goodness of the Almighty. No one's path is a perpetual darkness. The sun always rises again, through God's mercy. . . . Children suffer prodigiously but there is a spring and an elasticity about them which bears up against the misery they are exposed to; and no sooner is that actual pressure of sorrow removed, than the hoop and the marbles, and the top dry up their tears; and their trade allows them large time for these. But this is no reason why the sorrow should be wantonly inflicted. Who could stand by and see weakness borne down by savage power, and refuse relief because the suffering have an occasional intermission? ("The Trade of Chimney Sweeping Exhibited in its True Light," *Improving the Lot* . . . 20)

Rather than viewing the cheerfulness as a solace (for both child and adult viewer), Stevens—like Blake's lyric—cites it as grounds for indignation. If, in Schiller's term, the innocent enjoys free "determinacy," the child of Experience knows "determination," understands that he is a creature, "a little black thing" worked on by the forces of his society, from his parents on up to the King and to God. Recognizing that he is an object among other objects, moved by forces he does not control, the chimney sweeper of Experience is neither innocent nor invulnerable. Because consciousness is not all powerful, but linked to condition the child of Experience no longer feels safe and protected. He cannot stand against time though he obliquely threatens to stand against his persecutors. At once vulnerable and threatening, the chimney sweeper of Experience belongs to history. Like the sweepers in Montgomery's *Album* he has a palpable design on the reader just as the reader's world has imprinted its design on him. There is no sanctuary, no standing place outside the determining world.

Lamb's vision, however, will not tolerate such subjugation of a child to time. The determined child of Experience firmly set into history is antithetical to Lamb's own chimney sweepers. Though the climbing boy was the very archetype of the abused child, Lamb's own treatment disarms even that pain.

Unlike Blake, Montgomery, and the poet-contributors to *The Chimney Sweeper's Friend and Climbing Boy's Album,* Lamb is not interested in inciting his readers to action. His motives and treatment are not philanthropic. He makes no appeal out of the closed artifact of his composition, makes no move toward change. He never even uses the term "climbing boy," the term preferred to "chimney sweepers" by humanitarians because of its greater pathos. On the contrary, Lamb's terms (with the single exception of the "little Negroes" in a letter [*Letters* 2: 425]) tend to mitigate the pathos and emphasize vitality, incongruity, or visual interest: "tender novices," "young sparrow," "matin lark," "dim specks," "poor blots," "innocent blacknesses," "young Africans," "almost clergy imps," "sable phenomenon," "small gentry," "sable younkers." His interest is not in exacting pathos but in marking a comic distinctiveness through a distancing periphrasis or association ("clergy," "gentry," "novices," "phenomenon," the archaic "younkers," the non-human "sparrow," "lark," "blot," "speck") that makes the sweepers anything but weary children.

Lamb disarms any possible pathos associated with the sweep by an emphatically visual treatment. Though color is an important feature of the philanthropic treatments, the *blackness of the sweeps* is used there to emphasize their identity with *slaves*, Lamb entirely omits the slavery theme and instead turns the sweeps into arrangements in black and white. The very grinning freedom and roguish flexibility of the sweeps—most unservile qualities—point up the piquancy of their aesthetic value. The incongruity of the blackness or the intense contrast of black and white on a human body turn the sweeps into comic figures in William Hazlitt's sense that "the essence of the laughable . . . is the incongruous" ("On Wit and Humour" 644). Thus the sight of a black sweeper in a green rural meadow, is of itself a curiosity to be noted as "something dusky upon the grass" a something "discordant . . . like an artificial discord in music . . . a combination of *urbs in rure.*" "There is no reason in nature that a chimney-sweeper should not indulge a taste for rural objects, but somehow the ideas were discordant" ("A Sylvan Surprise," 1: 154). It is the allied joke of *discordia concors,* a sudden unexpected identity, rather like the English game of Snap, that influences the Creole boy's choice of trade in Mary Lamb's "Choosing a Profession." The black West Indian brought to England for an education displays no inclination to any profession until he one day proclaims:

> the same
> Trade he would be those boys of colour were,
> Who danc'd so happy in the open air.
> It was a troop of chimney-sweeping boys,
> With wooden music and obstrep'rous noise,
> In tarnish'd and grotesque array,
> Were dancing in the street the first of May. (3: 396)

Color calls to color, black to black. There is even a hint that both the sweeps' glee and the Creole's taste are "tarnish'd and grotesque" and thus comical because of their common blackness. Indeed blackness, which is the activating sign of the pathetic for the philanthropic writers, is for Lamb the sign of the grotesque. Totally unselfconscious in his color prejudice,[6] Lamb can "praise" the dehumanized and blackened sweeps only by finding piquant and incongruous the blackness of "these dim specks—poor blots—innocent blacknesses . . . these young Africans of our own growth—these almost clergy imps" ("The Praise of Chimney-Sweepers" 2: 109). Sharp contrasts of black and white—the teeth, "white and shining ossifications," in a filthy face, the "black head" of a sleeping sweep folded between "a pair of sheets whiter and softer than the lap where Venus lulled Ascanius" in Arundel Castle (2: 111-12)—contribute to the sense of the child as a comely decorative object rather like a blackface lawn-ornament.

Nor does Lamb's treatment emphasize the vulnerability of the child to exhort the reader to action. On the contrary, Lamb creates a reader who is a contemplative spectator of the picturesque prized diversity of life. Like a traveler from a time machine, Lamb's reader is expected to know better than to interfere with the pattern before him. Whereas Montgomery and his collaborators address a chosen collective audience with a possible sphere of action—the mothers of Britain who ought to protect the young or the "senators" of Britain who ought to legislate for the young or you middle-class readers whose "chimneys I sweep" who ought to clean your own chimneys with brushes and machines—in the interests of a change, Lamb has no such call to activity. Lamb addresses a contemplative, ambling, and solitary reader with no responsibilities, a reader who may happen to meet "one of these small gentry in thy early rambles" and may feel impelled to "give him a penny" or better "give him two pence" or even in very cold weather, sixpence, "a tester." This reader is advised to read, to meditate, the various postures of the sweeps so as to take from them a timeless "lesson of patience to mankind," to appreciate their almost feline susceptibility (in their poverty, in their hunger, in their cold) to the odor of sassafras (2: 109-10). Whereas the poems of Blake, Montgomery (especially his four soliloquies), and Bowles take a first person point of view within the chimney sweeper and force the reader to share the child's feelings, Lamb stations his rambling reader at a distance from the sweep and concentrates on analyzing the feelings of the adult who watches, not the child who suffers.

A distant, contemplative point of view is enforced by Lamb's transformation of the sweeps into the formal components of works of art—pictures, plays, tales. He chooses materials for prettiness and immovable fixity out of time. The focus is on fanciful prettiness; the chosen sweep is young: "old chimney-sweepers are by no means attractive—but one of those tender novices, blooming through their first nigritude." Distanced into adorable creatures, their hardships transformed to charm, the sweeps are like birds—like sparrows "with their little professional notes sounding . . . *peep-peep,*" like "the matin lark . . . in their aerial ascents not seldom anticipating the sun-rise"—or like cats, "those domestic animals," hanging "their black heads over the ascending steam" of hot sassafras tea. Indeed they are already parts of pictures or tales or plays: "Hogarth has got him already (how could he miss him?) in the March to Finchley, grinning at the pie-man—there he stood, as he stands in the picture, irremovable, as if the jest was to last for ever. . . .'"

Even more pictorially staged is the fanciful image of sweep's broom in the chimney: "'I seem to remember having been told, that a bad sweep was once left in a stack with his brush, to indicate which way the wind blew. It was an awful spectacle certainly; not much unlike the old stage direction in Macbeth, where the 'Apparition of a child crowned with a tree in his hand rises.'" This account primarily works to pile layer on layer of theatricality on the actual chimney sweeps so that the reader is at a fivefold remove from any actual dead climbing boy. Underlying the whole is a shadowy unmentioned sweep who died wedged in a chimney. That unseen victim (#1) becomes uncertain fiction (#2) through Elia's uncertain memories at three removes of a possible verbal account ("seem to remember being told"). That uncertain account produces a legendary "bad sweep . . . left in a stack with his brush" (#3). That legend is further transformed to the "awful spectacle" (#4) designed for mental theater. The spectacular sweep thus resembles the yet more fictitious "apparition of a child" within *Macbeth* (#5), another fiction built upon an absent child. Lamb de-realizes the unthinkable dead sweep by translating him from unseen reality into manifest theatricality.

Just as the sweeps are made fixedly theatrical, so are they assimilated to the folk tale pattern, used by Wordsworth as well, of the displaced noble child exiled from "that imperial palace whence he came." In the account of the lost sweep who napped "like a young Howard" in an Arundel Castle bed, Lamb argues a noble origin:

> Doubtless this young nobleman (for such my mind misgives me he must be) was allured by some memory, not amounting to full consciousness, of his condition in infancy, when he was used to be lapt by his mother, or his nurse, in just such sheets as he there found, into which he was now but creeping back as into his proper *incunabula,* and resting place. (2: 112)

Lamb's play on the language of bedding and early books (of "sheets" and "his proper *incunabula*") puts the unfortunate sweep squarely within an ancient tradition of story and makes him comfortably fictional.

These arrangements in black and white, the comparisons to the animal kingdom, the color patterning, the translation into picture and story and stage spectacles take the sweeps out of time. By assimilating the sweeps to lasting artifacts like pictures, to enduring species like cats and birds, and to permanent archetypes like lost princes, Lamb makes them a-historic. Lamb gives no sense that the chimney-sweepers of Regency London are a historical phenomenon, specific to a particular place and time with a particular way of building. Rather they are depicted as permanent features of the urban landscape whose place is no more to be questioned or reformed than sparrows or cats or fairy tales.

The picturesque timelessness and humorous incongruity of Lamb's portrayal impedes any significant sympathy for the plight of the sweeps. Yet as an alert city dweller, Lamb was entirely aware of the condition of the children of the poor. He knew that children who lived on the mean streets of London were knocked about, kept down, and "dragged up, to live or die as it happened" (2: 264). So terrible was the fate of these young human miniatures that Lamb flinched at giving them the honorific name of children. In one of several essays debunking "Popular Fallacies," Lamb writes of the children of the poor only to conclude that there is no such thing—only "premature reflecting persons." There is "no childishness" in the dwellings of the poor:

> The careless little darling of the wealthier nursery, in their hovel is transformed betimes into a premature reflecting person. No one has time to dandle it, no one thinks it worth while to coax it. . . . It grew up without the lullaby of nurses, it was a stranger to the patient fondle. . . . It was never sung to—no one ever told it a tale of the nursery. It was dragged up, to live or to die as it happened. It had no young dreams. It broke at once into the iron realities of life. A child exists not for the very poor as any object of dalliance; it is only another mouth to be fed, a pair of little hands to be betimes inured to labour. It is the rival, till it can be the co-operator, for food with the parent. It is never his mirth, his diversion, his solace; it never makes him young again, with recalling his young times. The children of the very poor have no young times. It makes the very heart to bleed to overhear the casual street talk between a poor woman and her little girl. . . . It is not of toys, of nursery books, of summer holidays . . . of the promised sight, or play; of praised sufficiency at school. It is of mangling and clear-starching, of the price of coals, or of potatoes. The questions of the child, that should be the very outpourings of curiosity in idleness, are marked with forecast and melancholy providence. It has come to be a woman, before it was a child. It has learned to go to market; it chaffers, it haggles, it envies, it murmurs; it is knowing,

acute, sharpened; it never prattles. ("That Home is Home Though It is Never so Homely" 2: 264-65)

The anxious young person brought up in an atmosphere of need, forced to calculate, to know, to exercise foresight, to recognize the force of circumstance is defined as a non-child, as a "premature reflecting person" or a mere "mouth" or "pair of hands" or "a woman, before it was a child."

As his essay evinces Lamb knows very well the discontinuity between the ideal of prattling, free-imagining, much-doted-upon childhood and the actual facts of real children's lives. Yet he recoils from any consideration of the social afflictions of childhood, from any empathetic consideration of the chimney sweepers, from any sympathetic depiction of the unloved children of need. Though he recognizes the power of environment to determine, he nevertheless asserts the self-preserving power of the essential childhood self. To support these contradictory insights, Lamb pulls childishness out of history even as he leaves the children there. Determined "little black things" and "premature reflecting persons" are not real essential children. Whoever is shaped and deformed by history ceases, in Lamb's interpretation, to be a child.

Lamb's own cherishing treatment of the chimney sweeps saves them as children though it extrudes them from history. By creating various kinds of aesthetic frames and distances around the children, he keeps terror and conditioning at bay though never entirely banished. It is aesthetic treatment rather than pathetic, and avoids extended scrutiny of the children's suffering and concentrates instead on the psychological and decorative uses of chimney sweeps for other people. The psychology of the children themselves is omitted in order to transform them into useful emblematic objects for adults. A private psychological rather than a public philanthropic strategy, it issues in an idealization of childhood without any activism on behalf of children. In all Lamb's writing on childhood, there is a will to draw the child—and the adult who remembers the self as child—into a pain-free neutral zone from which history and causality have been excluded.

In Neutral Space

In "The Child Angel. A Dream" (2: 244-46) Lamb sets forth a symbolic embodiment of "perpetual childhood," the "Tutelar Genius of Childhood," who lives outside of history set apart in a realm of neutral space. Ge-Urania, a "glorious Amphibium,"[7] is of neutral sex—an "It" being both, or neither, male and female—and, as the name indicates, both of heaven and of earth, but belonging fully to neither. Neither weak because immortal, nor strong because lame and "touched by the shadow of human imbecility," Ge-Urania, the Child-Angel, exists in a perpetual present, its portion "was, and is, to be a child for ever." As an amphibious neutral "it," Ge-Urania is one of a kind and cannot reproduce itself. Gender-neutral, it can never become a parent. As De Quincey remarked of Lamb's prose style, "it does not prolong itself—it does not repeat itself—it does not propagate itself" (*CW* 3: 88). It comes out of no where or perhaps even out of its own self-conception: "Whence it came, or how it came, or who bid it come, or whether it came purely of its own head, neither you nor I know—but there it lay . . ." In "New Year's Eve," Lamb had similarly allied with "my own early idea" as "my heir and favourite" (2: 29). This self-originating damaged being who shares Lamb's lameness (a flat-footed walk and a speech impediment) and "constitutional imbecility" ("Recollections of Christ's Hospital" 1: 146), exists in an eternal present. Indeed, it is a "young *present*" ("'Presents,' I often say, 'endear Absents'" ["A Dissertation upon Roast Pig" 2: 125]) who mediates between absent earth and absent heaven.

Like Keats' Psyche, Ge-Urania is a belated mythic figure born into a full hierarchy without a place of its own. Like Keats' Psyche too, it brings a new element into the moral universe, for it teaches the angels pity and sympathetic imagination. Yet despite its successful supplementarity, Ge-Urania, like Psyche in this too, exists precariously and subjectively, liable to dissolution from history or from death.

Childhood does not fit properly in earth with its coursing history or in heaven with its absolute knowledge. Thus Ge-Urania, coming out of no where, inhabits no place: "not the real heavens . . . but a kind of fairyland heaven," and even there "it might not press into the heart and inwards of the palace" but remains in "the purlieus of the palace." Neither father Nadir, the angel, nor dead human mother Adah, "who sleepeth by the river Pison" is present to the child. Indeed, their very names suggest absence, Nadir, an angelic neologism, is, astronomically, the point opposite the zenith, the height, of the heavens; the term is thus appropriate for an angel who has sunk to love a mortal. Adah, "brilliance" (Walker 8) or "ornament" (Monaghan 3), was one of the wives of Cain's fierce great-grandson son Lamech ("If Cain is avenged sevenfold / Then Lamech seventy-sevenfold" [Genesis 4: 24]) and the mother of Jubal the musician. "Nadir" chimes with "Adah" to produce "Nada," nothing.

Ge-Urania then is set in a safety zone of precarious antithetical existence, between the absence of its origin and the total presence of its semi-heavenly perpetual amphibious being. But Ge-Urania has a mysterious double, "the child by the grave," who is equally fixed in the precincts of death, a kind of dark commentator on Ge-Urania's seeming bliss.

The Tutelary Genius of Childhood is thus embodied in a creature who is arrested in fixity and is both cursed and blessed, damaged and invulnerable, lost and found. Without the necessity of going forward into time (and the sufferings of missing mother Adah) and without a remembered past, Ge-Urania is safe though frail in the perpetual present in the purlieus of the heavenly palace.

The beloved child whose experience is most cherished is typically placed by Lamb into walled and sheltered precincts, protected purlieus. The scatheless child in a walled utopia is a favorite motif. Though Lamb principally writes of his own early self, his finest poem, "To T. L. H., *A Child*" (1814), depicts and glorifies such another child. The poem is directed to four-year-old Thornton Hunt who spent his early childhood in prison. Thornton's father, Leigh Hunt, who was imprisoned in 1813 for libel, brought his wife and three-year-old son to share the captivity. The sweet-tempered Thornton eagerly played with his father in the narrow prison garden by day (Tatchell 37); by night, however, the child had terrible nightmares and eventually, at a physician's orders, was removed from the prison (Blunden, "Leigh Hunt's Eldest Son" 55). Though Lamb mentions Thornton's night horrors with seeming puzzlement in "Witches, and Other Night-Fears," written seven years after the poem ("this nurse-child of optimism will start at shapes, unborrowed of tradition" [2: 68]), he makes no connection at all between the boy's incarceration and his bad dreams. The prison's "Sights of fear and of distress" are thought invisible to the "harmless infant's guess." Indeed Lamb links the specters not to the immediate context of the prison, but to eternal "archetypes" within ("Witches, and Other Night Fears" 2: 68). In the poem Lamb's emphasis is on establishing little TLH's safely amphibious nature secured behind fortifications:

> Model of thy parent dear,
> Serious infant worth a fear:
> In thy unfaultering visage well
> Picturing forth the son of TELL,
> When on his forehead, firm and good,
> Motionless mark, the apple stood;
> Guileless traitor, rebel mild,
> Convict unconscious, culprit-child!
> Gates that close with iron roar
> Have been to thee thy nursery door;
> Chains that clink in cheerless cells

Have been thy rattles and thy bells;
Walls contrived for giant sin
Have hemmed thy faultless weakness in;
Near thy sinless bed black Guilt
Her discordant house hath built,
And filled it with her monstrous brood—
Sights, by thee not understood—
Sights of fear and of distress,
That pass a harmless infant's guess!
But the clouds, that overcast
Thy young morning, may not last.
Soon shall arrive the rescuing hour,
That yields thee up to Nature's power.
Nature, that so late doth greet thee,
Shall in o'er-flowing measure meet thee.
She shall recompense with cost
For every lesson thou hast lost.
Then wandering up thy sire's lov'd hill,
Thou shalt take thy airy fill
Of health and pastime. *Birds shall sing
For thy delight each May morning.*
'Mid new-yean'd lambkins thou shalt play,
Hardly less a lamb than they.
Then thy prison's lengthened bound
Shall be the horizon skirting round.
And, while thou fillest thy lap with flowers,
To make amends for wintery hours,
The breeze, the sunshine, and the place,
Shall from thy tender brow efface
Each vestige of untimely care,
That sour restraint had graven there;
And on thy every look impress
A more excelling childishness.

So shall be thy days beguil'd.
THORNTON HUNT, my favourite child. (5: 35-36)

As Lamb's "favourite," little Thornton appropriately enough is kin to "new yean'd lambkins," and "hardly less a lamb than" his admirer. Indeed, the quotation from Marlowe's "Passionate Shepherd to his Love" established the poem as a prison pastoral; here Lamb as shepherd addresses his beloved guarded lambkin. A type of Lamb in this poem, Thornton is "hemmed" in just as the young Elia had "been hemmed in by a yet securer cincture of those excluding garden walls" ("Blakesmoor in H____shire" 2: 155). The imprisoning enclave is perceived as benign. Indeed, Thornton's eventual liberation pleases only because external nature has been successfully transformed to a jail: "Then thy prison's lengthened bound / Shall be the horizon skirting round." Lamb's Edenic childhood recollections inevitably involve enclosures—cloisters, enclosed gardens, speaking walls ("all Ovid on the walls" [2: 155]), even the juvenile dungeons of Christ's Hospital. These enclosures almost all bear kindly associations. In "Recollections of Christ's Hospital" "the shelter of a care scarcely less tender than the paternal" is tied to "the numberless comforts, even magnificences, which surround [the student]; in his old and awful cloisters, with their traditions; in his spacious school-rooms, and the well-ordered airy and lofty rooms where he sleeps; in his stately dining hall" (1: 140). The walled Temple with the inner space of its urban garden, its rus in urbe, "place of my kindly engendure" (2: 83) is a "collegiate" shelter against time. The very walls and wall-hangings of "Blakesmoor in H____shire" were sustaining: "Why, every plank and panel of that house for me had magic in it. The tapestried bed-rooms—tapestry so much better than painting—not adorning merely, but peopling the wainscots—at which childhood ever and anon would steal a look . . ." (2: 154). James Scoggins has remarked how often Lamb places the child in a "temporal approximation of Eden," a "Goshen," an "Atlantis," "A sanctuary and quiet Alsatia," or the *hortus conclusus* of a quiet country house (Scoggins 202, 209, 205). "At the plucking of every panel I should have felt the varlets at my heart" (2: 154). This Edenic sanctuary is protected space, walled in and walled out. Lamb echoes Marvell's play on the possibilities of recapturing "that happy garden state" in "The Garden," a poem Lamb directly quotes in "The Old Benchers of the Inner Temple," especially dwelling on Marvell's "nectarine and curious peach" and his praise of the bliss of solitude: "Two Paradises 'twere in one, / To live paradise alone." He writes of the bliss of those Edenic "spacious old fashioned gardens, which I had almost to myself, unless when now and then a solitary gardening man would cross me—and how the nectarines and peaches hung upon the walls, without my ever offering to pluck them, because they were forbidden fruit, unless now and then" ("Dream-Children" 2: 102). The intensity of the bliss for Elia—as for TLH—seems to be intensified by its sense of possible rupture and time and guilt ("*almost* to myself," "*unless when now and then* a solitary gardening man *would cross me*," "*without* my *ever . . . unless now and then,*" "*forbidden fruit*"). To be contained, cinched into the girdling bounds of an inner garden space is paradise, but folly to pass "its strict [from *strictus,* past participle of *stringere* to draw tight] and proper precincts [from *cingere,* to gird]":

> Variegated views, extensive prospects—and those at no great distance from the house—I was told of such—what were they to me, being out of the boundaries of my Eden?—So far from a wish to roam, I would have drawn, methought, still closer the fences of my chosen prison; and have been hemmed in by a yet securer cincture of those excluding garden walls. I could have exclaimed with that garden-loving poet—
>
> > Bind me, ye woodbines, in your 'twines;
> > Curl me about, ye gadding vines;
> > And oh so close your circles lace,
> > That I may never leave this place;
> > But, lest your fetters prove too weak,
> > Ere I your silken bondage break,
> > Do you, O brambles, chain me too,
> > And, courteous briars, nail me through! ("Blakesmoor in H____shire"
> > 2: 155)

No motion has this imprisoned child, no force. Both the young Elia and the lambkin Thornton are privative figures, walled out from harm. Defined by what is excluded, Thornton is unfaltering, motionless, guiltless, unconscious, faultless, weak, sinless, uncomprehending, and harmless. Like young Elia within "the fences of my chosen prison," little Thornton within "gates," "chains," and "walls" is a passive figure made of negation. Absence of power, of consciousness, even of knowledge keep him safe in neutral space.

Thornton's "faultless weakness:" and powerful powerlessness figure him as an oxymoron, the appropriate inhabitant of a walled utopia. As a trope of simultaneous being and non-being, the oxymoron is the rhetorical equivalent of the utopian, the topos of no place. The oxymoron is the rhetorical figure that paradoxically asserts that a place may be no-place, a person may exist yet not exist. It is the figure that marks that amphibious existence in antithetical realms. Such oxymoronic utopianism marks Lamb's treatment of childhood.

Like Ge-Urania, the habitant of no place and no time, the child in Lamb is habitually depicted in a vocabulary that is antithetical and oxymoronic. The tendency of this paradoxical characterization is to prevent the child from merging into the social context. Neither fish nor fowl, the paradox-bedewed child thus is hemmed into a special precinct of verbal space. Just as the child-angel lives amphibiously in two realms, so does the child of Lamb's prose inhabit the borderland of paradox. To exist tentatively in a paradox is to be set apart from the rest of the world that lives in simpler categories.

Oxymoronic patterns emerge in word-play and in character traits. Lamb adapts habits of word play from the seventeenth-century poets he much admired, regularly counterpoising fragility and power, earnestness and lightness, plentitude and emptiness, art and life, and death and life. Lamb's three best childhood poems, "To T. L. H.," "On an Infant Dying as Soon as Born," and "Parental Recollections," all turn on metaphysically heterogeneous juxtapositions of opposite qualities. "To T. L. H." sets the boy apart oxymoronically as "serious infant," "guileless traitor," "rebel mild," "convict unconscious," "culprit child" endued with "faultless weakness." Even Lamb's choice of meter for the poem—the seven-syllable headless iambic line used by Ambrose Philips for his five "namby pamby" lyrics to the Carteret and Pulteney children—has an oxymoronic effect because juxtaposing the naivete and hypercorismatic simplicities associated with the meter with the darkness of the prison language. A similar antithetical patterning surrounds Thomas Hood's infant daughter, dead at birth. Human and yet not human, denatured and set apart, she is "A nameless piece of Babyhood," "a Human Bud." She embodies both life and death as she lies in her "coffin-cradle . . . Extinct, with scarce the sense of dying." Instantaneity and eternity are hers in the contrast between the rapid eyeblink of her life and her endless death: "She did but ope an eye, and put / A clear beam forth, then strait shut up / For the long dark." The antithesis between the brevity of the light and the eternity of the dark is picked up in the patent contrast between the colorful "pretty toys" of babyhood and the negativity of death that is both blank ("pale death") and black ("did late eclipse"):

> Rites, which custom does impose,
> Silver bells and baby clothes;
> Coral redder than those lips,
> Which pale death did late eclipse;
> Music framed for infants' glee,
> Whistle never tuned for thee;
> Though thou want'st not, thou shalt have them.
> Loving hearts were they which gave them.
> Let not one be missing; nurse,
> See them laid upon the hearse
> Of infant slain by doom perverse.
> Why should kings and nobles have
> Pictured trophies to their grave;

>And we, churls, to thee deny
>Thy pretty toys with thee to lie,
>A more harmless vanity? (5: 50-5l)

Similarly in "Parental Recollections" (3: 398) the sense of the fleetingness and intense energy of the "straggler into loving arms / Young climber up of knees" is contrasted with its unending preternatural power: "But I knew one, that to itself / All seasons could controul; / That would have mock'd the sense of pain / Out of a grieved soul."

The most powerful oxymoronic contrast—that of simultaneous guilt and innocence of the "guileless traitor," "rebel mild," "culprit child"—is carried forward in Lamb's ordinary focus on the terrors of childhood. Emphasizing *causeless guilt,* Lamb adds spiritual profundity to childhood by describing the intuition of evil accessible to the sweetest souled of children. Two tales from *Mrs. Leicester's School*—Charles' "The Witch Aunt" and Mary's "The Young Mahometan"—and "Witches, and Other Night Fears" treat childhood terrors. In each work, a seemingly trivial cause makes possible the child's intuition of sublime terror. Maria Howe misinterprets her old aunt's reading; Margaret Green in the solitude of an old library imagines the necessary damnation of her adored mother; and young Elia extrapolates from the Stackhouse Bible picture of Samuel raised by the Witch of Endor a chilling specter of "that old man covered with a mantle!" (2: 67) Though Lamb gives adequate circumstantial cause for childhood terrors—Margaret was left too much alone, Elia was susceptible to the Stackhouse illustration—he insists on distinguishing childhood terrors from their external causes. With a willful and tendentious discounting of the child's actual prison experience, he cites Thornton Hunt as an example of *archetypal childhood fantasy.* This nightmare-wracked prison-toddler becomes proof of the autonomy of childhood consciousness:

>Dear little T. H. who of all children has been brought up with the most scrupulous exclusion of every taint of superstition—who was never allowed to hear of goblin or apparition, or scarcely to be told of bad men, or to read or hear of any distressing story—finds all this world of fear, from which he has been so rigidly excluded *ab extra,* in his own "thick-coming fancies;" and from his little midnight pillow, this nurse-child of optimism will start at shapes, unborrowed of tradition, in sweats to which the reveries of the cell-damned murderer are tranquility. (2: 68)

This fear, Lamb holds, "is purely spiritual" and is strong "in proportion as it is objectless upon earth," predominating therefore "in the period of sinless infancy" (2: 68) probably because the child undistracted *ab extra* has readier access than the world-besotted adult to the "transcripts, types—the archetypes" that are in us and are eternal. The more guiltless the child, therefore, the more acute the sense of guilt for unknown sin, the more striking the oxymoronic contrast between the dreamer and his dreams. Even in infancy, childhood is thus double, looking toward heaven like Ge-Urania, but bending deathward like the child by the grave.

The oxymoronic structure is the companion of Elia's oxymoronic self, a self that joins childhood and old age discontinuously without the medium of manhood. Lamb's child is duplicitous, enacting a combination of roles that are discontinuous and opposite. As Randel, developing a point of De Quincey's, has indicated, the "world of Elia" is a world of *discontinuity* (Randel 21). Heterogeneous states are joined. This discontinuity is explicitly present in Lamb's persona and in his chosen characters, most of whom oxymoronically incorporate of the traits of age and youth. Old age and youth are virtually identified, so that to be old is a way to be young in disguise. More powerfully, it is a way to live in time yet to resist it.

Omitting depictions of the prime of life, Lamb privileges the boy-man, the childlike adult, the man-boy, and the wise child. Elia himself plays the boy; he "did not conform to the march of time, but was dragged along in the procession. His manners lagged behind his years. He was too much the boy-man. The *toga-virilis* never sate gracefully on his shoulders. The impressions of infancy had burned into him, and he resented the impertinence of manhood" ("Preface, by a Friend of the late Elia" 2: 153). In both "weakling infancy" and "foolish manhood" Elia is equally childlike under the "care" and "charge" of the maternal Bridget (2: 79).

Lamb is fond of the figure of the "changeling," the person who looks like one thing but is really another, especially the person who looks like an adult but is really a child. As a "stupid changeling of five-and-forty" ("New Year's Eve" 2: 28), Elia feels fallen away from his true self, much as the "poor changelings," the sweeps (2: 112) and Ann Withers, bereft heroine of Mary Lamb's "The Changeling" (3: 288-302), have also lost their childhood self-content. A similar discontinuity from real childhood identity is implicit in Lamb's characterization of his own adulthood as a ghost haunting his past: "Ghost-like I paced around the haunts of my childhood" (5: 23). Also a ghostly figure, "The Superannuated Man," argues himself into youth "for *that* is the only true Time which a man can properly call his own, that which he has all to himself; the rest, though in some sense he may be said to live it, is other people's time, not his" (2: 196).

Lamb's old men are habitually childlike. Old schoolmasters—"renewing constantly the activities that charmed their studious childhood"—are likened to the inhabitants of "their first garden, repeating harvests of their golden time" (2: 51). The "old Benchers" of the ancient Inner Temple are mostly childlike. Shy, tender Samuel Salt whom "a child might pose . . . in a minute" (2: 86) and his generous-minded servant (Lamb's father, James) who sank into senile reversion to boyhood memories "till I have wished that sad second-childhood might have a mother still to lay its head upon her lap. But the common mother of us all . . . received him gently into hers" (2: 88). The cloistered old bachelor dons of the Oxford colleges are great babies who "suck the milky fountains of their Alma Maters" ("Oxford in the Vacation" 2: 10-11). The old bachelor clerks of the decayed South-Sea are well-preserved elderly boys, especially Thomas Tame with his mind "in its original state of white paper. A suckling babe might have posed him" and "mild, childlike, pastoral M_____ . . . a gentle offspring of blustering winter" ("The South-Sea House" 2: 4, 6). These old men are yet younger than the sucklings of Oxford, for the decayed premises of South Sea House, layered with a "superfoetation of dirt" suggest that the old clerks, caught in this backwater of history, are mere foetuses, babes unborn. As critic Gerald Monsman has pointed out, the word "superfoetation" is a favorite with Lamb (*Works* 1: 283n, 2: 2, 259). A daring usage, superfoetation suggests "a pregnancy on top of a pregnancy, but in which there is no birth, no bringing forth, no life" (Monsman 18, 44-45). By likening these old men in an old house in an old trade to foetuses within the womb of time, Lamb deepens the connection between extreme youth and extreme age. Both states are separated off from the world of normal adulthood, that "darkness of sense and materiality" (2: 90).

Lamb regularly links childhood with ancient history, the long-outdated. Like the German Romantic Jean-Paul Richter who saw each child as beginning history again—"born without a past and without a future, beginning in the year one, and bringing with him a first new year" (Richter 31)—Lamb finds an affinity between childhood and the first dawn of human life. The appropriate haunts of the very young are thus old places long gone by which are haunted by the very old as well. The old Temple garden with its despoiled sundial, the old "artificial fountains of the metropolis" (2: 84) with their child-sized angelic guardians are all emblems of the childishly antique. All are odd antithetical spaces, which, like dreams, "reducing childhood," (2: 90), hold it in store in the midst of a hostile environment. Like the old, children are frail—Elia's boyhood "other me" is most vividly remembered in sickness—and in need of protection.

By conflating old and young, Lamb plays games with normal sequence and turns the past into the future. "Damn the Age," Lamb once jested, "*I will write for ANTIQUITY!*" (*Bon-Mots* 59). The affinity between the values and characteristics of the very young and the very old makes possible the paradox of declaring the "other me," "the child-self" as "heir" to the adult self, for the progress of age seems to be a growth toward the recapturing of childhood.

In his most systematic attempt to join youth and age, "Dream Children," Lamb attempts to tease the future out of the past, the not-to-be out of the all-but-gone. As in Coleridge's "Kubla Khan, A Vision in a Dream," in "Dream Children, A Reverie" the writer presents a dream of creation in which past, present, and future are held in suspension. Just as "Kubla Khan" empowers the dreamer with its antithetically balanced upper and lower regions, its sunlit greenery and moonlit chasms, its parturient fountain and river, its ancestral presences and its foreshadowed future, so does "Dream Children" bind past, present, and future. "Children love to listen to stories about their elders, when *they* were children; to stretch their imagination to the conception of a traditionary great-uncle, or grandame, whom they never saw" (2: 100). The stretched imagination makes the elders young and the young "by conception" the imaginative creators of their ancestors whose physical traits they already embody: Alice with her "mother's looks" and her grandmother's lively dancing feet; John with his uncle's intrepid spirit and his father's moral delicacy. Yet this imagined co-existence, co-creation of old and young—with young conceiving old, old imprinting young, and dreamer encompassing all—may be maintained only within the framework of the essay itself. But the essay is framed by the nothingness of reverie before and of wish after, the absent ancestor and the non-existent descendent. This delicate balance is upset, however, for the pressure of a real desire, a desired reality. In desiring to turn the balancing fiction into a sustaining representation of coexistent past and future, in desiring for childhood a historical rather than a conditional oxymoronic existence, the dreamer moves too close into the dream space and destroys the sustaining balance between past and future. Turning to the dream child for the consolations of reality:

> when suddenly, turning to Alice, the soul of the first Alice looked out at her eyes with such a reality of re-presentment, that I became in doubt which of them stood before me, or whose that bright hair was, and while I stood gazing, both the children grew fainter my view, receding, and still receding, till nothing at last but two mournful features were seen in the uttermost dis-

tance. . . . "We are not of Alice, nor of thee, nor are we children at all. . . . We are nothing; less than nothing, and dreams." (1: 103)

Elia has attempted to give the stability of life to his fictional childhood descendent whose only stability is the paradoxical oxymoronic stasis of being neither/nor in neutral space. The distinct, disjunct lovely childhood to which changeling Elia has access is his only by virtue of surrendering the possibility of continuity with his past and future and integration in the life stream. The perpetual child, a safe haven for the self, can exist for Elia only as discontinuous with the realm of daily adult life. Any attempt at creating a continuous historical context destroys the possibility of possessing that child self within neutral space.

The Child Within: "I am that Snake, that Annihilator"

In addition to the walls of gardens and the structures of utopian oxymorons, Lamb has yet another haven for his "other me." That haven is the incorporating body of the adult Lamb. The old self *introjects* the youthful self in order to protect it. Rather than *projecting,* that is throwing himself forward on the world or offering "offspring" that have sprung out of himself, Elia springs back, and throws himself inward to contemplate the past self as present within the present self: "being without a wife or family, I have not learned to project myself enough out of myself; and having no offspring of my own to dally with, I turn back upon memory, and adopt my own early idea, as my heir and favourite" ("New Year's Eve" 2: 28-29). Lamb introjects his unfallen childhood, incorporating it within. By virtue of what Lamb calls his "constitutional imbecility" that leads him, "too obstinately to cling to the remembrances of childhood," he attempts to replace what has been lost, for now "I belong to no *body corporate* such as I then made part of" ("Recollections of Christ's Hospital" 1: 146). To reproduce that containment, Lamb must incorporate himself.

The theory of introjection that has been set forth by Freud and Melanie Klein involves first the child's perception of "some figure in the environment either as exceptionally loving and benign or as singularly frightening and malign." In order to defend itself from the malign figure or—as is the case with Lamb—in order to protect the benign figure from harm, the child in fantasy "imagines himself taking the figure into his own body" (Wollheim 121-22). The introjected figure usually enters through the mouth in an act of what Freud calls "psychic cannibalism" (Wollheim 122).

Lamb's beloved object is the child self, perceived as most beloved within a walled enclosure. The pervasive oral voracity and yearning for containment in Lamb's works is a hunger to introject and possess the undamaged self in uninterrupted security. Lamb approaches the plenitude of childhood through the plenitude of consumption.

Lamb conceives himself both as eater and eaten, the consumer and the consumed, the container and the contained, as eater and piece of meat. Lamb as "Lamb-punnist" (*Letters* 3: 325) on his richly significant surname is well-known. Monsman notes (157-58n.) the titles Lamb somewhat sheepishly furnished for himself, titles running from "1. Mr. C. Lamb" through "4. Baron Lamb of Stanford" to "11th Pope Innocent which is nothing higher than the Lamb of God" (*Letters* 3: 35). In response to one of Mary's relapses, Lamb hopes that "the wind is tempered to the shorn *Lambs*" (*Letters* 3: 203, italics Lamb's). It is not only the connotations of innocence, vulnerability, and pastoral shepherdship (noted by Monsman) that are significant, however, but the associations with a hearty meat dinner. "MEAT, the only legitimate aliment for human creatures since the flood" ("Edax on Appetite" 1: 121) is everywhere present. There are beefsteaks, mutton chops, cutlets, roast beef, haunch of mutton, loin of veal, roast chickens, sweetbreads (1: 121), venison and turtle (2: 92), unctuous sausages (2: 113), pheasants, partridges, snipes, capons, plovers, brawn, oysters (2: 125). Most delicious of all, however, are the meaty sapors associated with roast hare and roast suckling pig, both Elian creatures, the former notable for their antic merriment, the latter for their guileless tenderness. Though this "Lamb-punnist" (*Letters* 3: 325) Lamb almost never mentions eating a dish of lamb, he uses the persona of "Lepus" (or Hare), comments on the affinity between hare-brained wit and savory hare ("The ancients must have loved hares. Else why adopt the word *lepores* (obviously from *lepus*) but for some subtle analogy between the delicate flavor of the latter, and the finer relishes of wit in what we most poorly translate *pleasantries*") and rhapsodizes over the consumption of "hare roasted hard and brown— with gravy and melted butter! ("Thoughts on Presents of Game, &c." 1: 343). The protagonist of Lamb's "damned" (5: 180) farce *Mr. H*____ bears the carnal name of Hogsflesh for which he is scorned and derided until he legally changes it to the more appetizing Bacon. Though Lamb writes as Hare, Hogsflesh, and Bacon, feasts on all manner of fowl, beef, pork, and mutton, the absence of lamb from his diet is hardly surprising. A character in a Borges story explains such omissions with a question: "In a riddle whose answer is chess, what is the only prohibited word?" ("The Garden of Forking Paths" 27). The answer is chess (or Lamb).

Lamb's obsessive concern with eating and drinking, his "gustatory raptures" as Lucas, Lamb's great editor, calls them (*Letters* 2: 213n), has been both thoroughly documented (Randel 113-137) and dismissively attacked (Thompson 206, 212-13). Randel's fine chapter, "Eating and Drinking," emphasizes Lamb's habitual use of "the gastronomic paradigm" (135) as his variant on the "typically Romantic attempt to assimilate the world of objects" (120). The most powerful sensuous experiences in Lamb's essays are oral. (Though the essays stress food, Lamb's own cravings were more for drink and tobacco. "Were it possible," Coleridge wrote, "to wean C. L. from the pipe, other things would follow with comparative ease, for till he gets a pipe, I have regularly observed that he is contented with porter—and that the unconquerable appetite for spirit comes with the tobacco—the oil of which, especially in the gluttonous manner in which he *volcanizes* it, acts as an instant poison on his stomach or lungs" [Blunden 58-59]. Such weaning was difficult, since Lamb wrote "For thy sake, TOBACCO, I / Would do any thing but die" [3: 35]). Lamb's "extraordinary concern with oral satisfaction" (Randel 117) and with "hunger (eldest, strongest of the passions!)" ("Christ's Hospital Five and Thirty Years Ago" 2: 13) issues in literal and metaphorical explorations and exhibitions of appetite. In an early essay, "Edax [the glutton, consumer, eater] on Appetite" (1811), Lamb takes as his persona a man all appetite, an adult who is arrested in self-proclaimed "Innocent Gluttony" (1: 124), a state of oral craving so primal that it has not yet given way to more mental appetites. There has been no displacement of a bodily interest on behalf of an intellectual: "My sufferings . . . have all arisen from a most inordinate appetite—Not for wealth, not for vast possessions . . . not for glory, not for fame, not for applause . . . nor yet for pleasure. . . . No, Sir, for none of these things; but an appetite, in its coarsest and least metaphorical sense,—an appetite for *food*" (1: 119).

A preoccupation with an appetite for literal food and drink is everywhere. To quote Randel's useful summary:

> One of Lamb's last essays, "Thoughts on Presents of Game, &c.," ardently proclaims in 1833 that Elia now prefers "a hare roasted hard and brown—with gravy and melted butter!' over his old favorite, roast pig. Within the Elia essays of the 1823 and 1833 collected editions, two pieces—"A Dissertation upon Roast Pig" and "Grace Before Meat"—deal unmistakably with food, and "Christ's Hospital Five and Thirty Years Ago" gives a detailed menu of what the schoolboys had eaten in Elia's childhood. Even if we exclude these essays, however, we find that the specific foods and beverages mentioned in the Elia volumes include muffin, cold mutton, punch, pies, the juices of meats and fishes, wine, beer, gooseberry, port, woodcocks, dotterels, cod's

> heads, French beans, lobster boiled, eels, fatted calf, nectarines, peaches, oranges, grapes, Saloop, sausages, hot meat and vegetables, butter, turbot, claret, soup, Madeira, pudding, salads, biscuit, broths, cordials, ale, roast fowl, salt, Cognac, water, beef, turkeys, custard, pancakes, cold fowl, tongues, hams, botargoes, dried fruits, tea, caudle, cold lamb, hare, grouse, Canterbury brawn, bread and cheese with an onion, cabbage, potatoes, a leg of goat, a horse's shoulder, pork, veal, Sherry, Malaga, and honey. (Randel 113-14)

The three essays excluded by Randel mention other edibles:

> tea and hot rolls, a penny loaf, small beer, milk porridge, pease soup., hot bread and butter from the "hot loaf of the Temple," millet with sugar and ginger or cinnamon, pickled beef, boiled beef, mutton scrags, overcooked or rare mutton, horse meat, roast veal, griskin, mutton, turnips, venison, minced veal, apple dumplings, asparagus, bread and cheese, smoking joints of roast meat, crackling, roast pig prepared with sage and its own liver and brains, pineapple, mutton chops, barbecued hog with shallots and garlic, partridges, snipes, chickens, capons, plovers, brawn, and oysters.

For Lamb the memory of appetite satisfied is the bliss of solitude. A well-stocked larder, like a well-stocked mind, furnishes memories and offers prospects of needs satisfied. Lamb recalls the appetitive texture, taste, attractions and repulsions. The accounts of food are sensuous and passionate. In the account of the Christ's Hospital meals Lamb juxtaposes the gustatory satisfactions of "L." to the austerities of "Elia" and the other schoolboys. Whereas L's food is "tea and hot rolls," "'extraordinary bread and butter'" from the "hot-loaf of the Temple," millet "endeared to his palate with a lump of double-refined and a smack of ginger . . . or the fragrant cinnamon," a "hot plate of roast veal, or the more tempting griskin," the other boys get coarse bread, "Crug" with "attenuated small beer" redolent of pitch, "blue and tasteless" porridge, "coarse and choking" pea soup, boiled beef "with detestable marigolds," and "scanty mutton scrags" or "rotten-roasted" mutton. In speaking of "our *half-pickled* Sundays," Lamb indicates the child's interassimilation of self and food, an assimilation that makes plausible the vivid recollection of a moral indignation rooted in a visceral loathing for "the fat of fresh beef boiled," an intolerable item frequently served. Lamb dwells convincingly on the disgust felt by children—even children as hungry as Christ's Hospital schoolboys—toward eating fat, a sensuous recoil so powerful that it generated a moral recoil. The onomatopoeic word *gag* with its suggestion of a occluded mouth and of gross retching evokes the childish distaste that made "a *gag-eater* in our time equivalent to a *goul*." The ostracism and persecution of the boy alleged to hoard gags indicates the emotional depth to which the oral experience reaches.

If gagging the mouth is associated with disgust, satisfying the mouth provides deepest comfort. For all the miseries of the chimney-sweeps, including "the fuliginous concretions, which are sometimes found (in dissections) to adhere to the roof of the mouth," sweet sassafras tea (Saloop) comes as "a sweet lenitive." As "a prodigious comfort" came the annual sausage feast sponsored by Jem White, a kind of redemption from slavery by mouth:

> O it was a pleasure to see the sable younkers lick in the unctuous meat, with *his* more unctuous sayings—how he would fit the tit bits to the puny mouths, reserving the lengthier links for the seniors—how he would intercept a morsel even in the jaws of some young desperado . . . how he would recommend this slice of white bread, or that piece of kissing crust, to a tender juvenile, advising them all to have a care of cracking their teeth, which were their best patrimony,—how genteelly he would deal with the small ale . . . with a special recommendation to wipe the lip before drinking. Then we had our toasts . . . every now and then stuffing into his mouth (for it did not do to be squeamish on these occasions) indiscriminate pieces of those reeking sausages, which pleased them mightily, and was the savouriest part . . . of the entertainment ("The Praise of Chimney-Sweepers" 2: 113-14).

Edax, the representative appetitive man, is a great infantile emptiness always yearning to be filled, he describes the "inanition which I experienced after the fullest meals." His intense internal craving and nervous awareness of himself as sensitive integument suggests a heightened infantile orality. Like an infant at the oral stage, living through mouth and tongue and touch and finding that "all's the world a breast and all that's in it good or bad milk" (qtd. in Rieff 49n) Edax has a desperate devouring relation to the world that he seeks to incorporate. He likens himself to a beast of prey ("*I am that Lion*"), yearning for large quantities of flesh, dispatching in an instant "the kind of suppers which elderly ladies . . . have lying in petto" (figuratively, "in reserve," but literally, "in the breast"). Edax also likens himself to a fabled reptile, a kind of elongated vacuum tube, capable of reducing its victim to absolute nothingness in an instant: "*I am that Snake, that Annihilator*" (1: 122-23). Disturbed by the violence of his appetites, ashamed and vulnerable for being nothing but skin, mouth, and gut, and with a preternatural consciousness of his own innards, Edax images his eventual dissection, the loss of his skin, as the punishment for "this unnatural craving," "the original sin of my constitution":

> I shudder when I contemplate the probability that this animal frame, when its restless appetites have ceased their importunity, may be cut up also (horrible suggestion!) to determine in what system of solids or fluids this original sin of my constitution lay lurking. What work will they make with their acids and alkalines, their serums and coagulums, effervescences, viscous matter, bile, chyle, and acrimonious juices, to explain that cause which Nature, who willed the effect to punish me for my sins, may no less have determined to keep in the dark from them, to punish them for their presumption. (1: 124)

On the tapestries of Blakesmoor, young Elia studied with interest the "almost culinary coolness of Dan Phoebus, eel-fashion, deliberately divesting of Marsyas" ("Blakesmoor in H_____shire" 2: 155). Awareness of the vulnerability of the encasing skin seems to have been a family trait. John Lamb, Charles' older brother, published a pamphlet about cruelty to animals, containing what E. V. Lucas calls "one red-hot sentence" about the maltreatment of eels, skinned alive by cooks who would "stick a fork into his eye, skin him alive, coil him up on a skewer, head and all, so that in extremest agony he could not move, and forthwith broil him to death" (2: 356n). This sense of being a creature primarily of mouth and skin and digestion, a creature like an eel or an infant, indicates a sensibility both vulnerable and desperately hungry.

Intense anxiety and violence, fear of being thwarted or deferred in this "holy rage of hunger" ("Edax on Appetite" 1: 120-121) are pervasive. In "Grace Before Meat" (2: 91-96) Elia writes of eating in the language of lust, noting the attendant "perturbation of mind," "desire and a distracted choice," and "the ravenous orgasm" of fulfillment. "The Last Peach" records the guilty desire of young Suspensurus (i.e. "the Man who is Going to be Hanged") for forbidden fruit in a childhood garden: "I know not by what demon of contradiction inspired, but I was haunted by an irresistible desire to pluck it . . . maddening with desire . . . with wilfulness rather" (1: 284). This appetitive lust foreshadows the life of crime to which Suspensurus feels himself fated. "The Gypsy's Malison" that urges the child to "suck, baby, suck," at the mother's breast, "kiss . . . kiss" the mother's lips, and "hang . . . hang" from the mother's neck forecasts a future in which by the same infantile appetites the man, a grown baby, will suck death, kiss poison, and hang from the gallows (5: 57).

William Godwin, who published the Lambs' children's books, expressed alarm at the Cyclops episode in Lamb's "The Adventures of Ulysses." Lamb's enthusiastic description of the way in which the Cyclops first ate gobbets of manflesh washed down with wine and them vomited up wine and flesh together made Godwin uneasy. "Amid the beauties of your manuscript," he complained, "what will the squeamish say to such expressions as these—'devoured their limbs, yet warm and trembling, lapping the blood,' page 10. Or to the giant's vomit, page 14" (3: 480). Such violent cyclopian, one-eyed appetite, a sensuality indifferent to all scruples, also marks Bo-Bo's fall into meat-eating, a fall represented in "A Dissertation upon Roast Pig" (2: 120-26) by his slaughter of the innocent, the newborn piglets. No sooner does Bo-Bo taste crackling for the first time, then "surrendering himself up to the newborn pleasure, he fell to tearing up whole handfuls of the scorched skin with the flesh next to it, and was cramming it down his throat in beastly fashion, when his sire entered ... and began to rain blows ... which Bo-Bo heeded not any more than if they had been flies. The tickling pleasure, which he experienced in his lower regions, had rendered him quite callous to any inconveniences he might feel in those remote quarters."

Lamb's sensibility, like Keats', is primarily oral. For him, as for infants at the oral stage, experience is mediated through the mouth. Intellection is appetitive, learning a matter of eating. He describes the safe settled masters of Oxford colleges as fortunate babes, "contented to suck the milky fountains of their Alma Maters" ("Oxford in the Vacation" 2: 10-11). Lamb, however, prematurely weaned, "defrauded in his young years of the sweet food of academic institution" (2: 9), seizes every appetitive opportunity. He cleaves to London where one "must have a rare *recipe* for melancholy, who can be dull ..." where "every appetite [is] supplied with its proper food ... Humour, Interest, Curiosity, suck at her measureless breasts without a possibility of being satiated" ("The Londoner" 1: 39-40). Even the derelicts of London are food-givers: "Much good might be sucked from these Beggars" ("A Complaint of the Decay of Beggars in the Metropolis" 2: 114), so much in fact, that Lamb wants never to stop feeding: "I do not want to be weaned by age" to drop into the grave ("New Year's Eve" 2: 29).

Learning is a preferred form of ingestion; Christ's hospital with a "care scarcely less tender than the paternal" dispenses "mental *pabulum*" (1: 140). Reading is habitually linked with eating. When Coleridge appropriates a volume, "You are sure that he will make one hearty meal on your viands, if he can give no account of the platter after it" ("The Two Races of Men" 2: 26). If the activities of reading and eating are sometimes opposed, they are still seen as cognate. In Mary Lamb's "The Two Boys" (quoted in "Detached Thoughts on Books and Reading") the child shooed away from the bookstall "wish'd he never had been taught to read" and the child starving outside a tavern is deemed to "wish he ne'er had learn'd to eat"; in her "Moderation in Diet" children are instructed to buy books for permanent nutriment instead of candy :

> Go buy a book; a dainty eaten
> Is vanish'd, and no sweets remain;
> They who their minds with knowledge sweeten,
> The savour long as life retain. (3: 404)

Reading is depicted as an intellectualized version of eating, governed by similar impulses. Memory is something "for cold and wintery hours to chew upon" ("The Old Margate Hoy" 2: 180). Taste and gust become for Lamb the metonymy by which all intellectual, aesthetic, and affective experience is presented. "Relish" is a favorite word of approbation (2: 13) because judgment to Lamb is oral: "I can look with no indifferent eye upon things or persons. Whatever is, is to me a matter of *taste or distaste* or when once it becomes indifferent, it begins to be *disrelishing*" ("Imperfect Sympathies" 2: 58, my italics). Among his distastes is one for assimilated Jews: "Jews christianizing—Christians judaizing—puzzle me. *I like fish or flesh*" (2: 62, my italics). Nor does he fancy Quakers: "I must have books, pictures, theatres . . . and a thousand whim-whams, which their *simpler taste* can do without. *I should starve at their primitive banquet. My appetites are too high for the salads which . . . Eve dressed for the angel, my gusto too excited*" (2: 63, my italics). Charles Cotton's fine seventeenth-century poem, "The New Year," quoted in "New Year's Eve" (2: 27-32), like the "smack of ginger" and the small beer "smacking of the pitched leathern jack" ("Christ's Hospital Five and Thirty Years Ago" 2: 12) is to be relished: "How say you reader—do not these verses *smack* of the rough magnanimity of the old English *vein?* Do they not *fortify like a cordial;* enlarging the heart, and productive of sweet blood, and generous spirits in the *concoction?*" ("New Year's Eve," 2: 32). Even more explicitly linking different kinds of entities that roll satisfactorily on the tongue, Elia praises Jem White's benefactions—sausages and jests: "O it was a pleasure to see the sable younkers lick in the *unctuous meat,* with *his* more *unctuous sayings*"; seeing Jem "[stuff] into his mouth . . . indiscriminate pieces of those reeking sausages . . . was the *savouriest part* of the entertainment" ("The Praise of Chimney-Sweepers" 2: 113-14, my italics). Objects are presented as beautiful or ugly in respect to their edibility—hence the "detestable Cinque Port" with its "starved foliage from . . . dusty innutritious rocks" (2: 181). In Mary Lamb's children's poem, "Breakfast," there is a similar transfer from the savor of tasting lump sugar to the visual satisfaction of relishing its appearance:

> . . . in idle mood he uses
> To sit and watch the vent'rous fly,
> Where sugar's piled high,
> Clambering o'er the lumps so white,
> Rocky cliffs of sweet delight (3: 397)

Though all eating is of interest to him, Lamb does distinguish two stages of ingestion: childhood vegetarianism and adult carnivorousness. Innocence and a vegetarian diet are made synonymous. Indeed, "*Hospita* on the Immoderate Indulgence of the Pleasure of the Palate" is a thumbnail *The Awkward Age* in which a mother fears to bring her ten-year-old daughter from her "happy state of innocence" in the vegetarian nursery to the adult dining table. Among adults the child will acquire knowledge of the flesh, that is, of meat-eating, from which her innate innocence will make her "recoil with horror" (though "I am in good hopes, when the proper season of her *debut* arrives, she may be brought to endure the sight of a roasted chicken or a dish of sweetbreads, for the first time without fainting" [1: 126]). The "simple and unprovocative repasts of children" belong, Elia writes, to a lost world. Though Coleridge is quoted to the effect "that a man cannot have a pure mind who refuses apple-dumplings," Lamb thinks such purity out of reach of his middle age: "With the decay of my first innocence, I confess a less and less relish daily for those innocuous cates. The whole vegetable tribe have lost their gust with me. Only I stick to asparagus, which still seems to inspire gentle thoughts" ("Grace Before Meat" 2: 95).

Food in general is associated with the intensity of carnal desire, but meat-eating in particular partakes of the fall. Bo-bo's discovery of charred pig, placed at the dawn of history, obtains the collusion of all mankind in his sin. Bo-Bo's descent into meat-eating is a descent into sexuality: his "ravenous orgasm" ("Grace Before Meat" 2: 92) of desire leads him to ignore the blows rained on his shoulders because of the "tickling pleasure which he experienced in his lower regions." At the same time he combines desperate "cramming . . . as if he would choke" with "barbarous ejaculations" ("A Dissertation Upon Roast Pig" 2: 121-22). The explicit connection between eros and appetite, between the aphrodisiac oyster and lust, is made the underplot of "A Bachelor's Complaint of the Behaviour of Married People" in which Elia protests the behavior of *Testacea* (whose name comes from "testa," shell-fish, but is also cognate with "testis," witness or testicle) who insists on saving the oysters for her husband. "Had *Testacea* kept the oysters back for me" that would have been true politesse (2: 131).

Associated with adult sexuality, eating is thus associated with guilt. Hence the title "Grace Before Meat" punningly suggests that a stage of innocence precedes and cannot coexist with meat-eating lust. Eden was vegetarian, and cooking the sign of the fall. Meat-eating in Lamb is thus associated with the end of childhood—both the end of the childhood of the race as in "A Dissertation upon Roast Pig" and the end of the individual childhood as in "Hospita . . ." and "Grace Before Meat."

A threat to childhood, meat-eating is often associated with cannibalism, a danger adumbrated in Hospita's double fear of her guest Edax, the hearty meat-eater. She fears for her entrees. When Edax sits at her table, he can hardly be trusted when the meat is served:

> His way of staring at the dishes as they are brought in, has absolutely something immodest in it: it is like the stare of an impudent man of fashion at a fine woman, when she first comes into a room. I am positively in pain for the dishes, and cannot help thinking they have consciousness, and will be put out of countenance, he treats them so like what they are not. Then again he makes no scruple of keeping a joint of meat on the table . . . till he has what he calls *done with it.*" (1: 125)

She also fears for her daughter. What will it mean to bring her tender vegetarian daughter to the table to confront "such a feeder as Mr. _____," this child who first heard of meat-eating and recoiled "with the same horror with which we listen to a tale of Anthropophagism" (1: 126). Fearing for her dishes—treated "so like what they are not"—and her daughter, Hospita hints at the danger of cannibalism and violation, dangers not disarmed by her less than innocent questions on the voracity of Mr. Edax: "Can he have read Mr. Malthus's Thoughts on the Ratio of Food to Population? Can he think it reasonable that one man should consume the sustenance of many?" (1: 126). The echo of Jonathan Swift hints that one may indeed consume the substance of many and thus ease the population problem. There is a suggestion, picked up elsewhere in Lamb, that the child herself is the most delicious object of ingestion, a notion substantiated by the apocryphal anecdote of Mrs. K. who asked "And how do *you* like babies,

Mr. Lamb?" "His answer, immediate, almost precipitate, was 'Boi-boi-boiled, ma'am'" (*Bon-Mots* 47).

Lamb depicts the childish innocent sometimes as a succulent fruit: "I could almost fancy myself ripening too along with the oranges and the limes in that grateful warmth" "Dream-Children" 2: 102). Little Caroline in Lamb's "The Dessert" is explicitly good enough to eat:

> With the apples and the plums,
> Little Carolina comes,
> At the time of dessert she
> Comes and drops her new last curt'sy;
> Graceful curt'sy, practis'd o'er
> In the nursery before.
> What shall we compare her to?
> The dessert itself will do.
> Like preserves she's kept with care,
> Like blanch'd almonds she is fair,
> Soft as down on peach her hair,
> And so soft, so smooth is each
> Pretty cheek as that same peach,
> Yet more like in hue to cherries;
> Then her lips, the sweet strawberries,
> Caroline herself shall try them
> If they are not like when nigh them;
> Her bright eyes are black as sloes,
> But I think we've none of those
> Common fruit here—and her chin
> From a round point does begin,
> Like the small end of a pear;
> Whiter drapery does she wear
> Than the frost on cake; and sweeeter
> Than the cake itself, and neater,
> Though bedeck'd with emblems fine,
> Is our little Caroline (3: 416)

The language of "A Dissertation upon Roast Pig" even more emphatically suggests pattern of incorporation by eating a child, an act once a source of continuing comfort and the mark of the fall. To preserve the child self within the adult is to consent to growing up into the adult social world and is thus, as in the essay, the beginning of civilization. It is also a strategy of self-protection, preserving what is most lovely in the original self and keeping it safe within enclosing walls of flesh. The characterization of the eating of the new-born piglets, giving "new-born pleasure" to Bo-Bo (2: 121) as an ingestion of childhood is emphatic. The roast pig is sinless human infancy, the chosen pig "under a moon old—guiltless as yet of the sty—with no original speck of *amor immunditiae,* the hereditary failing of the first parent, yet manifest—his voice as yet not broken, but something between a childish treble and a grumble" (2: 123). Its flesh—like little Carolina's—is like a flower, "in the first innocence—the cream and quintessence of the child-pig's yet pure food" (2: 124). As Randel notes, "the advantage of roasting a pig while he is still young is announced in words inexactly borrowed . . . from Coleridge's 'Epitaph on an Infant'" (123). Once cooked the infant piglet shows the sensibility of his "tender age," lying in the serving dish as in "his second cradle, "far better dead as an innocent"(2: 124) who would else grow into sin and "filthy conversation":

> Unlike to mankind's mixed characters, a bundle of virtues and vices, inexplicably intertwisted, and not to be unravelled without hazard, he is—good throughout. No part of him is better or worse than another. He helpeth, as far as his little means extend, all around. (2: 124)

The piquancy of this description is its obtrusive doubling of moral with culinary terms, a winking identification of purity of savor with purity of spirit. Implicitly, however, the pattern is that of the incorporation of an innocent new-born child self into the fallen adult self. The innocent and therefore vegetarian child is taken inside the protecting walls of the carnivorous older self. The full-grown Lamb takes in the little Lamb, the full-grown Lepus incorporates a hare, Bacon subsumes Hogsflesh.

Lamb is a desperate preserver of childhood against the forces that makes its faith, light-heartedness, and spontaneity impossible. Time, history, the ordinary terrible rigors of family life are the enemy of childhood. In recoil Lamb places the child into the superfoetation of an impregnable fortress—at once far out of time and deep within the body. The walled prison, the utopian oxymoron, and the inner space of his own body are all regions of safety, accessible to imagination but discontinuous with history.

Chapter Four

Little Mr. De Quincey and The Affliction of Childhood

> *He was a pretty little creature, full of wire-drawn ingenuities. . . . One of the smallest man figures I ever saw; shaped like a pair of tongs; and hardly above five feet in all: when he sat, you would have taken him, by candlelight, for the beautifullest little child; blue-eyed, blond-haired, sparking face, had there not been a something too, which said, "Eccovi, this child has been in Hell—."*
> —Carlyle on De Quincey, aged forty-two.

> *. . . it seemed to him as if he might still escape could he but surround himself with children.*
> —De Quincey on the madness of Charles Lloyd

> *He thought that by the hour of his death he would not even have finished classifying all the memories of his childhood.*
> —Borges, "Funes the Memorious"

De Quincey is a polymath who wrote vastly and well on a wide array of subjects. But his vocation was "the Affliction of Childhood"—experiencing it, collecting it, recapitulating it, evoking it, representing it, validating it, and generally living off it.[1] Afflictor and afflicted both, De Quincey found a career in the experience, documentation, and display of childhood suffering.[2] Though expressing with his Romantic contemporaries, a rapturous awe for the Eden of childhood, the experiential reality of childhood in his work is affliction, ostracism, and loss. He saw hell lying about us in our infancy and felt as presiding nursery presences not good fairies but the hulking Levana and her companion Eumenides, "our Ladies of Sorrow." With a paranoid vision that is the antithetical shadow, the "dark interpreter," of Wordsworth's vision of childhood blessedness, De Quincey devotes his considerable talents to a reconstruction of the torments rather than the raptures of childhood. Whatever the pains of this vocation, it furnished him with a political, literary, and even physical sanctuary by equipping him with a guiding ideology, a literary master, and a justification for being such a "little Mr. De Quincey." He is the most assiduous practitioner of the thrilling sado-masochism James Kincaid has connected to Romantic childhood.

"... this child has been in Hell"

That De Quincey loved the girl with a "love the most frantic" (*Recollections* 371) seems clear: "as often as I could entice her from home, [she] walked with me, slept with me, and was my sole companion" (371). And, as best he could recollect (for he wrote of her from a distance of twenty-eight years), she loved him back just as passionately:

> On the night she slept with me in the winter, we lay awake all the middle of the night—and talked oh how tenderly together: When we fell asleep, she was lying in my arms; once or twice I awoke from the pressure of her dear body; but I could not find [it] in my heart to disturb her. Many times that night—when she was murmuring out tender sounds of endearment, she would lock her little arms with such passionateness around my neck—as if she had known that it was to be the last night we were ever to pass together. (Jordan 265)

When, early in June 1812, he heard the news of her death, he broke down: "Never, perhaps... was there so fierce a convulsion of grief as mastered my faculties on receiving that heart-shattering news" (*Recollections* 372). He had chest pains; it hurt to breathe. All summer long he slept on her grave. All summer long he saw her ghost. Indeed, he deliberately invoked the specter of the girl's figure coming toward him "with the air of advancing movement" but always separated by the length of a field, always distant, unobtainable "at the opposite side" (373). By the end of that haunted summer, De Quincey had turned his occasional use of opium into a habit and became for the first time the Opium Eater. It is "likely," Grevel Lindop has speculated, that the girl's death "was the factor which turned De Quincey into a true opium addict" (Lindop 202).

De Quincey's unquiet love for Wordsworth's little daughter, Kate Wordsworth, dead at three, is characteristic of his habitually troubled, "convulsive" and aesthetically powerful relationship to childhood. As Alina Clej has shrewdly noted, "convulsion" is the form in which the Sublime encounters and energizes De Quincey (184); it is his capacity for "primary convulsions" that scoop out the depths of his nature (L 129) and authorize his claim for profundity. Though De Quincey makes insistent claims for the authority and autonomy of childhood: its privileged solitude, its "searching gaze" into "all the *elementary* feelings of man" (L 127), its "specific power of contemplating the truth, its emotional depths, its "distinct peninsula" (*CW* 1: 121), its "special revelations . . . authentic whispers of truth" (*CW* 1: 122), its "communion undisturbed" with God (L 114), that grandeur is always most profoundly evoked by disaster, by "the vast scale upon which the sufferings of children are found everywhere expanded in the realities of life" (W 189).

De Quincey emphasizes that his darkly ecstatic vision of childhood tied up with affliction, loss, and convulsion is both normal and normative—normal because commonplace; and normative because "the enormity of the convulsion" that was his (L 128), jolts him into reflecting and reinterpreting these experiences. He makes claims as a representative consciousness, standing "nearer to the type of the original nature in man" and "truer than others to the great magnet of our dark planet" (*L* 129) precisely because of his traumatic childhood experiences: "the *primary* convulsions of nature—such, perhaps as only *primary* formations in the human system can experience . . ." (*S* 154). Laying a claim to essential human nature, a "primary formation," De Quincey argues that a representative modern life must retrieve, organize, and illuminate such defining human events as these "primary convulsions."

De Quincey normalizes childhood suffering by "deciphering" virtually all childhood experience as affliction. A good classicist, De Quincey recruited the literal Latin original to his usage, always obliquely recalling that affliction derives from *affligo, afflixum, afflictum:* "to dash, to strike again"; "to dash to the ground"; and "to ill-treat, damage." One who is *afflictus* is either literally or figuratively damaged or shattered. De Quincey's afflicted children are manhandled, thrown down, marked down for ill treatment, and generally humiliated. From beginning to end of the De Quincey corpus, affliction is what is in store for children, so many "marked down in the unseen register as consecrated (dedicated) from their birth to an early death" (Eaton 346), so many "torn away from mothers and sisters" and dying of grief (L 148), their pain-wracked bodies "tossing in anguish, and weeping clamorously for death" (L 112), their vulnerability cowering before a gigantic nurse-Medea smiting them "senseless to the ground" (L 138), their broken skulls laid "in ruins" by the surgeons (L 108).

Affliction is what De Quincey looks for in childhood, what he finds, and what he dispenses. De Quincey even normalizes childhood affliction by deciphering virtually all childhood experience as painful and by assiduously collecting instances of childhood pain. De Quincey habitually read misery in lives of children, for example the Edinburgh "guisers," children who sang door to door in exchange for a small tip. A friend reports De Quincey's deep gloom at hearing the sweet voices of the children: "All that I have ever had of enjoyment in life, the charms of friendship, the smiles of women, the joys of wine, seem to rise up to reproach me for my happiness when I see such misery, and think there is so much of it in the world." Yet De Quincey's puzzled companions claimed to hear nothing but the cheerful giggles of "village children on an evening frolic" (Eaton 465-66). A notoriously easy mark for youthful beggars, De Quincey seemed to his friends so credulous of children's grief—real and fabricated—that even "the most nefarious of mothers" equipped with one or more "borrowed babies" could be sure of De Quincey's last shilling (Page 361-62).

It was the griefs of children that De Quincey collected with a Dostoyevskian attentiveness. His earliest literary plans included an updated Babes-in-the-Woods, a *"poetic and pathetic ballad* reciting the wanderings of two young children (brother and sister) and their falling asleep on a frosty night—moonlight among the lanes . . . and so perishing" (Eaton 91). Introducing Jean Paul to an English audience, De Quincey foregrounds two essays on childhood death: "On the Death of Young Children" and "The Prophetic Dew Drop" (*CW* 11: 284-85). He combed the newspapers with an eye for childhood catastrophes, noting the "three thousand children . . . annually burned to death [for the insurance money] . . . by their mothers" (*CW* 5: 249), recording the lamentable suicide (by an overdose of laudanum) of "a studious and meditative young boy" who had "languished, with a sort of despairing nympholepsy, after intellectual pleasures" (*Recollections* 272-73). Transcribing "anecdotes from the Edinburgh Advertiser," he notes "The dog of a boy that died paralytic from grief. Little child run over by a railway waggon and horse, clapping its hands when the shadow passed away, leaving it unhurt. Little girl of six committing suicide for fear of a stepmother's wrath" (*PW* 1: 275). During the crisis of the Sepoy Mutiny, De Quincey dreamed every night of the massacre of little English girls "five or six years old, who were standing in the air outside, but so as to touch the window; and I heard . . . always the same dreadful word, *Delhi*" (Lindop 383). Though careless of most social obligations, De Quincey would never miss a child's funeral. The one time he failed to attend, he wrote the bereaved father in recompense so ornate and passionate a letter that he "had it framed and hung over his chimney-piece" (Eaton 464).

Above all, De Quincey foregrounds affliction in his own autobiographical narratives. Whether written in the registers of realism or of myth—and De Quincey writes in both—the autobiography has a strong master narrative of affliction: persecution by a virago and the lost love of a second-self, figured as a beloved sister or sister-wife. De Quincey depicts his childhood as consistently desolate and afflicted. Even though he grew up as a rich boy in a luxurious household "not in solitude," one biographer insists, "but in a group of exceedingly lively contemporaries" (Eaton 9), De Quincey depicts a childhood of affliction by parents, brothers, and society.

The question of the literal misery of De Quincey's childhood is not merely unanswerable, but conspicuously unanswered. Whether De Quincey's autobiographical account is just to the facts of his biographical experiences is, as he makes emphatically clear, entirely irrelevant to his project of charting childhood affliction. Since the articulation of childhood experience is adult work, childhood is, for De Quincey, written in cipher; the gifted adult *deciphers* that past. The ability to infer certain events and feelings from childhood is for De Quincey the sole evidence of their historic reality:

> though a child's feelings are spoken of, it is not the child who speaks. *I* decipher what the child only felt in cipher.... Whatsoever in a man's mind blossoms and expands to his own consciousness in mature life, must have pre-existed in germ during his infancy.... I the child had the feelings, I the man decipher them. In the child lay the handwriting mysterious to *him;* in me the interpretation and the comment. (L 113)

In terms of biographical accuracy, De Quincey's deciphered memory needs to be accorded the same skepticism now paid to "recovered memory."

The main lines of De Quincey's childhood as he deciphers them are these: Thomas was the fourth of eight children of Thomas Quincey, a Manchester merchant, and his well-born, clear-headed Evangelical wife, Elizabeth Penson Quincey. Because Mr. Quincey was away from home on business or seeking to restore his heath for most of Thomas's early life, he was hardly a factor in the boy's rearing. When Thomas was seven, Mr. Quincey, hopelessly ill with tuberculosis, returned home to Manchester, but it was evident even to the children that their father was returning only to die. The children were present at the death bed; Thomas recalled "hearing him moan out to my mother a few minutes before he died—'Oh Betty Betty! why will you never come and help me to raise this weight?'" (Jordan 270). After his father's death, Thomas and his siblings were reared by his capable "intellectual" mother with some assistance from several male guardians named in the will.

Like Charles Lamb, De Quincey was a child who bonded more strongly with his siblings than his parents. Though his father was largely absent and his mother emotionally distant, the young Thomas recollects love and companionship among "the gentlest of sisters" though not his "horrid pugilistic brothers" (*CW* 1: 32). He was passionately close to his sister Elizabeth, older by two years. Before he was seven, however, two sisters had died: as in "We are Seven," the poem he read rapturously at fourteen, "the first that died was sister Jane,"[3] and then, disastrously, Elizabeth. In June of 1792, the summer before Mr. Quincey's death in July 1793, Elizabeth, eight years old, died of what was called "hydrocephalus" (probably cerebro-spinal meningitis). That loss remained with De Quincey all his life. It was, he wrote, the event that "drove a shaft for me into the worlds of death and darkness which never again closed, and through which it might be said that I ascended and descended at will" (L 92). This death is the keynote of the autobiographical writing, a note that is struck again in accounts of other childhood deaths—those of his father, his sister Jane, and of a pet kingfisher and a kitten.

After Elizabeth, De Quincey's most important sibling was his brother William, older by five or six years. Sent off to boarding school early—he was only five or six when deemed "unmanageable"—William returned home shortly after Elizabeth's death (Lindop 6). His presence—described by De Quincey in an autobiographical sketch titled "Introduction to the World of Strife"—intimidated the timid and depressed Thomas and drew him into sports, games, and competitions in which Thomas was the inevitable loser and from which he learned to take abjection as his role in life: "I had a perfect craze for being despised" (*CW* 1: 59).

Though physically inept, De Quincey was a fine student and made brilliant progress—so he recalls—especially in Greek when he was sent at age eleven to the Bath Grammar School, which he loved, and later to Manchester Grammar School, which he disliked. Increasingly desperate at his mother's refusal to permit his withdrawal from the latter school, Thomas, just short of his seventeenth birthday, ran away. After some weeks on his own he obtained grudging permission from his mother and went, with a very limited allowance, first to Wales (where he was reduced sometimes to living off the berries he could pluck from the hedges) and later to London where he also lived in poverty and hunger. It was in London that he befriended the young street-walker Ann who looked after him with sisterly kindness. Eventually, he reached a compromise with his mother and guardians, which enabled him to matriculate at Oxford. With his independent establishment in Oxford De Quincey's adulthood effectively begins.

De Quincey's autobiographical narrative thematizes childhood as an affliction narrative. The dominant notes are the tyranny of the mother, the sanctity of the sister, and the pariahhood of the self. De Quincey's mother is the villain of his resentful and unforgiving tale. In all Thomas' explicit recollections she is a cultivated, religious, intelligent, and forbidding woman, shrinking from human contact, ruling her servants through the housekeeper who alone was permitted to speak to the mistress. ("Speak to mistress!" a housemaid once protested, "Would I speak to a ghost?" [Eaton 20]). An "austere . . . rigid . . . upright, sternly conscientious" woman, fit to be "the lady president of rebellious nurseries," her relations with her children appeared to young Thomas as rigidly formal. The children were inspected each morning for cleanliness, neatness, posture, health, and dress: "As the mail-coaches go down daily to London to the inspector of mails," De Quincey recalls, "so we rolled out of the nursery at a signal given, and were minutely reviewed in succession" (Eaton 19). The mail system, here dominated by Mrs. Quincey, figures in Thomas' famous "The English Mail Coach" as the juggernaut crashing down helpless girlhood in the presence of a passive Thomas.

Though Mrs. De Quincey passed among her adult acquaintances as a benevolent and sociable woman, Thomas was convinced that she loathed children, especially her own: "She delighted not in infancy, nor infancy in her" (Eaton 19). An Evangelical later in life, Elizabeth De Quincey took as axiomatic the need to suppress the autonomy of children who are "sinfully polluted creatures," all too liable to the self-will that is "the root of all sin and misery" (Sangster 31, Moore 35). De Quincey shows his mother operating in the spirit of John Wesley's injunction to check anyone who praises children to their faces and to teach children that so far from deserving praise, they are "more ignorant, more foolish, and more wicked than they can possibly conceive" (Greven 59). A hanging judge, a gothic Grand Inquisitor, she assumed the guilt of her children:

> a peculiarity there was about my mother which is not found, or anything like it, in one mother out of five hundred. Usually mothers defend their own cubs, right or wrong; and they also think favorably of any pretensions to praise which these cubs may put forward. Not so my mother. Were we taxed by interested parties with some impropriety of conduct? Trial by jury, English laws of evidence, all were forgotten; and we were found guilty on the bare affidavit of the angry accuser. Did a visitor say some flattering thing of a talent or accomplishment by one or other of us? My mother protested so solemnly against the possibility that we could possess either one or the other,

that we children held it a point of filial duty to believe ourselves the very scum and refuse of the universe. (Eaton 19)

De Quincey declares that it was his mother's determination to keep her sons from praise that made her remove him from Bath Grammar School where he was a cosseted prize pupil much beloved of the Head Master. Suspicious of her sons' independent mindedness, bent on breaking their spirit and their pride, heeding no explanations because "predisposed to think ill of all causes that required many words" (*CW* 3: 315), she goaded them all into rebellion (two of the three ran away from home). As a spirit-crushing juggernaut, Elizabeth De Quincey models all the malevolent mother/no mother figures in De Quincey's corpus.

Under whatever name, De Quincey's mothers are hard-hearted, masterfully judgmental parental figures of fearful *"intellectual"* power (L 31). The unnurturing mother is embodied in institutions with parental claims. Of his "alma mater," De Quincey notes "Oxford, ancient Mother! hoary with ancestral honours, and, haply, it may be, time-shattered power—I owe thee nothing! Of thy vast riches I took not a shilling, though living amongst multitudes who owed to thee their daily bread" (*CW* 2: 10). And toward London, he also holds himself a neglected child: "Oxford Street, stony-hearted step-mother! thou that listenest to the sighs of orphans, and drinkest the tears of children" (L 34).

Another set of surrogate mothers, the bluestocking children's authors who foster the bookish child, are also faulted for their intellectual imposition upon the young. Though De Quincey's works are checkered with allusions to the children's books of his boyhood—especially to Anna Letitia Barbauld's and Maria Edgeworth's—he contemptuously classes the former as "a lady now very nearly forgotten" and the latter as "also now very nearly forgotten"; to identify Barbauld by a comparison to Edgeworth, once so famous, is "to explain *ignotum per ignotius,* or at least one *ignotum* by another *ignotum*" (*CW* 1: 127). "*That women have more imagination than men*" is one of De Quincey's "False Distinctions":

> What work of imagination owing its birth to a woman can he lay his hand on? . . . Who is the female Aeschylus, or Euripides, or Aristophanes? . . . where is Mrs. Shakespeare?—No, no! good women: it is sufficient honor that you produce *us*—the men of the planet—who produce the books (the good ones I mean) . . . (*CW* 10: 440-44)

De Quincey, like other members of the Wordsworth circle though even more testily, condemns as moralistic and unimaginative the children's works of Hannah More, Barbauld, Edgeworth, and other lady writers. This bluestocking crew are the enemies of childhood imagination. Relentlessly maternalistic, relentlessly judgmental, relentlessly bent on rooting out childhood, Barbauld and Edgeworth use their children's fictions—hardly fictions, little screeds of moral will and dull verisimilitude run wild—to annihilate all that is imaginative in children's experience and to hurry children into banal adulthood. Like Mrs. De Quincey in not doting on the darling *state,* Barbauld and Edgeworth see childhood as *continuous* rather than *distinct* from adulthood. They are thus largely uninterested in the Child, as childhood as a decontextualized state of being, and focus instead on social and ethical becoming. These literary mothers are blind to children's innate powers and seek to hurry on right action and facile moralizing in little books that "only told how Master Billy and Miss Ann spoken and acted . . . not only ridiculous but extremely hurtful" (S. T. Coleridge, *Lectures* 1: 587).

In general, parents are not to be trusted: "old age . . . is a miserable corrupter and blighter to the genial charities of the human heart," he remarks aphoristically of the parents of some young Welsh friends [L 16]). Mothers are tyrants, fathers are weak and futile.

Except for the bullying "pugilistic" William who for a time broke Thomas to his will, the father figures in De Quincey's childhood are impotent husbands unable to assert their superior wisdom against their virago wives: Mr. Hall is unable to protect his daughters from their mother's malignity; Thomas's father dies in a futile appeal to his wife for help.

But maternal power and paternal impotence are offset by sisterly love. The solace and source of De Quincey's childhood is his sister Elizabeth, represented in a vocabulary of transcendent visionary light. Childhood gave him access to paradise, for it gave him his beloved older sister: ". . . for me *ubi Caesar, ibi Roma*—where my sister was, there was paradise, no matter whether in heaven above or on earth beneath" (L 118). She is a saint with a glory round her head: "dear, noble Elizabeth, around whose ample brow, as often as thy sweet countenance rises upon the darkness, I fancy a tiara of light or a gleaming *aureola*" (L 99). She is the sign of God to the wandering Children of Israel: "Pillar of fire, that didst go before me to guide and to quicken—pillar of darkness, when thy countenance was turned away to God" (L 100). In their childhood paradise, she was Eve to his Adam, and like Eve irreplaceable. De Quincey appropriates Milton's words to describe his sense of his sister's loss:

> Loss of thee
> Would never from my heart; no, no, I feel

> The link of nature draw me; flesh of flesh,
> Bone of my bone thou art; and from thy state
> Mine never shall be parted, bliss or woe (L 101)

So much was Elizabeth his second self, his confidante, and his security that after she died he depicts himself plunged into hell: "for years—that is from seven or earlier up to ten, such was my simplicity, that I lived in constant terror" (L 129). Though the particular occasions of this perpetual anxiety were, he recalls, trivial—nothing more than a bookstore bill—the absence of Elizabeth made it unbearable. The world was now empty. There was no one left to ratify his existence by sympathizing with him:

> I durst ask no counsel; there was no one to ask. Possibly my sister could have given me none in a case which neither of us should have understood, and where to seek for information from others, would have been at once to betray the whole reason for seeking it. But, if no advice, she would have given me her pity, and the expression of her endless love; and, with the relief of sympathy, that heals for a season all distresses, she would have given me that exquisite luxury—the knowledge that, having parted with my secret, yet also I had *not* parted with it, since it was in the power only of one that could much less betray me than I could betray myself. (L 136)

As "one that could much less betray me than I could betray myself," Elizabeth is De Quincey's true self, his saving self. Elizabeth was notable above all for her extraordinary power of loving, "having that capacious heart overflowing, even as mine overflowed, with tenderness, and stung, even as mine was stung, by the necessity of being loved":

> Love, the holy sense,
> Best gift of God, in thee was most intense.
> That lamp lighted in Paradise was kindled for me which shone so steadily in thee; and never but to thee only, never again since thy departure, *durst* I utter the feelings which possessed me. (L 101)

From this ecstatic union in the paradise of childhood, De Quincey falls into the world. Her death, as the quotation from *Paradise Lost* indicates, ends paradise.

> At the beginning of that year, how radiantly happy! At the end, how insupportably alone!
> > Into what depth thou seest,
> > From what height fallen.[4]

> Forever I searched the abysses with some wandering thoughts unintelligible to myself. Forever I dallied with some obscure notion, how my sister's love might be made in some dim way available for delivering me from misery; or else how the misery I had suffered and was suffering might be made, in some way equally dim, the ransom for winning back her love. (L 136)

De Quincey suggests the whole religious apparatus of the fallen world at one fell swoop. He figures at once as sinner ("into what depth thou seest / From what height fallen") as recipient of the grace of redeeming love ("love . . . available for delivering me"), and even as redeemer through the assumption of suffering ("suffering . . . the ransom for winning . . . love"). This same mixture of roles—the role of fallen sinner, the role of redeemable sick soul, and the role of bringer of salvation—is evident in the most brilliant passage in all of De Quincey's writing: the description of the blazing spot of time at "exactly high noon" in Elizabeth's bedroom on the day of her death. Here De Quincey depicts his fall into guilt and his simultaneous awareness of the possibilities of redemption. As both Hillis Miller and Elizabeth Bruss have emphasized, self-consciousness itself is for De Quincey co-existent with the awareness of the loss of Eden; consciousness, selfhood, and time are tainted as soon as they are known.

De Quincey's fall is depicted in a scene as ambiguous as it is brilliant, for the genesis of despair is cast as a vision of glory, the loss of love as the triumph of understanding. On the day of Elizabeth's death, a June day of extraordinary beauty in 1792, De Quincey, six years old, with a clandestine sense of "hat[ing] the light and shrink[ing] from human eyes" waits for the hour when "I could steal up into her chamber" (L 103). This hidden moment, however, is the brightest hour of the day, "exactly high noon." When he enters his sister's room hoping for the last sweet secret glimpse of his sister's face, the intimacy is swallowed up in light:

> I sought my sister's face. But the bed had been moved; and the back was now turned. Nothing met my eyes but one large window wide open, through which the sun of midsummer at noonday was showering down torrents of splendour. The weather was dry, the sky was cloudless, the blue depths seemed the express types of infinity; and it was not possible for eye to behold or for heart to conceive any symbols more pathetic of life and the glory of life. (L 103)

As the boy turns to his sister's corpse and contemplates "the frozen eyelids, the darkness that seemed to steal from beneath them," he hears a mournful "Memnonian" wind begin to rise, "a wind that had swept the fields of mortality for a hundred centuries":

> Instantly, when my ear caught this vast Aeolian intonation, when my eye filled with the golden fulness of life, the pomps and glory of the heavens outside, and turning when it settled upon the frost which overspread my sister's face, instantly a trance fell upon me. A vault seemed to open in the zenith of the far blue sky, a shaft which ran up for ever. I in spirit rose as if on billows that also ran up the shaft for ever; and the billows seemed to pursue the throne of God, but *that* also ran before us and fled away continually. The flight and the pursuit seemed to go on for ever and ever. Frost, gathering frost, some Sarsar wind of death, seemed to repel me; I slept—for how long I cannot say; slowly I recovered my self-possession, and found myself standing, as before, close to my sister's bed. Oh flight of the solitary child to the solitary God—flight from the ruined corpse to the throne that could not be ruined!—how rich wert thou in truth for after years! (L 105-6)

This is the moment of exile and of self-consciousness. The images of paradise are still present to the child: "the golden fullness of life" and the glorious "throne of God" are expressed in the fullness of vision of the open window, the clear blue sky, the sun at noonday height, the bright shaft running up and up to God; but these are images that become fearful, suggesting both a terrifying loss of enveloping protection and with it a consequent visibility of the self and a displacement of paradise from the intimacy of his sister's bedroom to the zenith of the heavens. Heaven has "fled away" and can no longer abide in Elizabeth's "frozen eyelids," "stiffening hands," and "ruined corpse." Elizabeth has fled away too; she has successfully reached the throne of God, but De Quincey has returned from his vision of that impossible glory to his solitary self. He had yearned with Elizabeth, for the pronoun is intermittently plural ("*that* also ran before us and fled away continually") but had returned from his pursuit alone: "slowly I recovered my self-possession." In the solitude of his lonely self-possession, the boy feels himself forever shut out from paradise and consequently guilty. Exiled from Eden he takes on guilt and, at the sound of a footstep, "Hastily . . . I kissed the lips that I should kiss no more, and slunk like a guilty thing with stealthy steps from the room. Thus perished the vision . . . thus mutilated was the parting . . . thus tainted with fear was the farewell sacred . . . to perfect love and perfect grief (L 107). As a guilty exile, De Quincey puts on the mantle of the Wandering Jew: "O Ahasueras, everlasting Jew! . . . thou when first flying through the gates of Jerusalem . . . couldst not more certainly have read thy doom of sorrow in the misgivings of thy troubled brain than I when passing forever from my sister's room" (L 107). This "mutilated" farewell is the last farewell; the boy "crept again to the room, but the door was now locked—the key was taken away—and I was shut out for ever" (L 108).

This account of Elizabeth's loss clearly topples *Suspiria* into the register of myth. Brother and sister are a prelapsarian Adam and Eve who exist initially in an Edenic realm of love and safety. But the shadow of loss moves De Quincey's account from an Edenic Christian world in which love and safety are imaginable, a redemptive world, into the vengeful world of gothicized Greek myth.

De Quincey's tragic master narrative is inscribed on the brain where it can be overwritten but never erased. In a famous metaphorical exploration of memory, De Quincey describes the brain as a "natural and mighty palimpsest" (L 144). As "a membrane or roll cleansed of its manuscript by reiterated successions," the palimpsest, like the human mind, is capable of being inscribed with successive experiences each seeming to obliterate the former (L 139). In a trope at once bookish and anatomically elegant, experiences are said to be imprinted or inscribed on the brain much as a text might be written on a piece of fine vellum. The original manuscript, written in childhood on the virgin vellum, according to De Quincey's example, is Greek and tragic: "some Grecian tragedy, the Agamemnon of Aeschylus, or the Phoenissae of Euripides"; then some "bigoted" monk might wash away "the heathen's tragedy, replacing it with monastic legend . . . disfigured with fables"; this legend in turn might be rased to make way for "a knightly romance" (L 142). The clean vellum of our consciousness is successively inscribed with experiences, each seeming to obliterate the former. "Like the annual leaves of aboriginal forests, or the undissolving snows on the Himalaya, or light falling upon light, the endless strata have covered up each other in forgetfulness." But this apparent succession is illusion. Men and women forget nothing; their entire pasts are—under sufficient pressure—always available and legible. But most richly available to us are our childhood experiences—those first and most deeply inscribed on the vellum of the brain—that are as durable and as deep as our lives:

> In some potent convulsion of the system, all wheels back into its earliest elementary stage. The bewildering romance, light tarnished with darkness, the semifabulous legend, truth celestial mixed with human falsehoods, these fade even of themselves as life advances. The romance has perished that the young man adored. The legend has gone that deluded the boy. But the deep, deep tragedies of infancy, as when the child's hands were unlinked for ever from his mother's neck, or his lips for ever from his sister's kisses, these remain lurking below all, and these lurk to the last. (L 146)

Anatomizing the cause, uncovering the forgotten, wheeling "back into its earliest elementary stage" beyond the superficial blandishments and delusions of adulthood, De Quincey discovers tragedy at the heart of life, "the deep, deep tragedies of infancy." Childhood is to adolescence and manhood what tragedy is to legend and romance. Instead of Otto Rank's Family Romance of desire fulfilled, for De Quincey there is a Family Tragedy of fear realized. If in Rank's family romance, the child triumphantly discovers his royal birth and his welcoming true parents, in De Quincey's family tragedy the child ironically discovers his pariah birth and his murderous parents, discovers that all that is loving is intricately bound into in the guilt of incest and murder.

The tragic narrative that structures De Quincey's autobiography combines the claustrophobically domestic elements of "Grotto Gothic" (Mulvey-Roberts xvi)—nurseries, bedrooms, middle-class Mancunian households—with massive figures and great doomed names out of Greek tragedy. His tragic pattern features the dominant figure of a massive, torturing, even murderous mother. She has infinite power in a little room. She is resourceful and actively destructive: in De Quincey's misremembered version of Goethe's "Erl Konig," it is the Erl King's *daughter* who lures the child to his death. Such a killer disguised as helper is the monster in the nursery who killed his sister.

> Once again the nurse, but now dilated to colossal proportions, stood as upon some Grecian stage with her uplifted hand, and like the superb Medea standing alone with her children in the nursery at Corinth, smote me senseless to the ground. (L 138)

Embodied in Mrs. Hall, tormenter of daughters, she is the controller of domestic space, ordinary Mancunian households as bloody and evil as "the regal abode in Mycenae, destined to be the scene of murders so memorable" (*CW* 1: 108), a place where "noonday tragedies [are] haunting their household recesses" (*CW* 1: 109) She is at once the killer of her children and husband (Medea and Clytemnestra) and the vengeful scourge of childhood. She tortures the unfilial child:

> I was persecuted by visions as ugly, and as ghastly phantoms as ever haunted the couch of an Orestes . . . [My] Eumenides, like his, were at my bed feet, and stared in upon me through the curtains; but, watching by my pillow . . . sate my Electra. . . . (L 35-36)

In an astonishing conflation, De Quincey draws on Jean Paul's Levana, an entirely benign goddess of humanistic Kultur, only to amalgamate her with the retributive Eumenides. The *Suspiria de Profundis* introduces "Levana and Our Ladies of Sorrow." A little-documented Roman goddess, possibly Carthaginian or Phoenician in origin, Levana is mentioned glancingly in Varro's *Lingua Latina,* in Tertullian's *Ad Nationes,* and in Augustine's *City of God* (Black 42) as "Levana, that raises [the new-born child] from the ground to rear it" (Augustine 1: 122). There are no other extant classical accounts of this figure. In Lempriere's *Classical Dictionary,* De Quincey might have read the description of Levana as

> a goddess at Rome, who presided over the action of the person who took up from the ground a newly born child, after it had been placed there by the midwife. This ceremony was generally performed by the father, and so religiously observed was this ceremony, that the legitimacy of a child could be disputed without it. (442)

Though no other writers, not Varro nor Tertullian, not Augustine nor Lempriere, describe the special signs for Levana, De Quincey reports recognizing Levana in his Oxford dreams "by her Roman symbols" (L 146). Though De Quincey probably borrowed the name Levana from Jean Paul Richter's *Levana, or the Doctrine of Education* (1806), Richter himself barely embodies the goddess, treating her as the verb *levare,* to raise, personified, with an added tenderness of being "the motherly goddess who was formerly entreated to give a father's heart to fathers" (75). Richter's *Levana* is an exuberantly humane work with an emphasis on the pleasure, cheerfulness, playfulness, and physical activity of the normal childhood under the guidance of the true spirit of education, Levana. De Quincey, however, goes far beyond this nurturant Kultur goddess to a sinister characterization of Levana as one whose educational method is terror. Ezra Pound maintained that except for art, only torture could effectively teach anyone anything. De Quincey too places his educational goddess among the torturers. De Quincey's Levana, unique among other Levanas, is a "mysterious lady, who never revealed her face (except . . . in dreams)" who "watches over" human education, "that mighty system of central forces, hidden in the deep bosom of human life, which by passion, by strife, by temptation, by the energies of resistance, works for ever upon children" (L 147). Levana's force is *grief,* "she doats upon grief" and keeps as her handmaidens three sisters, the Sorrows, "mighty phantoms," each a massive being associated with the decimation of childhood: "These were the *Semnai Theai,* or Sublime Goddess—these were the *Eumenides,* or Gracious Ladies" (L 152). Levana and her three sisters, the *mater lacrymarum,* the *mater suspiriorum,* and the *mater tenebrarum,* the mothers of tears, sighs, and darkness, have the mission to torture De Quincey into consciousness, "to plague his heart until we had unfolded the capacities of his spirit" (L 153). The maternal educative mission, then, is to terrify and depress the child entrusted to her. The missing dead father in De Quincey's narrative has no power to protect the victimized children whether they are murder victims like Medea's children, or suicides like Menoeceus in *The Phoenician Women,* or tortured hostages to the maternal Eumenides like Orestes and Electra. Electra's famous lament accuses the mother of afflicting her children: "O Mother, / mother who gave me birth, / who killed and was killed, / you slew your husband, / you killed your children too. / By your death we died. / We are the living dead" (4: 203-4).

The cursed houses of Atreus and of Thebes imprint guilt on childhood—the sweet guilt of brother-sister love in *Electra,* the bitter guilt of fratricidal hatred in *The Phoenician Women.* These child victims are the principal members of De Quincey's vast category of pariahs. Although the term "pariah" had come into English by the seventeenth century, it gained wider currency in the early nineteenth century and was applied not simply to outcasts in India as in Casamir Delavigne's play *Le Paria* (1821) but metaphorically to all kinds of outcasts; the *OED* produces citations classing both sparrows as pariahs "among the feathered tribes" (1884) and Ibsen as pariah "of the English stage" (1901).[5] As John Barrell notes, De Quincey, like most of his contemporaries, used the term not in any technical sense of a particular Tamil caste but in the sense of a polluted outcast, an untouchable whose very touch—like a leper's kiss or a mad dog's lick—as fatally contaminating. De Quincey's concern with Pariah life—even at seventy he projected to new section for the *Suspiria* to be called "The Pariah Worlds" (H. Miller 25)—is lifelong. But he dates his fascination to earliest childhood, claiming childhood access to the "great idea" of pariah contamination as a form of negative election that, like imagination and its dark double, paranoia, gives organizing meaning to an otherwise vast and meaningless world.

Sometime after Elizabeth's death, "between my eighth and ninth years" (*CW* 1: 124), De Quincey found "the immeasurableness of the moral sublime" in his childhood reading.

> You have heard, reader, of pariahs. The pathos of that great idea possibly never reached you. Did it ever strike you how far that idea had extended? Do not fancy it peculiar to Hindostan. Before Delhi was, before Agra, or Lahore, might the pariah say, I was. The most interesting, if only as the most

mysterious, race of ancient days, the Pelasgi, that overspread, in early times of Greece, the total Mediterranean—a race distinguished for beauty and for intellect, and sorrowful beyond all power of man to read the cause that could lie deep enough for so imperishable an impression—*they* were pariahs. The Jews . . . *they* are pariahs to this hour. . . . The gipsies, for whom no conscious or acknowledged hope burns through the mighty darkness that surrounds them—they are the pariahs of pariahs. Lepers were a race of mediaeval pariahs, rejected of men, that now have gone to rest. But travel into the forests of the Pyranees, and there you will find their modern representatives in the Cagots. (*CW* 1: 100)

The pariah figure is found everywhere in De Quincey's work: "The Revolt of the Tartars" is the account of the flight of a pariah people across the steppes of Central Asia; "The Spanish Military Nun" recounts the triumph of a pariah; essays on Judas Iscariot, Joan of Arc, and "Walking Stewart" reveal his preoccupation with the outcast (Miller 25); while "The Theban Sphinx" examines Oedipus, vanished into "some wilderness of pariah eternities" (*CW* 6: 150), as embodying the "insupportable burthen of pariah participation in pollution and misery, to which his will had never consented" (*CW* 6: 142).

De Quincey bestowed pariahhood on many whose outcast state mirrored his own childhood isolation. In all his lost girls he saw pariah grandeur and contamination—in hydrocephalic Elizabeth with her big head, in the two scrofulous, deaf, and retarded daughters of his guardian (those sweetly loving "idiots . . . serfs, or slaves, strulbrugs or pariahs" [*CW* 1: 105]), in Ann the Outcast without a surname (whose lips "were not polluted" [*CW* 3: 342]).[6] In his flight from a vengeful nature embodied in the very waters of the River Severn, which flowed upstream to drown him, De Quincey recognized his own outlawry. (It was simply the tidal Bore but it felt like a manhunt.) And in others flying from the world's scorn De Quincey saw himself mirrored: in the mad dog who locked eyes with the boy as a brother from across a brook ("I looked searchingly into his eyes" [*CW* 1: 118]); in poor mad Charles Lloyd escaped from his asylum.

Even more emphatically abject, he structures the autobiography as the portrait of an English Opium Eater as a Young Pariah. De Quincey represents virtually all his childhood pursuits as pariah pastimes. Just as Levana's education functions through the torture of the boy's spirit, so the principal recreations of De Quincey's pariah childhood, his books and games, also model a horrible world of power politics, all vaunting persecution and cringing *ressentiment*.

De Quincey's most systematic discussion of his childhood reading is found in his 1851-52 essay on "Infant Literature." It is habitual to depict

146 Romanticism and the Vocation of Childhood

the Romantic claim for children's fantasy as gloriously empowering to the imagination: "Should children be permitted to read Romances, & Relations of Giants & Magicians & Genii?" is Coleridge's famous question; "I have formed my faith in the affirmative—I know of no other way of giving the mind a love of 'the Great' & 'the Whole.'" (*CCL* 1: 354). But De Quincey is less sanguine in defining the sphere of children's reading. Insisting on the separateness of childhood, "a distinct peninsula" (*CW* 1: 121), De Quincey sets up children's literature, "Infant Literature," as a pariah genre written by, for, and about pariahs. It is thereby a genre instinct with the "moral sublime" because it juxtaposes moral grandeur and worldly abjection. He cites three examples only: one writer, one contemporary fiction, and one fairy tale. The writer is Aesop, the slave fabulist. The fiction is a moral tale about revenge attributed to Thomas Percival, a friend of De Quincey's father, but actually principally based on Anna Letitia Barbauld's "Generous Revenge." The fairy tale is "Aladdin and his Marvellous Lamp" from the *Arabian Nights*. Taken together the three texts provide a boy's handbook to pariahdom: the first illustrates the Pariah as author, the second practical pariah ethics (or how worms should turn), and the third the Pariah as child victim. As a slave and also as a writer for children, Aesop is a "*a poor pariah slave*" sunk into the "awful chasm . . . the abyss . . . the pollution of slavery," but raised by his literary powers upon "an everlasting pedestal" (1: 125-26). De Quincey cites, with a minor inaccuracy, two lines by Phaedrus, the redactor of Aesop, in which he articulates his first experiences of the sublime with the authority of authorship:

> These were the two lines in which that glory of the sublime, so stirring to my childish sense, seemed to burn as in some mighty pharos:—
> "Aesopo statuam ingentem posuere Attici;
> Servumque collocárunt eternâ in basi";
> *A colossal statue did the Athenians raise to Aesop; and a poor pariah slave they planted upon an everlasting pedestal.* I have not scrupled to introduce the word pariah, because in that way only could I decipher to the reader by what particular avenue it was that the sublimity which I fancy in the passage reached my heart. This sublimity originated in the awful chasm, in the abyss that no eye could bridge, between the pollution of slavery—the being a man, yet without right or lawful power belonging to a man—between this unutterable degradation and the starry altitude of the slave . . . upon the unveiling of his everlasting statue. (*CW* 1: 125-26)

Despite his phenomenal memory, De Quincey here misquotes his source, substituting "*Aesopo statuam ingentem*" ("*a colossal* statue to Aesop") for Phaedrus' actual "*Aesopi statuam ingenio*" ("a statue to the genius of Aesop"). De Quincey inflates the size of the statue with a megalomaniac will to contrast.[7] Such an "*Apotheosis of the Slave*" (1: 127) is reworked in the Barbauld-Percival tale of what De Quincey describes as "noble revenge." His version is riff upon both Anna Letitia Barbauld's "Generous Revenge" and Thomas Percival's "A Generous Return for an Injury." But De Quincey suppresses any reference to Barbauld's version, which his strongly resembles, and gives full credit for the story to Percival whose *Parental Instructions* (1788) (also published as *A Father's Instructions to His Children*), he recollects under the title of *The Father's Assistant,* itself a patriarchal misprision of Edgeworth's *The Parent's Assistant.* In addition to eliding Barbauld's authorship, De Quincey takes further ignoble revenge upon this powerfully pedagogical maternal figure. He attributes to Coleridge a derisive gibe at Barbauld as "*that pleonasm of nakedness;* since, as if it were not enough to be *bare,* she was also *bald*" (1: 127). Subaltern resentment is the stuff of the Barbauld-Percival story. De Quincey finds the same pariah's "moral sublime" of justified resentment in the worm-turning sado-masochistic little story of "noble revenge" in which a soldier humiliated by an unprovoked blow from his officer is so gallantly selfless in battle that he humiliates the abusive officer by his magnanimity. "Crimsoned with glorious gore," the private leads a conquering party and sees at the battle's end the grateful admiring face of the officer who struck him. With "the gaze of armies upon them," the officer kisses the noble soldier but the noble soldier steps back, saluting: "'Sir', he said, 'I told you before that I would *make you repent it!*'" (*CW* 1: 133).

De Quincey's strange dislocation and distortion of "Aladdin" is a yet fuller revision of children's literature as pariah literature. Despite De Quincey's sympathy with the *Arabian Nights,* despite his Scheherazadean ability to spin labyrinthine, involuted, caducean tales within tales full of the "digressive but patterned movement" of the arabesque (Naddaff 112), his version of "Aladdin" is a radical divagation from the buoyant optimism of the *Arabian Nights.* As best I have been able to determine, De Quincey's version resembles *no* version current in his lifetime. Extolled as the "most renowned story invented by man" (Dawood 132), "Aladdin" first came to England in the anonymous "Grub Street" translation of 1721-22, which was reprinted in numerous editions for more than a century. Of all the tales, "Sinbad" and "Aladdin" were the most popular and the most frequently issued separately. They were also the tales that the six-year-old De Quincey and his older sister pronounced, in express defiance of Mrs. Barbauld's opinion, the worst stories in the collected tales because of their incoherent set of mere adventures and mere treasures. Though De Quincey almost certainly read the Grub Street translation as a child,[8] it is possible that he later encountered either the Torrens (1838) or the Lane (1839-42) translations. He may also have attended one or more Aladdin pantomimes that were performed at Christmastime in theaters throughout Britain. The first such Aladdin pantomime was presented at Covent Garden in 1788, beginning a popular tradition that has lasted two centuries.

All eighteenth- and nineteenth-century Aladdins *except De Quincey's* follow the same pattern. (The summary that follows is based on multiple versions of "Aladdin" though all quotations are drawn from the Grub Street translation.) Aladdin, the "careless and idle" son of a poor Chinese tailor, Mustapha, has "many vicious habits . . . wicked, obstinate, and disobedient." Refusing to settle down to work at his father's trade, Aladdin hangs out with "blackguard boys and such little vagabounds as himself." Mustapha chastises him, but Aladdin is incorrigible; and his father to his great grief is obliged "to abandon him to his libertinism." Mutapha dies of a broken heart but Aladdin, fifteen years old and bone-idle, lives off his widowed mother. One day an African magician, a talent spotter of young rogues, sees Aladdin and recognizes his potential for mischief. Passing himself off as a long-lost uncle, the magician promises to make Aladdin's fortune, takes him to an isolated rural spot where he knows a lamp of power is hidden in a subterranean cavern. Aladdin, now wearing a special ring of power, is sent into the cavern whence he retrieves the treasure. The rest is familiar and, especially in the Galland version, very protracted. Aladdin refuses to hand over the lamp unless he is helped out first. The magician gets testy, shuts Aladdin in the cavern, returns to Africa. Aladdin eventually gets out through the Genie of the Ring, eventually becomes rich through the Genie of the Lamp, eventually marries the king's daughter (this through a series of grossly cheerful tricks that involve locking a rival bridegroom all night in a freezing cold privy until his sexual member shrivels so he cannot consummate the marriage). The magician, learning of Aladdin's triumph and treasure, returns to trick the princess through the "New Lamps for Old" gambit and carries princess, lamp, and palace off to Africa. But Aladdin's ring enables him to recover the lost lamp, palace, and princess and to foil both the magician (poisoning him) and his brother, also a magician (stabbing him), and to live triumphantly as king for many happy years.

Except for De Quincey's version, all eighteenth- and nineteenth-century Aladdins, in storybooks and on the stage, share certain features. First, Aladdin is emphatically Chinese and the story is set in China. Most illustrated texts show Chinese characters and costumes; from 1813 the pantomimes heavily emphasize Chinese-ness. One frequently presented version names Aladdin's mother the Widow "Ching Mustapha" and the putative uncle "Quam Mustapha" (1826). In the most famous of all Aladdin pantomimes, H. J. Byron's 1861 Opium-War-era version, the supernumeraries are Mandarins; the chief courtier is called Pekoe; and Aladdin's mother is named Widow Twankey, after a brand of Green Tea (also slang for gin); and the Emperor toasts his son-in-law with a raised teacup:

> Let all the public sights be opened free;
> Pekin be wrapped in universal spree.
> Death to the publican who makes tea weak;
> Let the tea kettle to the trumpet speak,
> The trumpet to the cannonier without:—
> Now the king drinks to young Aladdin! (41)

Except for De Quincey's version, every other Aladdin is a layabout, a feckless juvenile delinquent, neither especially young—he is an adolescent not a child—nor especially good. Representative epithets make plain his character: "wicked, obstinate, disobedient" (1789, 943); "shiftless, idle, incorrigible" (1793); "many vicious habits" (*Oriental Moralist* 1800, 211); "Graceless, illiterate" (1826); "willful" (1855), "perverse and graceless from his earliest childhood" and "a good-for-nothing" (Payne 1889). (A breezy 1932 version even describes Aladdin as "a young rip with a taste for the beau monde" [Clinton-Baddeley]). Wealth eventually makes the adult Aladdin respectable—but too late to save Mustapha, dead of paternal heartbreak.

Except for De Quincey's, every Aladdin is lucky, hero of a story about easy money. It is Aladdin's effortless wealth and power that explain the popularity of the Aladdin name as shorthand for ease and plenty. Thus the Aladdin title to a number of turn-of-the-twentieth-century get-rich-quick adventure novels: Max Pembleton's *Aladdin of London* (1907; Polish mines); Herbert Quick's *Aladdin: A Romance of Yankee Magic* (1890; a Gilded Era land grab scheme); Fergus Hume's *Aladdin in London* (1892; a ring of power and Brahmin Slaves of the Ring give access to untold Indian wealth in a despoiled temple). Thus Aladdin stands for effortlessness in such areas as prefabricated houses (as in *Instructions for the Erection of your Aladdin Home* [1921] from the Aladdin Company of Bay City, Michigan); or Social Credit (in Gorham Munson's *Aladdin's Lamp: The Wealth of the American People* [1945]); or unbridled economic deregulation of public utilities (in Ernest Greenwood's *Aladdin USA* [1928]).

In all versions except De Quincey's, "Aladdin" is a cheerfully comic story, both funny and triumphant. In its incarnations as a Christmas pantomime (and more recently as a Disney film), "Aladdin" has generated multiple comic parts: the melodramatically evil Abanazar the magician; his deaf-mute assistant Kasrac, played in De Quincey's era by the celebrated clown Joseph Grimaldi; the lugubriously hysterical Widow Twankey. Aside from the textual shenanigans in the Galland version (the bridegroom in the privy), the story contains openings for broad stage humor as when Byron's Abanazar transports the palace to Africa and the Widow Twankey contemplates the empty pit center stage:

> Widow Twankey: Something's moved this house.
> Aladdin: Indeed! Ha! Ha!
> Our jokes have often moved this house, mamma. (50)

This comic exuberance and the triumphant shape of the plot help explain why an "Aladdin in Flanders" was produced by soldiers on the Western Front in 1915, and why Kipling's Stalky and his school-mate officers in "Slaves of the Lamp" can whip the fractious hill tribes of India's Northwest frontier while singing songs and sending coded messages from their schoolboy production of Byron's "Aladdin."

Though all other eighteenth- and nineteenth-century Aladdins are bad but lucky boys whose stories are comically triumphant, such triumphant comedy is antithetical to De Quincey's doleful recollection of the story he claims to have "despised" when he was a boy. In defiance of Mrs. Barbauld, "queen of all blue stockings,"

> my sister and myself pronounced Sinbad to be very bad, and Aladdin to be pretty nearly the worst . . . [In] Aladdin, after the possession of the lamp has been once secured by pure accident, the story ceases to move. All the rest is a mere record of upholstery; how this saloon was finished today, and that window the next day . . . (*CW* 1: 127-128)

For all that he despised it, he reclaims it in old age as a representative piece of infant literature. In making it representative, he recasts it as a pariah story. In recapitulating the story, De Quincey omits as boring *all* the elements of Aladdin's triumph—escape, genies, treasure, marriage, his active rescue of the princess, his active killings of the magicians, his subsequent "happily ever after" in prosperity and power. De Quincey focuses instead on two isolated figures: the "wicked" and "murderous" magician and the "innocent" and "solitary" Aladdin. De Quincey's Aladdin lives not in China (a realm always wicked in De Quincey's moral and political geography) but virtuously on the banks of the Tigris. Not a sociable Chinese adolescent hanging out "with other blackguards like himself," De Quincey's Aladdin is young and vulnerable, "an innocent child," "a solitary infant," the tender target of the magician's unique auditory surveillance. Unlike all other magicians in the Aladdin canon who are masters of "fumigation" and "geomacy" (divinations by fire and smoke and divination by sand diagrams), or—in the pantomimes—of a special "Book of Fate," De Quincey's unnamed sorcerer "in the central depths of Africa" is a supreme auditor:

> Where shall such a child be found? . . . The magician knows: he applies his ear to the earth; he listens to the innumerable sounds of the footsteps that at the moment of his experiment are tormenting the surface of the globe; and amongst them all, at a distance of six thousand miles, playing in the streets of Baghdad, he distinguishes the peculiar steps of the child Aladdin. Through this mighty labyrinth of sounds, which Archimedes, aided by the *arenarius,* could not sum or disentangle, one solitary infant's feet are distinctly recognized on the banks of the Tigris, distant by four hundred and forty days march of an army or caravan. These feet, these steps, the sorcerer knows, and challenges in his heart, as the feet, as the steps of that innocent boy, through whose hands only he could have a chance of reaching the lamp. (1: 128-29)

De Quincey emphasizes that the magician's interpretative terrorism can fasten a fixed and fixative "murderous attention" upon "one insulated tread" and "disarm Babel . . . of its confusion," by deciphering the "secret hieroglyphics uttered by the flying footsteps." Without moving his summary version beyond the poised balance of attentive hunter and fixed hunted, De Quincey leaves the Aladdin story as a vignette of a solitary child arrested in a static condition of terrified anticipation.

As a uniquely designated innocent, Aladdin becomes an isolate, a sequestered Wordsworthian child inhabiting a realm of difference, distance, and arrest. As the predestined object of the magician's irresistible art, Aladdin is marked out and contained in what Hartley Coleridge described as "mute simplicity of passive being" by an adult desire. Although this arrest accords with the powerful Wordsworthian pattern evident in packs of solitary children each "single in the field" in one way or another, Aladdin's arrest signifies not a protective detention but perpetual vulnerability. In De Quincey's version, Aladdin is translated from Experience into Innocence. The worldly and somewhat unlikable Aladdin loses all his pert insolent individuality and becomes another faceless Romantic innocent with his back to us (we see only "the hands of an innocent child," "the steps of that innocent boy"), another fungible Romantic victim. This erasure of personality is further enforced by De Quincey's refusal of narrative movement in an "Aladdin" that is more a predicament than a story. De Quincey's Aladdin never takes to his heels into a lived adventure but is held, contemplatively, a solitary, textual, readable being whose "secret hieroglyphics uttered by the flying footsteps" stand in need of reinterpretation, a process hardly distinguishable from torture. With all forward narrative movement truncated in De Quincey's vignette, the representative child-hero, child-pariah Aladdin is an arrested character in a fixed scene, forever available prey, bait, and lost self of the reconnoitering adult reader.

In addition to recollecting a childhood spent reading such resentful pariah texts of childhood persecution and revenge, De Quincey recalls playing games that he could never win against a brother-tyrant whose death he willed. These fratricidal games fought with and against a brother-tyrant were both class wars and imperial exercises that forecast the paranoid politics of his adulthood.

The psychology of imperial power and powerlessness is nowhere better set out than in sixty-five-year old De Quincey's memoirs, written in 1851-52, relating to the years 1793-96, "Introduction to the World of Strife." The memoir elaborates the games the Quincey brothers played from 1793 to 1796 while they lived in their parents' great house on the edge of Manchester. The memoir centers on Thomas' relationship with his overbearing brother William during the years immediately following the deaths of their father and two of their sisters when the little brother was eight to eleven and the older twelve to fifteen. William, four years his senior, served as his feared yet idolized mentor, his guide to the world of power politics.

As a sixty-five-year old xenophobic Tory journalist, a jingo imperialist beating the war drum during the Opium Wars, De Quincey looks back on himself as a frail child of eight in 1794, subjugated by his older brother William, recently returned home after a breach of years. The rambunctious William had been sent away to school to tame him but had been brought back home when his father was dying. William "very naturally despised" Thomas and rapidly took command of him and the other siblings, a sister and a toddler brother, the "swinish multitude" as he allegedly called them in the famous phrase drawn from Burke's *Reflections on Revolution in France* (1790) (*CW* 1: 59, 66). Within the nursery, William proved a bold, venturesome, and despotic impresario, "fertile in resources as Robinson Crusoe" with a repertoire of world-beating games and plays (*CW* 1: 61). William made magniloquent and magical claims—the ability to raise ghosts, the ability to walk on the ceiling—which the other children refused at their peril: Might made right. William wrote and staged plays, notably

"Sultan Selim" in which a bloody Sultan, played by William, massacres his entire family (played by the siblings) in Act 1 but generates a second family by magic to be slaughtered again in the second act.

Thomas' "perfect craze for being despised" (*CW* 1: 59) dovetailed nicely with this model of eternally recurring despotism—William Sultan forever slaughtering Thomas and the little girls and William Tory forever commanding the "swinish multitude," a multitude now impersonated by William's class enemies and now by his colonial subjects.

Thomas' memoir makes it clear that he and his brother were rich boys, so obtrusively well-dressed that they attracted a derisive "Jacobinism" in the attacks of the "unwashed," unkempt, cotton-fluff-covered boys of the local mill with whom they fought regular pitched battles (*CW* 1: 70). With a sneaking sympathy with the mill boys' independent-mindedness (they were Tories in respect to nation but Jacobins in respect to class) and delight in being coddling by the mill girls as a darling little boy, Thomas participated in William's assertions of class privilege with a bad conscience.

Thomas' wavering allegiances in this contest between capital and labor are even more obviously played out his participation in the game of empire he and William contrived. It was not surprising that the sons of a Manchester merchant would play the game of empire as well as the game of capital/labor. Britain's colonial power was a fact of life to the manufacturers and mill workers of Manchester. The late Mr. Quincey had been a textile merchant, a wholesaler, who had grown rich in the colonial trade, importing linen and cotton from Ireland and the West Indies. Manchester was the center of cotton manufacture in England. A city growing wealthy through the colonial trade, especially trade with India, with which they were in bitter competition,[9] Manchester textile manufacturers fought an unscrupulous and ultimately successful battle to extirpate the Indian textile industry from India and Indian textiles from Britain. William too dragged Thomas into a tale of two kingdoms locked in hopeless competition.

Thomas and William invented and ruled two "imaginary kingdoms" (*CW* 1: 88) but William set up the rules under which the kingdoms could operate. It was like a game of chess in which William always played white, Thomas black:

> since all the relations between us as independent sovereigns . . . rested upon our own representations and official reports, it was surely within my competence to deny or qualify, as much as within his to assert. But, in reality, the *law* of the contest between us, as suggested by some instinctive propriety in my own mind, would not allow me to proceed in such a method. What he

said was like a move at chess or draughts which it was childish to dispute. The move being made, my business was—to face it, to parry it, to evade it, and, if I could, to overthrow it. (*CW* 1: 90)

William's land was a vast northern kingdom named *Tigrosylvania* whose capital lay at sixty-five degrees North latitude. Thomas' kingdom was a small tropical island only 270 miles around which he placed at ten degrees South: it was called *Gombroon*. Thomas had waited for William to identify Tigrosylvania's coordinates before deliberately planting his kingdom far out of reach in the south. When William learned of Gombroon's location, he announced that, as it were, the sun never set on Tigrosylvania, that it extended eighty or ninety degrees southward and was very close to Gombroon. To counter a possible invasion, Thomas pointed out the poverty of Gombroon—it was hardly worth invading; William's counter-move was his announcement of the discovery of *diamonds* in the central forests of Gombroon, raw materials that the Gombroonians "from their low conditions of civilisation, did not value" nor know how to extract (*CW* 1: 90). Thus William, ruler of a more highly developed civilization, apprized of the modern laws of economies, "better able than the native to make its treasures available" moved to seize Gombroon—as Britain would force open China's ports—by right of eminent domain (*CW* 1: 90). During the Opium War, De Quincey would defend Britain's right and righteousness in doing to China what William had done to Gombroon; De Quincey cited the natural law of Free Trade which the Chinese, the "vilest and silliest amongst nations" (13: 349), "incapable of a true civilization" were too "savage" to understand. The Chinese, like the Gombroonians before them, were, in Nigel Leask's paraphrase, "infringing a natural right premised upon a *global* nervous system of free market" (219). Certain scarce goods, locally available, must be made available to the civilized even if the commercial nation must "*force* a commercial transaction" (qtd. in Leask 220). Just as commercial Britain triumphed over feudal China, so William triumphed over Thomas. In the war of nerves between the brothers and their kingdoms, William won every battle. Thomas had hoped to keep William's forces away by stressing the poverty of Gombroon. Thus, when asked by William how he raised taxes on Gombroon, Thomas felt in a double bind: he needed a system of taxation to support his standing army, the only bulwark against William's Tigrosylvanian army. But he could not raise much money lest William's greed be activated. The solution: Gombroonians, an island people, were "maritime" (1: 91): they caught herrings. But they did not know how to salt their herrings in order to preserve them, so King

Thomas collected his taxes in the form of rotten herrings that were sold abroad as fertilizer. This was a bad move on Thomas' part since it provided compromising biological evidence of the feebleness of his soldiers, frail from a herring diet: "a wretched ichthyophagous people must make shocking soldiers, weak as water, and liable to be knocked over like nine-pins; whereas in *his* army, not a man ever ate herrings, pilchards, mackerels, or, in fact, condescended to anything worse than sirloins of beef" (1: 91).

Worst of all, William dipped into the discourse of modern anthropology in Lord Monboddo's *Dissertations on the Origin of Language,* a reading Laura Roman has shown to be central to the whole Gombroon project. From Monboddo's quirky evolutionary theories, William acquired the damaging ethnographic ammunition against Thomas. Citing a recent traveler's report, William announced that "Gombroonians had not yet emerged from the early condition of apedom. They . . . were still *homines caudati*" (1: 98). At this stage of the game, the old De Quincey remembered he felt so degraded as king of this subhuman pariah people that he lost heart. The Gombroonians would not be fit for civilization for eons. The generations required for the Gombroonians to acquire a truly human posterior—either by gradually *rubbing off* "their ignominious appendages" (1: 99) or through compulsory sedentary occupations—seemed to stretch out to the crack of doom. With an account of his child-self as thrown once again into despair, sickened for and by his people, whom he simultaneously despised and identified with, De Quincey abandoned Gombroon without closure. Whether Tigrosylvania swallowed up Gombroon or whether Gombroon achieved its independence is never set out. Instead the narrative peters out in a vision in which the Gombroonians split endlessly into other specifically *pariah* peoples.

The Tamil term is closer to home in this usage than it usually is in De Quincey's texts. For William and Thomas' game of Tigrosylvania and Gombroon is a riff on the great game of empire and its various forms of submission and dominance. At one level, Tigrosylvania is Britain, ruling the whole world from its distant northern capital: "It seemed that vast thrones and promontories ran down from all parts of his dominions towards any country whatsoever, in either hemisphere—empire, or republic; monarchy, polyarchy, or anarchy—that he might have reasons for assaulting" (1: 89).

Tigrosylvania establishes its imperial dominance and hegemony in the ways familiar to the student of British imperial history. Economically, Tigrosylvania expropriates Gombroonian land just as Britain had recently forced open China's ports in the name of progress and free trade. In the spirit of the great British ethnographic survey of the peoples of India,

Tigrosylvania ethnographically classifies the Gombroonians and scientifically establishes their primitivism. Just as judicious John Stuart Mill had argued the need for authoritarian colonial rule over barbarous peoples for the duration of their barbarism, so De Quincey records the ineligibility for freedom of his savagely betailed subjects anytime in the imaginable future: "I was a king of a people that had tails; and the slow, slow process by which, in a course of many centuries, their posterity might hope to rub them off, a hope of vintages never to be enjoyed by any generations that are yet heaving in sight—*that* was to me the worst form of despair" (1: 99).

Tigrosylvanian science declares the biological superiority of beef-eaters to fisher-eaters in the same way that Kipling proclaimed the supremacy of meat-eating peoples (wolves, Englishmen, and martial tribes) over babu-vegetarians (monkeys, the bandurlog, Bengali babus, Hindus).[10] That the Gombroonians, as fish-eaters, are contrasted with the Tigrosylvanian meat-eaters in the same kind of binary that opposes vegetarian Hindus to meat-eating Muslims, probably owes something to De Quincey's "Indian Uncle" Thomas Penson of the East India Company whose domain lay in Bengal, famous in India as the home of fish-eaters. As Britain, Tigrosylvania is a realm of aggressive meat-eating rationalists in control of the apparatus of law, anthropology, science, and economics. Gombroon, as the East—especially India, motherland of Pariahs—on the other hand, is the realm of submissive, fish-eating, semi-human savages, mired by biological destiny in naked futility for countless ages. This sado-masochistic patterning is deepened by casting the "poor abject islanders" (1: 99) of effeminate Thomas (him of the "girlish tears" [1: 45]) into the mire of sexual perversity, that realm, to paraphrase Kaja Silverman, where the human and the animal are blended in bestiality, where pleasure and pain are blended in masochistic humiliation (35). The bestial Gombroonians are set up as nature's own catamites, defined by their embarrassing posteriors. Their apes' tails do not connote powerful phallic aggression but rather, hanging down behind, weakness and racial immaturity. These embarrassing appendages are veritable invitations to rape and aggression; they must be *rubbed away* by the forces of civilization.

The familiar binary of the masculine West, here enacted by manly aggressive William, and the feminine East, enacted by effeminate masochistic Thomas, is not the only binary of abjection. At a more literal historical level, Tigrosylvania stands not just for Britain but for Britain's deadly enemy. And Gombroon is very much just Gombroon, Britain's meanest possession. Indeed both Gombroon and Tigrosylvania were territories under the sometime control of the Indian Uncle's East India Company.

Though De Quincey scholars have long commented on the comic inventiveness of the name Gombroon (Rzepka notes that it rhymes with both buffoon and baboon), it may have been chosen as a genuine foreign place with a representatively ridiculous foreign name. There is an historically real Gombroon—a port in the gulf of Ormuz now called Abbas Bandar, a small port up against the island of Ormuz, metaphorically renowned in *Paradise Lost* where Satan's throne "far / Outshone the wealth of *Ormus* or of *Ind*." According to a Persian proverb "if the world was an egg, Hormuz . . . was its yolk" (Keay 105). But Gombroon, Portuguese for "place of shrimps," was as obscure as Ormuz was famous.

Gombroon was granted to the East India Company in 1622 by the Shah of Persia in recompense for British assistance in ousting the Portuguese from Ormuz. The East India company there established a "factory," that is, an entrepot for merchandise bound from Persia to India and from India; the company was also granted half the port-tax revenue. Gombroon was the site of a famous seventeenth-century British naval disaster, "a titanic engagement" between British and Portuguese fleets, "thought one of the greatest that ever was fought" (Keay 107). Gombroon remained in British hands from 1622 until 1760 when the expanding French trading interests, backed by warships, drove the English out. During the 140 years of British possession, Gombroon served as a conduit of a "negligible trade" (Keay 253) in Indian goods (mostly Bengal sugar and spices) into Persia and a trickle of trade out of Persia to Surat and Bombay—mostly thoroughbred horses and a small amount of European cloth carried overland from Turkey. It was a dreary place with a bad reputation. An eighteenth-century sailor's adage "had it that 'only an inch of deal stands between Gombroon and Hell,'" while a Victorian historian wrote: "You cannot get excited about Gombroon. It would be difficult to select a place less known or less calculated to awaken an interest of any kind in the reader" (Keay 253). Given Thomas' self-proclaimed "craze for being despised" (1: 59), no British territory would seem more appropriate to this shrimp of a child than this negligible "shrimp port" haunted by past defeats.

Gombroon, the mere flyspot, lay across the Arabian Sea from Tigrosylvania, the Land of the Tiger, that is, Mysore, the great South Indian state of the late eighteenth century. This was the kingdom of Tipu Sultan, also called Tipu the Tiger, who was Britain's Designated Oriental Enemy in the four fierce Mysore Wars, fought between 1767 and 1799. The Tiger of Mysore had concluded a treaty in the third Mysore War during 1792, the year before William's invention of Tigrosylvania. As Barrell reports, from at least 1790 until well into the nineteenth century, Tipu Sultan enjoyed a kind of cult status in Britain, "embedded in . . . nursery folklore" as the "oriental tiger the British loved to hate" (509). According to Barrell, the 1790s and early 1800s produced numerous paintings based on the Mysore Wars and some six plays or staged panoramas of Tipu's life and death including, in 1823, *Tippoo Sahib or the Storming of Seringapatam*. A version was marketed for children's toy theaters. Brought up on a court where tiger-wrestling was a court sport, Tipu consciously associated himself, as did brother William, with tigers (Bhattacharya 192-96). Though the popular British tradition that the name Tipu means "Tiger" in some Karnatic language is untrue, he did call himself "the Tiger of Mysore" (Swallow 187) and saw himself as God's own tiger, the devourer of God's enemies, "God's instrument for driving the infidel English out of India" (Swallow 187). Such an image is enshrined in the brilliantly painted wooden "Man-Tiger-Organ" that shows a huge Indian tiger mauling a European solider. The redcoat's groans issue from an internal bellows and the tiger growls when a handle in the shoulder is turned. (De Quincey probably saw this trophy that fell to the English at Seringapatam in 1799, now on display in the Victoria and Albert Museum, when it was exhibited in London in 1808). In addition, Tipu's throne was carved with tigers; his cannons were tigerform; his soldiers wore tiger-striped uniforms; and the walls of his palace in Seringapatam "were said to have been painted on his instructions with life-sized caricatures of Englishmen being devoured by tigers" (Swallow 188). Like Blake's "Tyger" (1793), also possibly associated with the Mysore Wars, Tipu might well offer a glamorous fearful symmetry to wild William.

Like the man-eating tiger of the jungles, the Tigrosylvanian Tipu was Britain's most dangerous—and worthy—enemy. Not only was he a figure of opposing force but an ally of the French—thus associated with Jacobinism. As a Muslim, inevitably described in contemporary histories as "fanatical," he signified Oriental despotism and was habitually labeled as blood-thirsty, false, and lascivious. Scott's *Surgeon's Daughter* (1825) depicts Tipu attempting to buy a Scottish surgeon's virtuous daughter for his harem; even so late an account as Edward Thompson's and G. T. Garrett's in 1934 describes him as perfidious, "a liar so ingrained that he never seems to have risen to the perception that a distinction between true and false exists" (67).

The Tigrosylvanian-Gombroonian pairing seen in merely colonial context offers a pair of sensationalized orientalized others: one the object of loathing, the other the object of fear. The abject Gombroonian—Thomas' role—is the colonial subject as bestial savage, pariah, slave, victim, masochist, both sexually available and sexually disgusting. The vaunting Tigrosylvanian is the colonial subject as barbarian supermale, as aggressor, as predator, as enslaver, as fanatic.

Although De Quincey's memoir put no term to the power of Tigrosylvania and the humiliation of Gombroon, the historical Tipu died bravely in 1799 at the siege of Seringapatam. His triumphant tiger-trophy was carried over to London and became in turn an ironic British counter-trophy, merely the ingenious futile toy of an ingenious futile enemy. The domestic Sultan, brother William, also died in 1797, at fifteen, unmourned by his brother: "I acknowledge no such tiger a friend of mine" (1: 115). Playmate but not friend, William initiated Thomas into games of power and humiliation that underwrote his vision of adult power.

The "Hidden Path" to Childhood: Being Wordsworth, Being Little

> It formed the main guarantee of an unmolested repose: and security there was not, on any lower terms, for the *latentis semita vitae.*

Thomas De Quincey spent most of his writing life rewriting his early life. The bulk of De Quincey's autobiographical writing makes up what Richard Coe has labeled a "Childhood," a form that carries the self "from first consciousness to full maturity over the allotted span (normally) of some fifteen to eighteen years" (7). Just as "the education of a child" is the only *action* included among De Quincey's "constituents of happiness," the real direction of all De Quincey's major work is along what he calls "the hidden path" ("latentis semita vitae" [*CW* 1: 59]) back to childhood.

In a curious aside in "Literature of Knowledge and Literature of Power," De Quincey draws a puzzling and labored comparison between children and great books. To ask what is the value of great literature is much the same as questioning the value of children:

> What is the effect . . . upon society of children? By the pity, by the tenderness, and by the peculiar modes of admiration, which connect themselves with the helplessness, with the innocence, and with the simplicity of children, not only are the primal affections strengthened and continually renewed, but the qualities which are dearest in the sight of heaven—the frailty, for instance, which appeals to the forbearance, the innocence which symbolizes the heavenly, and the simplicity which is most alien from the worldly,—are kept in perpetual remembrance, and their ideals are continually refreshed. A purpose of the same nature is answered by the higher literature, viz. the literature of power. (*CW* 11: 55)

As Charles Rzepka has demonstrated, De Quincey's claim to the "Literature of Power," the literature of the sublime, is a claim of authorial authority over the feared and despised mass reading public on which he was dependent. A writer of "the higher literature," unlike a hackwork purveyor of knowledge, does not receive a simple fee for service but achieves dominion over hearts and minds, subduing them to his will and imbuing them with a saving humanity. "A purpose of the same nature is answered" by following the hidden path to childhood, that separate space of intimacy and freedom.

A work of imaginative interior genius valid for all times, the "higher literature," like childhood, is a counterpoise to the much feared public world. Childhood is a timeless, solitary, and intimately loving place from which all powers flow. Like the isolated writer of power, De Quincey's child is a solitary, inhabiting a vast "solitude" (*CW* 1: 122):

> But in solitude, above all things . . . God holds "communion undisturbed" with children. Solitude, though silent as light, is, like light, the mightiest of agencies, for solitude is essential to man . . . Oh burden of solitude, that cleavest to man through every stage of his being. . . . Deep is the solitude in life for millions upon millions. . . . But deeper than the deepest of these solitudes is that which broods over childhood, bringing before it, at intervals the final solitude which watches for it, and is waiting for it within the gates of death. (L 114)

By means of "the mighty silence which infancy is . . . privileged by nature and position to enjoy" (CW 1: 122), the child become a register of greatness. "No man will ever unfold the capacities of his own intellect who does not at least chequer his life with solitude. How much solitude, so much power" (L 88).

On this "distinct peninsula" (*CW* 1: 121) where significant adult life originates, children with their "limited" privilege of strength" (1: 121) operate as the moral registers of humankind. All their senses and intuitive powers are more acute and profound: to his six-year-old self, De Quincey asserts "your heart was deeper than the Danube; and as was your love, so was your grief" (L 156). Children are visionaries, routinely in possession of hypnagogic vision:

> that power in the eye of many children by which in darkness they project a vast theatre of phantasmagorical figures moving forwards or backwards between their bed curtains and the chamber walls. In some children this

power is semivoluntary: they can control or perhaps suspend the shows; but in others it is altogether automatic. (W 187)

Visions of the eye are augmented by unsought visions of the mind: "special revelations . . . authentic whispers of truth" found in a particular text (*CW* 1: 122); a profound experience "of the relations subsisting between ourselves and nature—that not always are we called on to seek; sometimes, and in childhood above all, we are sought" (*CW* 1: 122), and even "communion undisturbed" with God who "speaks to children" in dreams, in signs, and especially in solitude (L 114). The qualities imputed to children are passive rather than active, apprehensive rather than constructive, affective rather than intellectual, unitary rather than multifarious ("the sensibilities are not scattered, are not multiplied, are not crushed and confounded . . . under the burden of that distraction which lurks in the infinite littleness of details" [*CW* l: l22]), solitary rather than social, mysterious rather than comprehensible.

Childhood solitude makes possible an intimacy unknown to adults in the teeming public world. In childhood all relationships are face to face. De Quincey remembers the lineaments of childhood, all lost—as hands, lips, necks, and faces: "the child's hands . . . unlinked for ever from his mother's neck" or "his lips for ever from his sister's kisses" (L 146). That intimacy is figured in the close-up presence of a unique and beloved face: Elizabeth's "ample brow," her "sweet countenance" sainted by "a tiara of light or a gleaming *aureola*" (L 99): Ann's uniquely "sweet expression of countenance" ("I have looked into many, many myriads of female faces. . . . I should have known her again amongst a thousand" [L 34]). Loss of that beloved face is a fall from intimacy into anonymity, from unity into multiplicity, always a source of terror.[11] Thus Elizabeth's death is figured as the replacement of Elizabeth's beloved face by the blank and terrible glory of the sun. As the six-year old enters his sister's room hoping for the last sweet secret glimpse of his sister's face, the intimacy is swallowed up in infinite light: "I sought my sister's face. But the bed had been moved, and the back was now turned. Nothing met my eyes but one large window wide open, through which the sun of midsummer at noonday was showering down torrents of splendour" (L 103).

"*Desiderium* (the yearning too obstinate after one irrecoverable face)" (*CW* 1: 56) is thwarted by the imposition of the public on the private. After Kate Wordsworth died, De Quincey lamented not having "seen my darling's face once again," not having "seen thy face and kissed thy dear lips again" (Jordan 263, 265) and with equal vehemence deplored the fact that other people were permitted to see her:

> One thing hurts me, when I think of this: I fear the custom of the country would oblige you to let many idle gazers look at our darling's face after she was dead—who never gave her a look of love or interest whilst she was living. (Jordan 266-67)

The public world wears away, dislimns the face of childhood. Chief among the pains of opium is the dream of "the tyranny of the human face"—a double curse that floods the consciousness with multitudes ("the sea appeared paved with innumerable faces, upturned to the heavens: faces, imploring, wrathful, despairing, surged upwards by thousands, by myriads, by generations, by centuries . . ." [L 72]) and "dislimn[s]" the irrecoverable particular face (L 116).

Just as it is the realm of intimate solitary power, so is childhood the space out of time, the very antithesis of chronology. Unlike Wordsworth's topographically and chronologically fixed "spots of time," De Quincey's "involutes" organize detemporalized childhood memories:

> The reader who may have accompanied me in these wandering memorials of my own life and casual experiences, will be aware that in many cases the neglect of chronological order is not merely permitted, but is in fact to some degree inevitable. There are cases, for instance, which, as a whole, connect themselves with my own life at so many different eras that, upon any chronological principle of position, it would have been difficult to assign them a proper place; backwards and forwards they must have leaped, in whatever place they had been introduced; and in their entire compass, from first to last, never could have been represented as properly belonging to any one *present* time, whensoever that had been selected: belonging to every place alike, they would belong, according to the proverb, to no place at all; or (reversing the proverb), belonging to no place by preferable right, they would, in fact, belong to every place; and therefore to this place. (*CW* 1: 287)

The peak memories of childhood are freed from the causal chain of Necessity and jumped out of History ("what hurts . . . what rejects desire," in Jameson's terse definition [102]) by De Quincey's organizing tactic of the "involutes." The intricate bundles of thoughts and feelings all originate in early childhood and take shape as "perplexed combination of *concrete* objects" that "pass to us as *involutes* (if I may coin that word) in compound experiences incapable of being disentangled . . ." (L 104). Such recurrent complexes as summer death, a child's labyrinthine footprints, the window as opening to lost union, the girl as the sun are "combinations in which the materials of future thought or feeling are carried imperceptibly into the mind as vegetable seeds are carried variously through the atmosphere, or by means of rivers, by birds, by winds, by waters, into remote countries" (*CW* 1: 128).

Although these involutes owe much to the "spots of time" De Quincey admired in Wordsworth's *Prelude,* there are differences. The term "spots of time" indicates Wordsworth's narrative concern with both space and time. Though the quality of the moments distinguishes them from ordinary clock time, the "spots of time" are inevitably localized, spotted, placed in particular places and often at particular moments. The exemplary demonstration spot in *The Prelude* 11 ("There are in our existence spots of time") specifies a single occasion at a specific place: the gibbet site where the murderer's name is cut in the turf. The boat-stealing episode of the 1805 *Prelude* focuses on a particular tree by the shore of Patterdale near the inn. Other spots of time that deal with repeated experiences, such as the account of the Boy of Winander, are localized by fixity of place: the lake below the school and the church. The involutes, however, are de-spatialized and de-temporalized; they consist of images cut loose from both particular places and particular times and interassimilated with emotions. The images are often literary or imaginary ideal creations rather than empirically observable concrete sites. The involutes have no origin in time or space. Thus summer-death complex, so powerful in De Quincey's work, has no definite beginning. In *Confessions* (L 75), De Quincey educes the poignance from general experience: "the contemplation of death generally is . . . more affecting in summer than in any other season of the year." In "The Affliction of Childhood," he describes Elizabeth's summer death as especially poignant but does not make this particular experience the originating point of power-laden juxtaposition. Rather he pushes it back to nursery readings of the Bible and then back still farther to ineffable musings too infantine and wordless to trace. Because Wordsworthian experience carried by the spot of time can be linked to the external world, it remains available for consultation and reuse by the adult who returns actually or in memory to the external marker. The De Quincean involute, however, floats freely in the psyche. From the first it is a complex of emotion and vision generated and abiding within the mind of the thinker. It has no lodging in the external world. Thus the Wordsworthian spot of time may change its meaning, or rather may be interpreted differently at different times, just as the enormous schoolroom of our sixth year may shrink to our adult eyes. Indeed it is typical for the experience of Wordsworth's spots of time to be one thing initially and something different in retrospect. The child terrified by the "visionary dreariness" of the moor near the gibbet becomes the young man who sees in the scene a "spirit of pleasure and youth's golden gleam." The adult can take a different meaning, an enhanced meaning, a "diversity of strength," different from the child's from the recovered spot of time, which is prized just for its aid in reconstructing a total later life. De Quincey, however, likens involutes to "seeds . . . carried variously combined through the atmosphere . . . into remote countries." The flowers the seeds bear are always the same—sunflower seeds always produce sunflowers—the emotional range and mystery of death in summer does not significantly differ from *Confessions* to *Suspiria* to the account of Catherine's death in *Recollections* to *The English Mail Coach:* always present are the sense of antithetical grandeur, the Christian promise of eternal life shadowed by the darkness of the grave, the heart and mind congested with the unsolvable paradox of the life-giving sun as death's harbinger. The "involute," primarily a creation of consciousness that is carried within the consciousness, neither itself changes nor does it have the power to change the consciousness bearing it. If the Wordsworthian spot of time is a way for an adult to retain contact with his past and yet chart his development, the De Quincean involute is a way to withstand change and to step back from the depredations of history.

The primary experiences in life carried in the involutes are fundamentally what human beings seek. "All of us ask not of God for a better thing than that we have lost; we ask for the same" (L 109). Randall Jarrell, the great twentieth-century poet of childhood's lost world, has observed that "The great CHANGE" is not for children who want everything to be the same always, but us adults only "dear to all things not to themselves endeared." ("Children Selecting Books in a Library"). For De Quincey, to whom his own childhood was endeared, change was the great enemy, the reconstitution of childhood the friend.

De Quincey's childhood narrative resists forward progress, enshrining childhood as the changeless and always available antithesis to chronological order. The static girl child—the English girl and the Malay, the girl smashed by the mail coach "going down with Victory," the anchoring English girls in their summer dresses who rescue their father form his swarming oriental dreams—authorizes De Quincey's political paranoia. She is the private place, the free space, and the unchanging realm endangered by and antithetical to modernity. She makes the project of retrieving childhood worthwhile and fundamental.

But the project is also impossible. If childhood is a perpetually gleaming realm of "the perfect peace of paradise," it is also the irrevocably lost world (1: 29). De Quincey constantly recapitulates versions of the departure from Eden. There is the primal "lion dream" that he attributes to Everychild, the timeless, dateless, unmotivated childhood dream of "lying down without a struggle before some all-conquering lion" (*CW* 3: 316). This surrender, repeated again and again in dreams, enacts the "secret frailty of human nature—reveals its deep-seated falsehood to itself":

> Perhaps not one of us escapes that dream; perhaps, as by some sorrowful doom of man, that dream repeats for every one of us, through every generation, the original temptation in Eden. Every one of us, in this dream, has a bait offered to the infirm places of his own individual will; once again a snare is presented for tempting him into captivity to a luxury of ruin; once again, as in aboriginal paradise, the man falls by his own choice; again, by infinite iteration, the ancient earth groans to heaven, through her secret caves, over the weakness of her child. "Nature, from her seat, sighing through all her works," again "gives signs of woe that all is lost"; and again the countersign is repeated to the sorrowing heavens for the endless rebellion against God. It is not without probability that in the world of dreams every one of us ratifies for himself the original transgression. In the sleeper, lighted up to the consciousness at the time, but darkened to the memory as soon as all is finished, each several child of our mysterious race completes for himself the treason of the original fall. (W 254-55)

The loss of Elizabeth also means that "*Life is Finished!*" . . . "*Life is Finished! Finished it is!*" (*CW* 1: 28). The departure from school also takes De Quincey "underneath the gloomy archway" into the irrevocable where "a Rubicon is placed between thee and all possibility of return" (*PW* 1: 25, *CW* 3: 297).

Not only is "*Nescit vox missa reverti* . . . a word once uttered is irrevocable," but a childhood once experienced is unparaphrasable (*CW* 3: 296). De Quincey understands his project as virtually impossible at least as a fixed textual literary achievement. In the phrase De Quincey so often quotes from Shakespeare, memories "dislimn" and become indistinct "as water is in water." In James Kincaid's fine variant, our childhood memories are like a teaspoon of milk mixed into a bowl of water, irretrievable except in contaminated or dilute form (*Erotic Innocence* 256). Memories are lost in the medium of memory. De Quincey's remembered child is irretrievable because available only in a distorting medium. The silent, solitary, encrypted, sublime cipher that is childhood can be deciphered only by a mutilating misrepresentation; the autobiography is a ruinous autopsy. As Vijay Mishra observes of the "Gothic Sublime" all representations of sublime objects of fear or desire tend towards dissolution: "Any idea that is in excess of language signifies the death of its own medium of representation, that is, of language itself" (23). De Quincey's regular representation of the beloved child is of failing representation—her steadily regressive, withdrawing movement over an expanding space; her perpetually dislimning countenance; her absorption into light. She is carried in free-floating involutes, in metaphors of infinite regress, infinite proliferations, infinite labyrinths, infinite number.

The writerly frustrations of representing and recapturing childhood in language bedevilled De Quincey throughout his career. Yet as early as in the diary he kept in adolescence, De Quincey proclaimed the "intimate connection which exists between the body and the mind" (qtd. in Lindop 98) and, in Paul Youngquist's formulation "that cognition is a material process, not just a mental one" (347). For De Quincey the body became at least as reliable a medium of expression as the mind. His campaign to grasp, articulate, and command childhood, so frustrating as a linguistic project, is also conducted on two corporeal fronts. He strives to remake himself as a surrogate Wordsworth, that master of childhood. And he seeks literally to embody himself as a child-man in a child's tiny form.

Being Wordsworth

Breaking his journey to the Lake District on August 18, 1805, three days after his twenty-first birthday, De Quincey paused at an inn just a few miles from Wordsworth's Grasmere and "jotted down a series of notes under the heading 'constituents of Happiness'" (Lindop 136). Now legally of age, De Quincey was in a position to chart his life's goals. His immediate and literal goal was this journey north, drawn by "a deep, deep magnet" [*CW* 3: 283], to satisfy his "nympholepsy," his "idolatrous" desire to visit Wordsworth, the object of his "adoration" but he shrank back—it was the second time he did so—"like a guilty thing" from actually approaching the great man's house (*Recollections* 119, 123). The larger goals were summarized in the "constituents of Happiness," which were also a journey to Wordsworth and a Wordsworthian identity. Cast in language that both forecasts and echoes *The Prelude,* that "Poem of my earlier life" of which Wordsworth had written De Quincey in 1804 but which De Quincey had not yet seen, ten of the twelve constituents set forth a Wordsworthian project "On Man, on Nature, and on Human Life / Musing in solitude . . . ," a project of reading, reflection, and the writing of a great work in a rural solitude. He will cultivate "an interest in all the concerns human life and human nature." He will settle "in some spot of natural beauty." To enjoy an "interchange of solitude and interesting society," "*Books*" will be crucial; the word is underlined as if De Quincey already knew that Wordsworth's poem of his life contained a section bearing the same title. He will enjoy in this life the same "vast predominance of contemplation" over action that Wordsworth's poetry emphasizes. And he will center his life, as has Wordsworth, on "some great intellectual project, to which all intellectual pursuits may be made tributary" (Lindop 136). To mold himself into a man who could live such a life—to live Wordsworth's life, was De Quincey's most fully articulated goal as he came of age. Wordsworth, the master poet of childhood, especially lost girls, is for De Quincey the keeper of the treasure and the lost lamp that was "lighted in paradise . . . for me" (L 101).

Before they even met, De Quincey "prefigured a connection" (Spector 502) between himself and Wordsworth as solitaries and pariahs ("Coleridge and Wordsworth, were the Pariahs of Literature in those days" [*CW* 3: 42]), and as contemplative recluses. De Quincey did not initially separate the poet from his work, but sought the same kind of solace from the man as from his poems. Indeed Wordsworth himself encouraged such an expectation. In offering to read his work in progress to De Quincey, Wordsworth implies that both his life and his work could be exemplary and useful to the young man, then himself unhappy and alienated at Oxford :

> I am now writing a Poem of my earlier life; and have just finished that part in which I speak of my residence at the University: it would give me great pleasure to read this work to you at this time. As I am sure, from the interest you have taken in the LB [*Lyrical Ballads*] that it would please you, and might also be of service to you. (qtd. in Lindop 118)

From the time the undergraduate De Quincey first began corresponding with Wordsworth in 1803 until the death of Catherine Wordsworth in 1812, De Quincey sought to make Wordsworth's life "of service" to him. It was only when the habit of Wordsworth failed that the opium habit became entrenched.[12]

That Wordsworth is a constant presence in De Quincey's work and De Quincey's consciousness is an axiom of literary history. Scholars such as Jordan, Devlin, De Luca, Tave, and Russett have emphasized to what a remarkable extent De Quincey's work and De Quincey's being are saturated with Wordsworth's language and ideas. His largest and smallest projects are Wordsworthian in conception and detail. De Quincey's autobiographical writings share with Wordsworth's a number of elements. Like Wordsworth, De Quincey is fascinated by the figure of the female waif: Wordsworth's include Margaret, Lucy, Martha Lee, the abandoned mother of "Her Eyes Are Wild," Ruth, even Emily Norton and her emblematic white doe; De Quincey's the dead Jane, the dead Elizabeth, the lost Ann, and the suffering Margaret. Just as Wordsworth habitually transforms the suffering child or woman to a "borderer," a creature immune from "human fears" who lives in an aesthetic rather than an historic realm, so De Quincey transforms his carriers of the burden of humanity into border figures (noble Ann in "the central darkness of a London brothel" [L 22] or dead-alive Kate Wordsworth haunting the "intacks") or symbolic beings such as the "Daughter of Lebanon" or "Our Ladies of Sorrow" who are at once Ann and Elizabeth and Margaret but also "mighty abstractions that incarnate themselves in all individual sufferings of man's heart" (L 149).

On a still larger scale, as Jordan and Devlin have observed, *The Prelude* is the model and inspiration of De Quincey's own autobiographical work. As Jordan has noted, both Wordsworth and De Quincey are autobiographers who emphasize childhood rather than adult experience and who limit their terrain principally to the country of the mind, Wordsworth choosing as his "haunt and main Region" the Mind of Man and De Quincey choosing "the shadowy world of Dreams" (Jordan 361). Both Wordsworth and De Quincey devote their lives to rewriting, reshaping, reinterpreting their early experiences. For both, the meaning and interest and *shaping power* of life lies in childhood experiences that are principally accessible to Wordsworth through his "spots of time" and to De Quincey through his analogous "involutes." Since these experiences are what is formative and redemptive in our lives—for Wordsworth the source of "a renovating virtue" by which "our minds are nourished and invisibly repaired" (*Prelude* 12: 211, 214-15), for De Quincey "our deepest thoughts and feelings" and "the materials of future thought or feeling" (L 104, *CW* 1: 128)—both repudiate the chronological organization of a life.

On the level of detail, Jordan has found more than two hundred allusions to Wordsworth scattered through De Quincey's works (Jordan 357); while Tave notes that the presence of quotations from Wordsworth in anonymous *Edinburgh Saturday Post* articles as "an aid to the identification of De Quincey's authorship of articles" (Tave 16). For every personal insight, De Quincey finds verification in Wordsworth. For every discussion of the attributes of childhood, Wordsworth appears as the source of wisdom. De Quincey notes Wordsworth as the expounder of axioms ("*The* child," says Wordsworth, "*is the father of the man*" [*CW* 1: 121]), as the discoverer of unknown resources ("another source of power—almost peculiar to youth and youthful circumstances—which Wordsworth also was the first person to notice" [*CW* 1: 122]), and the defender of childhood and liberty: "Ah, what avails heroic deed ? / What liberty? if no defense / Be won for feeble Innocence?" (*CW* 1: 295) No matter what the subject, De Quincey brings in passages from Wordsworth to strengthen his case: it can be an argument about war (*CW* 8: 392), about Robert Owen's New Harmony (Tave 106), or even about murder (W 284, 299). Wordsworth is pressed into service to furnish an appropriate epitaph for the hero of De Quincey's novel, the anonymously published *The Stranger's Grave,* which Lindop convincingly attributes to De Quincey. The stranger-hero consumed by grief and guilt for his incestuous love for his dead sister-wife dies in the Cumberland village of Wetheral and is memorialized in a masculinized version of "A Slumber Did My Spirit Seal." The dead De Quincey-figure, heartbroken for the love of his sister-bride, is mourned in Wordsworth's elegy for Lucy:

> No motion has he now, no force,
> He neither hears nor sees,
> Rolled round in earth's diurnal course
> With rocks and stones and trees (*SG* 271)

Even De Quincey's introductory notice to *Suspiria de Profundis* echoes Wordsworth's "Preface to *Lyrical Ballads.*" Just as Wordsworth complains of the violent and degrading overstimulation of modern life ("the increasing accumulation of men in cities . . . a craving for extraordinary incident . . . the rapid communication of intelligence" [Wordsworth, *PW* 792]), so does De Quincey complain of the "colossal pace of advance," the "hurry," and the "*dissipation*" of modern life (L 87-88). Wordsworth complains of "a state of almost savage torpor" that possesses the modern mind, De Quincey of "a reagency of fleshly torpor" (L 88).

De Quincey possessed himself of Wordsworth's poetry remarkably—certainly through impressive feats of memorization, probably through a feat of appropriation as well. If, as De Quincey told Emerson in 1848, he indeed "once possessed a manuscript copy" of the unpublished *Prelude* (Lindop 187), the poem could only have come into his hands as an unauthorized copy made of the manuscript version Wordsworth allowed him to read in 1810 or 1811 (Lindop 187). He had read the 1805 *Prelude* in manuscript shortly after first moving to Grasmere, probably in 1810 or

1811. In an 1839 article for *Tait's*—at a distance of almost thirty years—he was able to quote twenty-five lines from the poem with astonishing accuracy. Even the vocabulary of his prose is profoundly Wordsworthian. A single sentence from an essay on Coleridge reads like pastiche of Wordsworthian blank verse:

> Phantoms of lost power, sudden intuitions, and shadowy restorations of forgotten feelings, sometimes dim and perplexing, sometimes by bright but furtive glimpses, sometimes by a full and steady revelation, overcharged with light,—throw us back in a moment upon scenes and remembrances that we have left full thirty years behind us. (*Recollections* 92)

The echoes of Wordsworth's *Prelude* are striking: not "phantoms of lost power" but "hiding places of my power" (1805 *Prelude* 11: 336); not shadowy restorations of forgotten feelings" but "future restorations"; not "bright but furtive glances" but "see by glimpses now" (1805 *Prelude* 11: 337, 438); not "sometimes dim and perplexing" but "shadowy recollections / Which be they what they may" (Wordsworth, "Ode: Intimations of Immortality" ll. 150-51); not "throw us back in a moment . . . but "lovely forms / And sweet sensations that throw back our life, / And almost make our infancy itself / A visible scene on which the sun is shining" (1805 *Prelude* 1: 660-63).

De Quincey claims to have idolized Wordsworth from boyhood. Indeed he prided himself not only as one of the youngest but as one of the poet's earliest admirers. He was only fourteen when he read and intensely admired "We are Seven." "In 1799 I had become acquainted with 'We are Seven' at Bath. In the winter of 1801-2 I had read the whole of 'Ruth'; early in 1803 I had written to Wordsworth. In May of 1803 I had received a very long answer from Wordsworth" (*CW* 3: 302). De Quincey claimed he "only in all Europe" was "really quoting from Wordsworth" as early as 1802 (*CW* 3: 301-2). He further claimed that his appreciation for Wordsworth at Oxford put him in "one position in advance of my age by full thirty years" (*Recollections* 116).

In the diary De Quincey kept at seventeen he included a list of the twelve greatest poets of all time.

Edmund Spenser;
William Shakespeare;
John Milton;
James Thomson;
William Collins;

Thomas Chatterton;
James Beattie;
Robert Burns
William Penrose
Robert Southey;
S. T. Coleridge;
William Wordsworth!!! (exclamations De Quincey's)

The incongruous and overmatched Penrose, eventually expunged from the list, was a neighborhood poet whose Christian name, despite De Quincey's significant error, was Thomas (as in De Quincey), not William (as in Wordsworth). Shortly after composing the list, De Quincey sent an adulatory letter to Wordsworth in which he dedicated himself heart and soul to the great poet. Here and in a second letter written in response to Wordsworth's unusually cordial reply, De Quincey set forth his rapturous homage for *Lyrical Ballads,* which he identified as the greatest poetry of all time, or certainly as the poetry he most admired: ". . . I may say . . . without the smallest exaggeration, that the whole aggregate of pleasure I have received from some eight or nine other poets that I have been able to find since the world began—falls infinitely short of what those two enchanting volumes have singly afforded me" (Jordan 30). He would give all his fortune to preserve them: "I feel that, from the wreck of all earthly things which belong to me, I should endeavour to save that work by an impulse second to none but that of self-preservation" (Jordan 33-34). "Earnestly and humbly" suing for Wordsworth's friendship, De Quincey expresses his "admiration for your mental excellence," his "reverential love for your moral character" and already "bends the knee before you" and yearns to "lowly and suppliantly prostrate myself" and especially "to sacrifice even [my] life—whenever it could have a chance of promoting your interest and happiness" (Jordan 31). When the pleased Wordsworth invited De Quincey for a visit, the young man responded: "I believe that the bowers of paradise could hold out no such allurement" (Jordan 34).

Years later De Quincey described his admiration for Wordsworth, as "literally in no respect short of a religious feeling" (*CW* 3: 41). Before even meeting Wordsworth, De Quincey felt a holy dread of the idol and of his holy name. According to biographer Horace Eaton, De Quincey "could not even bring himself to mention [Wordsworth's] name in Oxford, for fear of having to encounter ridiculous observations or jeering abuse of his favorite . . ." (Eaton 113). "I have felt more than once that I can hear other poems [than the *Lyrical Ballads*] talked of by worldly men without such exquisite torture," but to hear Wordsworth's discussed was a profanation (Jordan 33). Indeed Charles Lamb was so amused by young De Quincey's adulation of Wordsworth and Coleridge, that he initiated a conversation about the two poets with the words: "If you please, sir, we'll say grace before we begin" (*CW* 3: 43). The same dread that inhibited De Quincey from hearing Wordsworth's name spoken in levity kept him from the Lake District and the company of Wordsworth. Though De Quincey found the thought of the Cumberland landscape rich with "secret fascination, subtle, sweet, fantastic . . . spiritually strong" (*CW* 3: 382), though he had dreamed as a run-away schoolboy in London to take "the road to the North, and therefore to _____, and if I had the wings of a dove, *that* way would I fly for comfort" (L 35), he found it difficult to face his idol. Though he twice came to the Lake District, "expressly for the purpose of paying my respects to Wordsworth," he dared not face him. "But the very image of Wordsworth, as I prefigured it to my own planet-struck eye, crushed my faculties as before Elijah or St. Paul." After catching one glimpse of Dove Cottage from afar, "I retreated like a guilty thing for fear I might be surprised by Wordsworth, and then returned faint-heartedly to Coniston, and so to Oxford, *re infecta* [without having done the thing]" (*Recollections* 122-23).

Regarding Wordsworth with the holy dread to be accorded to a divinity, De Quincey eventually served as this deity's acolyte for the years from their first encounter until after the death of Kate Wordsworth. His status as minor ministrant meant that Wordsworth never really took little Mr. De Quincey seriously as a possible friend and equal. De Quincey rationalizes his subjugation by commenting on Wordsworth's general want of friends: "He seemed to me too much like his own Pedlar in the 'Excursion,' a man so diffused amongst innumerable objects of equal attraction that he had no cells left in his heart for strong individual attachments . . . He told me so himself . . . that married people rarely retain much capacity for friendship" (*Recollections* 379). But Little Mr. De Quincey, so young and so small and so deferential, was even less an equal than others. Often Wordsworth "did not even appear to listen; but as if what [other people, especially De Quincey] said on such a theme must be childish prattle, turned away with an air of perfect indifference." The blind indifference of Wordsworth to De Quincey's qualities was intensely painful to him as on the occasion when Wordsworth refused to give some news of Charles Lloyd to Southey in De Quincey's presence because it "was a matter of some delicacy, and not quite proper to be communicated except to *near friends of the family*" (*Recollections*

320). In fact it was De Quincey who held himself the true friend of the Lloyds, while Wordsworth was a much-resented acquaintance.

But though De Quincey could not become Wordsworth's intimate, he did his best to become his surrogate and servile self. De Quincey instead took on more and more responsibilities as Wordsworth's surrogate. He likened himself to his idol by performing some of the deity's possible roles. He acted as Wordsworth's representative in London, taking on the thankless task of readying Wordsworth's "Convention of Cintra" pamphlet for the press. He was assiduous in his attentions to Mary, Dorothy and the children, especially Johnny and Catherine. He became Mary's and Dorothy's regular correspondent when away. His letters back to the family—some neatly printed so that the children, especially Johnny, who could not read cursive script, might themselves read the letters—are full of schemes for their welfare and their entertainment: how would the children like a pony; what would they think of having a special carriage—De Quincey had just seen one in Hyde Park—capable of holding six children yet so well balanced that one very small child could pull it; how would they like to learn to swim, to walk on stilts, to fly a kite, to build and sail their own boat? (Jordan 240, 128, 254) De Quincey arranged for the local carpenter to build the young Wordsworths a replica of the Hyde Park wagon and he seriously entertained the idea of establishing a commercial printing press in Grasmere, partly to print Wordsworth's poetry on the spot, but mostly to help Johnny Wordsworth learn to read. Johnny Wordsworth was slow in learning to read and De Quincey quite plausibly considered that the child might be inspired to learn by the delectable prospect of helping in typesetting. One of De Quincey's most engaging letters to Johnny details his encounter at a London print shop with "a boy sitting with a book that is about as big as you (only he is a little older than you, for I asked him how old he was; and he told me seven years old)." Recognizing that Johnny would be relieved that this child reader was *older* than he, De Quincey goes on to expound the connection between the task of reading and the privilege of printing:

> [One] day I said—"Well, Edward, you read very well for a boy that is only seven years old" (Edward is his name)—"I suppose you will soon begin to be a printer"—Edward only laughed; but Mr. Overseer, who heard what I had said to him told me—oh! yes! that he should make a printer of him *directly*. "Well, but Mr. Overseer," I said, "'how can that be?—It will take as long to learn how to print as to learn how to read; and Edward has been

more than a year learning how to read;—so he will be a year at least learning how to print;—and then that won't be *directly.*" Then Mr. Overseer said—"Oh no! it won't take a year—or half a year—or a quarter of a year—or anything like it;—it won't take more than 2 or 3 days to learn how to print." . . . So, as soon as ever you can read, then you will have no more trouble but a very little; and you may be a printer directly. (Jordan 126-27)

De Quincey here shows a delicate understanding for Johnny's feelings. He knows the boy feels self-conscious at being a late reader; Johnny must have been aware of his unsatisfactory progress since his father a few years later had no reservations about writing disparagingly to a stranger about him and his siblings: "As to their intellectual Powers they are none of them remarkable except the eldest [Johnny], who is lamentably slow. This is to me a mortification . . ." (*WLMY* pt. 2, 3: 8). But De Quincey soothes that pain by telling of a boy who, though an excellent reader (impressively so for *only* seven), is a full year older than Johnny. Further De Quincey disarms Johnny's possible discouragement at the prospect of as protracted an agony spent learning to be a printer as he has spent learning to be a reader; he tells the boy—on the authority of "Mr Overseer" himself—that a mere two or three days, a mere instant is required to be comfortable and competent. De Quincey's insight here reveals an adult who remembers perfectly a child's anxieties and a child's sense of the unending stretches of time. It is not surprising that Dorothy Wordsworth reported Johnny Wordsworth to be "passionately fond" of Mr. De Quincey (Lindop 163).

Not only was De Quincey vastly more attuned to Johnny's learning difficulties than his father, he was vastly more loving to the youngest Wordsworth girl, Kate, "noways a favourite" with her father (*Recollections* 371). His devotion was so intense that neighborhood gossip named De Quincey as the girl's father. De Quincey found her liveliness, her "witchery," her "radiant spirit of joyousness" (*Recollections* 371-72) so irresistible that he insisted that Catherine "is to be taught by nobody but *me*":

this promise Mrs. Wordsworth once made me; and therefore I shall think it an act of the highest perfidy, if anybody should attempt to insinuate any learning into Catherine—or to hint at primers—to the prejudice of my exclusive privilege. (Jordan 185)

Catherine and her "Kinsey" (Jordan 269) doted on one another, he with a "love most frantic." When the Wordsworths moved to a larger house at Allan Bank, De Quincey moved into the newly vacated cottage. In Wordsworth's house, in Wordsworth's landscape, with Wordsworth's womenfolk as his confidantes, and with Wordsworth's daughter as his daytime and nighttime companion, De Quincey lived for a while in the security of Wordsworth's life of protected solitude.

What so drew De Quincey? De Quincey's enthusiasm for *Lyrical Ballads* was extreme, even excessive. That De Quincey proclaimed the volume superior to the entire cavalcade of world poetry suggests that it spoke powerfully to his condition. The first poems of Wordsworth for which De Quincey expressed admiration—and he quotes them regularly throughout his life—are those he read at the ages of fourteen and sixteen, "We are Seven" and "Ruth." De Quincey records the "deep impression made on me" by "We are Seven," seen in manuscript at fourteen (Jordan 36-37). In the revised *Confessions* he recalls "read[ing]" in the clouds of North Wales "the very scene which six months before I had read in a most exquisite poem of Wordsworth's ["Ruth"] . . ." (*CW* 3: 301). De Quincey had been so struck by "Ruth" when it had appeared in a London newspaper that he had committed it to memory. These are the two texts from which the later admiration of Wordsworth is developed. De Quincey's first extended commentary on "We Are Seven" is a testimonial to its moral efficacy. He describes reading the poem at fourteen and then falling into a worldly, passionate state of mind. Seeking "for some guide to might assist and develop" his escape from worldliness, he remembers "We are Seven," looks to Wordsworth, and is "delivered" (Jordan 37). Later discussions of "We are Seven" treat it both in the usual Romantic manner as "a profound fact in the abysses of human nature—viz. that the mind of an infant cannot admit the idea of death" and in De Quincey's more personal manner as exemplifying the principle of creative antagonism: De Quincey construes "Ruth" as a sister's poem tied to Dorothy Wordsworth:

> A happier life, by far, was [Dorothy Wordsworth's] in youth, coming, as near of difference of scenery and difference of relations would permit, to that which was promised to Ruth—the Ruth of her brother's creation—by the youth who came from Georgia's shore; for, though not upon American savannahs, or Canadian lakes—
> > With all their fairy crowds
> > Of islands, that together lie
> > As quietly as spots of sky
> > Amongst the evening clouds—
> yet—amongst the loveliest scenes of sylvan England, and (at intervals) of sylvan Germany—amongst lakes, too, far better fitted to give the *sense* of their own character than the inland seas of America, and amongst mountains as romantic and loftier than many of the chief ranges in that country—her

times fleeted away like some golden age, or like the life of primeval man; and she, like Ruth, was for years allowed

> To run, though *not* a bride,
> A sylvan huntress, by the side

of him to whom, like Ruth, she had dedicated her days; and to whose children, afterwards, she dedicated a love like that of mothers. Dear Miss Wordsworth! (*Recollections* 198-99)

These two lyrics epitomize the theme in Wordsworth's work most important to De Quincey: solitary sisters-beloveds transmuted by nature into beings of lasting dignity and beauty or, in Russett's formulation, into an "appearance of intransigent and creaturely victimage" ("Wordsworth's Gothic Interpreter" 357). The protagonists, bereft young sisters, are De Quincey's own favorite second-self. The child of "We are Seven"—sister to the absent six—is eight years old, the age of Elizabeth when she died. Ruth, left "half-desolate" at six—De Quincey's age when his sister died—is in childhood a "slighted" and solitary child ("alone she seemed to live") as De Quincey had been himself; she ends in young womanhood as a crazed and childlike pariah. The experiences of the two children in "We are Seven" and "Ruth" are the very afflictions of De Quincey's own childhood: the deaths of siblings, the death of a parent, the emotional abandonment by the other parent ("a slighted child"), a solitary childhood, desertion by a trusted person ("the Youth / Deserted his poor Bride, and Ruth could never find him more"), and escape from constraint into a pariah's life of hunger and hardship ("She sleeps beneath the greenwood tree, / And other home hath none").

If these poems are uncanny renditions of the afflictions of childhood, they are also works of comfort. The little sister's comfort in her siblings' graves, which she cites confidently as proof of their continuity ("their graves are green, they may be seen"; "upon their graves I sit . . . and sing a song to them") bespeaks the same frame of mind that sees the grave as "the portal through which it may recover some heavenly countenance" (*PW* 1: 13). The principle of comfort here is that which will animate *Suspiria De Profundis,* that is, the principle of antagonism. Opposites engender each other. Just as "misery is a guarantee of truth too substantial to be refused" (*CW* 1: 56), so the consideration of death gives rise to the consideration of life, the consideration of childhood suffering to the consideration of childhood glory. Indeed De Quincey especially praises Wordsworth for his evocation of antithetical qualities by presentation of their opposites, showing skill at depicting the "reciprocal entanglement of darkness in light, and of light in darkness" (*CW* 11: 303), of his suggestion of saving presence in the seeming emptiness of "the breathless, mysterious Pan-like silence that haunts the noon-day" (*PW* 1: 15). In "We are Seven" the authority of the poet clearly supports the child against all numerical odds; while in "Ruth" there is a yet more striking transvaluation of desolation as Wordsworth transforms Ruth's misery to a form of triumph. Abandonment becomes beauty. In her earliest desolation she transforms herself into a solitary artist with her freedom, her bower, her living thoughts, her autonomy, "herself her own delight."

De Quincey sees in the poems what he reinscribes in his own life: the affliction of childhood, the solitude of childhood and the principle of *antagonistic knowing,* the generation of hope out of despair, the inference of presence from absence, of all ("the noonday Pan" [*CW* 11: 302]) from nothing ("the dead silence" [*PW* 1: 14]). "We Are Seven" and "Ruth" show Wordsworth transforming to art and to power the bereavement and solitude by which De Quincey was afflicted. By his insight into affliction, solitude, and sisterhood, Wordsworth must have seemed to De Quincey a second self, one who understood the experiences closest to him and who could build structures of comfort to contain and order those experiences. His idolatry of Wordsworth was a quest for self-preservation, a seeking for a way to endure and to use the memory of his childhood pain. By reading himself into Wordsworth's poems, De Quincey found—for a while—the immense comfort, lacking since Elizabeth's death, of being understood, "the relief of sympathy, that heals for a season all distresses" (L 136).

The mixture of attraction to and repulsion from Wordsworth, the mixture of love and fear, suggests that De Quincey both hoped and dreaded something that Wordsworth might give. There is a curious anecdote among De Quincey's hero-worshiping memorabilia of Wordsworth. In a fine edition of *Paradise Lost* De Quincey describes finding an engraving of the portrait of Milton reputed to be the most faithful of all likenesses: "Judge of my astonishment when in this portrait of Milton, I saw a likeness nearly perfect of Wordsworth, better by much than any which I have since seen, of those expressly painted for himself" (*Recollections* 140-41). Milton's picture looks more like Wordsworth than Wordsworth's pictures do. The image of Milton is the truest image of Wordsworth. As Wordsworth became Wordsworth by being Milton, might not De Quincey become De Quincey by being Wordsworth?[13] For the young De Quincey, Wordsworth was a double, a clearer image of his own identity than his own self-consciousness furnished. De Quincey's concept of "the dark interpreter" posits that anguish generates the power to create extra selves, "shadowy projections, *umbras* and *penumbras*, which the unsearchable depths of man's nature is capable, under adequate excitement, of throwing off..." (W 189).[14] As Karl Miller has shown the preoccupation with the duality of the self is a chronic period concern that touched virtually all Romantic writers. Concerned throughout his work with the nature of self-division (Maniquis 58) but also with the character of the authentic self, De Quincey seems to have superimposed on the figure of an exalted, improved De Quincey. Yet such a generation further destabilized De Quincey's identify by problematizing his selfhood, his work, his identity. Certainly the rapture, the guilt and the fear, the "nympholepsy," he felt toward Wordsworth (*Recollections* 119), suggest De Quincey's ambivalence toward this figure. As the god of De Quincey's idolatry who took so much devotion from his worshipper, as the confirming echo of De Quincey's lament for the lost girl, Wordsworth may sometimes have appeared as much De Quincey's creator as his master. The anxiety about the relationship is manifested in the dread admiration. Along with admiration for Wordsworth is his fear of Wordsworth as the potential devourer of De Quincey's selfhood. The fear is expressed ironically in De Quincey's wry account of Wordsworth's luck. Even his modest competency in the form of convenient legacies came virtually unsought with such magical convenience to Wordsworth much as De Quincey himself furnished books, aid, financial resources. De Quincey quips that he considered it very dangerous to be a person in possession of something Wordsworth might someday need. All the original owners of his legacies had been so conveniently dispatched by the goddess of Wordsworth's fortune that "had I happened to know of any peculiar adaption in an estate or office of mine, to an existing need of Wordsworth's—forthwith, and with the speed of a man running for his life, I would have laid it down at his feet. 'Take it,' I would have said—'Take it—or in three weeks I shall be a dead man'" (*Recollections* 197).

The ambivalence is also shadowed allegorically in the odd couple that appears in De Quincey's recapitulation of Aladdin. Here the usual autobiographical pair of adult/child, code-breaker/code is embodied in the pursuing Arabian Nights Magician and the fleeing Child, a paranoid couple who also model the Wordsworth/De Quincey relation.[15] The story functions as an enactment of self-justifying ressentiment by De Quincey-Aladdin against Wordsworth-Magician, the power who discovers and uses childhood. "Infant Literature" introduces the Aladdin narrative with a quotation from Wordsworth: "'The child,' says Wordsworth, '*is father of the man,*'" which establishes Wordsworth as the great talent-spotter of childhood, "the first person to notice" childhood has a privileged state on its "distinct peninsula"; the first to notice that childhood "is endowed with a special power of listening for the tones of truth" (1: 121-22). The literal talent-scout of Aladdin is the African Magician, a master "of all the mighty world / Of eye, and ear" Wordsworth described in "Tintern Abbey." The mage is endowed with this "special power of listening," a power of auditory divination. Sunk in the depths of Africa, 8,000 miles from Baghdad, he "applies his ear to the earth to distinguish the peculiar steps of Aladdin" walking the streets of Baghdad. So too on one memorable night in Fall 1808 on Denmail Rise during the Peninsular War did De Quincey watch Wordsworth "applying his ear to the ground so as to catch any sound of wheels that might be groaning along at a distance" with the news from the rim of Europe (*Recollections* 160). As Aladdin to the all-hearing Magician, so De Quincey to Wordsworth.

Just as Aladdin and the Magician seek the same hidden treasure, so De Quincey and Wordsworth seek the same elusive constituents of happiness, the same beloved sisters. Through the Aladdin figuration, De Quincey suggests the symbiosis of the figures who need each other. Neither can obtain the treasure without the help of the other. Wordsworth is the magician whose divination makes De Quincey conscious of the treasure he desires, for which he feels a prefigured affinity, a "peculiar destiny written in his constitution." Wordsworth is the authoritative discoverer of the life-treasures De Quincey most desired:

> he has possessed, in combination, all the conditions for their most perfect culture—the leisure, the ease, the solitude, the society, the domestic peace, the local scenery—Paradise for his eye, in Miltonic beauty, lying outside his windows, Paradise for his heart, in the perpetual happiness of his own fireside . . . (*Recollections* 195)

These were goods that De Quincey himself by "a peculiar destiny written in his constitution" and as wish list written in the "Constituents of Happiness" also desired. The sense of symbiosis was so powerful that De Quincey seems not to be able to distinguish what was innately "written on his constitution" and what had been written there by Wordsworth: where was the origin? Had he invented Wordsworth? Had Wordsworth invented De Quincey? As Russett notes of the psychological transaction enacted in De Quincey's early letter to Wordsworth: "it seems impossible to say whether De Quincey is correcting Wordsworth, or Wordsworth is correcting De Quincey, or whether indeed both identities have dissolved into merely characteristic textual effects" ("Wordsworth's Gothic Interpreter" 360). The

Aladdin fantasy suggests De Quincey's fear of Wordsworth's revenge—foreshadowed in the tale of "noble revenge"—for De Quincey's appropriation of his treasure: the treasure of his choice of life, the treasure of his intellectual property, and even the treasure of his daughter. De Quincey's anxious flight from Wordsworth-enchanter may signal his guilt at his actual appropriation of the unauthorized copy of *The Prelude;* or it may suggest that De Quincey's appropriation of the love of Kate Wordsworth, that light of his life, felt like an unauthorized seizure of a "new lamp for old" to replace that other "lamp lighted in paradise . . . for me" (L 101). It is at the very least a recognition that becoming De Quincey the writer of childhood reclamation meant constituting a Wordsworthian identity through both self-recognition and theft.

Being Little

If De Quincey's Wordsworthian identity was stolen, his little, wizened, "base, crazy, despicable, human system," his "crazy body" (*CW* 3: 467, 472) was irreducibly his own. It was also his most reliable and enduring stake in the childhood he sought to recapture and his visible resemblance to the children he sought to befriend.

For De Quincey loved children and was never so much his best self when among them. To become that self, assuming as much as possible the demeanor, the appearance and—through self-starvation—the size of a child is the crowning act of the self-mutilating project to open up the vile body and to scrape down through the *dura mater,* however cruelly, to reach the palimpsest child self.

In a neurasthenic life of mental and physical woes, making children happy was for De Quincey the single unalloyed pleasure. He himself was never so happy as when he was with children, making them happy. Thus "good" with children because happy with children. De Quincey often preferred their company to that of adults. In the diary De Quincey kept as a boy of seventeen, he several times mentions one "little William K. Williams," a small child "whom I ride on my shoulders" (*Diary* 183, 193). At twenty-three, in 1808, De Quincey began his long friendship with the Wordsworth family. Though it was William Wordsworth's poetry that drew De Quincey to Grasmere, it was his passionate friendship with the Wordsworth children that made his years there sweetest. Fond of all the children in the Wordsworth-Coleridge circle, especially Johnny and Catherine Wordsworth and Derwent Coleridge, De Quincey devoted time, energy, and imagination to pleasing and teasing and teaching them.

When Catherine died in 1812 at the age of three, De Quincey's grief was almost past bearing. He slept every night for months on her grave, hallucinated her specter, and fell prey to severe physical distress and psychological anguish that drove him into full-scale opium addiction (Lindop 202). Though De Quincey never gave his heart quite so passionately to any child again, he was a doting, if not judicious, parent to his own eight children. William, his eldest child and a brilliant boy was, De Quincey wrote, "the crown and glory of my life" (Lindop 320). A fine classical scholar, William was tutored by his father; "upon him I had exhausted all that care and hourly companionship could do to the culture of an intellect, in all stages of his life, somewhat premature" (Eaton 363). But William died terribly at eighteen in 1835 of granulocytic sarcoma, a then untreatable and undiagnosable malignancy that first deafened and then blinded him.[16] De Quincey believed William to have died of hydrocephalus, the same disease that had killed his sister Elizabeth forty-four years earlier. To his other seven children, De Quincey devoted less systematic intellectual training, but always displayed an affection that partly compensated for his habitual carelessness about the details of their physical well-being. He was especially tender with his daughters. His second daughter and fifth child Florence who grew to consciousness during the years when De Quincey's financial and psychological miseries were at their height, nevertheless remembered her father chiefly for his "love of children and power of winning their confidence." A restless sleeper as a toddler, she regularly enjoyed the dignity and delight of "sitting up with papa" who petted her and soothed her and comforted her with "coffee well loaded with sugar" and an unending stack of books with pages to cut and pictures to look at. As a middle-age woman Florence Baird Smith looked back on the years when she was her father's "constant and almost only companion, and . . . never so happy as with him," for he was always gentle, always tender (Page 278):

> One of my memories of him in bright summer mornings was his capturing my baby sister, fresh from her bath . . . and dancing her about the garden; the child, with its scanty white raiment and golden head, looking like a butterfly glowing among the trees. (Page 279)

De Quincey cultivated a childlike demeanor. His manners were strikingly childlike. All his life he retained the gentleness, carelessness, and even helplessness of extreme youth. Even the smallest children spoke to him as to an equal. Late in his life he befriended the four-year-old nephew of one of his servants. They walked daily in the garden where, one day, the child asked De Quincey "What d'ya ca' thon tree?" To which De Quincey earnest replied, "I am not sure, my dear, but I think it may be a *Lauristinus.*" But the child broke in, scornfully, "A *Lauristinus!* Lad, d'ye no ken a *rhododendron?*" (Page 279) Around the same time, De Quincey returned home from an evening party soaked to the skin. He had walked miles in the rain "because he could not find money to ride; he had met two street girls; one of these took his eight shillings out of his waistcoat pocket, and the other his umbrella. He told this sad story with utmost simplicity, as if he had been a child of seven, instead of seventy" (Eaton 452).

At some level De Quincey seems consciously to have chosen to play the child all his life, even to a childlike carelessness about money and possessions. The moral Southey wished that "he would not leave his greatcoat always behind him on the road" (Lindop 163), while his creditors had more serious reasons to complain of his inability to keep his debts straight. Though De Quincey wrote prolifically and lucidly on economic theory, he was incapable of managing household accounts and exercised not even the most elementary caution in paying and receiving payment. He displayed a child's incapacity to manage the practical affairs of life. Once at the age of forty De Quincey was a house guest in the home of Charles Knight who stopped by his bedroom to say good night. It was a cold evening, but De Quincey was sitting stripped to the waist. "Where is your shirt?" "I have not a shirt—my shirts are unwashed." "But why not tell the servant to send them to the laundress?" "Ah! how could I presume to do that in Mrs. Knight's absence?" (Page 190) Here is a well-brought up child who is too well-bred to wear a dirty shirt, too helpless to wash a shirt, and too timid to ask for help. De Quincey's first encounter with a tap of running water manifests his characteristic passivity, his tendency "to revert to a child-role" (Lindop 390). Left with a fellow guest to wash up in a room where the water tap had been turned on by the host, De Quincey stood by in "paralysed perplexity" lest "the basin should overflow and deluge the room." Making the "most amusing comparisons of himself to the hero of the German story *Undine,* overwhelmed by waters which he had conjured up but could not control" (Eaton 454), he failed to turn off the taps. In his later years, De Quincey emphasized his childlike demeanor by dressing in "a boy's duffel great-coat, very threadbare, with a hole in it . . ." Acquaintances likened him to a "street boy" (Lindop 365). Even his daughter Emily spoke of him in his last illness as "a delightful but naughty, wayward child that wanted a whipping at times, but always sweet and tender" (Eaton 507). Indeed, Grevel Lindop has argued that De Quincey "half-consciously adopted the role of a child" as soon as his conscientious and maternal daughters were old enough to manage the household. "It had been with reluctance that he had first undertaken adult responsibilities, and now that his children were grown up he retreated to become once more the baby of the family" (Lindop 365).

If the role of a child was attractive to De Quincey, it was also easy for him to play because he was a notably small man. Childlikeness remained a physically accessible disguise all his life. Even at fifteen he was conscious that his size linked him to much younger children as, for example, his later travelling companion the ten-year-old Lord Westport whom he noted was "a very nice boy, about my size" (Page 1: 37). "The dwarf opium eater," as Carlyle spitefully called him (Carlyle 1: 263), "one of the smallest men you ever in your life beheld. . . . Poor little fellow!" (Tave 6-7). Very thin, short, with a large head (Lindop 366), he seems to have made people more than a little uncomfortable by his appearance. Indeed he himself claimed to despise his own body: "I hate it," he wrote and even proposed that his "worthless . . . base, crazy, despicable human system" be dissected by the "gentlemen of Surgeons' Hall" like the cadavers of "the worst malefactors" (*CW* 3: 472, 467, 472). Among his constituents of happiness, the last and most wistful, is

> one which, not being within the range of any man's control, I should not mention, only that experience has read me a painful lesson on its value—a personal appearance tolerably respectable. I do not say attractive . . . but so far not repulsive, *and on level with the persons of men in general*. . . . (Page 77, italics mine)

He was too short, however, to reach to that level. Accounts of his height differ slightly, but only among degrees of smallness. His Edinburgh acquaintance Findlay called him "a very little man (about 5 feet 3 or 4 inches)" (Eaton 441). The Carlyles reduced even this figure, Thomas claiming he was "hardly five feet in all" and Jane likening him to a pet homunculus: "What would one give to have him in a box, and take him out to talk" (Lindop 288). The vituperative attack on De Quincey as one of the "Humbugs of the Age" by William Maginn in the *John Bull Magazine and Literary Recorder* depicts him as a foetal grotesque with a huge head and a tiny body:

> Conceive an animal about five feet high, propped on two trap-sticks, which have the size but not the delicate proportion of rolling pins, with a comical

sort of indescribable body, and a head of most portentous magnitude, which puts one in mind of the queer big-headed caricatures that you see occasionally from whimsical pencils. (qtd. in Lindop 270)

Even less splenetic observers than Maginn seemed to have been troubled, indeed irritated, by his size. Lamb sneers at "the animalcule" and Dora Wordsworth at the "little Monster" (Lindop 220, 315). At best, there is a note of condescension in Coleridge's kinder description of De Quincey as a "very short & boyish-looking modest man" (Lindop 166), while there is something close to disquiet in Dorothy Wordsworth's description: "His person is *unfortunately* diminutive, *but* there is a sweetness in his looks ... which soon overcomes the *oddness* of your first feeling at the sight of *so very little* a Man" (Lindop 163, italics mine). Southey's comment indeed hints a *moral* disapproval of De Quincey's size as if he were somehow short on purpose, as if his height were just another of his careless habits: "Little Mr. De Quincey is at Grasmere. ... I wish he was not so little, and I wish he would not leave his greatcoat always behind him ..." (Lindop 163).

"I wish he was not so little, and I wish he" was not so careless with his clothes. De Quincey's acquaintances found something *willful* in the childlike, even foetal, appearance that disquieted them. Further, the insistence on De Quincey's size is in itself peculiar. Though Keats was very short, his acquaintances were not forever *complaining* about his size. It is clear that De Quincey willed his literary preoccupation with his childhood past, his childlike manners, and his passionate friendships with children. Could De Quincey whose literary purpose as autobiographer was the reconstitution of the Eden of Childhood also have willed his little body? Could his childlike physique be as much a construction of his will as his childhood autobiographies? Could he have *made* his body *childlike?*

There is some evidence that De Quincey suffered for much of his life from anorexia nervosa and thus may have stunted his growth by self-induced starvation at crucial periods during childhood. De Quincey was the frailest and probably the smallest of his brothers. The accounts both of William—who was vigorously fond of boxing, fighting, swinging, and horseback-riding (all of which frightened young Thomas) and of "Pink"—who ran away to sea, withstood the rigors of captivity by pirates, and had "loud, unrepressed" manners (*CW* 3: 59)—indicate that they had a good deal more physical energy and stamina than Thomas. This suggests, though it does not prove, that they were larger and heavier than he. About the sizes of De Quincey's parents and other siblings I have been able to find no relevant information.[17] At least two of his children, however, are known to have been substantially larger than he. This is hardly surprising since his wife Margaret, "taller and larger than he" (Lindop 206) was described by Dorothy Wordsworth as a blooming English rose, a strapping woman capable of carrying her diminutive husband. His eldest child William was observed at eighteen as "much taller than most young men of the same age" (Balfour 319). His daughter Emily, youngest of his eight children, wrote of her father's weakness during his last illness and of her strength that was enough to "lift him in my arms like a child and carry him to the armchair and he told the doctor I was a 'female Hercules.' He did not know how light he was" (Eaton 507n). Even assuming that the five-foot De Quincey weighed no more than seventy or eighty pounds in his wasted last days, it would still require more strength than most five-foot women could muster to carry such a weight. It seems reasonable to assume that Emily was substantially larger than her father.

The evidence and suppositions about family size are not conclusive, but they do suggest that the De Quincey *family* was not especially small and that De Quincey's own smallness may not have been genetically determined but induced by some external cause such as poor nutrition. It is known that poor nutrition was characteristic of De Quincey's adulthood: "I have in the course of my misfortunes fasted for thirty years" (Lindop 364). De Quincey seems to have been a man with an equivocal attitude toward food, a simultaneous interest and aversion. The adult De Quincey was an austere but particular eater who subsisted on soup, coffee, and laudanum (Page 1: 360). Because he was troubled for years by stomach pains and had lost his teeth early, in middle life "bread in soup or tripe was all the nourishment he could take" (Eaton 457). Though he ate little, he was nonetheless very conscious of that little. As a house guest in John Wilson's home, De Quincey proved to be very fussy in his asceticism:

> For example, he rarely appeared at the family meals, preferring to dine in his own room at his own hour, not infrequently turning night into day. His tastes were very simple, though a little troublesome; at least to the servant who prepared his repast. Coffee, boiled rice and milk, and a piece of mutton from the loin, were the materials that invariably formed his diet. The cook, who had an audience with him daily, received her instructions in silent awe, quite overpowered by his manner; for, had he been addressing a duchess, he could scarcely have spoken with more deference. He would couch his request in such terms as these:—"Owing to dyspepsia afflicting my system, and the possibility of any additional disarrangement of the stomach taking place, consequences incalculable distressing would arise, so much so indeed as to increase nervous irritation, and prevent me from attending to matters of

overwhelming importance, if you do not remember to cut the mutton in a diagonal rather than a longitudinal form." The cook—a Scotchwoman—had great reverence of Mr. De Quincey as a man of genius; but after one of these interviews, her patience was pretty well exhausted, and she would say, "Weel, I never heard the like o' that in a' my days; the bodie has an awfu' sicht o' words. If it had been my ain maister that was wanting his dinner, he would ha' ordered a hale tablefu' wi' little mair than a waff o' his haun, and here's a' this claver aboot a bit mutton nae bigger than a prin" [pin] (Eaton 325).[18]

Solitary eating and elaborate attention to minute portions of particular foods are characteristic of anorexia (Bruch 9). So too is the habitual "denial of hunger" along with the consciously cultivated "inability to recognize nutritional needs" (Emmett 22). His friend Hogg blamed De Quincey's habitual stomach aches on his sparse diet and told of one occasion when Wilson responded to De Quincey's complaints of "rats gnawing in his stomach" by ordering up some soup and forcing him to swallow it. "The gnawing disappeared; and we heard no more of the creature in the stomach'" (Eaton 457). The inability to recognize as hunger what were evidently hunger pangs is characteristic of the anorectic patient who usually trains herself (or, more rarely, himself) to ignore hunger or reinterpret it as "pleasant and desirable" (Bruch 4). De Quincey's perpetual feeling of cold is also a characteristic accompaniment of self-starvation. Though Youngquist plausibly ties De Quincey's abstinence to his wish to mitigate the horrible constipation induced by opium, the self-starvation evidently preceded the addiction. Austerity at table goes back to De Quincey's youth, certainly to the period of enforced starvation in Wales and London recounted in the *Confessions* and possibly even earlier. He maintained in fact that "the extremities of hunger suffered in my boyish days" produced the "derangement of the stomach" (W 28) from which came all his later troubles, especially his opium habit. The diary he kept at Everton in 1803 shortly after he returned from his travels in Wales and London opens with a meditation on the "intimate connection which exists between the body and the mind" (*Diary* 141) and then records among his social activities, his dreams, his literary plans, and a series of notes on eating. The comments on his diet, in fact, are considerably more detailed than any other remarks in the diary. In the two months between late April and mid-June 1803, De Quincey, then seventeen, makes the following observations on his diet:

April 30: dined by myself at C's.—drank 1 cup of coffee at W's
May 4: dined alone without C

May 5: dined alone at C's
May 7: introduced to 2 vulgar belles; and eat a few shrimps.
May 10: stomach aches—drink coffee
May 11: dine at W's . . . drink 1 cup and a half of coffee
May 12: drank 1 cup of tea
May 15: dine alone w. C . . . drink 1 half cup coffee
May 16: drink 1 cup of tea
May 17: drink 2 cups tea
May 20: drink at Mr. Williams's a few teaspoons of ginger wine . . . walk home with the ladies—sit till past 10 o'clock;—then come in sandwiches . . . and after them, Mr. W. and Mrs. Daltry—I eat nothing—I drink nothing, but I read the King's *Declaration*.
May 26: walk with ladies to Mr. Williams's . . . the ladies eat tart and drink ginger wine;—I drink or eat nothing . . .
May 27: drink 1 cup of tea . . . supper is announced;—I eat a few mashed potatoes;—and a mouth full of bacon . . . I walk home in a state of exquisite misery.
June 2: supper is announced;—I am asked to stay but do not.
June 5: walk—first to toffee house where 6d worth of toffee is got (of which I eat none) and thence to Liverpool; go to Benterjak's—eat a bit of raw lamb;—drink half a tumbler of porter and 3 or 4 glasses of port wine—complain of being ill;—go home.
June 7: sup on cold meat and 3 or 4 glasses of wine.
June 8: eat a little salmon and bread—drink some porter and a few glasses of wine.
June 10: Feel ill about the head; drink coffee
June 11: drink 1 large cup of coffee but eat nothing . . . they drink coffee and afterwards tea;—I drink or eat nothing more nor talk at all.
June 12: then I made tea—drank 1 cup myself—but eat nothing. (*Diary* 132-208)

At the time of this diary, De Quincey is seventeen, but he is as careful as a dyspeptic man four times his age. He measures his allotment carefully, notices every half-cup of tea, and seems to grudge his every mouthful ("I eat a few mashed potatoes . . . walk home in a state of exquisite misery") as if he feels remorse at having eaten at all. The pattern here is of watchful abstinence, with pride in abstinence, shame at relapsing, and superiority to the gourmandizing company. In his *Confessions* the boy De Quincey appears as one who eats barely enough to keep alive. In Wales he soon runs out of money and finds himself reduced to "only one meal a day":

> From the keen appetite produced by constant exercise, and mountain air, acting on a youthful stomach, I soon began to suffer greatly on this slender reg-

imen, for the single meal, which I could venture to order, was coffee or tea. Even this, however, was at length withdrawn, and afterwards . . . I subsisted either on blackberries, hips, haws, etc., or on . . . casual hospitalities. (L 14)

In London, a "famishing scholar" (W 41) in a "hunger-bitten" house (*CW* 3: 351), De Quincey endures steady, grinding hunger, grateful to receive a few broken bits of bread left over from Brunell's table. This sustained deprivation deprives him of the power to eat fully at all when he is invited to breakfast with "Lord D____" at Eton, the "first regular meal . . . that I had sat down to for months." Unable "scarcely to eat anything":

> On the day when I had first received my 10l. Bank-note, I had gone to a baker's shop and bought a couple of rolls . . . [but] my appetite was quite sunk, and I became sick before I had eaten half of what I had bought. This effect, from eating what approached to a meal, I continued to feel for weeks: or, when I did not experience nausea, part of what I ate I rejected, sometimes with acidity, sometimes immediately and without any acidity. On the present occasion, at Lord D_____'s table, I found myself not at all better than usual; and, in the midst of luxuries, I had no appetite. (L 31-32)

Though De Quincey traces his uncertain appetite at Lord D_____'s table and throughout later life to the hardships of his wanderings, one of his major complaints about Manchester Grammar School before he ran away was that he could not eat properly there. In the revised *Confessions* and in De Quincey's letters of complaint to his mother written in 1802, he complains of the haste with which school meals had to be eaten. The boys had only half-an-hour for their breakfast of bread and milk ("a pace fitter for the fowls of the air than students of Grecian philosophy" [*CW* 3: 273]) and somewhat less than the officially specified two hours for dinner. De Quincey resented "the short time one has to eat one's dinner in; I have barely time to push it down, and as to chewing it, that is out of the question" and considered this would eventually ruin his health. This complaint suggests that De Quincey had unusual eating habits for a teen-age boy, an unusual lingering over his meal, a methodical chewing over of every bite. His reference to a separate process of "chewing" his food recalls his alleged instructions to the Wilsons' cook to cut his mutton—a piece no bigger than a pin—"in a diagonal rather than a longitudinal form." A contemporary student of anorexia notes that patients with anorexia "often dawdle, are finicky, eat odd combinations, and toy with the food a long time before they eat it. They often develop rituals around food" (Dwyer 28). De

Quincey's two-hour well-chewed dinners sound like obsessional behavior designed to minimize the amount eaten.

Thus from the time he was sixteen De Quincey was a man who ate little and who was self-conscious about that little. The eating habits of the child Thomas De Quincey are unknown, but it is likely that the child was father of the man, that the habits of his adolescence were an extension of those of his childhood. De Quincey describes himself as lapsing into a depression after the death of Elizabeth, a depression unnoted and uncomforted by his mother. His descriptions of his longing to join Elizabeth, the perception of the absence of "any sympathy at all . . . in the desolating grief I had suffered" (L 123), his sense of guilt associated with her death, and the "constant terror" that accompanied him "from seven or earlier up to ten" (L 129), his self-imposed isolation in "the most silent and sequestered nooks" (L 111) all evince that child's depression. Given De Quincey's later fussiness about food it seems likely that he responded to Elizabeth's death as children often respond to grief: he stopped eating.[19] With a mother so distant as Elizabeth Quincey, it is possible that a pattern of picky eating could persist undetected for years and become so much second nature that the child might not even recognize or even feel the signs of hunger.

Chronic undernourishment stunts growth. According to the current authoritative pediatric text, "Height-for-age . . . serves as an indicator of the chronicity of undernutrition" (Figuero-Colon 194). Children who are malnourished during the vulnerable period of the adolescent growth spurt (for males, the key period is sometimes between ten and sixteen years but with growth often continuing as late as twenty-one) can be seriously stunted. During this period in which adolescent boys generally grow between twelve and fifteen inches and "often require double the nutritional intake of the remainder of the adolescent period," De Quincey was starving in Wales and London (Parr 93). The boys "most vulnerable to unanswered nutritional requirements" (Parr 93) are "early and late maturers." Whatever Thomas De Quincey's case, it is known that his notably tall son William had a late adolescent growth spurt between sixteen and eighteen, the years corresponding to his father's period of deepest austerity (Balfour 319). By self-induced malnutrition, Thomas De Quincey may have been the architect of his own size. De Quincey's small childlike stature may thus evince a hidden will to remain in the world of childhood.

In his diary the seventeen-year-old De Quincey noted that "the intimate connection, which exists between the body and the mind, has never (to my knowledge) been sufficiently enlarged on in theory or insisted on in practice." His alertness to the interactions of mind and body makes it at least arguable that on some level of the conscious or unconscious will De Quincey wished to be "so very little a Man" as "little Mr. De Quincey." The austerity of his diet, the years of the gnawing rats of hunger indicate his willingness to endure suffering toward a goal of remaining, in every sense and in every way, as little a man as possible and as much a child. Anorexia is usually regarded today as "an effort to make time stand still, not to grow but go back to childhood size and functioning" (Bruch 74), as "a pathological response to the developmental crisis of adolescence" (Brumberg), especially among teenage girls who wish to seize control of their bodies and keep their bodies childlike and immature. Part of such childhood identity is an evasion of conventional gender, "a narcissistic, sexless existence . . . providing a refuge from feminine, genital sexuality" (Thoma qtd. in Spignesi 15). To be thus "neuter . . . neither boy nor girl" (15) restores to the adult the unproblematic bodily space of childhood.

A predominantly female disease, anorexia in our era is frequently decoded as a tactic of resistance to patriarchy, a jiu-jitsu revenge of the weak upon the strong. De Quincey's choice of a girl's malady and a child's body performs his allegiance to his lost sister. His starvation works to feminize him, making him weak, small, and self-consciously bodily. His oft-stated nympholeptic goal to rejoin his dead, "to go to *them,*" to join his lips with "the lips that we could hang on for ever" (*PW* 1: 13) is a will toward the lost small sister. By molding a body that is small, weak, and girlish and habits that are self-torturing, he establishes a union with the lost childhood second self and becomes strong in that union. De Quincey's will to childhood is not merely inscribed in his works of power and works of knowledge but upon his living, suffering, and self-starved body, the body of a child who "has been in Hell."

Chapter Five

The Case of Hartley Coleridge: The Designated Genius

> "Don't ask me so many questions, Papa! I can't bear it."
> —Hartley Coleridge, age 6, to S. T. Coleridge

Afterwards; or Remembering the annus mirabilis

On the 4th of November 1806 my dear Father presented this book to me—little thinking I guess that some pages of it would be still blank in 1830—and still less foreseeing through what dark and miry ways, what dark vicissitudes of ill my own Fancies would lead me before the last leaf was written. High were his hopes for me, for his love was strong, and finding an understanding and creative spirit in the ready tears, repentance close upon offence and simple notions of the nature of ill he never thought the heart could be wrong. (*Hartley Coleridge Papers,* Notebook 13)[1]

Already gray at thirty-four, already "loveless and confined" to a Grasmere banishment as a "hopeless" case, Hartley Coleridge looked back from 1830 to his glory days as a ten-year-old prodigy.[2] In the very notebook his father had given him at ten, the self-proclaimed loser in "the race I never ran" recalled his *annus mirabilis* with his great father in the great world.

When Hartley was ten years old, he alone among the Coleridge children was chosen to accompany his father and the Wordsworth menage—William, Mary, and Sara Hutchinson—to Coleorton and London. The six months Hartley spent in intense contact with Samuel Taylor Coleridge were the last time the boy was ever to live with his father who thereafter effectively abandoned his family. A striking passage of Derwent Coleridge's "Memoir" compares Hartley's life to "an Australian river, wide at first, a flow of hopeful waters, which speedily contract into a feeble, narrow stream and are insensibly lost in the sand" ("Memoir," *PHC* xlix). But these six months with Coleridge, "the *annus mirabilis* of my brother's childhood" ("Memoir" xxxi) were the wide-water mark of that life and were remembered with an glad enthusiasm strangely at odds with what Coleridge's biographers report of this dark period of STC's return from Malta in an almost psychotic state (Lefebure, *BO* 447).

Thirty years after the event, in the 1830s and 1840s, Hartley Coleridge's journals and marginalia recur to this peak time of 1807 as a comforting refrain: "It was in 1807 . . ." that he met famous poets, scientists, novelists, public men, writers; that he saw tragedians and comedians; that he knew London; that he had his portrait painted; it was in 1807 that he saw draft riots in the streets and heard of political crises and glorious military expeditions. In Hartley's recollections this six-month period is notable for the qualities so lacking and so longed for in his adult life: privileged access to metropolitan artists and intellectuals; privileged communion with his brilliant and omniscient father; and privileged admiration as a celebrity—albeit a celebrity child.

He lived among the famous: he knew George Beaumont, the great philanthropist; he sat for David Wilkie, the future academician; and he "once saw HD (nundum Sir Humphrey Davy) in the spring of 1807. I think at Sir George Beaumont's. Ὁ Μακαρίτης was vexed that I did not know him" (*HCP,* Marginalia, *Universal Magazine,* February 1807: 139).[3] He visited London in a whirl of activity and for the rest of his life he recalled seeing the sights of London "with a freshness of recollection, as if the circumstance occurred only yesterday." A Grasmere friend recalled how Hartley would describe his never-to-be-forgotten trip to the Tower of London with both Scott and Wordsworth. But Wordsworth's "economy" would not "allow us to see the Jewel Office" ("Memoir," "Appendix C," *PHC* cciii). With Charles and Mary Lamb, Hartley visited Barthelmy Fair and saw a satisfyingly gory painting of the Battle of Hastings: "Harold is just pierced with the arrow and falling from his horse" (*HCP,* Marginalia, *The Atheneum,* April 17, 1847: 416). London in 1807 was the powerhouse of national politics and living theater:

> It was in 1807, the memorable year of Mother Goose, the Wood Demon, Slave Trade abolition, No Popery, Sir Francis Burdett, the Battle of Jutland and Freedland [sic?], the Expeditions to the Dardanelles, to Buenos Ayres and to Copenhagen, the death of Opie and the return of the Tories to Office . . . (*HCP,* Marginalia to *Atheneum,* March 27, 1841: 459)

He went to the theater. He saw the famous Joseph Grimaldi in "Mother Goose." He went once to "Town and Country" (whose paper moon "STC compared to a warming pan" [(*HCP,* Marginalia to *London Magazine* March 1822: 190-91]), and twice to see Monk Lewis's "The Wood Demon." Hartley "was in a great passion" with Sara Hutchinson for being "disgusted" at the melodramatic claptrap that delighted him at ten—and delighted him always because "it makes me such a child again" ("Memoir," "Appendix C," *PHC* cxcix-cc).

During this wonderful six months, Hartley was uniquely close to his father. They even shared a bed in Coleorton and possibly in London as well. In the decade after 1807, Coleridge saw his children briefly and infrequently and wrote them hardly at all. (Hartley's sole letter from his father in this period tells him principally "what *worms* we all are" [*CCL* 3: 54]). But in the wonderful year of Hartley's recollection, the boy felt himself the focus of his father's attention. Whether or not Hartley was ever more than a passive listener to his father's talk, he liked to remember himself and his father as conversational partners and even literary collaborators. Hartley's recollections evoke a time of vanished intimacy, of chat about Coleridge's pet books and favorite themes. Thus certain writers, in particular Laurence Sterne, recall 1807. In a late undated notebook entry, Hartley records "my dear father at Coleorton taking down a volume of Tristram Shandy to enforce his opinion about the aggravation of death-bed sufferings" (*HCP,* Notebook 8). Of Sterne's *Sentimental Journey* Hartley's remembers "'Ο Μακαρίτης as to its inferiority to the better parts of Tristram Shandy" (*HCP,* Marginalia, *London Magazine* January 1, 1824: 39). He recalls learning prosody from STC: "It was at Coleorton in the winter of 1806-07 that I first saw the Bath Guide. . . . The galloping anapestic movement was easy and rememorable. My father had just then explained to me the names and quantities of the simple feet . . ." (*HCP,* Marginalia, *London Magazine* January 1822: 25). His father explained "the conversion of Gasses from the aeriform to the fluid and in one instance directly to the solid state. It was on a walk from the Manor Farm House at Coleorton to Ashby de la Zouch. He set the wonders of Chemistry above all the wonders of Romances and all the miracles of Legend" (*HCP,* "Essays and Marginalia" u). And he "once explained the fire and smoke" of the Exodus journey "By supposing a Volcano casting forth smoke by day and fire by night but this was in 1806 or 7" (*HCP,* Marginalia, *The Atheneum* July 27, 1844: 691). Or again, "I remember STC pointing out a passage in Shevlocke's Voyages touching Juan Fernandez as more interesting than Robinson Crusoe." But Hartley never followed up on the suggestion because "it was an early infirmity of mine never to read a book with delight which was put in my hand" (*HCP* "Omnium Gatherum"). Evidently basking in his father's attention, the complacent ten-year-old told Anna Montagu that he and his father were writing a tragedy together and that "he should inform the public that the only bad lines in the Tragedy were written by Mr. Coleridge Senior" (*HCP,* ALS to Derwent Coleridge, April 4, 1849).

He was, moreover, the direct recipient of works expressly tailored to his needs and character. A focused paternal attention is evident in the fragment of a Greek Grammar Coleridge composed expressly for Hartley in Fall 1806. A lesson in cases underlines Hartley's status as the chosen son:

> . . . we often meet with a noun substantive either by itself, or with a noun adjective, which shows that it is spoken or called to, either as really present, or as if it were present, as, Come to me, *my son.* This is called the vocative case, from the Latin *voco,* I call; and may always be known my prefixing the word O, as, O my Son! . . . there are five cases enumerated: 1. the precedent, 2. the dependent, 3. the motive, 4. the objective, 5. the vocative. Example: (1) His father gave (4) this book (3) to Hartley do not dirty it, (5) O Derwent, for it is (2) Hartley's. ("Memoir," "Appendix A," *PHC* cxci)

Although Coleridge furnished as his Greek example of the middle or self-reflexive voice the standard grammarian's τύπτομαι ("I beat myself"), his English instance called on the verb *to wonder* for his "young Philosopher" son, noting that "When we say, 'I wonder at myself'" we are adverting to "the self-contemplative faculty of man" ["Appendix A, " *PHC* cxcii]. Coleridge's most sustained text for Hartley is a letter of character analysis and advice, composed to prepare Hartley for an anticipated but thwarted visit with his Coleridge kin in Ottery. As a moral recipe to correct the boy's irritating habits and dangerous tendencies, this letter, as biographer Rosemary Ashton notes "would be comic if it were not so painful" (242). But however ineffective as character education, the letter that "could equally apply to myself" is Coleridge's explicit and implicit admission of his deep affinity with his child. The resemblances stand out in Coleridge's list of Hartley's defects: the boy's habit of elaborating ingenious excuses for wrong doing, which "may show your ingenuity, but they may make your *honesty* suspected"; his procrastination; his active and absorbing mental life that makes him "less impressible both to the censure of your anxious friends, and to the whispers of your conscience"; his avoidance of pain by "shoving aside all disagreeable reflections, or losing them in a labyrinth of day-dreams, which saves you some present pain, [but] has, on the other hand, interwoven with your nature habits of procrastination, which, unless you correct them in time . . . must lead you into lasting unhappiness" (*CCL* 4: 10). However critical this letter, it testifies both to paternal concern and to paternal identification with Hartley.

Hartley was no mere passive spectator to the wonders of the wonderful year. Like the intellectuals around him, he too was galvanized into creation. Acting on his father's prompting and imitating his father's practice, he began a lifelong habit of journal keeping. The notebooks he started in 1807 continued intermittently but steadily for the rest of his life. Inspired by the London theater, he planned his own play for the Montagues' back garden and "set my little arts to contrive a pantomime if possible still more marvellous and really thought to perform it in a theatre of our own creation on the mould heap with the assistance of automatic actors—Happy days of Thornhaugh Street" (*HCP,* Marginalia, *London Magazine,* March 1822, 290-91). Anna Montagu's 1849 recollections confirm his boyhood rhetorical prowess:

> . . . he had found a spot upon the Globe which he peopled with an imaginary nation gave them a name, a language, laws, and a Senate where he framed long speeches which he *translated* as he said for my benefit, and for the benefit of my neighbours who climbed the garden wall to listen to the surprising child whom they supposed to be reciting pieces from memory. . . .—He called his nation *Ejuxini* and one day when walking very pensively, I asked him "what ailed him," he said "My people are too fond of war, and I have just made an eloquent speech to the Senate, which has not made any impression and *to war they will go.*" (*HCP,* ALS to Derwent Coleridge, April 4, 1869)

When Hartley returned to Greta Hall, he carried with him recollections of London and Sterne's Uncle Toby's hobby-horse battlefield. Like Uncle Toby he desired to replicate his glory days—Toby in a battlefield model of Flanders, scene of his wound and his honors; Hartley with a metropolitan model of a child-governed London. Desiring "to reproduce whatever he saw in London," Hartley upon his return home took possession of a "spot of waste ground":

> This was divided into kingdoms, and subdivided into provinces, each of the former being assigned to one of his playmates. A canal was to run through the whole, upon which ships were to be built. A tower and armoury, a theatre and a "chemistry-house," (under which mines were expected to be formed), were to be built, and considered common property. War was to be declared and battles fought between sovereign powers. . . . [He] had a

scheme for training cats and even rats for various offices and labours, civil and military. ("Memoir" xli-xlii)

The wonderful year may have remained so vividly wonderful in retrospect because Hartley was loved, approved, and lionized. Whether he was directly praised by the adults around him 1807, it seems likely that he was aware of an atmosphere of approval from those who found him so "delightful" (Dorothy Wordsworth [*WLMY* pt. 1, 125]) and, "extraordinary" (Anna Montagu). And to be drawn—twice—by the renowned David Wilkie was both flattering and fixative. The two Wilkie images gave back to the child a double image of himself in thought and in action, as thinker and as artist—in repose in the pencil sketch and in motion in "The Blind Fiddler," an oil painted on commission for Sir George Beaumont. The sketch, labeled "Hartley Coleridge Aet. 10," shows a small round shouldered boy in a ruffled open-necked shirt and dark jacket. At ten, he still has a babyish look—round cheeks, a wide flat nose, huge dark eyes, and fragile bone structure. What biographer Earl Leslie Griggs acutely describes as the boy's "stunned expression" (and interprets as Hartley's "subdued astonishment at the existence of a world of reality" [*HCLW* 31]) suggests a child wistful, sensitive, thoughtful, and above all vulnerable. This tender ten-year-old was also the model for the irrepressible child fiddler in Wilkie's famous "Blind Fiddler," a painting later donated by Sir George Beaumont to the National Gallery and housed today in the Tate. This genre scene shows an itinerant musician, a blind fiddler, playing for a family of cottagers, country people like those who populate Wordsworth's *Lyrical Ballads.* Just outside the rapt circle of the cottage family listening to the blind fiddler's music jumps a "deformed mischievous jackanapes" (Hartman 45) mimicking the adult musician. The child pretends to bow with a poker a make-believe violin made from a bellows. Of all the tranquil group, only the child refuses childlike passivity; he does not sit still as a member of the audience but attempts to rival and supplement the adult artist. As parodic miniature of the tranquil adult musician, the Hartley figure has large eyes, a mobile twisted mouth, a stumpy jumpy body suspended for an instant on one foot. Perpetually in motion, he seems either praeternaturally bold or praeternaturally fearful. Here is the elfin Hartley who at three had seemed to dance on an aspen leaf and who thwacked the dolorous "Mr. Gobwin," Godwin the philosophic determinist, on the shins with a bowling pin in a spirit of noisy free play. Here is Wordsworth's "exquisitely wild" H. C. energetically mocking the adult world and miming his "unutterable" thoughts.

Such images and such memories of himself as the companion and collaborator of his famous father, the admired of the famous, and the aesthetic inspiration of the Royal Academician[4] made the wonderful year stand out from "The Waste Book and Daily Chronicle" of the later years of Hartley Coleridge's life.[5]

Hartley, thirty and forty years on, recalled the most minute details of "the memorable year" (*HCP,* Marginalia to *The Atheneum,* March 27, 1841: 459). Hartley's memory is prodigious and seems to validate Coleridge's complacent praise of Hartley at six for possessing like his father before him "a memory both quick and retentive" (*CCL* 2: 802). Remembering all the minutiae, however, he leaves out the one big thing. Of 1807 he remembers all the details of his father's conversation but forgets the overwhelming fact of his father's wreck. Hartley does not, or will not, or cannot remember Coleridge's shattered state. According to all accounts, the Coleridge who returned from Malta in 1806 was in a state that shocked all old friends who welcomed him back. Coleridge had returned from Malta entirely morphine-dependent, "utterly changed" (Lefebure, *BO* 447). He was flabby like "a person in a dropsy." According to Southey:

> His countenance is more changed for the worse than I could have believed possible. His eyes have lost all their life, partly from fat and still more from the quantity of laudanum which he takes, and the quantity of spirits. Nothing intoxicates him and he is not sensible and will not be easily convinced that he drinks enough to kill anybody—frequently when he was home nearly a bottle of rum a day (qtd. in Doughty 291).

Molly Lefebure dates Coleridge's "most advanced stage of morphine reliance" to the winter of 1806-7 calling his condition "one of organic psychosis" (*BO* 447). First at home in Greta Hall in November 1806, the month of the notebook presentation to Hartley, and later at Coleorton, Coleridge continued to drink heavily, brandy mostly, and to take large doses of laudanum. The Notebook entries of winter 1806-7 contain the telltale psychedelic musings on candle flames (*NB* 2933, 2994), frequent markers of his habit, and also explicitly remorseful observations on his inability to live with or without opium. Coleridge blamed his misery explicitly on his unrequited love for Sara Hutchinson, *Elpixomene, the hope-for one,* and hardly less explicitly on his jealousy of Wordsworth, both as the consummate poet and Sara's putative lover. On December 27, six days after his arrival at Coleorton with Hartley, Coleridge had an hallucination (so he later believed) of William and Sara in bed together. Later he wrote that he *knew* the horrid phantasm to be mere phantasm: "and yet what anguish, what gnawing of despair, what throbbings and lancinations of positive Jealousy!" (*NB* 2: 3128). While suffering through this agony, falling "asleep each night watching that perpetual feeling to which Imagination . . . has given . . . a shechinah in the heart" (*NB* 2: 2999), Coleridge was sharing the bed with Hartley. Coleridge was deeply miserable, despairing in soul and opium-saturated and brandy-soaked in body. His behavior was volatile; he felt awful and, flatulent and costive, he also smelled bad. But according to all contemporary reports, Hartley was oblivious and happy. Happier than ever and even more oblivious—more careless, more likely to drop things, more likely to lose himself in a fantastic tale of his own making, more likely to sweep like a whirlwind through the house, "absolutely in a dream when you tell him to do the simplest thing—his Books, his Slate, his Pencils, he drops them just where he finds them no longer useful" (*WLMY* pt. 1, 125). Coleridge the great good father could be remembered as the mainstay of Hartley's exquisitely happy childhood only through an all-points obliviousness to Coleridge the bad father. But as Bellow's Augie March famously notes: "Everybody knows there is no fineness or accuracy of suppression; if you hold down one thing you hold down the adjoining." To retain Coleridge the wonderful father, Hartley regressively suppresses everything he knows about Coleridge the bad father.[6] But such an evasion of knowledge and remembrance blocked the possibility of the child's own maturation and growth since he could not bear to separate from a merely life-sized, merely human father. A willed obliviousness to the conditions of his childhood existence was the very condition of keeping alive the happiness of that childhood and the greatness of his father.

But the willful obliviousness of Hartley's boyhood necessitates the compulsive retrospection of his age. Hartley at thirty, at forty, at fifty continues to remember the boy of 1807 and in many respects even to remain that boy. Hartley Coleridge's adult years are principally devoted to despairing retrospect and recapitulation of his glory days. Writing in the same notebook STC had given him in his eleventh year and in a series of other notebooks to follow, Hartley all his life continues the process of casual poetry, random jottings, and intermittent introspection that had marked the ten-year-old's work. The adult Hartley in thought and behavior rackets back and forth between a sense of youth and a sense of age. Indeed, he habitually conflates extreme youth with extreme antiquity. His "Nursery Lecture Delivered by an Old Bachelor" links the earliest ages of history to early childhood and presents an alienated childhood at once ancient, youthful, and untouchable:

> When I see a numerous small family at play, my mind sinks back . . . to the world's infancy. In the life, the innocence, the simple bliss before me, I hail a something that is not changed. The furniture of a well-littered play-room reminds me of Chaldea, Egypt, Etruria, and the Druids . . . (*EM* 1: 305)[7]

He describes himself as being as "Strange in the wide world as if . . . like the mammoth and megatherion, a relic of a perished system, or dropped like a selerite from the moon" (*HCP,* "Autobiography of a Quizz").

Always temporally dislocated, he alternatively impersonates premature age and superannuated youth, always surprised by the one ("I waked to sleep no more . . . I find my head is grey" [*CPW* 7]) and desiring the other ("I would be treated as a child / And guided where I go" [HCP, Notebook C]). As the "Old Bachelor," his frequent nom de plume, he is "Untimely old, irreverently grey / And like a patch of dusky snow in May" ("How shall a man foredoomd to low estate" [*HCP,* Poems—Transcriptions, Notebook A]). His age is unseasonable, incongruous: "My locks were very black in May / But now in August growing grey" ("Valentine by an Ancient Lover" *HCP,* Notebook E). The grey hairs make a piquant counterpoint to his consciously cultivated demeanor of extreme youth. In appearance and in affect, "in some sort an infant still" (Drinkwater in HC, *Essays on Parties* 6-7), "with in intellect and appearance of a man, but with the heart and emotion of a child" (Griggs 155), "a pure minded, single-hearted, childlike being over whom *almost* everyone was ready to have a care" (D. Coleridge, "Memoir" xc), Hartley Coleridge demanded to be perceived as a child—and most of his acquaintances complied. The testimonies are virtually universal: "in most of the simple delight of country life he was like a child" (*HCP,* Blackburn, AL); "he lived as a child and therefore was loved as only a child is loved" (*HCP,* Sarah Fox, AL letter); one of those who are "children through life" (Bagehot 46), "an interesting and wayward Child . . . never fit to go alone . . . to walk as other men do, in the prospect of gain, or ambition, or even self-preservation" (*HCP,* Anna Montagu, AL); "gay as 'a three-years' child; whose head was midwinter, while his heart was green as May" (*HCP,* John Richardson, AL, 11 Nov 1850). Known by the local country people as "Li'le Hartley," called "Hartley" even by the schoolboys he briefly taught ("That will give you an idea," Dorothy Wordsworth noted, "of the nature of the discipline exercised by him" [*WLLY* 1: 162-63]) and "Poor Hartley" by virtually all of his old friends, he was consistently treated with the indulgence meted out to sweet-natured but naughty children. So settled was the tendency to label Hartley as a child, that Derwent eventually refers to it contemptuously as an all-purpose excuse manufactured as a cover-up. Late in Hartley's life, after he had set fire to his bedcurtains—perhaps through clumsiness, probably because he was drunk—his brother exploded. For once, he would not drop the subject and avoid speaking the truth: "Would not this be playing a part, justifiable only toward a child, or a lunatic? My dear, dear Brother, there are those who regard you in one or both of these lights—some with kindly feelings, that they may excuse, that which they must else condemn . . . And would you shelter *yourself,* would you wish *me* to shelter you under such a plea?" (*HCP,* ALS September 28, 1846).

But the shelter was so tempting and the role was so easy as to be irresistible. Physically, Hartley Coleridge was a natural for the part. He was a tiny man, barely five feet tall, who sometimes used the pen name Tom Thumb the Great and who could sign a letter to tall Thomas Poole "Your very grateful and sincere little friend" (*LHC* 23). His clothes emphasized his boyishness:

> Extremely boyish in aspect, his juvenile air was aided not a little by his general mode of dress—a dark blue cloth round jacket, white trousers, black silk handkerchief tied loosely round his throat: sometimes a straw hat covered his head, but more frequently it was bare. (qtd. in *CPW* xl)

Another contemporary description puts him in a "quite short jacket, which made him look like a boy in an Eton jacket . . . But, one thing I remember . . . was that he always wore, or seemed to wear, two waistcoats, one above the other. Then around his neck was a blackstock, his collar, like a Gladstone, standing above it" (qtd. in Griggs 154). The schoolboy's clothes worn with schoolboy carelessness emphasized the boyish demeanor, little changed from the impetuous movements his father had chided in the ten-year-old. Caroline Fox was startled on her first acquaintance with him to see "a little being standing hat in hand, bowing to the earth round and round, and round again, with eyes intensely twinkling" (Fox 20). Just as he had larked and whirled at ten, Hartley at eighteen, so his mother reported, was seen "flying about in the open air, and uttering his poetic fancies aloud: this he constantly does when the fit is on him . . . we hear him whizzing by, and sometimes his uncle [Southey] calls out to him 'Whither so fast, Endymion?'"(*Minnow* 34-35). Even in his forties he was seen "running alone in the fields with arms outstretched, and talking to himself" (*HCP,* Blackburn, ALS). When Aubrey de Vere met the middle-aged Hartley, this "white-hair apparition-wearing in all other respects the semblance of youth" was still the whirling boy:

> He could scarcely be said to have walked for he seemed with difficulty to keep his feet on the ground, as he wavered near us with arms extended like wings . . . After fifty years of ill fortune the man before us was still the child described by Wordsworth . . . It was a strange thing to see Hartley Coleridge floating about the room, now with one hand on his head, now with both arms extended like a swimmer's. There was some element wanting in his being. He could do everything but keep his footing . . . One might have thought he needed stones in his pockets to prevent his being blown away. (DeVere 133-34)

The childlike demeanor corresponded to childlike taste. He loved puppet Punch-and-Judys (Drinkwater 7) and nonsense words and silly jokes. A talented improvisational poet, he once tossed off for Sarah Fox a set of rhymes he claimed were a sample lot of those he proposed to write eventually as Poet Laureate to the Royal Nursery:

> Lolly pops and nice mint drops
> They are my dear delight.
> For sugar candy I'm the Dandy -
> I have both brown and white.
>
> A toffee stick will make me lick
> Like any Pup, my chops,
> On gingerbread I would be fed
> And dainty sugar pops.
>
> And figs and prunes and macaroons
> And oranges also
> And raisins dry, and nuts, my eye!
> But they are all the go![8]

Childlike, he loved children and animals, especially donkeys with whom he claimed cousinship. Hartley was remembered by the local people for his affectionate interest in their children. "Won't you give me one of your pretty curls," he would say, stroking a child's hair (Hartman 146). Like Lewis Carroll who liked "all children except boys," Hartley shunned boisterous schoolboys: "I have an instinctive terror of big boys . . . If I am at all unwell or feverish . . . these are always at me in my dreams, hooting, pelting, spitting at me" (*LHC* 127-28). He liked girls, preferably small ones below the age of puberty who had not yet become the "Miss in her teens" with an "antipathy to quizzes" (*HCP* Marginalia, *London Magazine* September 1822: 253). He especially adored infants. He had many godchildren and always had a pet "baby idol—I cannot do without one" and longed for more: "How I should . . . squeeze Christabel," "dandle your little Fanny" (*LHC* 278, 88). He studiously kept up with the welfare of all his friends' children, writing in what his biographer Earl Griggs regarded as an unmanly and even "morbid" way about childbirth, suckling, and weaning (Griggs 225). Like his father, he had what he called "the Coleridge love of babies" and found it easy to project himself back to earliest infancy: "When I was a baby I have often been in the greatest terror, when, to all appearances I was quite still;—so frightened that I could not make a noise" ("Memoir" cxxxiv). This empathic recourse to infancy made him an attentive and sympathetic inquirer after nursing infants, "the little tugging piggie-wiggies" whose intuited experiences at the breast give him "such a reality of sympathetic bliss" (*LHC* 129). On his deathbed Hartley was comforted by holding a tiny baby on his chest; and mused as he died that "I should not mind little girls running over my grave" ("Memoir" cxxxvii).

Generally avoiding contemporaries, Hartley warmed to his elders, those old enough to look upon most grownups—and especially Hartley—as still being children themselves. "Whether it arose from my breeding up under Jacky and Wilsy I know not, but I can generally agree better with old folks . . . than with men of, or under my own age (*HCP,* Marginalia, *London Magazine* 5: 285*).* This fondness for older people was expressed in his warm relationships with a number of old women—first his nurse Mrs. Wilson (Wilsy) and later Mrs. Fleming who looked after him in Rose Cottage; Quaker Sarah Fox; and the stunningly non-judgmental Eliza Fletcher: "Only once I saw him not quite sober, & then he came in that state, & stretched himself at my feet in the drawing room & when he rose after an hour's sleep sober and quiet as a lamb" (*HCP,* AL, January 18, 1849).

The decision to inhabit childhood is also evident in Hartley's journals, which he kept mostly in school children's soft-backed notebooks with covers picturing animals, multiplication tables, Robinson Crusoe, soldiers, and alphabets. Although Hartley outlines many earnest literary projects, he also maintains a steadily anti-pedagogical schoolboy ragging of the system. There are collections of riddles, comic verses, nonsense rhymes. He coins derisive jingles about educators with funny names: thus *Butter's Etymological Spelling Books* receives the riposte of "Butter's books I ne'er have read / I hope they butter him his bread." On the front cover of one notebook containing a fragmentary essay on Aristotle he jots "Aristotle / mottle /

gottle / bottle / throttle / wattle / pottle." In his notebook titled "Notes on Shakespeare," Hartley devises a whimsical list of "Sobriquets of Shakespeare's commentators," including Theobald Tibbald (i.e., Theobald) as "Good Man Dull," Pope as "Hoxantes the Little," Warburton as "Justice Overdo or the Bishop of Laputo or Parson Piston," Malone as "Pastorophilis," Hazlitt as "Staccanto," STC as "Phosphoros," and "H.C." himself as "Mystagogus."

Much of Hartley's reading focused on the books of his childhood. His letters and notebooks often cite fairy tales. Architect Perrault he considered nothing to fabulist Perrault:

> The Louvre is, I dare say, a grand palace yet how little good it does compared to Blue Beard and Cinderella! How much better to make a story which may delight the hearts of good little children from generation to generation for sixpence than a huge pile of stone or wood at the enormous expense of an oppressed people for an overgrown tyrant! (*HCP,* "Untitled Essay on Books")

Nursery rhymes, Mrs. Barbauld's tales (loved despite his father's derision), and "Goody Two Shoes" haunt his memory.

Childhood retrospect in the notebooks appears side by side with self-contempt for his failure ever to develop beyond childhood. Laments over lost chances punctuate the notebooks over the years: "Alack for my Valentine days"; ". . . my father's gift—eheu"; "Alas that I have made such little use of my opportunities for seeing [the Isle of Wight] . . . How different might be my present state"; "the English Bosphorus [Oxford] . . . φεῦ φεῦ φεῦ [woe! woe! woe!]"; "I burn with shame . . . I am . . . a Dead Sea below the level not only of the Mediterranean but of the Fleet Ditch. Is it too late?" (*HCP,* Marginalia, *London Magazine* February 1823: 145; *The Atheneum,* November 20, 1841: 896). His notebooks reveal a pattern of destructive self-criticism. Their titles proclaim futility: "Dry Leaves Dropp'd on the Surface of Lethe," "Omnium Gatherum," "Another Brick from Babel," "Bricks without Mortar from the Ruins of Babel," "Gripes and Grumblings," "Horae Otiossime," "The Waste Book and Daily Chronicle." He self-consciously devotes the notebooks to killing time. On the inner cover of the STC gift notebook of 1806-30, "DUNCE" is printed in neat capitals; page two bears a dedication:

> To whomsoever it be that the following exhalations of idleness (which, if anybody, will be of the same time-killing disposition as the author) the said author devotes his brain maggots with all due respect, wishing him health, prosperity, and better employment. (*HCP,* Notebook 13)

The self-contempt inscribed in the titles is replicated in Hartley's choice of abject noms-de-plume (Poor Pillgarlick, Caliban, Tom Thumb the Great, Mystagogus), which depict him as something less than a man. At most he is a physical and spiritual homunculus: "I am a man of small reading and small experience... loiterer out of the daily paths of men" (*HCP,* Notebook 3). More often he is a freakish midget, a "quizz." "Next to being born a Queen, the greatest misfortune in the world is to be born a Quizz... who is out of the pale of human sympathy... who is an inexplicable riddle to his fellow-creatures, whose thoughts and feelings have no intelligible language" (*HCP,* "Autobiography of a Quizz," "Historical Collection"). He boasts of founding of the "Ugly Club." He spins out self-mocking anecdotes:

> I once travelled in a six inside coach with the following select company. A dancing Bear and his keeper, a lunatic and ditto, a resurrection man and a subject. I being then—(and ever since)—of small weight and stature was thrown into the bargain as Nobody (tho' paid full price) and was obliged to sit on the Bear's knee. (Notebook 13)

At times he wove a series of tales of his metempsychosis into the souls of various lowly creatures: he had lived in Troy as a louse in Helen's "bright yellow hair. I was pointed out to her by Paris, and she crushed me with her pearly nail." He had been an irritable donkey in Elizabethan days and his bad behavior led to his punitive rebirth as "a man *such as you see me*" (*HCP,* Sarah Fox, Notes).

The incompletion and unfulfillment of his ever shifting soul, the narrative of a being who never succeeded in becoming a separate person, is evident in Hartley's obsessive self-identification as "an embryo incomplete" (*HCP,* Undated sonnet), "the loved abortion of a thing designed" or a seed "for ever ever ever / It sought to plant itself, but never never never, / Could that poor seed or soil or water find" (*HCP,* Sonnet 1850). In a letter to his brother on their father's death, Hartley wrote of the mind of God in which "the very abortions of lives, the thoughts which we think we never thought... live everlastingly" (*LHC* 120). Such a life lived for God only but otherwise abortive is his representation of his own. Hartley regularly depicts adult life as unformed and unborn, abortive:

> Youth, love, and mirth, what are they but the portion,
> Wherewith the Prodigal left his Father's home,
> Through foreign lands in search of bliss to roam,
> And find each seeming joy a mere abortion... (*CPW* 7)

In another poem addressed to Derwent, Hartley suggests that his life never comes to fruition and production but aborts: "Oh—why my Brother, are we thus apart / Never to meet but in abortive dreams" (*NP* 71).

As a lamentable quizz, abortion, louse, donkey, dunce, Hartley is able to write only by positioning himself as a "small poet." Indeed his single volume of poetry bears an epigraph from the Elizabethan poet Michael Drayton: "I write, endite, I point, I raze, I quote, / I interline, I plot, correct, I note, / I make, allege, I imitate, I feign." Boasting himself an instant poet who seldom revised, seldom spent more than ten minutes on a sonnet, and never planned a single poem "with any definite purpose," Hartley subscribed himself among the "poetae minimi" (*LHC* 168; *HCP*, Notebook 11; *EM* 1: 304) and both formally and thematically stakes out the territory of the miniature, the youthful, and the minor.

Formally, Hartley frequently adopts the persona of a schoolchild or youth. He writes "In the Manner of a Child of Seven Years Old" or in the voice of an adolescent at a dance watching the pretty girls from his corner: "Like little Jack Horner / Curled up like a Cat / When she smells a big Rat" (*NP* 110). In a long unpublished comic poem, "The Dunce's Execration of Latin," Hartley speaks as a persecuted schoolboy struggling with his lessons:

> What a plaguey old Gammer
> Is that Madam Grammar
> With her moods and her tenses
> To bother one's senses . . .
> I wish Captain Rock
> Would burn Hic, Haec, Hoc,
> I never will choose a
> Wife that sings Musa . . .
> As a Papist hates Lent I
> Hate Ars in Praesenti.
> And no more I love Syntax
> Than a drunkard the gin-tax . . .

A favorite form is the anti-wisdom poem that turns on the adult speaker's refusal to be an authority or even an author. "To Elizabeth Anne Burns" protests:

> In truth I know not what to write
> To suit a maid of heart so light
> For I have little skill to teach—

> To warn, to lecture, or beseech,
> As age should so that speaks to youth (*HCP,* Notebook DF)

Addressing his tiny niece Christabel Rose Coleridge, Hartley begs off from serving her in any more intimidating capacity than that of Uncle Toby:

> Yet though the name of uncle, in the mind
> Of childhood, be with horrid deeds combined
> Of bloody Richard, and that covetous man
> That left the poor babes in the wildering woods,
> I would be Uncle Toby if I could . . . (*CPW* 193)

Hartley's lyrics, often brief instantaneous products of a moment's ebullience, play out in their rapid creation and constricted form his leading theme: the greatness of littleness, especially of childhood. Out of a published corpus of 390 poems, 60 explicitly concern infancy and childhood. About half the unpublished manuscript poems also treat childhood directly or metaphorically. Even Hartley's considerable body of nature poems dwells mostly on expressly frail flowers such as "The Anemone" or "The Lily of the Valley," on slighted animals like donkeys, or on transient creatures like butterflies, bees, ants, gnats, fleas, frogs, toads, and glowworms. One lyric fragment on Lucretius honors the value even of "an atom, motion, aim, or flame / Whose essence perished by the change of form."

But of all little beings, children are the most precious. Hartley's poems represent the most unqualified and extravagant vision of the beatitude of childhood to be found in all Romantic literature. Only Swinburne and Francis Thompson rival Hartley Coleridge in their longing to lounge about what Thompson calls "the Nurseries of Heaven" ("To My Godchild" 14); but neither Thompson nor Swinburne has so desperately and monotonously celebrated childhood sanctity.

To Hartley, the child—preferably an infant, but certainly a child conceived as infantilized—is a holy object. The appropriate stance of adult toward the child is worshipfully on his knees because a baby such as "Jeannette, Six Weeks Old" in her "mute simplicity of passive being" is "A co-essential symbol of the life / Which God hath made a witness of Himself." Though the human race has fallen from Deity, the child, however limited, is the most divine being we can reach:

> . . . methinks, sweet babe! If I should kneel
> And worship thee for thy meek innocence,
> I less should err than Egypt's white-swathed priest,

> Who bade the prostrate toiling race adore
> The one great life incarnate in the bull,
> Ibis, or cat, monkey or crocodile (*CPW* 185-86)

Not simply an embodiment of the mindless life-force equally apparent in bird, bush, and bull, however, each new-born recalls Christ "Who steeped in baby tears—his Deity." Each is the image of "the baby god" and thus the "fair type and pledge of all redemption given."[9] It is not merely the recollection of the infant Christ that contributes to Hartley's sense of the child's sanctity. A series of praeternatural attributes combine to glorify the baby in the ways that Hartley himself had been glorified. Like Wordsworth in the all-pervasive Immorality Ode, Hartley in "The First Birthday" emphasizes the "sweet infant mystery" of birth (*CPW* 12). Coming as an emissary "from the unknown place / Of unborn souls" or "from some distant Paradise," the infant is "a mysterious thing."[10] Drawing on Wordsworth's musings on pre-existence, Hartley asks:

> Where dwells the Soul through all the dateless years
> Ere the doom'd moment of the Infant's birth?
> Comes it a stranger from the radiant sphere,
> A naked exile to the shores of earth?
>
> Or was it e'en from nature's natal day
> A life in wood, or wild, or sunny stream,
> That like a dream would lightly pass away
> And still return a many-coloured dream?
>
> Or slept the Spirit in the Almighty mind
> Among the forms of fair and awful things,
> High in eternal light and love sustained
> Beneath the shadow of the Seraph's wings? (*CPW* 196-97)

Such rhetoric of mysterious origins works to suggest the baby's grandeur. Infancy is the saving grace of mortal life, the "perpetual Messiah," as Emerson called it (54); it temporarily undoes the fall of man, giving all human beings, "once in their life fair Eden's simpleness." "Sinless" childhood hardly needs the blessing conferred by the adult world ("To an Infant" *CPW* 177). Though a frequent godfather, he regularly greets that honor with discomfort at presuming to guide a spiritual superior:

> Would I were good enough to bless
> Thee child, so early motherless . . .

> If Innocence were like the measles,
> If pure thoughts stuck to us like teazles . . .
> Could I remain—what holding thee
> My little maiden, on my knee
> E'en to myself I seem to be,
> Then like a Seer—
> With voice and power of prophesy
> I'd bless thee, dear ("To Little Annie Gibson," *NP* 106)

But adult blessings are superfluous since the tide of blessing flows the other way: "Would I might give thee back, my little one," Hartley tells a god-child, "But half the good that I have got from thee" ("The God-Child," *CPW* 179).

Innocence and mystery combine in the infantine intelligence, an intelligence lacking articulate speech, Hartley perceives in the seemingly passive baby. In a fine sonnet "To an Infant, Written on a Snowy Day," Hartley draws on memories of "Frost at Midnight"—the quiet baby, the winter scene, the presence of a saving under-life—and the paternal repudiation of Locke—to emphasize the latent mind of childhood:

> Some say, sweet babe, thy mind is but a blank,
> As white and vacant as the level field
> Of unsunn'd snow, that passively must yield
> To human foot . . .
> I deem not so of any human child,
> Nor can believe our nature ever sank
> To such a lowness. Nay, my pretty boy!
> In thy shrill laugh there is intelligence;
> And though we can but guess, or how, or whence
> Thy soul was wafted—from what realm of joy
> Or mere privation thou hast hither come,—
> Thought has come with thee, happy thought, though dumb. (*CPW* 178)

Similarly the lovely sonnet contemporary with this, "To a Deaf and Dumb Little Girl," praises the child's beautiful self-sufficiency. Her privation is presence not absence with "All her little being / Concentred in her solitary seeing" (179). Mind unuttered is mind unspent.

Because Hartley's infants seem to possess intelligence without articulate speech, to possess the defining attributes of humanity without specific and limited content, the baby represents the grand embodiment of undifferentiated human life itself, the "purest abstract of humanity" ("To an Infant," *CPW* 178). The very qualities that make babies dull to many make them precious and sacred to Hartley. In their beautiful lack of individuality, their similarity to each other, in their monotony of burbled sounds and needs and affection, in their unity of mind and body—a quality that endeared infancy to STC as well—Hartley sees the embodiment of pure Being, life without the self-division that so tormented him.

Hartley frequently focuses on the seeming uniformity of infants: "All babies are so much alike / 'Twere easier to single out a spike, / The fairest spike in all a field of barley" than to distinguish one beautiful baby from another. Such uniformity seems blessed, for to possess the attributes of humanity without limiting, frustrating, alienating individuality is to come as close as any individual can to union with the all-encompassing God-Man. Hartley's vision of beatitude is a return to this state of infant uniformity:

> So ancient fathers deemed, and wisely deem'd.
> Or, if not so, yet beautifully dream'd,
> At the last day of God's consummate love,
> The cherish'd nestlings of the mystic dove
> Shall spring from earth and meet the promised skies
> All in one shape, one feature, and one size,
> Welcome alike before the Almighty throne,
> Each in the Saviour's likeness, not its own,
> Alike all blessed, and alike all fair,
> And only God remember who they were ("To Dear Little Katy Hill,"
> *CPW* 191)

The infant is also a perfect emblem of Being because of its integrated consciousness. The child is unselfconscious and loves without knowing that it loves. As a boy, Hartley recalls, he rejoiced ignorantly in "the unknown joy which knowing kills" ("To a Friend," *CP* 3). To be unselfconsciously young is to live in a timeless moment "like one not born to die" ("Long time a child, and still a child, when years," *CPW* 7). Children inhabit an affective joyous atmosphere:

> Joy that is not for this or that,
> Nor like the restless joy of gnat,
> Or midge in moty beam so rife,
> Whose day of pleasure is its life;
> But joy that by its quiet being
> Is witness of a law foreseeing ("On an Infant's Hand," *CPW* 183)

It is in earliest childhood—before the infant becomes a child—that we enjoy unconditional, unqualified love. In a curious and wistful lyric, Hartley distinguishes between infancy and childhood. Babyhood enjoys unconditional life, childhood is all contingency:

> Fain I would dive to find my infant self
> In the unfathom'd ocean of the past;
> I can but find a sun-burnt prattling elf,
> A froward urchin of four years at least.
>
> The prettiest speech—'tis in my mind engrain'd—
> The first awaked me from my babyhood—
> 'Twas a grave saw affectionately feign'd—
> "We'll love you, little master—if you're good."
>
> Sweet babe, thou art not yet or good or bad,
> Yet God is round thee, in thee, and above thee;
> We love, because we love thee, little lad,
> And pray thou may'st be good—because we love thee (*CPW* 189)

This desire for unqualified love is associated with Hartley's recurrent pleas to remain as a child. He begs that his friends give the respect due to an adult to his father but to himself the unqualified love due to a child: "I had rather / You'd give your love to me, poor elf, / Your praise to my great father" ("Lines" *NP* 93). It is to remain lapped in this love that he advises a young child to "Stay where thou art, thou canst not better be" (*HCP*, undated sonnet) and prays to God to grant him approval and that he be "less careful to serve thee much / Than please thee perfectly" (*HCP* "My Times Are in Thy Hands," Notebook C). To be approved of rather than to achieve is to be a satisfactory beloved child.

Though to the eye of common sense the baby may seem frail and vulnerable, though he may be growing and changing daily, Hartley nevertheless finds in this baby the divine attribute of immutability. Much like Keats' deathless nightingale, the baby is a source of stability and permanence in a changing world. Hartley attributes to the infant's "brook-like gurglings" the blissful and comforting monotony of nature. The babbling baby language, "the catholic speech of infancy," is ever the same:

> But well for us that there is something yet,
> Which change cannot efface, nor time forget,
> The patient smile of passive babyhood....
> Let mutability, then, work its will,
> The child shall be the same sweet creature still
> ("To K.H.I., the Infant Grandfather of a Blind Grandfather" *CPW* 181–82)

In the sleeping baby of "The Sabbath-Day's Child," Hartley finds an overwhelming image of unified life. It is a life so deep that he apostrophizes it in the language of paradox, the language that allows life to contain its opposite:

> Thou breathing image of the life of Nature!
> Say rather, image of a happy death—
> For the vicissitudes of vital breath,
> Of all infirmity the slave and creature,
> That by the act of being perisheth,
> Are far unlike that slumber's perfect peace
> Which seems too absolute and pure to cease,
> Or suffer diminution, or increase,
> Or change of hue, proportion, shape, or feature;
> A calm it seems, that is not, shall not be,
> Save in the silent depths of calm eternity (*PHC* 1: 105)

The union of stillness and process in the "sleeping life of infancy" is able to contain the antitheses of death and life, suggesting a stability beyond either.

In the infant's mystery, innocence, unselfconscious psychic harmony and unindividuated fullness of life, the child is a sacred being to Hartley Coleridge. So sacred that Hartley consistently identifies religious salvation with man's re-attainment of the infant state. While the Fatherhood of God is a traditional and ancient concept, Hartley's heavy emphasis on the special childishness of man is his own. The image of ultimate fulfillment for Hartley Coleridge is not the attainment of the maturity of one's adult powers bolstered by the energies of one's childhood faculties. Salvation, for Hartley, is a return to protected childhood: "I would be treated as a child / And guided where to go" (*HCP*, "My Times are in Thy Hands," Notebook C). This is especially striking in the poem, "'Of Such is the Kingdom of God,'" Adam, "our great Parent," was perfect in his manhood; "but Adam fell before a child was born." Since then each child has been born in weakness, "in human shape without the strength of man." All fallen mortals, whose weakness exacts loving protection from God, are like sleeping babies: "O sleep, sweet infant, for we all must sleep, / And wake like babes, that we may wake with Him" (*CPW* 28-29). However much Hartley longs like Jesus to hold "By filial right / O'er all the world alike of thought and sense / The fulness of his Sire's omnipotence" (*HCP* "Jesus Praying," MS), his identification is always with the fallen child-man rather than "our greater Parent," prelapsarian man. Maturity is depicted as irrevocably out of reach. At the Last Day, man will be fathered in and comforted by the fostering, fathering God. At Judgment we shall all be children together:

> The babe that drew but once its breath on earth
> And the grey chronicle of ninety years,
> Shall meet together in one family,
> Coeval children of the one great Sire ("To Jeannette, Six Weeks Old,"
> *CPW* 186)

Childhood is thus not only mankind's beginning, but its goal as well.

Adulthood as Hartley depicts it, is not the usual Wordsworthian trade-off of the goods of the philosophic mind for the glories in the flower and splendors in the grass. Rather it is banal, mechanical, and emptied out. Adulthood is neither the worthy nor the natural extension of the childhood Hartley depicts. Rather it is a surprising betrayal. Childhood was, is, and ever will be the time of Being—being whole—of unity of thought and feeling; but adulthood is the period of Becoming—becoming less and less—of subdivision and calculated prudence. In Hartley's excruciating poems of adulthood, he signals deep distress through the use of the language of time, measure, and classification. Such language represents the betrayal of childhood unity. His most famous sonnet juxtaposes the timelessness of childhood with the measured existence of adulthood:

> Long time a child, and still a child, when years
> Had painted manhood on my cheek, was I,—
> For yet I lived like one not born to die;
> A thriftless prodigal of smiles and tears,
> No hope I needed, and I knew no fears.
> But sleep though sweet, is only sleep, and waking,
> I waked to sleep no more, at once o'ertaking
> The vanguard of my age, with all arrears
> Of duty on my back. Nor child, nor man,
> Nor youth, nor sage, I find my head is grey,
> For I have lost the race I never ran:
> A rathe December blights my lagging May;
> And still I am a child, tho' I be old,
> Time is my debtor for my years untold (*CPW* 7)

Another poem of remorse, "Written in a Bible," draws painful contrast between Hartley at seventeen, "When it was hoped I should be all / Which once, alas! I might have been," and Hartley at thirty-five (*CPW* 223). In one of a series of remorseful New Year's poems, measurement and pain go together.

> Could I have known that the first new year's sun
> Could rise upon me—and so little done—
> Not any worthy work performed of mine
> While thirty-eight has turned to thirty-nine
> How much myself I had myself abhorred
> Too like the thriftless servant of the Lord—
> That thriftless servant of a Lord austere
> That wrong'd his Lord from sloth and selfish fear ("To the Old Year," *NP* 90)

Beguiled by the moral and aesthetic superiority of the timeless childhood state to the thrifty calculated adult state, Hartley finds no possibility of surviving into adulthood. A doggedly retrospective reader, recapitulating, "chewing the cud" of blissful images, Hartley read and wrote for return to the static sites of his childhood reading: "Robinson Crusoe . . . on his island still . . . Don Quixote . . . still walking in the Sierra Morena . . . Dear Uncle Toby . . . yet riding his Hobby Horse . . . and little Goody . . . still trudging about with . . . her lame Billy, and her raven Ralph" (*HCP*, "Untitled Essay on Books"). Reading for stasis, writing without a plan, Hartley evades thinking about the future.

How did the infinitely promising boy with all the world before him in 1807 become the remorseful old man producing abject whimsies in his tiny northern cottage? To chronicle Hartley Coleridge's life and its movement from hope to despair is to reveal the exorbitant human costs of making a life as a perfect Romantic Child.

The first child of Sara Fricker Coleridge and Samuel Taylor Coleridge, David Hartley Coleridge was born on September 19, 1796. A month premature, he was a small baby who remained a small, almost elfin figure all his life. As he would be for his daughter's birth Coleridge was away when Hartley was born, but returned home to greet the infant in three sonnets of such emphatic paternal ambivalence that he even dallies imaginatively with the baby's death: "As sometimes, through excess of hope, I fear" (*PW* 1: 154).[11] Spotted early as gifted, a "Pisces rarissima," "a genius" by his father and friends, Hartley gave childhood signs of the unusual intellectual quickness and emotional sensibility that soon made him the subject of Romantic poems and anecdotes. Educated at home, Greta Hall shared with the Southeys, until his twelfth year, Hartley from three until six received tender loving attention from his father, especially in the years between 1799-1804, after Coleridge returned from Germany and before he went to

Malta. After 1806-7, however, Hartley saw little of his father. Starting in 1808, at twelve, Hartley and his brother Derwent were sent to school at Mr. Dawes's academy in Ambleside—Hartley for free because of Dawes's delight in teaching so brilliant a boy. Though Hartley never really played with his schoolmates—he was physically maladroit and never played games—he kept on good terms with the other students by telling them a nightly serial, "The Tale," about virtuous robbers and a father-son rivalry. Hartley was a brilliant Greek scholar but his other training, both socially and intellectually, was erratic: his Latin was limited, his mathematics was shaky, his manners were bohemian. By the time Hartley was ready to go up to Oxford, Coleridge off in London was too distracted, depressed, and addicted to be able to do anything for his son. Through the efforts of Southey, Wordsworth, Poole, and other friends of the family, Hartley was able to matriculate at Merton College, Oxford in May 1815. His undergraduate career was successful: he struck his contemporaries as brilliant, unworldly, eccentric, and eloquent beyond all living men "except his father" (H. Hartman 65). Hartley's Oxford years were crowned by his election to a fellowship at Oriel College. Though Hartley had taken only a second-class degree (the spottiness of his preparation had tarnished his otherwise brilliant performance), the Fellows of Oriel were impressed by his sheer brain power and great promise. All Hartley needed to do to be assured of a secure position for the rest of his life was to complete a probationary year (literally six months of residency at Oriel). But against all precedent, he was removed from the fellowship at the end of his probationary year on the grounds of "intemperance." Whether Hartley had in fact done much more than get tipsy several times with non-Oriel drinking friends (Fellows were expected to chose their companions from members of the College) remains in question. What is clear is that Oriel was in 1820 the most priggish and rigid of Oxford colleges, while Hartley Coleridge was the least priggish and most whimsical of possible Fellows. Hartley ignored the injunction to choose his associates from among Oriel men; he was erratic in chapel attendance and undependable in delivering assigned lectures ("declamations"); and he was whimsical. Thomas Mozley's *Reminiscences, chiefly of Oriel College* include an anecdote of a rebuke given to Hartley for appearing in the Senior Common Room looking as if he had not shaved in a week. He protested and claimed to have been misjudged, and "presented himself unmistakably shaven and shorn the next day. He was then absent from the common room for a week, in spite of repeated summons. He then appeared with such growth on his face as clearly proved the former charge of a week's neglect to have been a gross exaggeration"

(1: 86). Hartley's harmless whimsy prejudiced the Fellows against him. Despite the eloquent and assiduous pleas of S. T. Coleridge and Hartley's courteous and closely-reasoned brief in his own defense, he was removed from the fellowship at the end of the probationary year. This disappointment, which might have been nothing but a minor set-back in the life of another young man—STC had botched his own Cambridge career, Shelley was expelled, J. S. Mill had a breakdown—was the crucial failure of Hartley's life. First his father and eventually Hartley himself treated the loss of the fellowship as a cataclysm from which Hartley could hardly be expected to recover. And he did not.

The loss of the fellowship marked the beginning of Hartley's lifetime pattern of wandering, despondency, and desultory literary activity. He spent two years in London as a journalist writing for *The London Magazine* and other periodicals. Though he met with some professional success as a hack journalist, he periodically went missing on drinking sprees that left him remorseful and unable to face friends and family. In 1822 in response to this pattern a newly responsible Coleridge insisted that Hartley return to Ambleside as Mr. Dawes's assistant schoolmaster. Hartley did not want to return. He thought, correctly, that he would deteriorate and stagnate back in the Lakes. But he was not strong enough to stand out against his father's insistence and his own remorse. He returned to the north in 1822 and remained there until his death in 1849; he never saw London—or his father—again. After a brief unhappy stint as a schoolmaster, he passed a short sojourn in Leeds where he managed, under contract and under his publisher-landlord's watchful eye, to produce the *Biographia Borealis* (1833), a creditable volume of biographies of "Northern Worthies." One fine volume of poetry, *Poems,* was published in 1833, but he composed hundreds of other poems still unpublished at his death.[12] Except for two brief periods of teaching, he was largely unemployed, supported by the bounty of his mother, the legacy of his father, the kindness of friends, and an occasional pittance from his journalistic efforts. In 1837 he settled permanently in tiny Nab Cottage, the rent paid by his family, and cared for the doting Mrs. Fleming. He spent the Nab years partly in study, partly in companionable conversation in middle-class drawing rooms and country pubs. He talked so well that he became a minor tourist attraction for visitors to the Lakes. He drank ever more heavily as the years went by, often to excess. He slept in barns and sometimes in ditches but never alienated his many friends and well wishers. "Li'le Hartley," as the country people called him, died at fifty-two on January 6, 1849, a figure of charm and pathos to the end. He left no wife, no children, no literary name, only a cache of some ninety volumes of unpublished poems, essays, reading notes, speculations, and marginal doodles.

The Designated Genius

But thou, my babe! shalt wander like a breeze
By lakes and sandy shores, beneath the crags
Of ancient mountain, and beneath the clouds . . .
Great universal Teacher! He shall mould
Thy spirit . . .
—S. T. Coleridge, "Frost at Midnight" (1798)

I fear that if he lives, he will dream his life away like his father, too much delighted with his own ideas ever to embody them, or suffer them, if he can help it, to be disturbed. I gave him Robinson Crusoe *two years ago. He never has read, nor will read, beyond Robinson's departure from the island. "No," he says, "he does not care about him afterwards, and never will . . .*
—Robert Southey on Hartley Coleridge, age eight.

Thy prayer was heard: I "wander'd like a breeze,"
By mountain brooks and solitary meres . . .
—Hartley Coleridge, "Dedicatory Sonnet to S. T. Coleridge" (1833)

Literally and figuratively David Hartley Coleridge was the first-born son and heir of English Romanticism. Though no one consciously willed Hartley's destiny the boy was elected in infancy, principally because of his intense sensibility and possibly because of his intention-bearing name to lead an experimental childhood in the spirit of the new poetry. Almost from his birth, poems by Coleridge and Wordsworth marked Hartley as a chosen child both of Nature (in the spirit of the philosopher for whom he was named) and of the self-reflective philosophic mind[13] He appears as the infant of "Frost at Midnight" and "The Nightingale," and later as the small boy of the conclusion to "Christabel," and of "To H.C., Six Years Old" and "Ode: Intimations of Immortality from Recollections of Early Childhood." He stars in the powerful version of Romantic childhood produced by Wordsworth and Coleridge. Finding in Hartley the winning qualities of Romantic childhood and then projecting back upon Hartley an augmented version of those qualities, Coleridge made of Hartley the prototype of the Romantic child. By the time Hartley first went to school, at the age of eleven, he had already inspired the texts that were to serve as his scripts for the remainder of his life. The beloved child of a loving and empathetic but seductive and abandoning father, Hartley desperately longed to please his great father. He lit upon the desperate expedient of reproducing his childhood practices in order to re-invoke the loving pleasure STC had once taken in his pleasant childish ways. Hartley's gladhearted and all-too-filial assent to STC's brilliant characterization gave him a lifetime role as arrested child. The role demanded a renunciation of adulthood but offered the compensatory gratification of returning to his father what he had good reason to believe his father most desired. For his father had embodied that desire in many ways: enacting it in intense father-son dialogues, retailing it in eloquent anecdotes of the child genius, and publishing it in stunning poems starring Hartley as the living symbol of creative nature and imaginative mind.

When Coleridge chose to name his son *David Hartley Coleridge* after the great philosopher of Associationism, the name carried with it the implication of an experimental life in store for the child, to "compound the mind out of the senses" according to the eighteenth-century materialist project (Willey 149). In Philosopher David Hartley's spiritualized Associationism, sensation proceeding from natural beauty automatically leads on to sympathy, morality, and Christian love. Because human beings in Hartley's "wise passiveness" version of materialist determinism are largely the passive products of their circumstance, it is crucial for the developing mind to be properly situated so as to be open to nature's "vibrations." As befitted the namesake of the philosopher who taught how the mind is compounded out of the senses (Willey 149), little David Hartley (initially "David Hartley," then and evermore "Hartley"; never "David") had a role as "Nature's playmate" already waiting for him. During Hartley's infancy, Coleridge wrote frequently of his intention to give the child an exemplary associationist rearing in an exemplary rural Hartleian environment, his mind stocked with the joyous natural imagery—"that with the night / He may associate joy" ("Nightingale"). Coleridge knew what he wanted in a child, knew what he admired in childhood, and baby Hartley proved extraordinarily successful from the first as a Hartleian register of sensation—Coleridge would liken him to that delicate instrument of physico-spiritual sensation, the Eolian Harp.[14] Fascinated by this psycho-spiritual borderland of the material, nature spiritualized, Coleridge wrote during Hartley's first year "The Foster's Mother's Tale," an account of the psychopathology of a Natural Child who grows to a Natural Man. A mysterious foundling is discovered, like Geraldine of "Christabel," under a great oak:

> Well, he brought him home,
> And rear'd him at the then Lord Velez's cost.
> And so the babe grew up a pretty boy,
> A pretty boy, but most unteachable—
> And never learnt a prayer, nor told a bead,
> But knew the names of birds, and mock'd their notes,
> And whistled, as he were a bird himself... (*PW* 1: 183, ll. 26-32)

This "unteachable" child is an instinctive ornithologist, a poet with nature's own voice, and an innate anti-theologian. This "doted-on Hartley," this "darling of the Sun and of the Breeze," this child of nature resists religious orthodoxy: "Shall I suffer the Toad of Priesthood," Coleridge demands of Godwin, "to spurt out his foul juice on this Babe's Face?" (*CCL* 1: 625). Mimicking birdsong like Wordsworth's Boy of Winander, the "pretty boy" is a figure of authentic knowledge (thus his association with natural science and poetry) rather than rote authority (thus his resistance to papist fol-de-rol). He hungers for the freedom of natural man: "How sweet it were on lake or wild savannah, / To hunt for food and be a naked man, / And wander up and down at liberty" (61-64). Eventually, by the light of the Moon, that presiding sign in Coleridge of unified consciousness and Hartley's special emblem, the Boy disappears into infinite potential among the trackless fields and waters and "savage men" of America.

Some years after composing this poem, Coleridge exultantly matches Hartley at ages seven and ten to this literary model. Coleridge's obvious pleasure in the congruence between the live boy with his textual precursor seems partly an admiration for the charm of his literary and human offspring and partly pride at successful prognostication. In a display of paternal and authorial achievement, Coleridge tacitly woos the beloved Sara Hutchinson with an account of his double creation:

> Some time ago, I watched Hartley under the Trees, down by the River—the Birds singing so sweetly above him / & he evidently lost in thought. I went down, & asked him what his Thoughts were—and so he hugged me, & said after a while, "I thought, how I love the sweet Birds, & the Flowers, & Derwent, and Thinking; & how I hate Reading, & being wise, & being Good." Does not this remind you of "the pretty Boy" in my Foster-Mother's Tale....
> (Summer 1802, *CCL* 2: 804)

Four years later, Coleridge again glosses ten-year-old Hartley's restlessness on a trip as the same as the "pretty Boy's," a "hatred of confinement (in which in fancy at least 'Doth sing a doleful song about green fields, / How sweet it were in Woods and wild Savannas / To hunt for Food and be a naked man / And wander up and down at Liberty')" (*CCL* 2: 1204-5). In a notebook written in the 1830s, Hartley indicates that he knew from early childhood the poem in which he was prefigured: "I cannot tell whether it was from ["Ruth"] or from my father's Foster-Mother's Tale—that I first learned the word Savannah . . . one of the noblest sounding words that I know in any language—and presents the most beautiful image of any landscape world whatever" (*HCP,* "Untitled Essay on Books").

During the first eleven years of Hartley's life, Coleridge consistently depicted him as a Nature child operating in harmony with the formative creative principle of "Natura Naturans," the natural energies that continually generate all the material world. Hartley is regularly represented as buoyantly spontaneous and impatient of all restraint. His embodiment as nature is evident both in his animist harmony with nature as well as in his self-impelled and "breeze-like" impatience of external governance. Thus Coleridge delights in recording Hartley's conscious sense of kinship to natural objects, both passive as in his "intense wish to have Ant-heaps near [?a/our] house/his *Brahman* love & awe of Life . . ." (*NB* 1: 959) and active as in his "shouting to some foxgloves and fern, which he has transplanted . . . telling then what he will do for them if they grow like good boys!" (*CCL* 1: 614).

The assumption of pre-existing harmony between Hartley as infant and the natural world undergirds "Frost at Midnight" and "The Nightingale," both written well before Hartley's second birthday. In "Frost at Midnight," Hartley, as silent infant whose quiet breathings merely supplement and heighten the poet's conscious articulation, seems simply a representative infant whose sleeping life is an unconscious emblem of the numinous life of nature that is also evident in frost, the flapping ash of the fire, and all the processes of the turning year. For this sleeping and not-yet-conscious child, Coleridge prays a later life of conscious kinship with the nature to which he is already unconsciously allied:

> Dear Babe, that sleepest cradled by my side,
> Whose gentle breathings, heard in this deep calm,
> Fill up the interspersed vacancies
> And momentary pauses of the thought!
> My babe so beautiful! it thrills my heart
> With tender gladness, thus to look on thee
> And think that thou shalt learn far other lore,
> And in far other scenes! . . .
> But *thou* my babe! shalt wander like a breeze

> By lakes and sandy shores, beneath the crag
> Of ancient mountain . . .
> . . . so shalt thou see and hear
> The lovely shapes and sounds intelligible
> Of that eternal language, which thy God
> Utters, who from eternity doth teach
> Himself in all, and all things in himself
> Great universal Teacher! he shall mould
> Thy spirit, and by giving make it ask.
> Therefore all seasons shall be sweet to thee . . . (*PW* 1: 242)

The Hartley of "Frost at Midnight" is really Everychild with little to individuate him. He is a sleeping tranquil bundle of potential life, manifesting no more intellect or individuality than the frost itself. Although Hartley talked early and burbled incessantly, in this poem he is silenced. Indeed, Coleridge's excision of the manuscript lines describing Hartley's excitement at the sight of a melting icicle (he would "shout / And stretch and flutter from [his] mother's arms / As [he] wouldst fly for very eagerness") indicates a will to quiet Hartley down in order to equate him with the very ground of nature's being, what Schiller describes as "the tacitly creative life, the serene spontaneity of their activity, existence in accordance with their own laws, the inner necessity, the eternal unity with themselves" (85).

"The Nightingale," written two months after "Frost at Midnight," represents an advance in Hartley's role as Nature. He is no mere representative baby, a role Coleridge would later assign somewhat condescendingly to "fat, healthy, hungry, pretty" Derwent, "the abstract idea of a Baby—a fit representative of Babe-borough" (*CCL* 2: 668). He no longer merely embodies Nature but explicates it. His developing powers of speech ("mars all things with his imitative lisp") and agency ("would place his hand beside his ear . . . and bid us listen") declare the pre-established harmony between Man and Nature. Sometime in the fall of 1797 according to Coburn's estimate (*NB* 1: 219n), when Hartley was little over a year, Coleridge records an episode that he glosses as an uncanny revelation of microcosmic and macrocosmic correspondence between the infant and the universe: "—Hartley fell down & hurt himself—I caught him up crying & screaming—& ran out of doors with him—The Moon caught his eye—he ceased crying immediately—& his eyes & the tears in them, how they glittered in the Moonlight!" (*NB* 1: 219)[15] Attachment psychologists would gloss the scene as a good moment of both "sensitive attunement" (Stern) and "joint attention" (Dunham & Dunham). Here Coleridge is so sensitively attuned to the child's distress that he matches the infant's intensity of action and feeling: the baby is hurt ("crying & screaming"), the parent hurriedly "caught him up crying & screaming—& ran . . ." in a syntactical turn that suggests the father's involvement in "crying and screaming" too. As he watches the baby watching the moon, there is "shared attention" to their common object. Father and son mutually acknowledge a shared experience: Hartley sees the moon, Coleridge sees the moon and also sees Hartley seeing the moon; there is an exchange of vision as the father's eyes gaze at the child's eyes bright with the moonlight. The child's comfort comes not simply from the beauty of the moon but from the *shared* sight of the moon; the moon thus can function as a surrogate parent to the baby and mirror back a comfortable image because the parent is participating in the sight with the baby. A moment such as this explains the powerful bonding between the attentive noticing father and this close-watched beloved baby.

This Notebook entry illustrates why Coleridge, as a sometimes deeply intuitive parent, was so lovingly remembered by Hartley in later years. The reworking of the episode in "The Nightingale," however, shows Coleridge's prising Hartley out of the collaborative shared occasion and staging him as a fully autonomous child. In "The Nightingale," the reciprocity between baby and father is displaced by a reciprocity between the child and the moon. This baby is an active wise child who "knows well the evening star" and is capable of agency even though "capable of no articulate sound": "How he would place his hand beside his ear, / His little hand, the small forefinger up, / And bid us listen!" (*PW* 266-67). This strong child is not shown as liable to the ordinary material accidents of childhood; he does not "fall down & hurt himself" but is rather the inexplicable sensitive receiver of "that strange thing, an infant's dream." The dream is "strange," that is, incongruous because an innocent and inexperienced infant would have committed no wrongs to merit a terrifying dream.[16] Indeed, Kathleen Coburn argues that the dream was Coleridge's transferred to Hartley's, a transferal that suggests both Coleridge's promotion of psychic woe above physical misfortune and also his unselfconscious projection of his own feelings onto the infant. Uncannily agitated by this "strange" dream, the child is also uncannily comforted by the moon:

> I hurried with him to our orchard-plot,
> And he beheld the moon, and hushed at once,
> Suspends his sobs, and laughs most silently,
> While his fair eyes, that swam with undropped tears,
> Did glitter in the yellow moon-beam! Well!—
> It is a father's tale . . . (*PW* 1: 267)

The comfort of shared attention, so notable in the Notebook entry, is deemphasized and replaced in the poem by the child's autonomous power through his allegiance with the magical moon. The moon-child axis is a paradoxical Romantic image in which antithetical elements are brilliantly suspended—the light-filled eyeball and the moon; the microcosm and the macrocosm; laughter and tears; brightness and darkness; sound and stillness; intimacy and vast distances. The glamour of the scene establishes the supreme adequacy of the solitary child who has no need for paternal support. The child with praeternatural authority needs no nurturing.

Represented here as the intersection of the human with the natural, Hartley is frequently represented as an airy spirit, an Ariel figure who inspirits dull matter as a spirit, a soul, an anima, a breath or breeze, air or motion. "He was not fully aware he had a body at all" (Griggs *HC* 50). Small, thin, delicate—unlike the "fat baby" Derwent—indifferent to food and drink ("Southey says, that all Hartley's Guts are in his Brains, and Derwent's Brains in his Guts" [*CCL* 2: 1022]), Hartley was always in motion, a hyperkinetic child whose "nerves are as wakeful as the Strings of an Eolian Harp" (*CCL* 2: 909). Coleridge often read Hartley's perpetual motion as marking him as thing, as a natural force or praeternatural being rather than a human being. His mobility even made his father assume Hartley the toddler as indifferent to pain:

> Never was more joyous creature born—Pain with him is so wholly transsubstantiated by the Joys that had rolled on before, & rushed in after, that oftentimes 5 minutes after his Mother has whipt him, he has gone up & asked her to whip him again. (*CCL* 1: 612)

Above all Hartley in infancy and boyhood is associated with the breeze and with wind-tossed leaves and flowers. Virtually all references to the child stress his mobility and interpret his mobility as cognate both with his own joy and the joy of the natural world. Coleridge makes this analogue psychedelically vivid in his observations of Hartley, six, and Derwent, two, at play in the windy splendor of a September day:

> It is in very truth a sunny, misty, cloudy, dazzling, howling, omniform Day / & I have been looking at as pretty a sight as a Father's eyes could well see— Hartley & Little Derwent running in the Green, where the Gusts blow most madly—both with their Hair floating & tossing, a miniature of the agitated Trees below which they were playing / inebriate both with the pleasure— Hartley whirling round for joy—Derwent eddying half willingly, half by the

force of the Gust—driven backward, struggling forward, & shouting his little hymn of Joy. (*CCL* 2: 871-72)

Embodying a principle of energy, Hartley is represented as spirit breathing a finer air: "the air, which yonder sallow-faced & yawning Tourist is breathing, is to my Babe a perpetual Nitrous Oxyde" (*CCL* 1: 612). Drunk on air, Hartley is "all Health & exstacy—He is a Spirit dancing on an aspen Leaf—unwearied in Joy, from morning to night indefatigably joyous" (*CCL* 1: 615). Coleridge repeatedly describes the boy as "a fairy elf—all life, all motion—indefatigable in joy—a spirit of Joy dancing on an Aspen leaf. From morning to night, he whirls about and about, whisks, whirls, and eddies, like a blossom in a May-breeze—" (*CCL* 2: 668), one who uses "the air & the Breezes as skipping Ropes" (*CCL* 2: 746). Wordsworth's "To H.C., Six Years Old" augments this characterization of Hartley as inhabitant of air, a "fairy voyager" with "breeze-like motions" moving in air rather than on "an earthly stream." So "exquisitely wild," Wordsworth's H.C. is an object of prophetic anxiety. Unlike the familiar *senex puer,* the Wise Child too grave and somber to live long, Hartley is too light, too quick, too fleeting to live. Thus for the years "when Pain might be thy guest," Wordsworth predicts:

> Nature will either end thee quite;
> Or, lengthening out thy season of delight,
> Preserve for thee, by individual right,
> A young lamb's heart among the full-grown flocks.
> What hast thou to do with sorrow,
> Or the injuries of tomorrow? ("To H.C. Six Years Old," *PW* 290)

This "restless, whirling, self-sufficing creature," as Dorothy Wordsworth called him (*WLMY* 1: 125), invites presentation as a figure of nature in his seeming self-sufficiency and as a human being interassimilated with nature. Though Coleridge himself was emotionally voracious and siphoned off sympathy from all those around him, he represented little Hartley—otherwise seen as so much like himself—as virtually autonomous, as one whose self-sufficiency needed no others. Between four and six, Hartley is represented by Coleridge as "a thing sui Generis," "his own Self—piscis rarissima"; "a strange strange Boy—*'exquisitely wild!'*[17] An utter Visionary! like the Moon among thin Clouds, he moves in a circle of Light of his own making—he alone, in a Light of his own" (*CCL* 2: 802, 960, 1014).

The images in which Hartley is represented—though never by the mother who regularly tended and attempted to guide him—all remove him from the sphere of possible or necessary adult responsibility or control. If he is "sui generis" and a unique "piscis rarissima," then no prior rule need apply. Like the breeze blowing where it listeth, like the spirit of which the breeze is an emblem, the whirling, spontaneous, and ungovernable child "always finds and never seeks" without the need for a parent. Like the exhilarating new anaesthetic Nitrous Oxide, an air fresher than fresh air, this airy sprite offers a new pure-minded high to those who contemplate him as he spins his airy dance. Like the cool moon, always for Coleridge an image of unique self-sufficiency, "who comforts those she sees / But knows not what eyes are upward cast," Hartley needs no human comfort.[18] Thus Hartley is habitually represented by his tragically proud and needy father more as a self-complete object than as a growing child in need of friends and teachers and parental guidance. Southey worried over Hartley's seeming indifference to the sufferings of others, noting that when Mrs. Wilson was sick, "He never manifested the slightest uneasiness or concern about her nor would ever go near her"(1: 311). But Coleridge read Hartley's happy self-sufficiency and seeming obliviousness to complicated adult anxieties as a triumphal state:

> ... never can I read De la Motte Fouqué's beautiful Faery Tale ... of Undina, the Water-Fay, before she had a Soul, beloved by all whether they would or no, & as indifferent to all, herself included, as a blossom whirling in a May-gale, without having Hartley recalled to me, as he appeared from infancy to his boyhood ... (*CCL* 5: 110-111)

But this "seemingly constitutional insensibility" to the direct and obvious needs and feelings of others and to the scene before him (*CCL* 5: 110), was linked to a key characteristic that made him even more the exemplary Romantic Child: the primacy of the idea, the "need of having [sense impressions] generalized into *thoughts* before they had an interest, or even a distinct place, in his Consciousness" (*CCL* 5: 110). In his joyful nonstop whirl of activity, Hartley might be manifesting in a heightened degree, the qualities assumed to belong to all children. But what most startled his friends and family, and led to his being "considered as a Genius by Wordsworth, & Southey—indeed, by every one who has seen much of him," however, was the combination of these qualities with a special kind of Romantically-modulated intellectual precocity, not cram knowledge ("He is very backward in his Book-learning") but a gift for self-reflexive philosophical idealism, a fascination with thinking about the process of thinking (*CCL* 2: 1022). The "young philosopher," seemed designed by nature to be a philosophic Idealist, one for whom the world discovered or created by thought was considerably more real and more interesting than the world of corporal objects. Both Wordsworth and Coleridge considered such a temperament, which both had manifested in their own childhoods, as the cornerstone of Romantic perception. Wordsworth's explanatory note to the Immortality Ode is well known:

> I was often unable to think of external things as having external existence, and I communed with all that I saw as something not apart from, but inherent in, my own immaterial nature. Many times while going to school have I grasped at a wall or tree to recall myself from this abyss of idealism to the reality. (*Prose* 3: 194)

In the autobiographical letters, Coleridge drafted during Hartley's first year, he emphasizes that in his own childhood he ". . . never regarded *my senses* in any way as he criteria of my belief. I regulated all my creeds by my conceptions not by my *sight*—even at [eight years of age]" (*CCL* 1: 354). He boasted that abstraction—of social conduct and of intellectual process—defined him: "From my very early childhood I have been accustomed to *abstract* and as it were unrealize whatever of more than common interest my eyes dwelt on . . . (*Friend* 1: 521n) Hartley's temperamental affinity towards "obstinate questionings / Of sense and outward things" was therefore welcome.

Nicknamed "Philosopher" by Lamb and "Moses" by Southey, Hartley seemed to Southey "as miraculous a boy as ever King Pharaoh's daughter found his namesake to be" (*SL* 1: 241). "The boy's great delight is to get his father to talk metaphysics to him," Southey wrote just after Hartley's seventh birthday:

> Few men understand him so perfectly;—and then his own incidental sayings are quite wonderful. "The pity is,"—said he one day to his father, who was expressing some wonder that he was not so pleased as he expected with riding in a wheelbarrow—"the pity is that *I'se* always thinking my thoughts." The child's Imagination is equally surprising; he invents the wildest tales you every heard,—a history of the Kings of England, who are to be. "How do you know that this is to come to pass, Hartley?" "Why you know it must be something or it would not be in my head," and so because it had not been, did Moses conclude that it must be, and he prophesies of his King Thomas the 3rd. Then he has a tale of a monstrous beast called the Rabzeze Kallaton,

whose skeleton is on the outside of its flesh; and he goes on with the oddest and most original inventions, till he sometimes actually terrifies himself, and says "*I'se* afraid of my own thoughts." (*SL* 1: 241-42)

Hartley's interest in thinking about thinking, in pursuing metaphysical questions, is unusual but by no means unknown, as Gareth Matthews has pointed out. In *Philosophy and the Young Child,* Matthews cites Tim, aged six, who tries to reason out such questions as "how can we be sure that everything is not a dream"; and Denis, six, who critiques his brother's comment about "the fuss people make about getting up early, and things" saying "Early and late *aren't* things. They're not things like tables and chairs and cups—things you can move" (14). Michael, seven, son of a computer programmer and a mathematician worries about the infinitude of the universe: "I don't like to [think] about the universe without an end. It gives me a funny feeling in my stomach. If the universe goes on forever, there is no place for God to live, who made it" (34). These ruminations suggest to Matthews that "for many young members of the human race, philosophical thinking—including on occasion, subtle and ingenious reasoning—is as natural as making music and playing games, and quite as much a part of being human" (36). As Matthews notes, most of the children he cites have been taken seriously by parents who are willing to play speculative games with them and to respond respectfully to children's thoughts. Hartley, evidently gifted at thought games, had, in addition, a father who confessedly could "understand & sympathize with, his wild Fancies—& suggest others of my own" (*CCL* 2: 804).

This father explicitly recalled his own early idealism in the days of Hartley's infancy, early introduced him to philosophical thinking. Indeed Coleridge sought to educe evidence of his emerging idealist philosophical position from the child Hartley during the years from 1801 to 1803. If little Hartley Coleridge intuitively and spontaneously thought like a philosophical idealist, then Kant was right and John Locke and David Hartley were wrong. Between the winter of 1801 when Coleridge records his first serious conversation with Hartley, then four, and winter 1803, when Coleridge left for Malta, the Hartley of Romantic folklore emerges from Coleridge's accounts of those conversations. Hartley is at once joyous fairy sprite and philosophic genius, the living embodiment of joy and of the creative mind. The theme of these father-son dialogues is Thinking Thoughts. This is also the theme of Coleridge's philosophical studies during 1801 and 1802. It is during 1801 and 1802 that Coleridge writes the "Metaphysical Letters" to Josiah Wedgwood; it is during this period that

Kant "took possession of [Coleridge] as with a giant's hand"; it is during this period that Coleridge renounces Hume's and Hartley's empiricism for a new system: "The pith of my system is to make the senses out of the mind—not the mind out of the senses, as Locke did" (Ashton 195). During Hartley's fifth year, Coleridge was on the alert to notice, to educe, and to understand—perhaps in Hartley's telling later phrase to *over-understand*—the boy's comments on "thinking my thoughts." On Monday, February 9, 1801—in the midst of drafting his Kantian letters to Wedgwood—Coleridge sat the four-year-old on his lap and drew him out on the subjects of "Life, Reality, Pictures, & Thinking":

> He sate on my knee for half an hour at least & was exceedingly serious . . . he pointed out without difficulty that there might be five Hartleys, Real Hartley, Shadow Hartley, Picture Hartley, Looking Glass Hartley, and Echo Hartley / and as to the difference between his Shadow & the Reflection in the Looking Glass he said, the Shadow was black, and he could not see his *eyes* in it. One thing, he said, was very curious—I asked him what he did when he thought of any thing—he answered—I look at it, and then go to sleep. To sleep?—said I—you mean, that you *shut your eyes*. Yes, he replied—I shut my eyes, & put my hands so (covering his eyes) and go to sleep—then I WAKE again, and away I run . . . the notion of that state of mind being Sleep is very striking, & he meant more, I suspect, than that People when asleep have their eyes shut—indeed I *know* it from the tone & *leap up* of Voice with which he uttered the word 'WAKE.' (*CCL* 2: 673)

Coleridge evidently had given the child cues to think hard and self-reflexively. The father probably suggested the topic of Hartley's identity. The father certainly formulated a question about thinking about thinking: "what he did when he thought of anything." Shepherds' children think sheep; musicians' children think melodies; philosophers' children think thinking. Six weeks later, Coleridge gives another account of Hartley as a mental gymnast in training. In response to the child's questions about the mountain landscape—"Will yon Mountains *always* be?"—Coleridge problematizes the meaning of *being*. To show Hartley that existence is complex and possibly constructed by thought, "I shewed him the whole magnificent Prospect in a Looking Glass, and held it up, so that the whole was like a Canopy or Ceiling over his head, & he struggled to express himself concerning the Difference between the Thing & the Image almost with convulsive Effort.—I never before saw such an Abstract of *Thinking* as a pure act & energy, of Thinking as distinguished from *Thoughts*" (NB 1: 923). It does not take away from Hartley's merits to note that Coleridge was evidently conducting a thought experiment with the child and that he took pride in the boy's ability to manipulate the elements of the experiment: introspection, a metaphysical vocabulary of being/non-being, selfhood, and identity.

At six, Hartley pleased Coleridge by his announcement "that he was thinking all day—all the morning, all the day, all the evening—'what it would be if there were *Nothing* / if all the men, & women, & Trees, & grass, and birds & beasts, & the Sky, & the Ground, were all gone / *Darkness & Coldness*—and nothing to be dark & cold'. . . . [His] motto from infancy might have been *not me alone!* 'My *Thoughts* are my Darlings!'" (*CCL* 2: 804) But Hartley's darling thoughts made him Coleridge's darling. The shared discourse bonded father and son: the six year old knew how interesting to his father were Thoughts and Thing, Non-Being and Nothingness (especially in the frame of "Trees & grass").

For Hartley to be abstracted in thought and "always Dreaming" was a source of mock disapproval but obvious pride to Coleridge who boasted to Poole of the seven-year-old:

> He said very prettily about half a year ago—on my reproving him for some inattention, & asking him if he did not see something—"My Father!" quoth he with flute-like Voice—"I see it—I saw it—I see it now—and tomorrow I shall see it when I shut my eyes, and when my eyes are open & I am looking at other Things; but Father! It's a sad pity—but it can't be helped, you know—but I am always being a bad Boy, because I am always *thinking of my Thoughts.*" (*CCL* 2: 1014)

The self-consciousness implicit in Hartley's locution "thinking *of* my thoughts" shows how early he learned, was coached, to contemplate his consciousness in action. The Hartley of Romantic anecdote is the Hartley of agonizing self-consciousness. Thus Crabb Robinson reports being told by a vaunting Coleridge that Hartley "used to be in an agony of thought, puzzling himself about the reality of existence, as when someone said to him: 'It is not now, but it is to be'; 'but,' said he, 'if it *is* to be, it is'" (Crabb Robinson 1: 44).

Hartley is consistently remembered by his father and those his father has briefed as dreamily abstracted—too abstracted ever to play games with other children—because he was so philosophically absorbed. Thus in Hartley's twenties, Coleridge cites Thomas Poole that notably reliable witness as remarking twenty years earlier of the infant Hartley "when he was not a year old" that "the little fellow never shewed any excitement at the *thing,* whatever it was, but afterwards, often when it had been removed, smiled or capered on the arm as at the *thought* of it" (*CCL* 5: 113). It is likely that this memory and this formulation are Coleridge's and not Poole's, however. The rational bachelor Poole was no great observer of infant development. He had indeed written to Coleridge in Germany dismissing the death of infant Berkeley as merely the loss of a not-yet-fully-human unformed being for whom Coleridge could feel no more than a merely instinctual sub-rational affection:

> Doubtless the affection found to exist between parents and infant children is a wise law of nature, a mere instinct to preserve Man in his infant state.... But the moment you make this affection the creature of reason, you degrade reason. When the infant becomes a reasonable being, then let the affection be a thing of reason, not before. (Lefebure, *BL* 115)

Poole had urged Coleridge not to distress himself irrationally by recalling the "merely instinctive attractions of an infant a few months old," reminding him that "I myself within the last months have experienced disappointments more weighty than the death of ten infants" (115). Such a friend, however well disposed, was not likely to be interested in why any speechless baby was smiling and still less likely to couch the reasons for such smiles in the idiom of "thoughts and things," a *vocabulary that Coleridge himself did not use until after Hartley's infancy.*

Just as Hartley's whirling, mobile behavior marked him as a bridge between mind and nature, just as his self-reflexive "thinking of my thoughts" marked him as the demonstration model for intuitive Idealism, so Hartley's childhood temperament marked the rightness of his mode of being. A child of Joy is the normative child—and, according to most reports including his own, Hartley's childhood was joyous. Hartley is the exemplary Romantic child in his affective role as a child of joy, brought up to associate the natural world with joy, brought up "vault[ing] & jubilat[ing]" (*CCL* 1: 625), "unwearied in Joy, from morning to night indefatigably joyous" (1: 615).

Not to say that Hartley was consistently cheerful and serene. Indeed he was a high-strung child with "nerves ... as wakeful as the Strings of an Eolian Harp" [*CCL* 2: 909]) subject to "presentiments," a favorite word, and dreads. But his sensibility was merely the defect of the quality that made his boyhood so interesting both to himself and others. Thus Coleridge's curious anecdote in a letter to Sara Hutchinson of Hartley, six, and "*crazy* Peter Crosthwaite" who visited the house:

> Hartley soon found out that he was crazy, turned pale & trembled—& Mrs W. snatched him up & brought him in to us / as soon as he came in, he cried aloud in an agony, nor could we appease him for near a quarter of an hour.

Why had Hartley cried? His explanation of the pain of incongruity delighted his father:

> Well, says he, you know, I am always frightened at things that are not like other things. But, Hartley! Said I—you would not be frightened if you were to see a number of new Beasts or Birds or Fishes in a Shew—Yes—said he! When I was a little Boy, I was frightened at the Monkey & the Dromedary in London (*so he was, poor fellow! God knows*)—but now I am not frightened at them, *because they are like themselves*. What do you mean, Hartley?—"Don't ask me so many questions, Papa! I can't bear it. I mean that I am frightened at men that are not like men / a Monkey is a monkey—& God made the Dromedary—but Peter is a crazy man—he has had a chain upon him!"— Poor fellow! When he recovered he spent the whole afternoon in whirling about the Kitchen, & telling Mrs Wilson wild Stories of his own extempore composition about mad men & mad animals. (*CCL* 2: 827-28)

As in so many of Coleridge's letters to Sara Hutchinson, the episode shows both father and son—the son a miniature STC—as intellectually and emotionally irresistible: The father is attentive, interested, engaged, sympathetic ("poor fellow" . . . "poor fellow"), and delighted at the boy's "whirling" and "wild" recovery into creation; the son, like his father, exhibits intense emotional range (moving from "agony" to "whirling" exhilaration) with subtle self-reflexive intellectual powers ("I am frightened at men that are not like men"), with spontaneous creativity ("wild Stories of his own extempore composition"). The father draws out the son's latent powers: "Don't ask me so many questions, Papa! I can't bear it." But Hartley's agonized distinctions, drawn from him by his persistently interrogative father, show him as a young genius as he contrives a juvenile version of Coleridge's distinction between Imitation and Copy: Imitations please, Coleridge would eventually argue, because the more they are contemplated, the more unifying resemblances can be discerned; but Copies disgust because their immediately and merely superficial resemblance to their original gives way on further examination to important differences. Thus, Hartley is "frightened of men that are not like men," men who are external physical copies of human beings but who lack the formative and essential quality of human beings—a controlling intellect. Hartley's very pain—soon turned to exuberant creative play—is evidence both of the delicacy of his sensibility and the acuity of his perception of difference.

Both adult observers and the retrospective Hartley represent his childhood as exuberantly and consciously happy. The joyous exuberance of the three-year-old who boldly rapped William Godwin on the shins with a ninepin (*CCL* 1: 553) , the four-year-old "happy as a young lamb" (*WLEY* 1: 330), the "thoroughly happy" ten-year-old (*WLMY* 1: 128) is never contradicted by the grown Hartley who confirms the contentment of his early years in endless retrospective praises of the books, the toys, the pursuits of his boyhood. Thus he invokes the reading of the "books of his childhood" because "They carry me back to childhood, and the journey is as salutary to the soul as native air is to a constitution broken by long residence in foreign climes" (*HCP,* "Untitled Essay on Books"). Thus he bestows his childhood shell collections on his cousin Cuthbert Southey with a benediction for equal childhood happiness: "I wish I could bequeath to him, a tithe of the pleasure . . . a little of the pride" (*LHC* 99). Indeed, Hartley recalls that unlike most children, he was so happy in boyhood that he never wished to grow up: "Distant hopes were never the stuff of my daydreams . . . [Yet] in my earliest childhood, I was not without a sense, a praesentiment, that I was enjoying more freedom than I could ever expect again" (*LHC* 159).

Hartley's conscious recollection of his childhood as happy in its freedom and its affections, was confirmed by all adults who knew him. If in adulthood, Hartley was morbidly sensitive to criticism and disapproval, in childhood he had basked in an almost universal approval. As a man, short of money and consumed with guilt, he noted his desire to please: "Next to money, my great excitement is to please those whom I love" (*HCP* Notebook 11), but in childhood he basked in universal approval and gave universal pleasure. He was a cosseted baby, suckled by his mother for about eighteen months until her next pregnancy intervened. Indeed Sara Coleridge so much enjoyed nursing and comforting her children—all three were suckled well into their second years—that Dorothy Wordsworth criticized her as a "sad fiddle faddle" for all the time she took feeding and dressing and playing with her two young children. Physically affectionate, Sara Coleridge cuddled her children and gave them the emotional mirroring necessary to growth; "Hart.[ley] seemed to learn to talk by touching his mother" (*NB* 1: 838). According to his father, "Love followed him like his Shadow" (*CCL* 5: 229). "My doted-on Hartley . . . the darling of the Sun and of the Breeze" (*CCL* 1: 625), and also "the *Darling*" "of the Village" (*CCL* 2: 1022), "a universal Darling . . . seems to have administered Love Philtres to the whole Town"(*CCL* 2: 662). Hartley was approved of—it seems—by everyone. Mr. Jackson the landlord doted on him; Mrs Wilson,

Wilsy, the housekeeper adored him and read to him by the hour. The Wordsworths and Southey called him genius. His schoolmaster, John Dawes, insisted on educating him gratis and gave him favored treatment. According to Derwent

> Mr. Dawes does not *love* him because . . . he ain't such a genius as Hartley—and that though Hartley should have done the same thing, yet all the others are punished, and Mr Dawes only *looks* at Hartley and never scolds *him,* and *all* the boys think it very unfair—he *is* a genius. (*LHC* 9)

Most of the adults he met in childhood smiled on him: Wilkie drew him, Anna Montagu was stunned by him.

Above all, Hartley's childhood was blest by "my great father." The approval of STC meant more to Hartley than the praise of all other adults together. In Hartley's journals and letters, his father is mentioned ten times as often as anyone else—more often than mother, than siblings, than Southey, than Wordsworth. Even though Coleridge was only intermittently present after Hartley's eighth year, he remained, even after his death, the dominant force for approval and disapproval. Though Sara Fricker Coleridge's steady conscientious mothering was the principal stable ground of his life, Hartley did not consciously find anything useful in her strength. In a high patriarchal era, Mrs. Coleridge's position in Southey's household had little public authority. Further, Sara Coleridge was careful always to give at least lip service to her husband's primacy. Derwent's "Memoir" gives an account of the preparations for his father's return from Malta. Needing some extra pillows for their father's bed, Sara Coleridge asked Derwent to surrender a pillow. He replied: "I would lie on straw for my father." As a grown-up Derwent would commend this fostering of filial respect for the father: "How well does this that speak for my mother. I was then just at the close of my 6th year" (*CCL* 2: 1199n). The whole menage at Greta maintained the fiction that Coleridge was not only a great man but a conscientious father. Southey, therefore, never filled the role as surrogate father for Hartley but was rather condescendingly regarded a pedantic goody-goody and nicknamed "Philagathos" (lover of goodness) in Hartley's journals.

The approval of the father was the source of the son's childhood happiness but also the source of his adult despair. Coleridge's over-identification with his brilliant son, his brilliantly empathetic passion for this chosen child fixed Hartley inescapably into the role of perpetual child. Because Coleridge found in Hartley what he wanted to find in a child, because Hartley matched Coleridge's conception of normative childhood, because

Hartley matched Coleridge's conception both of what he had himself been in childhood and might have been in a happier childhood, he felt authorized to represent this boy he understood so well. And the eloquence of that representation so fixed the boy that he could not separate an independent adult self off from the gorgeous creation his father had made. All his life he remained a text inscribed by the father, a hollow dummy, a literal child *persona* amplifying his father's voice.

In one document, at least, Hartley sketches a veiled account of his takeover. After Coleridge's death, Hartley was asked to prepare a biographical essay as introduction to a new edition from Moxon of the *Biographia Literaria*. Though Hartley talked for years of the essay as virtually ready for publication, it was found at his death among his papers as a series of fragments titled "Coleridge the Poet." Hartley's incomplete account of Coleridge is couched in his usual filial tone of adulation ("how paternally he watched over my childhood, how anxiously he plucked out every weakness, how hopefully he cherished every germ" [Griggs 1931: 1248]) but the analysis is uncharacteristically sardonic. He describes Coleridge as an "overunderstander" who unconsciously turned sympathetic companions into ventriloquist's dummies. Hartley gives the process the most affectionate of interpretations:

> My father, of all men whom I ever knew, was the readiest to love any one in whom there was but an appearance of goodness, and no man so egregiously over-rated the understanding of those whom he loved. In fact, he put his own sense in their nonsense, inspired their very common-place with his own transcendent meaning; if by any chance a stray word struck a new train of thought in his mind, he attributed the fulness of his own ideas to the unconscious speaker. In the kingdom of the intellect, he had no notion of meum or teum; he mistook the sympathy of affection . . . for a sympathy of intelligence, and would sometimes, in describing a conversation, repeat as the veritable speeches of his company, such bursts of eloquence, such revelations of Truth, as they could no more of [*sic*] uttered or conceived than they could have talk'd the language of paradise—no more than the *Bos loquitur* of Livy's epitomizer could have cultivated the words which the ventriloquist made to proceed from its muzzle. (Griggs 1931: 1249)

Such affectionate ventriloquism was "not even conscious . . . these forgeries always proceeded from some short observation, couched in words which might vent the meaning which he infused from his proper store— he galvanized a dead frog and fancied that it was a living cherub[?]" This "propensity to overunderstand (for he seldom misunderstood) the words of others" required only a sympathetic listener willing to give sympathetic prompts (1250). Allied to Coleridge's affinity for a sympathetic listener was his admiration for the quality that makes a willing listener: "Next to the love of truth for its own sake, the quality he valued most was docility. He had a distaste of disputatiousness . . ." (1249). He sketches his father as a self-engrossed thinker who mistook emotional sympathy (the loving child's eagerness to please, for example) for intellectual comprehension and assent. Since a conversation between Coleridge and a sympathetic but ignorant listener is here figured as the exchange of a ventriloquist and his dummy, the self-application is clear. A child, adoring his father, full of the "sympathy of affection," docilely fluent in his father's idiom, was sympathetically "overunderstood" and unconsciously ventriloquized leaving him as his father's imitative "zany" and attenuated "spectre."

Coleridge has a magical and virtually supernatural role in Hartley's life and work. As father, prophet, and muse Coleridge had made Hartley, scripting his life and inspiring his works. He is the only begetter—father and mother both. "But for him my things would either not have been conceived, or have been still born and perished in the infancy of neglect" (*HCP*, "Alan Cunningham's Opinion," "Essays and Marginalia"). That Hartley feels his life to have been prophetically scripted by his father and Wordsworth is everywhere apparent: ". . . after all, what can we call our own but energy, power, will? Could I point out all that I myself owe to my great fore-runners and contemporaries truly there remains but little over" (*HCP*, Notebook 40). Although he once denied that poets are prophets, he is conscious of his father's voice uttering his life, nowhere more strikingly than in the dedicatory poem to his sole published book of poetry:

> Father, and Bard Revered! To whom I owe,
> Whate'er it be, my little art of numbers,
> Thou, in thy night-watch o'er my cradled slumbers,
> Didst meditate the verse that lives to shew,
> (And long shall live, when we alike are low)
> Thy prayer how ardent, and thy hope how strong,
> That I should learn of Nature's self the song,
> The lore which none but Nature's pupils know.
> Thy prayer was heard: I "wander'd like a breeze" . . .
> . . . If good therein there be,
> That good, my sire, I dedicate to thee (*CPW* 2)

Knowing his life to have been charted with uncanny accuracy by Coleridge's "Frost at Midnight" and Wordsworth's "H.C., Six Years Old,"

Hartley lived a consciously textualized existence. An awareness of his life as a text in process of inscription may help to explain his fondness for and ease with Sterne's *The Life and Opinions of Tristram Shandy*, a work he quotes constantly.

I would argue that from reading *Tristram Shandy*, the domestic staple of Greta Hall and the literary model for Southey's *The Doctor*, Hartley learned to read himself as text.[19] Certainly Hartley knew the book well and aped its style. He cites his father's frequent praise of the book. Further, as Molly Lefebure notes, Southey was "a lifelong devotee of *Tristram Shandy*" (*BL*) who encouraged a Sternean absurdity of names at Greta Hall: Mrs. Coleridge as "Snouterumpater," young Sara as "Namput." Further, the boundaries between the inhabitants of Greta Hall and the inhabitants of Sterne's novel were blurred. Both realms were dominated by "My Father" and "My Uncle." In both realms, "My Father" is deeply contemptuous of his literal-minded wife and disappointed in his inadequate son. In both realms "My Father" is "a philosopher in grain,—speculative— systematical" (*TS* 49). In both, he is eloquent:

> But indeed, to speak of my father as he was;—he was certainly irresistible, both in his orations and disputations—he was born an orator;— θεοδίδακτος—Persuasion hung upon his lips, and the elements of Logick and Rhetorick were so blended up in him,—and withall, he had so shrewd a guess at the weaknesses and passions of his respondent,—that NATURE might have stood up and said,—"The man is eloquent." (37)

In both realms "My Father" is a monumental procrastinator:

> Every day for at least ten years together did my father resolve to have it mended.—'tis not mended yet;—yet no family but ours would have borne with it an hour,—and what is most astonishing, there was not a subject in the world upon which my father was so eloquent, as upon that of door-hinges.— And yet at the same time, he was certainly one of the greatest bubbles to them, I think, that history can produce: his rhetorick and conduct were at perpetual handy-cuffs.—Never did the parlour-door open—but his philosophy or his principles fell a victim to it;—three drops of oyl with a feather, and a smart stroke of the hammer, had saved his honour for ever. (147-48)

Uncle Toby, gentle, hobby-horsical, frightened of women partly resembles Uncle Southey in gentleness but even more Hartley himself who once told his sister that he would never "act Uncle" unless it be "my Uncle Toby" (Stephens 65). Even more, Tristram with his ill-starred name is a type of

Hartley with his: "I am as superstitious about names as Mr. Shandy. I have known more than one Hartley and none of them were all that could be wish'd either in themselves or their circumstances" (Stephens 67). Tristram and Hartley are both defined as sons and nephews without lives of their own. The record of their lives and opinions comes down to a record of *my Father's* and *my Uncle's*. In the evasive, intricately delaying, intricately digressive and regressive structure of Sterne's novel, the actual opportunity for Tristram to live a life is indefinitely delayed. The book is structured as an evasion of forward narrative motion; the life of Tristram Shandy is an endless regressive and self-reflexive deferral of living.

As a self-reflexive text, *The Life and Opinions of Tristram Shandy* constantly calls its mimetic task into question by its repeated references to itself as artifact: the scratchiness of the pens that inscribe it, the typographical and mechanical games (the famous black page for Yorick), the chats with resistant readers. Books that call attention to their own status as books rather than slices of life create for most readers, as Norman Holland has argued, "a deeper, inner sense of uncertainty, an uncanny feeling such as seeing my reflection in a mirror move and act by itself would produce. Because we fuse with a work of art, to call its reality into question is to question our own" (99). Poststructural theorists tend to deride, as Catherine Belsey does, the cozily "conservative" and "ultimately reassuring" experience of reading realistic texts. By "effac[ing] their own textuality," realistic texts seem to "reflect the world" and thus ratify it (51); but self-reflexive texts that problematize their textuality are deemed to destabilize and thus radicalize received conceptions of reality. Yet Hartley fits into unstable structure of *Tristram Shandy* as into an old unproblematical slipper. Philosopher Alasdair MacIntrye has argued that human beings through practice and action are story-telling animals who organize their lives using the stories they tell. The key question for each of us is "'Of what story or stories do I find myself a part?' We enter human society, that is, with one or more imputed characters—roles into which we have been drafted—and we have to learn what they are" (201). The ease with which Hartley enters and accommodates to a world of textual creation and suspension of a constantly deferred self suggests that he has normalized the condition of being written. His natural habitat, as it were, is in the middle distance between the "seer blest" inscribed on the poet's page and the flesh-and-blood dailiness of life. "Of what story . . . do I find myself a part?" Hartley finds himself most comfortable playing Tristram Shandy's liminal part—part child, part voice, part text.

The Muse who governs both text and boy is the voice of Ho Makarites, the absent father.[20] In "Adolf and Annette," a curious fairy tale unpublished in Hartley's lifetime, he represents Coleridge as Muse and subtly critiques his baleful effect.[21] Although the manuscript of the tale is undated, it is certainly written after Coleridge's death and no earlier than 1835 when the journals begin to show extensive interest in fairy stories. It may have been written in response to his sister's *Phantasmion* (1837). The story follows a familiar fairy-tale pattern. Infant twins, Adolf and Annette, are carried off to safety in their cradle-ark by the same icy flood waters that sweep away their parents' valley cottage. In the safety of the mountains, companioned by bees and birds who feed them, cheered by the clear "rattling sykes" and fair "red & purple berries" of the "short mountain turf," the twins are nurtured by the androgynous "White Lady" who is simultaneously the spirit of maternal nature and the spirit of paternal poetry. The White Lady (who speaks only in the paternal tetrameter of "Christabel") is nurturing during the twins' earliest years, then increasing distant, and eventually absent. She takes her leave as the twins approach puberty and enjoins them against growing up; they should remain docile and never leave their mountain home "to see the vale that lies below." But the Vale is so tempting, glittering white with the very whiteness of the White Lady—and the voice of the White Lady rings in the air—and the twins descend "the white abyss" of a terrible waterfall to a glittering and dead land of salt—the land of the Cities of the Plain— where the white fruit on the trees is salt as Sodom apples. "Everything was white and shining, but everything except they two, was dead." On the point of death, the twins hear the voice of the White Lady in a hidden stream and are guided to a patch of scruffy moorland by a pool. Here, banished forever from their edenic home but rescued from the salt plain, they can remain in perpetual exile. The fairy tale is a parable of Hartley's life—boyhood in Eden; descent to the glittering prizes of Oxford, that Dead Sea Sodom; protective detention in Grasmere—with Coleridge functioning as absent guiding spirit. The White Lady whose voice is Coleridge's is a thoroughly ambivalent figure, attentive and neglectful, affectionate and abandoning, beautiful and absent, dictatorial and unreliable. A figure whose *words* are heard more often than she is herself present,[22] she echoes Coleridge's most famous poems: twice she cites "Kubla Khan" in urging the children to "Beware! Beware!" in lines metrically identical to Coleridge's source line "And all should cry Beware! Beware!" (The "Adolf and Annette" lines are "But yet I say—Beware— Beware—" and "Regard it not. Beware! Beware!"). As in "Kubla Khan" rushing waters are associated with both life and icy death. As in *The Ancient Mariner,* the children are parched in the midst of salt plenty, and solitary in the midst of dead bodies: "beside the cottage doors strange white forms lay huddled together." The seemingly benevolent White Lady is closely tied to the sinister Geraldine of "Christabel," that self-tortured seductress of the girl she claims to protect. Both are magical, praeternaturally-bright, white-clad; both are associated with a "far countree." Geraldine is "beautiful exceedingly" and so is Hartley's deadly valley, "white and glistening, and 'beautiful exceedingly.'" There is an echo from "Christabel" of "So free from danger, free from fear" in the White Lady's parting words to Adolf and Annette: "With much of love and much of fear." An androgynous mother-father figure—embodied as woman, but distant in the symbolic through the words of the Father, the White Lady presides over the eden of childhood, the regrets of adulthood, and the music of both.

The music Hartley thus learns to make is always the music of a Son and a Child. Hartley takes his father and friends as his mother lode and patrimony. Hartley took for granted his role as "Coleridge the Less" (Blunden's phrase), a miniaturized version of Ho Makarites, his great and blessed father. Indeed, virtually every one who saw the boy growing up noted the resemblance in his "Gift of the Gab" (Sara Coleridge's wry phrase [*Minnow* 18]), "which I question if any man . . . living, except his father, could have surpassed," in the admiring words of an Oxford contemporary (H. Hartman 65). Like but less, Hartley both accepts but miniaturizes the heritage. Though some like Robert Fox hymn Hartley as the "Scion of Genius!—on whose favour'd head / *His* wondrous mantle fell" (*HCP*, AMS, 1837*)*, Hartley himself wore the mantle with a difference: "I had rather / You'd give your love to me, poor elf, / Your praise to my great father" (*NP* 93) He's an attenuated version:

> Full well I know—my Friends—ye look on me
> A living spectre of my Father dead—
> Had I not borne his name, had I not fed
> On him, as one leaf trembling on a tree,
> A woeful waste had been my minstrelsy . . .
> . . . Still alone I sit
> Counting each thought as Miser counts a penny,
> Wishing to spend my penny-worth of wit
> On antic wheel of fortune like a Zany:
> You love me for my sire, to you unknown,
> Revere me for his sake, and love me for my own (*NP* 69)

An airy weightless "elf" without mass; a "living spectre" less substantial than the great Father who endures in death; a fragile last leaf of a mighty tree;

a "Zany," pitifully imitating his great master, Hartley represents himself as a much enfeebled and degraded version of "my great Father." Unable to cut the knot that binds him to the father who defines him, he enacts a Zany's imitations of his father's practices and his father's themes. The non-stop monologue unsuited to his listeners; the notebooks—written like STC's from both front and back—filled with a mixture of observations on books, extracts from his reading, sketches of possible works, autobiographical musings, the occasional drawing, the occasional one-line jottings; the marginalia as intensely addressed to the trivia of twenty-year-old magazines as those STC addressed to Eichorn.[23]

Just as Hartley felt himself inscribed and enunciated by Coleridge, so Coleridge saw himself replicated in Hartley. The "over-understanding" Hartley perceived as a general paternal trait was hypertrophied toward Hartley. Coleridge so over-identified with the boy, so readily and rapaciously empathized with the child's feelings that corrective dialogue between parent and child was swept away. Attachment theorists such as Daniel Stern have tracked the "development of the infant's sense of self" through a process of child-parent "joint attention" to objects of attention. Children—infants and toddlers—develop most successfully when their parents practice an accurate and attentive "mirroring" or "sensitive attunement" to the child's perceptions and feelings. Correct parental attunement is neither the inattention that completely tunes out a child's feelings nor the intrusive overstimulating attention that overestimates ("overunderstands") the child's feeling. Such attunement is a continuing process of reciprocal interaction between parent and child, an exchange that validates the child's feeling. This process requires empathy, what psychiatrist Heinz Kohut calls "vicarious introspection . . . the capacity to think and feel oneself into the inner life of another person" (Bouson 17) but also objective self knowledge and attention to the other, which tests the validity of the empathetic reading. The psychological literature suggests that the line between empathy (an accurate assessment of the other's feelings) and projection (an attribution of one's own feelings to a chosen and resonant other) is difficult to discern (Berger 32), so that empathy must be habitually tested by reciprocal exchange.[24] There is also reason to believe that empathetic sensitive parents who are much preoccupied with their own experiences are likely to be better at the "mirroring" that validates the legitimacy of their child's feelings than they are at "coping with the affect" (Fonagy et al. 242). To weep with a weeping child instead of cuddling her is to mirror the feeling but not to ease the pain. These "preoccupied" empathists are also likely to misinterpret their child's signals and "misconstrue their child's affective state" and fail to respond to it (Fonagy, et al. 242).

Hartley was clearly Coleridge's most dearly beloved child, singled out *because of his presumed resemblance to his father.* That Hartley is the "darling" of his father as well as of Village, Nature, and Breeze is obvious. Even if Coleridge had not explicitly tied all his paternal hopes to Hartley—"if I were to lose him, I am afraid, it would exceedingly deaden my affection for any other children I may have" (*CCL* 2: 728)—the ranking is clear in the distinctions he habitually draws between Hartley that genius "sui generis" and "fat Derwent," "the abstract idea of a Baby—a fit representative of Babe-borough" (*CCL* 2: 668). Hartley will have a remarkable life, "a thing that cannot be forgotten" but Derwent

> very unlike Hartley—very vain & much more fond & affectionate—none of his Feelings so profound—in short, he is just what a sensible Father ought to wish for—a fine, healthy, strong, beautiful child, with all his senses & faculties as they ought to be—with no chance, as to his person, of being more than a good-looking man, & as to his mind, no prospect of being more or less than a man of good sense & tolerably *quick parts.* (*CCL* 2: 1014-15)

Coleridge barely knew or sought to know his third child Sara at all.[25] Except for a few months' contact during her childhood (Mudge 2), Coleridge knew and inquired little of his daughter's amazing progress though he greeted her with genuine pride and pleasure upon her move south. Hartley was the chosen one.

Kathleen Coburn has praised the "empathy that distinguished Coleridge's relation to his children, Hartley in particular" (*NB* 1: 205n). In moments of tension, Coleridge saw his children's lives ("I think oftentimes that my children are my Soul" [*NB* 2: 2332]) as coextensive with his own: "There are moments in which I have such a power of Life within me, such a conceit of it, I mean—that I lay the Blame of my Child's [Berkeley's] Death to my absence—*not intellectually;* but I have a strange sort of sensation, as if while I was present, none could die whom I intensely loved" (*CCL* 1: 490). And he found it hard to disengage himself from identifying with Hartley, that perfect ringer. In infancy the resemblance was seemed just physical: at two months Hartley was "the very miniature of me" (*CCL* 1: 243) But by the time Hartley was six, the boy was designated as true intellectual successor for possessing "that, for which, I believe, *I* was somewhat remarkable when a child, namely a memory both quick & retentive" (*CCL* 2: 802), and definitely "a Poet, spite of the Forehead '*villainous low,*' which his Mother smuggled into his Face" (*CCL* 2: 847). The identification is so complete that in "The Nightingale" he even attributes what Kathleen Coburn says is his own dream to the infant Hartley. The remarkable autobiographical letters Coleridge sent to Poole are written just after Hartley's first birthday, as if the father's close attention to his infant's development connects seamlessly to a consideration of his own early development. Hartley was still tiny, a mere "2 & 3 months old" when Coleridge spotted him—or designated him—as a soulmate who shared his own habitual resistance to duty. Neither father nor infant resisted from moral dereliction—such a concept could hardly apply to a babe at the breast—but because they were temperamentally thoughtful and associative:

> That *Interruption* of itself is painful because & as far as it acts as Disruption / & then, without any reference to or distinct recollection of my former theory, I saw great Reason to attribute the effect wholly to the streamy nature of the associating Faculty and especially as it is evident that *they most* labor under this defect who are most reverie-ish & streamy—Hartley, for instance & myself / (*NB* 1: 1833)

In a father-son reversal, Coleridge even looks to Hartley as forecasting his own life. Sometimes "[have] I said, when I have seen certain tempers & actions in Hartley, That is *I* in my future State" (*NB* 2: 2332).

Coleridge assumes that he can read Hartley's temperament so well as to make other playmates unnecessary and undesired: "Play fellows are burthensome to him / excepting *me* / because I can understand & sympathize with, his wild Fancies—& suggest others of my own" (*CCL* 2: 804). He also so takes for granted the affinity between Hartley's mental process and his own that in a moment of high anxiety of despairing love for Sara Hutchinson, a desire so long meditated but not actualized, he quotes Hartley: "What did he say, speaking of some Tale & wild Fancy of his Brain?—'It is not yet, but it will be—for it *is*—& it cannot stay always, *in* here' (*pressing one hand on his forehead and the other on his occiput*)—'and then *it will be*—because it is not nothing'" (*NB* 3: 3547). With this assumption of the reality of mental things, Hartley functions as his father's ratifying second self in this moment of spiritual dearth.

As these examples indicate, Coleridge's empathetic insights into Hartley usually minister to the father, testifying to the adult's basic innocence, deep sympathy, pure-hearted idealism. However accurate Coleridge's reading of his children's feelings, his empathy most often was a tool of self-analysis. In general, Coleridge's empathy sent him back to his own needy childhood and led him to use his children to help fill his need. His daughter Sara's brief childhood contact with her father was largely devoted to comforting *him* for *his* sense of abandonment. Though Coleridge had left his daughter in her infancy, he clearly cast himself as bereft and underloved. Six-year old Sara was expected to act both the surrogate mother and loving daughter and was punished when she failed at her roles. Her autobiographical memoir of her visit, at six, with her long-parted father to the Wordsworth's is a tragi-comedy of role reversal. The father shared a room with the little girl whose fearful need for a nightlight to keep the night-terrors at bay he perfectly intuited just as he had comforted Hartley with a nightlight to cure "the seems." But the empathetic father who so well understood the child's need for a candle (the Notebooks testify to his own fascination with candleflames) woke the exhausted girl up every night when he came to bed at midnight or one A.M. He kept her up telling the fairy stories that *he* had loved so much as a child. Delightful as this should have been, "I preferred sleeping with Miss Hutchinson at Allan Bank to sharing my Father's bed because he was so late in joining me" ("Autobiography" in Mudge 266). Neither did Coleridge's empathy extend to an understanding of the little girl's love for the mother from whom she had never before been separated:

> ... some of my recollections are tinged with pain. I think my dear Father was anxious that I should learn to love him and the Wordsworths & their children, and not cling so exclusively to my mother and all around me at home. He was therefore much annoyed when on my mother's coming to Allan Bank I flew to her and wished not to be separated from her any more. I remember his showing displeasure with me, and accusing me of want of affection. I could not understand why. The young Wordsworths came in and caressed him. I sate benumbed; for truly nothing does so freeze affection as the breath of Jealousy. The sense that you have done wrong, or at least given great offence, you know not how or why—that you are dunned for some payment of love and feeling which you know not how to produce or to demonstrate on a sudden—chills the heart & fills it with perplexity and bitterness. (qtd. in Mudge 261)

Even though Sara did not bear Hartley's burden of election as the favorite, she too found in her relationship with her father a mixture of guilty love and pain. Much more than Derwent or Sara, Hartley was drafted to serve as his father's second chance, his breath of fresh air, his shot of Nitrous Oxide. That Hartley, seemingly impervious to suffering ("Pain with him is so wholly trans-substantiated by the Joys that had rolled on before"), is repeatedly equated with "a perpetual Nitrous Oxyde," the "laughing gas" anaesthetic discovered as a compound by Joseph Priestley in 1772 but first named by Davy and sampled by Coleridge in Bristol in April 1799—is richly suggestive (*CCL* 1: 612). As a new element in the chemical universe, Nitrous Oxide proved perfectly and pleasantly breathable, useful as an anesthetic, delightfully heady and exhilarating as a lark, a sustainer of brighter fires than ordinary air, but fatal after prolonged inhalation. Hartley who was to ordinary phlegmatic children as Nitrous Oxide was to ordinary air, seemed to promise his father a movement into an ampler air. "Frost at Midnight" explicitly contrasts all that is limited, lonely, and urban in the father's life with all that will be right in the son's life. Hartley's life will make good the losses of his father's life. The father was reared far from home, lonely in the city, bereft of his family and playmates, dependent on the fantasized kindness of "the fluttering *stranger.*" "But *thou,* my babe!" will have an opportunity to lead the right life, the joyous life in a stable home with permanent companions "By lakes and sandy shores," taught by the most benign and wise of schoolmasters: "Great universal Teacher! he shall mould / Thy spirit."

So bound up did Coleridge feel with Hartley that he unconsciously made Hartley a stalking-horse in his wooing of Sara Hutchinson. From the earliest days of his infatuation, Coleridge uses Hartley as an emotional go-between as he enters into a highly-charged correspondence with Sara Hutchinson. He writes to Sara regularly about the boy; about half of his surviving letters to Sara contain elaborate accounts of Hartley's loveableness, his sensitivity, his intellectual acuity, his thoughtfulness, his instinctively religious sensibility, his high spirits, and his intense relationship to the father he so resembles. It is to Sara Hutchinson that he recapitulates the father-son conversation, so creditable to them both, about a Renaissance drawing of "Adam & Eve rising out of a Chaos!"

> But I asked Hartley what he thought of it—& he said—"it is *very* curious! A Sea not in a World, but a World rising out of a Sea! (these were his own unprompted word, & entirely his own idea)—There they all are—Adam & all!—Well! I dare say, they stared at one another finely!" This strikes me as a most happy image of the Creation. (*CCL* 2: 827)

That Hartley speaks so originally and acutely in the domestic vocabulary of a little child but with the intellectual freedom of an adult makes him a striking figure of the high thinking and tenderly domestic plain living so prized in the Wordsworth circle.

In all the Coleridge letters of 1802 to Sara Hutchinson, portraits of

Hartley are love tokens from his father and double: "[His] motto from infancy might have been *not me alone!* 'My *Thoughts* are my Darlings!'— [His] *attachments* are excessively strong" (CCL 2: 804). The anecdotes of Hartley and Peter Crosthwaite, Hartley "under the trees, down by the River," and other instances of Hartley thinking and feeling so passionately woo Sara. The child's charm and affection substantiate the father's charm and affection: the father is both the boy's begetter and his textual explicator, bringing his thoughts forward much as an adult autobiographer brings to consciousness his otherwise unrecorded childhood experiences.

The interassimilation with Hartley is so great that within a day or two of the epochal bedroom hallucination, Coleridge jots down an idea for a poem, associated with Sara Hutchinson, to be called "the Soother of Absence." The animus of the poem is Coleridge's love-longing for Asra but the text will come from Hartley: "Of the Passion of Love in very young Children, describe, paint, & explain, & deduce, for the Soother of Absence / " (*NB* 2: 2980). Coburn claims this passage shows "Coleridge's awareness particularly of Hartley's sensibilities and affections" (*NB* 2: 2980n) but it seems a clear example of empathy gone awry, of Coleridge projecting his own erotic longings upon Hartley rather than observing Hartley's feelings. Rather than Kohut's "vicarious introspection," which might allow a parent to understand the inner life of a child, Coleridge is engaging in cooptive introspection, seizing on what he can intuit of Hartley's feelings and finding in them the mirror of his own. Coleridge is eager to make Hartley his surrogate, too easily assuming that a congruence in vocabulary and manner means an identity in feeling. Thus he cites Hartley's puzzled idealist plaint that the fancies of the mind "cannot stay always, *in* here" (*NB* 3: 3547) to validate his own anguished longing for Sara Hutchinson.

Ventiloquizing Hartley, "over-understanding" this lovable child of the "very sweet and docile Disposition" (*CCL* 2: 802), Coleridge inadvertently set Hartley up as a miniature Coleridge destined to fail. Finding a ready mirror in Hartley, Coleridge initiated the boy early into his own pursuits. Even before Coleridge presented Hartley at ten with a notebook, four-year old Hartley was scribbling with "his pencil jabbings" in his father's notebooks (*NB* 1: 649n). The notebooks of Coleridge senior were to be recapitulated by Hartley in format (often begun at both ends), content (self-analysis, reading notes, writing plans, memos), and even handwriting (uncannily similar).

Finding Hartley "reverie-ish" by disposition, Coleridge consciously "fostered his habit of Introition" (Coleridge's word). Sometime in 1801, at four, Hartley, taken on his father's knee, becomes a sometime interlocutor on metaphysics. Their conversations are "about Life, Reality, Pictures & Thinking" (*CCL* 2: 673). It is clear that Coleridge introduces Hartley early to the practice of thinking about thinking:

> Hartley . . . struggled to express himself concerning the difference between the Thing & the Image almost with convulsive Effort.—I never before saw such an Abstract of *Thinking* as a pure act & energy, of *Thinking* as distinguished from *Thoughts*. (*NB* 1: 923)
>
> Hartley told his Mother, that he was thinking all day . . . "what would it be if there were *Nothing.*" (*CCL* 2: 804)
>
> I . . . asked him what his Thoughts were—so he hugged me, & said . . . "I thought, how I love the sweet Birds, & the Flowers, & Derwent, and Thinking . . ." (*CCL* 2: 804)
>
> "The pity is," he said one day to his father, who was expressing some wonder that he was not so pleased as he expected with riding in a wheelbarrow—"the pity is that *I'se* always thinking my thoughts." (*SC* 1: 241)
>
> "*I'se* afraid of my own thoughts." (Hartley qtd. in *SL* 1: 142)
>
> "[B]ut I am always being a bad Boy, because I am always *thinking of my Thoughts.*" (Hartley qtd. in *CCL* 2: 1014)

Hartley's ingenious skill in the discourse of idealism clearly delighted Coleridge. That the child reveled in this delight is clear from Hartley's few childhood literary remains. According to Derwent and the Montagues, Hartley's imaginary kingdom dates from 1806-7. Ejuxria (is the name, a coinage—i.e. Jackie's—from Mr. Jackson the landlord of Greta Hall?) survives in a map and in one episode of its history, "The history of Saint Malo," related in a letter, dictated by Hartley, eleven, to his mother, acting as amanuensis. Augurias Malo, "wild and enthusiastic" from childhood achieves authority over his father and later his countryman as a dreamer of dreams: "I have dreamed a dream, said the Son. . . . His father wondered much, but believed him" (*LHC* 6).

Approval followed Hartley like his shadow. Even the faults that shadowed his youth and might have darkened a boyhood spent in another family were treated lovingly and even reinforced. His faults were not really faults but the defects of the excellence of his childhood. He was evidently careless, disorganized, and restless. Dorothy Wordsworth noted of Hartley at ten:

> Poor thing! . . . [W]e find some trouble in checking him, that is, making him keep silent and *still* in the sitting room, and never having done any offices for others or for himself, except putting on his cloaths, he is absolutely in a dream when you tell him to do the simplest thing—his Books, his Slate. His Pencils, he drops them just where he finds them no longer useful. (*WLMY* pt. 1, 125)

Even at eighteen, going off to Oxford, Hartley received—and presumably still needed—detailed instructions from his mother about how exactly to pack his trunk and how exactly to address a letter. He was clumsy and maladroit ("two left hands," said Southey). He had bad table manners, picking a little bit of this and a little bit of that out of the common dish and sometimes putting pieces back. He had little pertinacity; he did not follow through on his projects: he tended not to read books all the way to the end (he claimed *never* to have completed the story of Robinson Crusoe); he never wrote down the Ejuxrian chronicle (the only written episode was dictated to his mother); he never actually built the elaborate model city he planned on his return from London—that, Derwent noted, was nothing beyond words, "*Vox et praeterea nihil*"; "the smallest portion was never actual commenced" ("Memoir," *PHC* xxxvii, xli). He seemed inattentive, even oblivious, to what was going on around him.

But within the Coleridge circle, especially in STC's eyes, these habits were merely the negligible side-effects of admirable qualities. A boy whose capacity for "introition" was expressly cultivated by his father might be expected to prize thoughts over things, to be "thinking my thoughts" instead of attending literally to the concrete. The father who gently mocked his "Fat Baby" Derwent as literal and gluttonous ("any story that has no Pie or Cake in it, comes very flat to him" [*CCL* 2: 1022]); the husband whose scarcely veiled contempt for his wife as "deficient in organic sensibility" and banausically literal (Lefebure *BO* 93) welcomed every evidence of thoughtfulness and self-reflexive preoccupation in the brilliant Hartley. Hartley's whirling inattention to the world around him, however irritating, evinced his link both to his idealist father and, indeed, to "the one life within us and abroad" that was the subject of Coleridge's early poetry. That Hartley was faulted by Mr. Dawes for "his procrastinating ways, and habits of doing *anything* rather than the *right* thing" was certainly lamented by his father (*Minnow* 18) but also glossed by an explanation (the "reverie-ish streamy nature of thought" that resists interruption in proportion as the thought stream is swift and powerful) that casts both father and son as men of intellect. That Hartley seemed ruminative rather than purposive, retrospective rather than prospective, that he did not follow up mental projects with literal embodiments fit with Coleridge's praise of the uses of reverie. Even Hartley's seeming absence of concern for other people—his avoidance of his beloved Wilsy during her illness, for example—was evidence that Hartley was a boy of intense sensitivity. Like Dorothy Wordsworth whom Coleridge so admired as a "perfect electrometer" (*CCL* 1: 331), Hartley was so finely calibrated to pain and pleasure that he often feared opening a letter. The boy was a sensitive, possessing what Wordsworth called the meditative, that is, self-reflexive, imagination rather than the dramatic or sympathetic imagination. Thus in a notebook entry dating from about 1835, Hartley gives an elaborately circumstantial account of Caspar Hauser, the abandoned child—possibly a lost royal heir—reared to manhood in total isolation. After recapitulating the miseries of Caspar's life and death, Hartley concludes: "Such is the mysterious tale. I am too heartily glad that I did not hear it when I was a little one. It would have haunted me cruelly . . ." (*HCP,* "Odds and Ends" 15). Hartley's intense response is an identification with the potential terror to *himself* when young rather than with the actual sufferings of the pitiful child Caspar. Such a response is consistent with what Hartley's elders took as a praeternaturally fey and sensitive temperament that disengaged him from the life around him. Furthermore, Hartley's obliviousness was useful not so much to the child himself but to the adults around him. By the time Hartley was five, the Coleridge marriage was a going bad and Coleridge's opium addiction was out of control. By the time Hartley was ten, Coleridge was a wreck. But Hartley, from all reports, was happily, dizzily self-absorbed.

Hartley's obliviousness was a very useful shield for every member of the menage—for the adults who did not want the child to notice his father's despair and for the child who did not wish to notice. As Southey was to remark of Hartley in his teens, "no one dared" to speak to Hartley about his father's conduct and Hartley himself "contrives to keep it out of his sight" (Griggs, *HCLW* 65). Thus Hartley's faults were either glossed as the defects of his excellence or welcomed with relief as part of a collaborative operation to protect children from the sight of their father's deficiencies.

By the time Hartley was eleven, the era of his father's permanent departure from the family, the pattern of Hartley as the chosen Romantic child—brilliantly metaphysical, unshakably retrospective, piously filial, whirlingly mobile, and airily oblivious—is set. These are qualities that do not drop away with age. Rather, after Coleridge's virtual abandonment of his children, Hartley's childlike qualities intensify and provide a life-long pattern. Rather than maturing, Hartley becomes more and more childlike as he grows old, more whirlingly eccentric and disorganized at eighteen than at ten, more strangely childlike at forty than at eighteen. Carrying on his father's commission of "carrying the feelings of childhood into the powers of manhood," Hartley consciously elects the vocation of childhood as a debt of honor. Like his sister Sara who felt "dunned" by her father "for some payment of love and feeling which you know not how to produce" (Mudge 261), Hartley considered himself permanently in debt to his father for his exquisitely happy childhood. Living off childhood capital that had been heaped up and accumulated by his great progenitor, Hartley feels obliged to pay off the debt rhetorically, by testifying to childhood as source of all:

> Could I disburse from the treasure of my memory, but one farthing in the pound of the mighty debt of happiness which I owe to dream-nourish'd childhood, and pay the dividend to the heirs and assignees of childhood. (*HCL* 99)

"[To] whom," he heart-brokenly asks Derwent at Coleridge's death, "can I pay the huge debt of duty which I owe him" (*HCL* 163). He pays it back recapitulating the child whom STC so dotingly approved.

Hartley's Case: The Self-Deconstructing Child

> But I never forgot him—no, Derwent, I have forgot myself . . . but I never forgot my father.
> —Hartley Coleridge on STC's death

Hartley's case is commonplace enough in the annals of childhood. Without their fathers' blessings, sons falter. Children who are alternately overwhelmed and neglected do not thrive. Abandoned children, distracted from their right life of growth and achievement, spend their lives seeking the lost parent. And Hartley certainly felt his abandonment always. In middle age, he recounts the great "misfortune" of "what is practically to be without a father" (*HCL* 202, 260). Abandoned by the father he continued to adore, Hartley enacted the familiar role of the abused child: clinging to the abuser, and clinging to childhood. Winnicott has argued that mature individuation, which comes only through separation from the parent, is impossible for a child "inconsistently neglect[ed] and overwhelm[ed]." Such a child cannot risk separation into individuation lest the parent either totally disappear or totally "invade his inner space" (Holmes 35).

But the form of Hartley's sad life is not simply any failure, it is a failure that both embodies and judges the Romantic discourse of essential childhood. The Romantic Child, so formative when conceived heuristically as an interior aspect of a developing self, is fatally fixative as a representative model for the individual child. The model is internally psychological and not externally pedagogic. Alone among the instances of Romantic childhood I have examined, Hartley is *written* rather than *writing,* the created text rather than the creator. In the works of Wordsworth, Lamb, and De Quincey childhood and adulthood are mutually constitutive. The childhood self, anterior and interior, coexists with the adult self in perpetual conversation with that self. But Hartley as present and active living child is neither an anterior nor interior aspect of his own adult self. He functions instead as his father's *persona,* a ventriloqized dummy of a praeternaturally eloquent adult who stages pseudo-conversations, dialogic but not dialogues, with and for the sleeping baby, the moon-struck toddler, the philosophical child.

Although Hartley criticized the powers of philosophers as teachers and poets as prophets, he accepted his father's definition of him. He agreed with and remembered his father's analysis of his character flaws (as stepping through a chair seat, he noted that ". . . my poor father . . . used to say that I could get through nothing; but, in all events I am clean through this chair" [HCP, Richardson, AML, Nov 1850]); he remembered and embraced his father's poetic paeans, acknowledged—fatalistically—that his father's prayers were answered: "Thy prayer was heard: I 'wander'd like a breeze.'" The godlike Coleridge, with his magisterial intellect always seemed to Hartley the master of those who know and what he knew to its depths was his son's character, for indeed he had written that character into being.

There is an illuminating contrast in the account of another loving father-son team. In Edmund Gosse's *Father and Son: A Study of Two Temperaments* (1907), young Edmund loses his mother early and is reared by his scholarly father, a devout member of the Plymouth Brethren. Brought up as lovingly as Hartley and, like Hartley an "infant Samuel" prodigy, Edmund nonetheless finds grounds on which to revolt. In an episode from his seventh year, which forecasts his adult separation from his father, young Edmund—thoroughly indoctrinated in the Ten Commandments—deliberately commits idolatry by worshipping an idol in the form of a chair: "I knelt down on the carpet in front of the table and looking up I said my daily prayer in a loud voice, only substituting the address 'O Chair!' for the habitual one" (37). When nothing happens, no bolt from the blue, no other evidence of divine irritation, the result "was not to make me question the existence and power of God" but rather to "lessen still further my confidence in my Father's knowledge of the Divine mind" (38). From this point, though still a loving son, young Edmund starts his separation from his no-longer-omniscient father and becomes capable of resisting him.

Hartley, however, never achieved such a moment of separation from paternal omniscience but always remained subject to Coleridge's overwhelming knowledge and devouring empathy. During the Oriel affair, Coleridge proclaimed "Oh! If he knew how much I feel *with* him as well as how much I suffer for him, he could not so forget that he has a most affectionate Friend as well as a Father in S. T. Coleridge" (*HLC* 34-35). But Coleridge was wrong about Hartley, who could not ever forget anything about his father: "But I never forgot him—no, Derwent, I have forgot myself . . . but I never forgot my father" (163). Hartley took for granted both his father's love and his father's knowledge, assuming that his identity was completely known, completely understood, and completely constructed by Coleridge and Wordsworth.

The Hartley constructed by Coleridge and Wordsworth has proved metaphorically irresistible to the readers of Romantic poetry as it proved literally irresistible to Hartley himself. However much the fairy elf, the child of joy, the "pretty boy" who runs with the savage men was a portrait of young David Hartley, that being became reified and fixed and usurped the being of the living man. Adorable, brilliant, active, ethereal, the Romantic child role offered no way for Hartley to grow. The unqualified success of Hartley as childhood model for this beautiful discourse made it only too likely for the child-man to shelter under the discourse that kept him in a state of perpetual readiness for his father's return.

"Poets are not Prophets," Hartley asserts in a rare moment of resistance, but in fact, Coleridge never more prophetically allegorized his lovingly abusive relationship with the son whose life he scripted than in the lines that eventually were incorporated into the unfinished "Christabel." Writing in May 1801 to Southey, Coleridge includes a portrait of Hartley couched in the terms he used so often: here is the "little child," "limber Elf," whirlingly mobile and self-absorbed; here is the meditation on thoughts and things that are "tender," "pretty," "wild," and giddy. The prettiness and giddiness are, however, associated with the bittersweet pleasure won from inflicting pain on a child:

> A little child, a limber Elf
> Singing, dancing to itself;

> A faery Thing with red round Cheeks,
> That always *finds* and never *seeks*—
> Doth make a Vision to the Sight,
> Which fills a Father's eyes with Light!
> And Pleasures flow in so thick & fast
> Upon his Heart, that he at last
> Must need express his Love's Excess
> In Words of Wrong and Bitterness.
> Perhaps 'tis pretty to force together
> Thoughts so all unlike each other;
> To mutter and mock a broken charm;
> To dally with Wrong, that does no Harm—

Calling this, apologetically "A very metaphysical account of Fathers calling their children rogues, rascals, & little varlets" (*CCL* 2: 728-29), Coleridge both registers and then evades as commonplace the co-existence of parental love and parental sadism. It is fitting that this portrait of the horrors of love stands in for a conclusion to "Christabel," also a narrative, "beautiful exceedingly," of a parent's folly and a child's pain in which nothing is concluded.

Notes

Notes for Preface

1. De Quincey labels the girl Wordsworth's "little mountaineer," noting that this poem and this child *"delivered"* him (De Quincey, *CW* 11: 303; Jordan 37).
2. I am especially indebted to Kincaid, Rose, and Steedman.
3. Except for Riewald, all commentators link the caricature to "We are Seven." Riewald, however, sees it as "an ironic comment on 'It is a beauteous evening, calm and free,' especially the last six lines" (*Beerbohm's Literary Caricatures* 42). Though the lakeland landscape argues against Riewald's claim of the seaside sonnet, Riewald does pinpoint the Wordsworth topos of adult poet and unsatisfactorily responsive child.
4. See Hartman's "Wordsworth and Goethe in Literary History" and Kincaid's *Child-Loving: The Erotic Child and Victorian Culture.*
5. De Quincey numbers first among his "False Distinctions" "*That women have more imagination than men* . . . What work of imagination owing its birth to a woman can he lay his hand on?"
6. See Myers, "Little Girls Lost"; Plotz, "In the Footsteps of Aladdin."

Notes for Chapter One

1. If Scudder (1838-1902) was not the most brilliant Boston critic of the spirit of the age, he was at least one of the most prolific and typical. The author of some ninety books, he was a power in American literary circles during the later nineteenth century. He had a particular interest in juvenile literature, editing *The Riverside Magazine for Young People* (1867-70), compiling numerous anthologies of fables and fairy tales (most successfully *The Children's Book: A Collection of the Best and Most Famous Stories and Poems in the English Language* [1881], a handsomely illustrated anthology still found

in the children's rooms of municipal libraries), and writing numerous original works for children, notably the Bodley Family Series. He wrote two much-reprinted sweetly lachrymose books of tales for and about children, heavily influenced by Charles Lamb: *Seven Little People and their Friends* (1862) *Dream Children* (1864). A series of *Atlantic* articles in 1885 was collected as *Childhood in Literature and Art* (1894). He was the author of biographies of James Russell Lowell and Noah Webster and the editor of dozens of collections of the works of American and British Poets. He served as editor of *The Atlantic Monthly* from 1890 until 1898.

2. Such claims of discovery originate, I believe, in the mid-eighteenth century with Rousseau who claimed childhood as a newly discovered territory now being explored for the first time. In *Emile*, Rousseau depicts all earlier child study as blind ignorance: "We know nothing of childhood; and with our mistaken notions the further we advance the further we go astray" (1). Thomas Day, author of the heavily Aemilian *Sandford and Merton*, held that Rousseau had looked into childhood and had been able to "discover the secret sources and combinations of the passions" (Edgeworth 1: 226). Ranking *Emile*, the latter-day gospel of childhood, as a third sacred text along with the gospels of God and of Nature, Day wrote to his friend Richard Lovell Edgeworth, author of *Practical Education:*

> Were all the books in the world to be destroyed, except scientific books . . . the second book I should wish to save, after the Bible, would be Rousseau's Emilius. It is indeed a most extraordinary work—the more I read, the more I admire. Rousseau alone, with a perspicuity more than mortal, has been able to look through the human heart, and discover the secret sources and combinations of the passions. Every page is big with important truth. . . . Excellent Rousseau! First of human kind! (qtd. in Edgeworth 1: 226)

It is customary to date the so-called cult of childhood to the late-eighteenth century when, as Peter Coveney notes, "the child emerges from comparative unimportance to become the focus of an unprecedented literary interest, and, in time, the central figure of an increasingly significant proportion of our literature" (Coveney 29). Like most originary dates, this one is also dubious. Many earlier texts—Traherne and Earle in the seventeenth century, for example—set up a normative child. There are precursor texts as far as the eye can see. Note, for example, M. H. Abrams' discussion of links between Romantic childhood and the New Testament in *Natural Supernaturalism* (381-82). Boas collects many Early Modern examples of blessed children, notably the child in John Earle's *Microcosmographie* (1628) (Boas 42-43). What is original perhaps is the *claim* of originality.

3. After about 1840, idolatry becomes a period idiom especially in elegiac works with a regular "substituting the dead child for God" (39) to cite

William Logan's *Words of Comfort for Parents Bereaved of Little Children* (1867), one of many comfort books intended for bereaved parents. Even in explicitly religious texts, such idolatrous substitution takes place. Again and again, writers identify a child as "the idol of my heart" (Prime, *The Smitten Household* 1); "She was my idol" (Anon. qtd. in Smyth, *Solace for Bereaved Parents*); "I . . . hungered for my idol's kiss / Before she went to bed" (Stoddard in Foxcroft, *Our Glorified* 29). See Dinah Mulock's address to a baby, "Philip My King" (Brownell 202-5) and Canton's rapturous chant: "Take the idol to her shrine; / In her cradle lay her! / Worship her—she is divine; / Offer up your prayer" (*IP* 23). Such hyperbole belongs to the high Wordsworthian tradition manifested in such tributes as "mighty Prophet! Seer blest!" (Wordsworth), as the "Type of the Divinity" (Alcott), as "the world's deliverer" (Chapman #27). As "[God's] small interpreter" (Whittier qtd. in Meynell ii), as "director of the parent's education" (Froebel in Dusinberre 15), as a "a lively representation to us of the ideal" (Schiller 87), as a "latter revelation" (A. Smith qtd. in Russell 77).

4. For various anatomies of a unitary Romantic childhood, see Carpenter; Coe; Coveney; Garlitz, "Immortality Ode"; Knoepflmacher; Kuhn; Pattison; Plotz, "The Perpetual Messiah"; Richardson. For a deconstruction and multiplication of the unitary Romantic Child, see Myers, "Little Girls Lost" and "Reading Children"; Rose; Warner.

5. In *The Education of Man* (1885) Froebel metaphorically equates young children to "nature, in field and garden . . . how perfectly it conforms to law" (8) but also demands the concrete experience of external activity—digging, making things—as the cornerstone of his developmental educational method. The mind of the child grows by self-revelation that can alone come from the child's concrete activity and exertion of its own powers.

6. Louisa May Alcott satirically depicts Bronson's metaphysical bent in the exchanges between grandson Demi and Grandfather March in *Little Women* (1868). To his wife's complaint that the child was overtaxed and "learning to ask the most unanswerable questions":

> "If he is old enough to ask the question he is old enough to receive true answers. I am not putting the thoughts into his head but helping him unfold those already there. These children are wiser than we are, and I have no doubt the boy understands every word I have said to him. Now Demi, tell me where you keep your mind?"
>
> If the boy had replied like Alcibiades, "By the gods, Socrates, I cannot tell," his grandfather would not have been surprised; but when, after standing for a moment on one leg, like a meditative young stork, he answered in a tone of calm conviction, "In my little belly," the old gentleman could only join in Grandma's laugh and dismiss the class in metaphysics." (423)

7. Except where otherwise indicated, all references to the *Confessions of an English Opium Eater* are to Grevel Lindop's World's Classics edition of *Confessions of an English Opium-Eater and Other Writings* (designated L).
8. In his *The Growth of Biological Thought: Diversity, Evolution, and Inheritance*, Ernst Mayr notes the nineteenth century as an era of intense biological thought. Even "the word 'biology' is a child of the nineteenth century" (36). Mayr notes that the privileging of biology, a life science, meant the privileging of a vocabulary in which certain vitalist qualities are emphasized. Among these qualities are individuality ("The uniqueness of biological individuals means that we must approach groups of biological entities in a very different spirit from the way we deal with groups of identical inorganic entities" [46]), complexity and organization, quality, uniqueness and variability, emergence ("We live in a universe of emergent novelty" [Popper qtd. in Mayr 63]), and holism-organicism (Mayr 45-67).
9. "For children of the first stage, everything that is in any way active is conscious, even if it be stationary. In the second stage consciousness is attributed only to things that move. The sun and a bicycle are conscious, a table and a stone are not. During the third state an essential distinction is made between movement that is due to the object itself and movement that is induced by an outside agent. Bodies that can move of their own accord, like the sun, the wind, etc. are henceforth alone held to be conscious, while objects that receive their movement from without, like bicycles, etc., are devoid of consciousness. Finally, in the fourth stage, consciousness is restricted to the animal world" (Piaget, *CCW* 197).
10. Hartley Coleridge argues that adults who forget their childhoods are morally impoverished: "Ingratitude, sensuality, and hardness of heart all flow from this source. Men are ungrateful to others only when they have ceased to look back on their former selves with joy and tenderness. They exist in fragments" (*HCP* "On Pride / In continuation"). Samuel Taylor Coleridge considers the difference between mere talent and genius to lie in the extent to which childhood is retrievable: the more childhood, the more power. The one who is able "to carry the feelings of childhood into the powers of manhood; to combine the child's sense of wonder and novelty with the appearances which every day for perhaps forty years had rendered familiar" possesses "the character and privilege of genius" (*The Friend* 1: 109-10). De Quincey holds that for most people growing up represents diminution since "*whatsoever is seen in the maturest adult blossoming and bearing fruit, must have pre-existed by way of germ in the infant*" but that "the killing frost of counter forces" in the social environment blast and shrivel potential gifts so that most adults are shrunken parody versions of their youthful selves: "Most of what he has the grown man inherits from his infant self; but it does not follow that he always enters upon the whole of his natural inheritance" (*CW* 1: 121).

11. This literary prodigy was the subject of two rapturous and widely reprinted essays: John Brown's "Pet Marjorie" (1858) and Mark Twain's "Marjorie Fleming: The Wonder Child" (1909). The Brown essay introduces the otherwise unknown nickname "Pet," and the unfounded myth of Marjory's (Brown spells it Marjorie) friendship with Scott. Both Brown and Twain quote extensively from her writing. Fuller versions of the Fleming oeuvre are available in MacBean, *The Story of Pet Marjorie (Marjorie Fleming)* and, even better, in Sidgwick: *The Complete Marjory Fleming: Her Journals, Letters, & Verses* (1934). Her poetry was widely anthologized early in the twentieth century. Two poems—"A Sonnet" and "A Melancholy Lay"—remain available in major anthologies: Oscar Williams' *Silver Treasurer of Light Verse* (1957) and Russell Baker's *The Norton Book of Light Verse* (1986). For two shrewd critiques of the cult of this "Pet," see Myers and Johnson ("It's as if Little Nell had left a Diary" [104]). See also Plotz, "The Pet of Letters."
12. This discussion is indebted to Cunningham's *Children of the Poor*, especially to his account of the priceless/worthless paradox arising from systematic campaigns against child labor.
13. According to the OED, these terms emerge in the mid-nineteenth century. As an English word, the French *gamin* comes into English about 1840, probably drawn from Victor Hugo's use in *Les Miserables* (III.i.7). Emile Littre's *Dictionaire de la langue française* asserts *gamin* to be of eighteenth-century origin. Originally applied to adults, it is transferred to children sometime early in the nineteenth century. According to Littre, "Victor Hugo . . . claims that the word came into popular usage [as applied to a street child] in 1834 in a work called *Claude Gueux*" (2027). The earliest OED citation is to Thackeray's *Paris Sketch Book* (1840): "There are the little gamins mocking him." *Guttersnipe,* applied both to adult refuse gatherers and to children "brought up 'ii ˋ gutter'; one of the lowest class; an urchin" is also a nineteenth-century term. The earliest citation is from an 1869 Mark Twain essay: "Unfurl yourselves under my banner, noble savages, illustrious guttersnipes." Patridge's *Dictionary of Slang and Unconventional English* cites both *gutter-slush* and *guttersnipe* as synonyms for *street arab* and dates them respectively to 1885-1910 and c. 1880. *Mudlark,* in the sense of "a gutter child, street urchin" is exemplified in the OED by a 1865 citation. The earliest citations of *street arab* in the sense of "A homeless little wanderer; a child of the city" are to works published in 1848: Guthrie's *Plea for the Ragged Schools* and Shaftesbury's parliamentary speeches.

Notes for Chapter Two

1. The interrogation of romantic innocence is Bowen's project from *The Death of the Heart* (1939) through *Eva Trout* (1968). She casts a cold eye on the innocent: "The innocent are so few that two of them seldom meet—

when they do meet, their victims lie strewn all around" (*Death of the Heart* 110); "It is not only our fate but our business to lose innocence, and once we have lost that it is futile to attempt a picnic in Eden" (Heath 99).

2. For the skepticism of Wordsworth's contemporaries about Wordsworth as "nursery bard" (Rehder 211), see Garlitz "The Baby's Debut"; Rehder, chapter 7; Myers, "Reading Children." For Victorian and Modern celebrations of Wordsworth as expositor of childhood as state or as process, see the line of writers including Babenroth, Coveney, Garlitz, Knoepflmacher, McGavran, Pattison, Plotz, Richardson.

3. Few would any longer share Coveney's view that Wordsworth and the Romantics are uniquely original in the quality of their representation of childhood. As Pollack and others have established, there is ample early evidence both of parental devotion to children and of transcendentalizing symbolism, a view recently set out in Richardson's "Romanticism and the End of Childhood" (23-43). But in quantitative terms, nineteenth-century writers do foreground childhood. Babenroth's tally of child words in Wordsworth (child, babe, baby, infant, girl, boy) makes clear a real preoccupation: he cites approximately 1,000 instances, including 400 citations of "child" and 250 of "boy" (but a mere 50 of "girl") (383). Further, Wordsworth has been consistently described in the language of source and origination. In *The Spirit of the Age* (1825), Hazlitt nominates Wordsworth as the "most original poet now living" for the radical "levelling" egalitarianism that made *children,* like peasants, eligible poetic subjects (89, 87). In John Keble's influential lectures as Oxford Professor of Poetry from 1832 until 1841, the decade in which Wordsworth's reputation was soaring (the collected volume of lectures was eventually dedicated to Wordsworth), he defines genuine poetry as the exclusive creation of "the Primary Poet." Though the Ancients had their Primary Poets who were responsible for all the major works of poetic genius (Keble discusses works such as *The Iliad, The Odyssey,* and *The Aeneid),* there is little doubt that the conception is modeled on Wordsworth. Keble's Primary Poet is a thinly veiled portrait of Wordsworth. Though the great man's name is not mentioned, he is so deeply interfused into the characterization of the Primary Poet and his world that identification is inevitable. Keble argues that major "primary" poetry emanates from a writer who has an acute feeling for the numinous in natural home places, a rigorous simplicity cognate with a distaste for social and rhetorical pomp, total sincerity, and a childlike modest reserve (1: 56-85). Only such a poet is capable of true "primary" originality. Later commentators have found Wordsworth's originality in his project to trace the origins of identity. Ward's important account of Wordsworth's influence on Victorian education represents Wordsworth as the fountainhead from which progressive education flowed. ("Who shall point as with a wand and say / 'this portion of the river of my mind / Came from yon fountain'?"

[*Prelude,* 1805, 2: 213-15]), noting that Wordsworth on childhood development became part of the air nineteenth-century children breathed, a kind of education revenant haunting nineteenth-century readers with "the odd feeling of Wordsworth's presence even when he is not cited" (Ward 414). More recently B. Hopkins has twinned Wordsworth with the twentieth-century attachment theorist Winnicott as a pioneer originator and explorer of the childhood origins of meaningful life itself—Wordsworth unacknowledged, Winnicott renowned, "of what it is that makes life worth living in the first place and of how the conditions that make life worth living could be made more generally available" (184). Analogously Edmundson's reading of the Intimations Ode as an allegorical struggle between poetry and philosophy, identifies Wordsworth's visionary child, the best and blest philosopher and seer, with the principle of unsystematic destabilizing originality, the something new in the world that is antithetical to death (747).
4. He is the main subject of one essay only but still receives more index citations (forty-four) than any other writer.
5. See the discussion of the essentializing discourse of Romantic childhood in chapter one.
6. Keble's "Pebbles on the Shore," *Lyra Innocentium* (1846) features children, "a fairy band," dancing "on the twinkling sand" and picking up the sea's gifts, pebbles and shells, emblems of God's equally free and accessible and delightful grace. Arnold's "To a Gipsy Child by the Sea-Shore" is a darker version.
7. The motif of the crusty old gent softened by winning child is pandemic: see Alcott's *Little Women* and Juliana Ewing's "Mary's Meadow." Kipling appropriates the latter for "Fairy Kist," a post–WWI tale of shellshock, repressed memory, and redemption by a return to childhood via children's literature.
8. The infanticidal masterpieces of the nineteenth century such as *Wilhelm Meister, The Brothers Karamazov, The Possessed, Little Eyolf, Tess of the D'Urbervilles,* and *Les Miserables,* link adult security to the process William Canton glosses in his historical anecdote of the founding of Copenhagen: "how when the walls of Copenhagen . . . crumbled and fell as fast as they were built, an innocent little girl was set in her chair beside a table, where she played with her toys and ate the rosy apples they gave her while twelve master-masons closed a vault over her; and then the walls were raised, and stood firm ever after. And so it may sometimes be in the dispensations of providence that the lives of men can only be raised high and stable in virtue of the little child immured for ever within them" (225). Serge Laclaire has argued in *On tue un enfant* (1975) that adult sanity requires each adult to murder (metaphorically) the child within (Kuhn 178).
9. Emerson attributes this observation to an "Orphic Poet," generally thought to be Bronson Alcott. Alcott's view on childhood ("Nothing is too meta-

physical for the mind of a child") are admirably treated by Charles Strickland. Chapter 45 of *Little Women* gives a playful account of a philosophic grandfather leading his grandson in metaphysical discussion. The same task for children—serving as transcendental mnemonic—is assigned by Corelli to the angelic eponymous hero of *Boy* (1906):

> The enormous difference between the very young and their elders exists not only on account of the disparity in years—but also because the elders have retained, for the most part, nothing more on their minds than the quickly crowding and vanishing impressions of this present world,—while children are, we may imagine, busy with vague recollections of something better than the immediate condition of things,—recollections which occasionally move them to wonder why their surroundings have become so suddenly and strangely altered. It is impossible not to see, in the eyes of many of these little human creatures, a look of infinite perplexity, sorry and enquiry,—a look which gradually fades away as they grow older. . . . (16)

10. This line of comfort may lead to such strained praise of, for example, Wordsworth's "Surprised by Joy" as Lerner's: "We can even entertain the thought that little Catherine's death was worth while if it produced so splendid a poem as this (after all, we can add limply, she would by now be dead anyway)" (73).
11. I am grateful to Marilyn Gaull for allowing me to see the draft version of "Wordsworth and the Six Arts of Childhood" before its publication in *1800: The New Lyrical Ballads*. Gaull's is the fullest account of the diversity and toughness of Wordsworthian children.
12. In "Wordsworth, Lost Boys, and Romantic Hom(e)phobia," McGavran sees inscribed a conflict between male "autoerotic and homoerotic tendencies, and of 'normal,' patriarchally controlled domesticity" (131).
13. See Beer's similar argument in *Wordsworth in Time* 17-22.
14. Indeed Byatt, Wordsworth critic as well as novelist, said in a conversation in 1981 that Marcus' experience was connected to the "Being spread" passage in *Prelude* 2 which she recalled as employing not the noun substantive "Being" but the present progressive "being spread." Thus she recollected the boy Wordsworth as "being spread" across the landscape like butter on bread. For a fuller discussion see Plotz, "A Modern 'Seer Blest'" in Alfer and Noble.
15. Pasternak's context, however, is historical and political. In the closing section of *Dr. Zhivago,* a friend of Zhivago's speaks of the child victims of the Russian Revolution and civil war and cites the Blok line: "We the children of Russia's terrible years." Blok, he notes, "meant it figuratively, metaphorically. The children were not children, but the sons, the heirs of the intelli-

gentsia, and the terrors were not terrible but apocalyptic; that's quite different. Now the figurative has become literal, children are children and the terrors are terrible." Wordsworth criticism has so effectively assimilated Wordsworthian traumatic moments to the category of the Sublime that without any deliberate intent to soften childhood experience, the effect has been Panglossian.
16. In Barnardo's *Memoirs*, "Some Queer Children I Have Met" are mediated through Wordsworth via Whittier: "I think I may say of a truth I have never seen a really ugly child! There is always to my mind something beautiful in the little ones, however disfigured they may be with sin and suffering, something that looks out of their young eyes and half-formed features, and that pathetically appeals to one's pity and sympathy and love—something, too, that fills one with reverence for childhood. It may be as the poet Whittier sings, that the young child is 'latest from God's hand and nearest unto him'" (356).
17. Although a conscientious and admirable boy, Johnny Wordsworth seemed to his Aunt Dorothy "as far as scholarship goes the greatest Dunce in England" (*WLMY* 2: 141). Although dyslexia as a syndrome was not described until 1896 (Miles & Miles vii) and although retrospective diagnosis is always, as Huston notes acerbically, "precarious" (188), there is some evidence that points to such a diagnosis. John did reverse letters and numbers, put letters in words in faulty sequence, and had difficulty in "processing, interpreting, and recalling visual images," the three leading indicators of visual dyslexia (Huston xvii). He had enormous difficulty in learning Latin and was a very slow worker. In 1819, Wordsworth notes of the sixteen-year-old John that he has a great love and knowledge and interest in instructive conversation, "catches at it from all quarters, when the trouble is not imposed upon him of seeking it *himself* in books." But he is a worse reader at sixteen than his aunt Dorothy had been at four: "I'll give you a slight specimen of his way of reading English . . . 'Oh! That,' (he read '*On* that'), 'requite' he read rightly—the *same* word in the next line he read '*require*' though four lines lower 'meagre stores of verbal gratitude,' he read *stories*—and so on" (*WLMY* 2: 514).
18. Though earlier editors place the letter in 1806, Moorman argues for an 1804 date and thus during the composition of the 1805 *Prelude*.
19. See Garlitz, Kerrigan, and Ward on its educational influence. But Myers ("Reading Children") is skeptical.
20. See for example Bushnell, Levinson, Hartman, Collings, and Manning.
21. See Collings (160-62) and Eilenberg (47-49).
22. Eilenberg demonstrates multiple usurpations: 1) "Michael" usurping the place originally intended for Coleridge's "Christabel" in the second edition of *Lyrical Ballads;* 2) both "Michael" and "Christabel" focus on fathers who permit the displacement of their own children by the children of others; 3) Wordsworth usurps Luke and becomes heir to Michael's story.

23. *The Oxford Dictionary of English Proverbs* places the first use of "Abraham's Bosom" in 1533. Early uses are all earnest but post–*Richard III* uses are generally sardonic as in Horace Walpole's account of "Two or three old ladies who are languishing to be in Abraham's bosom" (*ODEP* 1).
24. See Plotz, "Literary Ways of Killing a Child," for an account of the Madame Tussaud's waxworks of the Princes in the Tower, installed in 1865 and still on view. For an account of the multiple pictorial treatments of the Princes in the Tower (he cites nineteen) as evidence of "the Victorian obsession with violated children," see Strong's *And when did you last see your father?* (104).
25. See Schapiro, chapter 4.
26. Duncan Wu's account of Wordsworth's reading makes clear his reading in Percy's *Reliques* from the 1780s, through the 1790s and at least until the late 1820s (Wu 1800-1815, 165). Gaull points out the immense importance of folkloric materials in "Awake in Araby" and "Wordsworth and the Six Arts of Childhood."
27. Gaull and Wiener suggest an affinity between the protagonist of *The Prelude* and the boy hero of the British Jack tales. "The boat-stealing episode, for example, bears a remarkable similarity to the tale of Jack and the beanstalk" (Wiener 214).
28. Brooke Hopkins has argued for applying a frame drawn from Winnicott in his eloquent "Wordsworth, Winnicott, and the Claims of the 'Real'," noting that Wordsworth's project is the same as Winnicott's: to construct "a life that has reality in it instead of futility." Yet despite Winnicott's claim, in a charming anecdote retold by Hopkins, that "[Wordsworth] seems to have read my books," I would argue for a darker Wordsworth who read Bowlby even more assiduously than Winnicott, whose drive for "reality . . . instead of futility" is underwritten by loss.
29. In one Bowlby study, 42.5 percent of the children who lost their mothers before the age of eleven developed a depressive disorder; of the unbereaved control group 14.1 percent developed such a disorder (*Loss* 258).
30. See *Loss,* chapter 19, "Children's Response When Conditions are Unfavorable."
31. 1850 text only.
32. According to the reading of "We are Seven" in the Cornell edition, the 1798 version is uncapitalized: "A simple child, dear brother Jim." In the edition of 1815, the line is truncated and the adjective promoted: "A SIMPLE child." But "Child, 1827—and A simple Child MS 1819D MS" (Butler and Green 73).
33. 1850 text only.
34. Owen's *Fourteen-Book Prelude* shows that Wordsworth labored hard over the "dwarf man" passage. Two excluded versions show Wordsworth playing with upper- and lower-case versions of "A child, no child" and "a Child, no child"

(611). The Cornell texts show a clear pattern of changing words referring to children from lower to uppercase (e.g. Butler and Green 363-70).
35. E. Nesbit has some fun with the universally-desired radiant cynosure baby in chapter 3 ("Being Wanted") of *Five Children and It* (1902). As long as the (highly literary) spell lasts, everyone in the children's world (noblewomen, coachmen, gypsies) worships, desires, dotes upon, and serves the radiant baby, the so-called Lamb. When the spell wears off, however, they cannot get rid of the grubby kid quickly enough.
36. Hartman's "Wordsworth and Goethe in Literary History" makes clear that Wordsworth might have read translations of Monk Lewis of both the ballad "Erl-King's Daughter" and Goethe's "Erl-King" included in the fourth edition of *The Monk* (1798). Wu notes Wordsworth's reading of *The Monk* but not in the 1798 edition.
37. In Hartman's rich essay linking Wordsworth's "The Danish Boy" and Goethe's "Erl-Koenig," he suggests that the Erl King is a lover of eudaemonia, "eternal youth . . . sought for its own sake, not for the sake of a productive life" and thus the enemy of culture (195). Hartman suggests the lover of youth is often the enemy of culture.
38. Wordsworth, Abrams, and Gill in their Norton Critical Edition are very positive: "Book VII belongs almost certainly to November 1804" (519).
39. Alice is inexplicable to the narrator in the same way Bowlby's three-year-old Patrick seemed indecipherable to the staff of the children's home where he was warehoused during his mother's long illness. Bowlby eventually decoded the child's strange finger motions. When initially left, the boy comforts himself with the scenario that "My mother will put on my overcoat and take me home again." When his mother fails to show up, Patrick develops a more elaborate sequence: "She will put on my overcoat and my leggings, she will zip up my zipper, she will put on my pixie hat." When the adult attendants tire of this endlessly repeated mantra and tell him to stop, Patrick "moving his hands and lips with an absolutely tragic expression on his face" eventually substitutes "gestures that show the position of his pixie hat, the putting on of an imaginary hat, the zipping of a zipper, etc." gestures eventually reduced "to a mere abortive flicker of his finger" (*Loss* 12). As Patrick's dressing in his own outdoor clothes, eventually reduced to the merest finger flicker, signifies his mother, so Alice's cloak signifies all affective possibility.
40. Bowlby found aggressive blaming of the surviving parent to be a frequent strategy of loss.
41. Roe and Simpson have emphasized the Thelwall presence in "Anecdote for Fathers." Simpson reads Kilve as a displaced Racedown and Liswyn Farm both as Alfoxden (characterized as "a rentier's embarrassingly opulent residence") and Thelwall's actual working farm at Liswyn in Wales. Roe argues cogently that the absence of contextual information in "Anecdote for

Fathers" works against any choice between the two sites, but he urges *both* as types of rural retreat against the dangers of radical political participation after the Gagging Acts of 1795.

42. Goldstein cites the wind vane passage of 1805 to underscore his argument that Wordsworth's child "is an infant of the French revolution," a potentially fearful figure betokening destruction who is eventually repudiated (87). Richardson notes this as the only explicit comparison of child to Revolution in Wordsworth's works (36).

43. In his essay on epitaphs, Wordsworth makes clear his hostility to antithesis as a rhetorical posture: "In the minds of the truly great and good," there is an inner consistency where "everything that is of importance is at peace with itself; all is stillness, sweetness and [?stable?] grandeur" ("Celebrated Epitaphs Considered" Grosart 2.61).

44. Marcus discussed "Ruth" in these terms in a seminar sponsored by the Washington Psychoanalytic Institute in Spring 1983.

45. Not only did Socrates die from hemlock but "Children are sometimes poisoned when they make whistles or pea-shooters from the hollow stems" (*World Book* 9: 1733-34).

46. Douglas, for example, has noted that Wordsworth's poetry regularly incorporates "not the external mother . . . but rather the inner mother, the possessively absorbed object of life and need":

> The decisive fact is that Wordsworth's self has been constituted as a depository of attitudes, values, and feelings taken from his mother. Wordsworth's self was enough like what he felt his mother was and wanted so that she was in feeling (if not in fact) contained within him. (Douglas 133)

Since Onorato's important study of maternal loss in *The Prelude,* many have explored the interplay of presence and absence, connecting presence to the earliest experience at the breast. Friedman, Douglas, Schapiro, along with Onorato have associated Wordsworth's sense of meaningful Presence in nature with the "oceanic feeling" of infantile bliss, the "small child's psychic sense of his vastness and omnipotence" (Friedman 6). See especially Beer, Caruth, Douglas, Easthope, Friedman, Jacobus, Onorato, Spivak.

47. According to the line of argument pursued by Beer, Caruth, Douglas, Easthope, Hopkins, and Onorato, virtually all of Wordsworth's expositions of "presence" are empowering internalizations of the Body of the Mother.

48. This is a key distinction between Wordsworth and the other figures treated in this book. See especially Hartley Coleridge's raptures on littleness. Steedman has brilliantly documented how much the nineteenth-century discussion of children is stuck on "littleness itself and the complex register of affect that has been invested in the world 'little'" (9). Wordsworth notably avoids synonymizing childhood and littleness. On the contrary, littleness

often has a grotesque spin as in the Pedlar's stunted dear, "a little girl ten years of age, / But tiny for her years, a pretty dwarf, / Fair-hair'd, fair-faced, and though of stature small / In heart as forward as a lusty child" ("Ruined Cottage") or, notoriously, "the six years Darling of a pigmy size."

Notes for Chapter Three

1. Unless otherwise indicated, citations of Lamb's works refer to the Lucas edition: *The Works of Charles and Mary Lamb.* Ed. E. V. Lucas. 5 vols. 1903. New York: AMS Press, 1968. Citations will be made parenthetically simply by volume number and page. Where appropriate, titles of individual works will be indicated parenthetically as well.
2. Coleridge, "This Lime Tree Bower My Prison" lines 11, 75; Elton in 2: 404n.; Lloyd in Blunden 93-94; Blunden 66.
3. To distinguish the Lucas edition of Lamb's correspondence from the Marrs, citations to the Lucas edition will be noted parenthetically as *Letters,* those to the Marrs as Marrs.
4. Though critics agree that any full identification of Elia with Lamb is seriously mistaken, there is considerable difference of opinion in assessing the relationship, some arguing that Lamb and Elia are antithetical, others that they are supplementary. Morley has argued that after 1799 Lamb splits into "an original personality, which becomes more and more silent as hope is lost . . . [and] an assumed character, which becomes more and more vocal as defense is needed" (215). This "assumed character," eventually solidified as Elia, is, Morley holds, no more than "a device, a conscious dramatization, a method of cheering one's self up" (299). Riehl, on the other hand, speaks for most Lamb scholars in suggesting that "Elia gave Lamb freedom to be himself at his best" (52).
5. McFarland links Lamb's choice of a consciously "Little" person (he glosses Elia as the initial L with a diminitive "ia" ending "that indicates hetereogeneous fragmentation, as in juvenilia or trivia" [46]), as a consequence of his intense psychic twinning with Coleridge. McFarland holds that Coleridge's role in Lamb's psychic economy was to be great; consequently "Coleridge was large, Lamb was small" (41). Jane Aaron sees Lamb's rejection of the adult male role, enacted partly in his childlike persona, as his resistance to the strongly polarized gender system of the mid-nineteenth century. This resistance Aaron links to Lamb's "double singleness" with Mary and to his class and occupational position.
6. Lamb had a distinct color prejudice, which he regarded as mere common sense. His objections to staging, rather than privately reading, *Othello* are well known:

> Nothing can be more soothing, more flattering to the noble parts of our natures, than to read of a young Venetian lady of the high-

est extraction, through the force of love and from a sense of merit in him whom she loved, laying aside every consideration of kindred, and country, and colour, and wedding with a *coal-black Moor*—(for such he is represented in the imperfect state of knowledge respecting foreign countries in those days, compared with our own, or in compliance with popular notions, though the Moors are now well enough known to be by many shades less unworthy of a white woman's fancy)—it is the perfect triumph of virtue over accidents, of the imagination over the senses. She sees Othello's colour in his mind. But upon the stage, when the imagination is no longer the ruling faculty, but we are left to our poor unassisted senses, I appeal to every one that has seen Othello played, whether he did not, on the contrary, sink Othello's mind in his colour; whether he did not find something extremely revolting in the courtship and wedded caresses of Othello and Desdemona; and whether the actual sight of the thing did not over-whelm all the beautiful compromise which we make in reading;—and the reason it should do so is obvious, because there is just so much reality presented to our senses as to give a perception of disagreement, with not enough of belief in the internal motives,—all that which is unseen,—to overpower and reconcile the first and obvious prejudices. ("On the Tragedies of Shakespeare, Considered with Reference to their Fitness for Stage Representation" 1: 108)

In "Imperfect Sympathies," Lamb gives an account of his distaste for Scotchmen because they are dry, unimaginative, and humorless; for Jews because they are too "separative"; for Quakers because they are too literal and unspontaneous; and for Negroes simply "because they are black" (2: 62).

7. The source for Lamb's *amphibium* is probably Thomas Browne's *Religio Medici,* one of Lamb's favorite books. Lamb applies to the child alone the glorious ambivalence Browne imputes to humankind:

We are alone that amphibious piece between a corporal and spiritual Essence, that middle form that links those two together, and makes good the Method of GOD and Nature, that jumps not from extreams, but unites the incompatible distance by some middle and participating natures. That we are the breath and similitude of GOD, it is indisputable and upon record of Holy Scripture; but to call ourselves a Microcosm, or little World, I thought it only a pleasant trope of Rhetorick, till my better judgment and second thoughts told me there was a real truth therein. For first we are a rude mass, and in the rank of creatures which only are, and have a dull kind of being, not yet privileged with life, or preferred to sense and reason; next we live the life of Plants, the life of Animals, the life of Men, and at last the life of Spirits, running on in one mysterious nature those five kinds of existences, which comprehend the creatures, not onely of the World, but of the Universe. Thus is Man that great and true *Amphibium,* whose nature is to live, not only like other creatures in divers elements, but in divided and distinguished worlds. . . . (Browne 38-39)

Notes for Chapter Four

1. "The Affliction of Childhood" is the first and longest section of *Suspiria de Profundis*. Except where otherwise indicated, all references to the *Suspiria* and to the *Confessions of an English Opium Eater* are to Grevel Lindop's World's Classics edition of *Confessions of an English Opium Eater and Other Writings* (designated L). (Lindop's biography, *The Opium-Eater: A Life of Thomas De Quincey,* is designated as Lindop.) In several instances, however citations are to the Aileen Ward NAL edition (designated W).
2. Any claim to defining De Quincey's career is problematic: is he a major Romantic with an psychotropic vocation rather than a career (see H. Miller, Clej, Rzepka, Porter, Platzner, Jordan)? Is he a consummate professional writer with an eye for the market (McDonagh, Black, Goldman)? A genius? A hack? A pathology? Russett's recent compelling study of De Quincey as a consciously *minor* writer (*De Quincey's Romanticism: Canonical Minority and the Forms of Transmission* [1997]) has considerable explanatory power and supplements my argument that De Quincey's strategic literary choices—"minority" choices in Russett's view—of forms, themes, subjects and self-representations are grounded in an identification with childhood in trouble.
3. According to De Quincey, Jane was a year younger than himself. Barrell notes that she was actually a year or more older (25-26).
4. De Quincey by quotation ventriloquizes Satan addressing Beelzebub. He speaks to another creature in hell, both now "joined / In equal ruin; into what pit thou seest / From what highth fallen" (*Paradise Lost* 1: 90-92). Loss and guilt are intertwined, as always in De Quincey's autobiographical ruminations. For De Quincey to be weak, like a helpless child or a fallen cherub, is not simply to be miserable but to be guilty.
5. Yule and Burnell's extensive entry on Pariah in *Hobson-Jobson* notes that although the word is properly "the name of a low caste, of Hindus in Southern India, constituting one of the most numerous caste, if not *the* most numerous in the Tamil country," the English and other Europeans used the word "as applicable to the whole body of the lowest castes or people without any caste." However mistaken, this "use of *pariah* as synonymous with out-caste, has spread in English parlance [i.e. as spoken by the English] all over India" (678-79). By extension, the word comes into com-

mon English usage, according to the *OED*, as "any person (or animal) of a degraded or despised class; a social outcast" in the early nineteenth century. The first *OED* citation is from Shelley in a letter of 1819.

6. Barrell remarks the insistent and repetitious defensiveness of DQ's claim for the purity of Ann's polluting lips, a defensiveness that makes the pollution and the purity cognate (30).
7. Among the several projected sections of the *Suspiria* is one surviving simply as a title: "The Nursery in the Desert" (*PW* 4). Developing the motif of childhood isolation, the title plays on the contrast between the delicacy, littleness, and vitality of children and the rigor, vastness, and stillness of the desert.
8. An abridged children's version, *The Oriental Moralist*, appeared in 1781. But no less an authority than Brian Alderson maintains that "the dominance of Galland's version for so long makes it almost certain that his is the edition that children would have read" (Caracciolo 83).
9. In India, by the eighteenth century the machine-produced goods from Manchester were driving out the more expensive indigenous hand-woven goods. Though Indian raw cotton was imported in quantity to Britain, Indian fabrics were either so severely taxed as to be uncompetitive or barred from Britain altogether. C. H. Philips records that the "the Manchester manufacturers demanded that their goods should be received duty free in India and that the wearing of Indian cotton goods in England should be prohibited; the Glasgow interest sought legislation to prohibit the use of machines in the manufacture of India piece goods. After studying these demands, a relatively impartial contemporary writer was led to remark that 'Manufacturers with regard to one another have more of the savage than any other class of man'" (75).
10. See MacKenzie's account of the inferiority of vegetarians to carnivores in the moral and military hierarchy of British India.
11. De Quincey, a life-time headache sufferer (Dr. Balfour's autopsy report on William De Quincey notes "head complaints" as a family malady [325]) had reason to long for the unchanged faces of his dead. Both Elizabeth and his son William died of brain diseases and were subjected to autopsies. De Quincey alludes tersely to "the dishonors of this scrutiny" (S 134), the opening of William's skull—William whom he held his own "crown and glory." The references to the "mutilated parting" and the "ruined corpse" of Elizabeth as well as the reference to the "Memnonian" wind (said to come from the shattered head of Memnon's statue) all point to an obsession with the lost and damaged face of the beloved.
12. Grevel Lindop connects Catherine Wordsworth's death in 1812 both to De Quincey's opium addiction and to his break with the Wordsworths (202-8).
13. Russett argues that the "erasure of boundaries" between De Quincey and Wordsworth was a crucial "part of De Quincey's project," viz. to penetrate

the Wordsworth circle in the guise of Wordsworth's *child* ("Wordsworth's Gothic Interpreter").

14. See Herbert, "De Quincey and Dickens" for a helpful comparison between the two on the theme of guilt and self-division.

15. Noting De Quincey's citation of Wordsworth's dream of the Arab in *Prelude* 5, Russett demonstrates the doubling of the Arab and the poet-dreamer who sets his *ear* to the Arab's shell: "This is as close as Wordsworth comes in the *Prelude* to encountering a *doppelganger*. Does the Arab personate Wordsworth, or De Quincey? Neither, and both at once" (196).

16. The description of the course of William's disease and an account of the findings of the post-mortem examination appear in Balfour, "Case of peculiar Disease of the Skull and Dura Mater," *Edinburgh Medical and Surgical Journal* 43 (1835): 319-25. For an interpretation of the case in the light of contemporary brain pathology, I am grateful to Dr. Marius Valsamis, Professor of Neuropathology, New York Medical College, Valhalla, NY.

17. Dr. Grevel Lindop in a personal letter (October 16, 1985) notes that while he imagines De Quincey's mother as "rather large" and his father as "rather small," "these ideas rest on no evidence whatsoever." Though there is no hard evidence of family size, Dr. Lindop notes "that whilst De Quincey was laughed at for his smallness . . . as far as we know none of the rest of the family were. He may therefore have been the only conspicuously small one." For an analysis of De Quincey's self-hating attitude toward his own body, see Plotz, "On Guilt Considered as One of the Fine Arts" and Youngquist.

18. That Wilson was struck by De Quincey's eating habits is clear. The April 1830 entry of *Noctes Ambrosiae* features a dinner party at which "The Opium Eater" fusses over the meal, eating only the first course, vermicelli soup, and rejecting the roast meat as "transverse" rather than "longitudinal": "I shall dine to-day entirely on soup, for your Edinburgh beef and mutton, however long kept are difficult of mastication,—the sinews seeming to me to go all transversely, thus,—and not longitudinally,—so—"(4: 433).

19. See John Gould, *The Withering Child*. Of his five year old son who wasted away from homesickness, Gould observes, "young children, faced with an overwhelming loss—of a home, of a parent or sibling—have stopped eating. Five-ear-old children *do* have eating disorders, despite what our English doctor said" (226).

Notes for Chapter Five

1. The Hartley Coleridge Papers (henceforth *HCP*) constitute a largely unpublished treasure for scholars. I am very grateful to Mrs. Joan Coleridge and to the Harry Ransom Humanities Research Center of The University of Texas at Austin for permission to quote from these materials.

2. Hartley identified himself with a Spanish exile poet whose work he annotated sometime in the early 1830s in the margins of *London Magazine,* July 1823: 54-55 (*HCP*):"Alas, I can feel it too, for I am far from all my kindred, not friendless indeed, but loveless and confined . . . Che sera sera . . . Better to mourn for Spain than for myself." (In this instance, as in most others, Hartley annotates a periodical a decade or more after its publication.) Dorothy Wordsworth comments in April 1830 on Hartley's "hopeless state" of uncontrolled drunkenness and aimless wandering "till some charitable person leads the vagrant home" (*WLLY* Pt. 2, 248).

3. The use of 'Ο Μακαρίτης, sometimes in Greek letters, sometimes transliterated as *Ho Makarites,* dates this annotation to after Coleridge's death in 1834. Hartley regularly used this Homeric Greek expression for one who is departed (in Liddell and Scott's Greek-English dictionary HO MAKARITES SOU PATER is glossed as "late father"). Besides implying the subject's death, *Ho Makarites* carries the additional connotation of a great man who is "blessed, happy" in the manner of the gods rather than of mortal men.

4. David Wilkie (1785-1841) was elected an associate of the Royal Academy in 1809, a full academician in 1811. "The Blind Fiddler" was exhibited at the Royal Academy in 1807 and presented to the National Gallery in 1826.

5. The title of a journal begun in 1843. The opening observation: "Every day discovers more & more of my ignorance. Would that I could say that every week and month did work to remove it."

6. By splitting off the good father from the impossible father in the manner of the regressive mode of very early childhood, Hartley consciously or unconsciously willed regression. According to Object Relations Theory, maturation requires "the integration of idealized objects (the Ideal Good Father) and bad objects (the Bad Father) into a whole person." This occurs in early childhood. "Any splitting that occurs after reaching the whole object relation is a falling back on the infantile modality of object relations, serving a defensive aim and representing a primitive stage in the emotional life of the individual" (Blos 110).

7. *EM* signifies the posthumously published *Essays and Marginalia* (1851). The collection headed "Essays and Marginalia" found among the Hartley Coleridge Papers will be designated *HCP,* E & M.

8. Among Hartley's other comic poems is a Latin version of "Hey Diddle Diddle": "Hi diddle dides / Felis et fides / Vacca transiluit lunam / Talus lusus ut videt / Parvus catulus ridet / Patinaque surripuit spoonam" (*HCP,* Notebook D).

9. "Of Such is the Kingdom of God," *CPW* 28; "Lines suggested by a Cast from an Ancient Statue of the Infant Hercules, Strangling the Serpents," *CPW* 205; "The Sabbath Day's Child," *CPW* 68.

10. "The First Birthday," *CPW* 12; "To an Infant," *CPW* 178; "To Jeannette, Six Weeks Old," *CPW* 185.
11. Anya Taylor has written persuasively of the ambivalence in these early poems.
12. Derwent Coleridge published a selection of Hartley's posthumous poems in the two-volume *Essays and Marginalia* of 1851. Griggs' edition of *New Poems* (1942) includes sixty-one previously unpublished and uncollected poems. Almost 200 more poems and fragments in the *Hartley Coleridge Papers* still remain unpublished.
13. John Rea has argued Hartley's presence in Wordsworth's Lucy poems. Lucy Newlyn (among others including Derwent Coleridge, J. Plotz, J. Rea) has made a convincing case for "pygmy" Hartley as both the "Seer blest" and the little man with the "little plan or chart" in Wordsworth's Intimations Ode.
14. Coleridge calls him "a child whose nerves are as wakeful as the Strings of an Eolian Harp, & as easily put out of Tune!" (*CCL* 2: 909) and insists that Sara not allow him any tea no matter how dilute.
15. This important image of reflected moonlight as an emblem of microcosmic / macrocosmic correspondence recurs at the conclusion of "Frost at Midnight," in Part VI of "The Ancient Mariner," and in the figure of the blind man and the moon in "Limbo."
16. Lamb makes a similar assumption about Thornton Hunt's inexplicable (to Lamb) bad dreams while confined with his father in debtor's prison. The child is deemed invincible even though the dreams attest his vulnerability.
17. The allusion is to Wordsworth's 1802 "To H.C. Six Years Old": "O blessed vision! Happy child! Thou art so exquisitely wild / I think of thee with many fears / For what may be thy lot in future years."
18. In a Notebook entry (#3130) of Summer 1807, Coleridge quotes with approval a Sanskrit poem by Trivedi Servoru Sarman, which he had just read in a memoir affixed to *The Works of Sir William Jones* (1807). "To you there are many like me; yet to me there is none like you, but yourself; there are numerous groves of night flowers; yet the night flower sees nothing like the moon, but the moon" (*NB* 2: 3130n). Hartley knew the formulation, possibly from one of those 1807 conversations, because in a letter of October 1833, he describes his sister Sara as similarly incomparable: "She was always so completely unique . . . 'There is nothing like the Moon but the Moon'" (*LHC* 156).
19. Before Southey's authorship of the pseudonymously published *The Doctor* was revealed, Hartley Coleridge's name was suggested as a plausible author. The Shandyesque style adopted by Southey for this work is one in which Hartley habitually wrote.
20. Estecean themes are everywhere. Hartley's essay on Hamlet is a virtual commentary on his father's treatment of Hamlet. Like his father, Hartley

remarks on Polonius as "haunted with the spectre of his departed abilities" (*EM* 1: 164) and extensively on Hamlet's noble ascendancy of thought over action. Like his father, Hartley draws a self-portrait in drawing Hamlet, "still meditating mighty works, and urged by all motives and occasions to the performance,—whose existence is nevertheless an unperforming dream" (1: 153). Similarly, Hartley's "On Pride" develops Coleridge's emphasis on fidelity to childhood memory. The father's version: "Men are ungrateful to others only when they have ceased to look back on their former selves with joy and tenderness. They exist in fragments" (*Friend* 1: 40). The son's version: "But grave practical men whose feelings are not like an Aeolian harp . . . acquire a fixation and permanence, and they have not imagination enough to recall their former selves. . . . There is no 'natural piety,' no filiation between their former and latter selves" (*EM* 1: 320). Coleridge filiation and Wordsworthian Natural Piety mark Hartley's poetry emphatically. Among many examples, the unpublished "No Doubt 'Twere Heresy or Something Worse" is striking for its evocation of the marine creatures of "The Ancient Mariner":

> But who may count with microscopic eye
> The multitude of lives, that gleam and flash
> Beyond the sounding keel, and multiply
> In myriad millions when the white oars dash.
> Through waves electric, or at stillest night
> Spread round the bark becalm'd their milky white?

21. For a complete text of "Adolf and Annette" and a critical account see Judith Plotz, "Childhood Lost, Childhood Regained: Hartley Coleridge's Fable of Defeat," followed by "Varia: Adolf and Annette." *Children's Literature* 14 (1986): 133-61.
22. After Hartley's loss of the Oriel Fellowship, Coleridge noted that he had done everything a father could do, or rather had *said* everything a father could say. The eloquent admonition stands in for the whole duty of fatherhood: "Since the time of Hartley's first arrival at Calne to the present day I am not conscious of having failed in any point of duty, of admonition, persuasion, intreaty, warning, or even (tho' ever reluctantly, I grant) of parental injunction—and of repeating the same whenever it could be done without the almost certain consequence of baffling the end in view" (*CLL* 5: 231).
23. The impossibility of Hartley ever succeeding in Coleridge's vein, however, is evident in Coleridge's own acerbic marginalia on Hartley's *Worthies of Lancashire*. Here Coleridge notes and repeatedly rebukes his son's penchant for being always "witty, or rather *hitty*—i.e., giving a sly hit," which is "sadly vulgar" and works to "anger & mortify me" (*Marginalia* 56, 79, 54). He blames Southey's influence.
24. In Rogerian analysis and in popular discourse generally, empathy is an

unproblematically positive term. What after all can be bad about "the capacity to think and feel oneself into another person" (Kohut)? Yet ever since the term entered English from German it has been of uncertain valence. From 1903 "empathy" has been used as the English equivalent of the German *Einfuhlung,* "to feel into" or "to feel within" (Berger 5). But in German the word *Einsfuhlung* means an *identification,* a "being at one" whereas *Einfuhlung* means the *projection* of an aspect of the self on another. The English "empathy" begs the question as in Piaget's 1913 formulation that calls it the merging of "the activities of the perceiving subject with the qualities of the perceived object" (Reed 1). Empathy has several drawbacks as an agency of therapeutic or moral beneficence: first, it is as much a kinaesthetic and aesthetic quality as a moral quality. It means, says Buber, "to glide with one's own feeling into the dynamic structure of an object, a pillar, or a crystal or the branch of a tree or even an animal or man, and as it were, to trace it from within." As such it has no more moral significance than the circulatory system: as John Shlien puts it, "it happens." As a skill, empathy is the quality useful to shoppers in crowded aisles, to fliers of kites, to deer-hunters and even to torturers who need to "feel your pain" in order to increase it. Second, one-way empathy is indistinguishable from projection: the tickled child may be screaming with laughter. I may feel the screams as agony; the tickler may feel the laughter as delight. Closer attention to the child may resolve the ambiguity; closer attention to my feelings and the tickler's will not.

25. Mudge emphasizes Sara's always wistful relation to her father and traces her diminished sense of self to a sense of neglect and abandonment she could never articulate or acknowledge. See especially the Introductions and chapters five and six.

Works Cited

Aaron, Jane. *A Double Singleness: Gender and the Writings of Charles and Mary Lamb.* Oxford: Clarendon Press, 1991.
Abrams, M. H. *Natural Supernaturalism: Tradition and Revolution in Romantic Literature.* 1971; Oxford: Blackwell, 1991. New York and London: W.W. Norton & Co, 1973.
Aladdin and the Enchanted Lamp. Trans. John Payne. London: Villon Society, 1889.
Aladdin and the Wonderful Lamp. New York: Hewet, 1855.
Aladdin, or The Wonderful Lamp. Altemus Banbury Cross Series. Philadelphia: Henry Altemus, 1905.
Aladdin; or, The Wonderful Lamp. A Delightful story selected from the Arabian Nights Entertainments and on which the Pantomime of the Name is founded which is now performing, with universal applause, at the Theatre Royal, Convent Garden. London: Hardy and Co., 1789.
Aladdin; or, The Wonderful Lamp. A Grand Romantic Spectacle, in Two Acts. Ed. D. D. London: John Cumberland, 1826.
Alcott, Amos Bronson. *Essays upon Education.* Gainesville, Florida: Scholars Facsimiles & Reprints, 1960.
———. *Sonnets and Canzonets.* Boston: Roberts Brothers, 1882.
Alcott, Louisa May. *Little Women.* 1868; New York and Scarborough, Ontario: NAL, 1993.
The Arabian Nights. Trans. Edward Foster. 5 vols. London: William Miller, 1803.
The Arabian Nights' Entertainment. Trans. Richard Burton. 2 vols. New York: Heritage Press, 1955.
The Arabian Nights' Entertainment. Trans. Edward William Lane. London: John Murray, 1853.
The Arabian Nights' Entertainment. Trans. Jonathan Scott. 6 vols. London: Longman, Hurst, Rees, Orme and Brown, 1811.
The Arabian Nights' Entertainment. Vols. 3 and 4. Montrose, 1793.

Ashton, Rosemary. *The Life of Samuel Taylor Coleridge: A Critical Biography.* Oxford and Cambridge, MA: Blackwell, 1996.

Augustine, Saint. *The City of God.* Trans. John Healey. Ed. R. V. Tasker. 2 vols. New York and London: Dent and Dutton, 1945.

Babenroth, Charles A. *English Childhood: Wordsworth's Treatment of Childhood in the Light of English Poetry from Prior to Crabbe.* New York: Columbia University Press, 1922.

Babrius and Phaedrus. Ed. and trans. Ben Edwin Perry. Loeb Classical Library. Cambridge, MA and London: Harvard University Press and William Heinemann, 1975.

Bagehot, Walter. *Literary Studies.* 2 vols. London: Longmans, Green and Co., 1879.

Balfour, J. H. "Case of peculiar Disease of the Skull and Dura Mater." *The Edinburgh Medical and Surgical Journal* 43 (1835): 319-25.

Barbauld, Anna Letitia and Dr. Aikin. *Evenings at Home; or, The Juvenile Budget Opened.* London: George Routledge and Sons, 1870.

Barnardo, Mrs. and James Marchant. *Memoirs of the Late Dr. Barnardo.* London: Walter Scott Ltd., 1900.

Barnardo, Thomas John. "A City Waif: How I Fished for and Caught Her." London: J. F. Shaw, 1885.

———. "My First Arab; or, How I Began my Life Work." London: Shaw and Co., 1893.

———. "The Seed of the Righteous among the Children of the Poorest." London: Shaw and Co., 1893.

Barrell, John. *The Infection of Thomas De Quincey: A Psychopathology of Imperialism.* New Haven: Yale University Press, 1991.

Barton, Barnard. *Poems and Letters by Bernard Barton. With a Memoir.* London: Arthur Hall Virtue and Co, 1853.

Beer, John. "Fragmentations and Ironies." *Questioning Romanticism.* Ed. John Beer. Baltimore and London: Johns Hopkins University Press, 1995: 234-64.

———. *Wordsworth in Time.* New York and Boston: Faber and Faber, 1979.

———. *Wordsworth and the Human Heart.* New York: Columbia University Press, 1978.

Beerbohm, Max. *Beerbohm's Literary Caricatures from Homer to Huxley.* Selected, introduced, annotated by J. G. Riewald. Hamden, CT: Archon, 1977.

Belsey, Catherine. *Critical Practice.* London and New York: Methuen, 1980.

Berger, David. *Clinical Empathy.* Northvale, NJ and London: Jason Aronson Inc., 1987.

Bewell, John. *Wordsworth and the Enlightenment: Nature, Man, and Society in Experimental Poetry.* New Haven: Yale University Press, 1989.

Bhattacharya, Bhabani. "Hyder Ali." *Glimpses of Indian History.* New Delhi: Sterling Pub, 1976: 192-96.

Black, Joel D. "Levana: Levitation in Jean Paul and Thomas De Quincey." *Comparative Literature* 32 (1982): 42-60.

Blainey, Ann. *Immortal Boy: A Portrait of Leigh Hunt*. London and Sydney: Croom Helm, 1985.

Blake, William. *The Complete Poetry and Prose of William Blake*. Rev. ed. Ed. David Erdman. Commentary by Harold Bloom. Berkeley: University of California Press, 1982.

Blos, Peter. *Son and Father: Before and Beyond the Oedipus Complex*. New York and London: Free Press/Collier Macmillan, 1985.

Blunden, Edmund. *Charles Lamb: His Life Records by his Contemporaries*. 1934; Folcroft, PA: Folcroft Library Ed., 1975.

———. "Coleridge the Less." *Votive Tablets: Studies Chiefly Appreciative of English Books and Authors*. London: Cobden-Sanderson, 1932: 306-16.

———. "Leigh Hunt's Eldest Son." *Essays by Divers Hands*. Transactions of the Royal Society of Literature of the U.K. New Series. 19. London: Oxford University Press, 1942: 53-75.

Boas, George. *The Cult of Childhood*. Studies of the Warburg Institute 29. London: Warburg Institute, 1966.

Bohart, Arthur and Leslie Greenberg, Eds. *Empathy Reconsidered: New Directions in Psychotherapy*. Washington, DC: American Psychological Association, 1997.

———. "Empathy and Psychotherapy: an Introductory Overview." *Empathy Reconsidered,* Ed. Bohart and Greenberg: 3-31.

Borges, Jorge Luis. *Labyrinths: Selected Stories and Other Writings*. Ed. Donald A. Yates and James E. Irby. New York: New Directions, 1964.

Bouson, J. Brooks. *The Empathetic Reader: A Study of the Narcissistic Character and the Drama of Self*. Amherst: University of Massachusetts Press, 1989

Bowen, Elizabeth. *The Death of the Heart*. New York: Vintage Books, 1959.

———. "The Easter Egg Party." *The Collected Stories of Elizabeth Bowen*. London: Jonathan Cape, 1980: 529-38.

Bowlby, John. *Attachment and Loss*. Vol. 1: *Attachment*. 2nd Ed., 1969; New York: Basic Books, 1989.

———. *Attachment and Loss*. Vol. 2: *Separation*. New York: Basic Books, 1973.

———. *Attachment and Loss*. Vol. 3: *Loss*. New York: Basic Books, 1972.

"Brenda." *Froggy's Little Brother*. Intro. Gillian Avery. 1875; London: Victor Gollancz, 1968.

Brewer, E. Cobham. *Brewer's Dictionary of Phrase and Fable*. Rev. Ivor H. Evans. New York: Harper and Row, 1970.

Brown, John. "Marjorie Fleming." *Rab and His Friends and Other Papers*. 1858. London and New York: Dent and Dutton, 1934.

Browne, Thomas. *The Religio Medici and Other Writings*. London and New York: Dent and Dutton, 1906.

Browning, Elizabeth Barrett. *The Poetical Works of Elizabeth Barrett Browning*. New York: Hurst and Co, 188-?

Bruch, Hilde. *The Golden Cage: The Enigma of Anorexia Nervosa*. New York: Vintage-Random House, 1979.

Brumberg, Joan Jacobs. *Fasting Girls: The Emergence of Anorexia Nervosa as a Modern Disease.* Cambridge, MA and London: Harvard University Press, 1988.

Bruss, Elizabeth. "Thomas De Quincey, Sketches and Sighs." *Autobiographical Acts: The Changing Situation of a Literary Genre.* Baltimore: Johns Hopkins University Press, 1976: 93-120.

Bushnell, John P. "'Where is the Lamb for a Burnt Offering?': Michael's Covenant and Sacrifice." *The Wordsworth Circle* 12 (1981): 246-52.

Byatt, A. S. *The Virgin in the Garden.* London: Chatto and Windus, 1978

Byron, H. J. *Aladdin.* Ed. Gyles Brandreith. 1861; London: David Pounter, 1971.

Canton, William. *The Comrades: Poems Old and New.* London: Ibister and Co., 1902.

———. *The Invisible Playmate W.V., Her Book, and In Memory of W.V.* London and New York: Dent and Dutton, 1912.

———. *A Lost Epic and Other Poems.* Edinburgh and London: William Blackwell & Sons, 1887.

Caracciolo, Peter L. *The Arabian Nights in English Literature: Studies in the Reception of The Thousand and One Nights into British Culture.* New York: St. Martin's Press, 1988.

Carlyle, Thomas. *Reminiscences.* Ed. J. A. Froude. 2 vols. London: Longman, 1881.

———. *Sartor Resartus.* Ed. Charles Frederick Harrold. New York: Odyssey Press, 1937.

Caruth, Cathy. "Past Recognition: Narrative Origins in Wordsworth and Freud." *MLN* 100.5 (1985): 435-48.

———. "'Unknown Causes': Poetic Effects." *Diacritics* Winter 1987: 78-85.

Chamberlain, Alexander Francis. *The Child and Childhood in Folk-Thought (The Child in Primitive Culture).* New York and London: Macmillan, 1896.

———. *The Child: A Study in the Evolution of Man.* London: Walter Scott Ltd., 1900.

Chapman, Elizabeth Rachel. *A Little Child's Wreath.* Flowers of Parnassus XXI. London and New York: John Lane, 1904.

Chaudhuri, K. N. *The Trading World of Asia and the East India Company 1660-1760.* Cambridge: Cambridge University Press, 1978.

Clej, Alina. *A Genealogy of the Modern Self: Thomas De Quincey and the Intoxication of Writing.* Stanford: Stanford University Press, 1995.

Clinton-Baddeley, V. C. *Aladdin.* London: S. French, 1932.

Coe, Richard. *When the Grass Was Taller: Autobiography and the Experience of Childhood.* New Haven and London: Yale University Press, 1984.

Coleridge, Derwent. "Memoir," *Poems of Hartley Coleridge with a Memoir of His Life.* Ed. Derwent Coleridge, 2 vols. London: Edward Moxon, 1851.

Coleridge, Hartley. "Adolf and Annette." *Children's Literature* 14 (1986): 151-61.

———. *The Complete Poetical Works.* Ed. Ramsay Colles. London: George Routledge and Sons, 1908.

———. *Essays and Marginalia.* Ed. Derwent Coleridge. 2 vols. 1851; Plainview, NJ: Books for Libraries Press, 1973.

———. *Essays on Parties in Poetry and on the Character of Hamlet.* Ed. John Drinkwater. 1925; Folcraft, PA: Folcroft Library Editions, 1973.

———. *The Hartley Coleridge Letters: A Calendar and Index*. Ed. Fran Carlock Stephens. Austin, TX: Humanities Research Center, 1978.

———. *The Hartley Coleridge Papers*. Harry Ransom Humanities Research Center, The University of Texas at Austin.

———. *Letters of Hartley Coleridge*. Ed. Grace Evelyn Griggs and Earl Leslie Griggs. London: Oxford University Press, 1936.

———. *New Poems*. Ed. Earl Leslie Griggs. London: Oxford University Press, 1942.

———. *Poems by Hartley Coleridge, with a Memoir of his Life*. Ed. Derwent Coleridge. 2 vols. London: Edward Moxon, 1851.

Coleridge, Samuel Taylor. *Aids to Reflection*. Ed. H. N. Coleridge. 2 vols. London: William Pickering, 1843.

———. *Anima Poetae*. London: William Heinemann, 1895.

———. *Biographia Literaria*. Ed. James Engel and W. Jackson Bate. *Collected Works of Samuel Taylor Coleridge: 7*. Bollingen Series LXXV. Princeton: Princeton University Press, 1983.

———. *Coleridge on Logic and Learning*. Ed. Alice D. Snyder. 1929; Rpt. Folcroft, PA.: Folcroft Library Editions, 1973.

———. *Collected Letters of Samuel Taylor Coleridge*. Ed. Earl Leslie Griggs. 6 vols. Oxford: Clarendon Press, 1956-71.

———. *Complete Poetical Works of Samuel Taylor Coleridge*. Ed. Ernest Hartley Coleridge. 2 vols. 1912; Rpt. Oxford: Clarendon Press, 1968.

———. *The Friend*. Ed. Barbara Rooke. 2 vols. *Collected Works of Samuel Taylor Coleridge: 4*. Bollingen Series 75. Princeton: Princeton University Press, 1969.

———. "Hartley Coleridge, *The Worthies of Yorkshire and Lancashire.*" *Marginalia II: Camden to Hutton*. Ed. George Whalley. *The Collected Works of Samuel Taylor Coleridge 12*. Bollingen Series 75. Princeton: Routledge & Kegan Paul and Princeton University Press, 1984: 49-85.

———. *Inquiring Spirit: A New Presentation of Coleridge from his Published and Unpublished Writings*. Ed. Kathleen Coburn. New York: Pantheon Books, 1951.

———. *Lectures 1818 - 1819 On Literature*. Ed. R. A. Foakes. 2 vols. *Collected Works of Samuel Taylor Coleridge: 5*. Bollingen Series 75. Princeton: Princeton University Press, 1987.

———. *Logic*. Ed. J. R. de J. Jackson. *The Collected Works of Samuel Taylor Coleridge 13*. Bollingen Series 75. Princeton: Routledge & Kegan Paul and Princeton University Press, 1981.

———. *The Notebooks of Samuel Taylor Coleridge*. Ed. Kathleen Coburn. 3 vols. Bollingen Series 50. New York: Pantheon, 1957-73.

———. *The Poems of Samuel Taylor Coleridge*. Ed. E. H. Coleridge. London: Oxford University Press, 1960.

Coleridge, Sara F. *Minnow among Tritons: Mrs. S. J. Coleridge's Letters to Thomas Poole, 1799-1834*. Ed. Stephen Potter. London: Nonesuch Press, 1934.

Coleridge, Sara, ed. *Memoirs and Letters of Sara Coleridge (Mrs. S. T. C.)*. 2 vols. London: Henry S. King & Co, 1873.

Collings, David. *Wordsworthian Errancies: The Poetics of Cultural Dismemberment.* Baltimore and London: Johns Hopkins University Press, 1994
Conrad, Peter. *Everyman History of English Literature.* London and Melbourne: J. M. Dent and Sons Ltd., 1985.
Cooper, Lane. *A Concordance to the Poems of William Wordsworth.* London: Smith, Elder and Co, 1911.
Corelli, Marie. *Boy; A Sketch.* Philadelphia: J. B. Lippincott Co., 1900.
Coveney, Peter. *The Image of Childhood: The Individual and Society: A Study of the Theme in English Literature.* 1957; Rev. ed. Harmondsworth, Middlesex: Penguin, 1967.
Cunningham, Hugh. *The Children of the Poor: Representations of Childhood since the Seventeenth Century.* Oxford: Blackwell, 1991.
Dawood, N. J., tr. *Tales from the Thousand and One Nights.* Harmondsworth: Penguin, 1985.
Day, Thomas. *The Poetical Works of Thomas Day.* Ed. Thomas Park. *The Works of the British Poets.* Vol. 27. London: J. Sharpe, 1828.
De Luca, Vincent. *Thomas De Quincey: The Prose of Vision.* Toronto: University of Toronto Press, 1980.
———. "'The Type of a Mighty Mind': Mutual Influence in Wordsworth and De Quincey." *TSLL* 12 (1971): 239-47.
De Quincey, Thomas. *The Caesars.* Boston: Ticknor, Reed, and Fields, 1851.
———. *The Collected Writings of Thomas De Quincey.* Ed. David Masson. 14 vols. Edinburgh: Adam and Charles Black, 1889-90.
———. *Confessions of an English Opium-Eater and Other Writings.* Ed. Grevel Lindop. Oxford and New York: Oxford University Press, 1996
———. *The Confessions of an English Opium-Eater and Other Writings.* Ed. Aileen Ward. New York: NAL, 1966.
———. *A Diary of Thomas De Quincey.* Ed. H. A. Eaton. London: Noel Douglas, 1925.
———. *Posthumous Works of Thomas De Quincey.* Ed. Alexander Japp. 2 vols. London: William Heinemann, 1891.
———. *Recollections of the Lakes and the Lake Poets.* Ed. David Wright. Harmondsworth, Middlesex: Penguin, 1970.
———. *The Stranger's Grave.* Exeter: S. Graves, 1928.
De Vere, Aubrey. *Recollections of Aubrey de Vere.* London: Edward Arnold, 1897.
Devlin, D. D. *De Quincey, Wordsworth and the Art of Prose.* New York: St. Martin's Press, 1983.
Dickens, Charles. *Our Mutual Friend.* New York: Thomas Crowell, 1904.
Doughty, Oswald. *Perturbed Spirit: The Life and Personality of Samuel Taylor Coleridge.* Rutherford, Madison, Teaneck, London and Toronto: Farleigh Dickinson University Press and Associated University Press, 1981.
Douglas, Wallace. *Wordsworth: The Construction of a Personality.* Kent, OH: Kent State Press, 1968.

Dunham, Philip J. and Frances Dunham. "Optimal Social Structures and Adaptive Infant Development." *Joint Attention: Its Origins and Role in Development.* Ed. Chris Moore and Philip J. Dunam. Foreword by Jerome Bruner. Hillsdale, NJ & London: Lawrence Erlbaum Associates, 1995: 159-88.

Dusinberre, Juliet. *Alice to the Lighthouse: Children's Books and Radical Experiments in Art.* London: Macmillan, 1987.

Dwyer, Johanna. "Nutritional Aspects of Anorexia Nervosa and Bulimia." *Theory and Treatment of Anorexia and Bulimia: Biomedical, Sociocultural, and Psychological Perspectives.* Ed. Steven Wiley Emmett. New York: Brunner-Mazel, 1985: 20-50.

Easthope, Antony. *Wordsworth Now and Then: Romanticism and Contemporary Culture.* Buckingham and Philadelphia: Open University Press, 1993.

Eaton, Horace Ainsworth. *Thomas De Quincey: A Biography.* New York: Oxford University Press, 1936.

Edgeworth, Richard Lovell. *Memoirs of Richard Lovell Edgeworth.* 2 vols. 1820; Shannon, Ireland: Irish University Press, 1969.

Edmundson, Mark. "Vital Intimations: Wordsworth, Coleridge, and the Promise of Criticism." *South Atlantic Quarterly* 91.2 (Summer 1992): 739-64.

Eilenberg, Susan. "'Michael,' 'Christabel,' and the Poetry of Possession." *Criticism* 30.2 (Spring 1988): 205-24.

Emerson, Ralph Waldo. "Nature." *Selections from Ralph Waldo Emerson: An Organic Anthology.* Boston: Houghton Mifflin, 1960: 21-56.

Emmett, Steven Wiley, Ed. *Theory and Treatment of Anorexia and Bulimia: Biomedical, Sociocultural, and Psychological Perspectives.* New York: Brunner-Mazel, 1985.

Erdman, David V. "Coleridge, Wordsworth, and the Wedgwood Fund." *Bulletin of the New York Public Library* 60 (1956): 489-91.

Euripides. *The Medea.* Trans. Rex Warner. *Complete Greek Tragedies.* Ed. David Grene and Richmond Lattimore. Chicago: University of Chicago Press, 1959: 3: 55-108.

———. *Orestes.* Trans. William Arrowsmith. *Complete Greek Tragedies.* Ed. David Grene and Richmond Lattimore. Chicago: University of Chicago Press, 1959: 4: 185-288.

Figuero-Colon, Reinaldo. "Clinical and Laboratory Assessment of the Malnourished Child." *Textbook of Pediatric Nutrition.* 2nd edition. Ed. Robert M. Suskind and Leslie LeWinter-Suskind. New York: Raven Press, 1992: 191-205.

Fleming, Marjory. *The Journals, Letters, & Verses of Marjory Fleming.* Ed. Arundell Esdaile. London: Sidgwick and Jackson, 1934.

Fonagy, Peter, Miriam Steele, Howard Steele, Tom Leigh, Roger Kennedy, Gretta Mattoon and Mary Target, "Attachment, the Reflective Self, and Borderline States: The Predictive Specificity of the Adult Attachment Interview and Pathological Emotional Development." *Attachment Theory: Social, Developmental, and Clinical Perspectives.* Ed. Susan Goldberg, Ro Muir, John Kerr. Hillsdale, NJ and London: Analytic Press, 1995: 233-78.

Fox, Caroline. *Memories of Old Friends.* Ed. Horace N. Pym. London: Smith, Elder, 1882.

Foxcroft, Elizabeth Howard, ed. *Our Glorified: Poems and Passages of Consolation, especially for those Bereaved by the Loss of Children*. Boston: Lee and Shepard, 1889.

Frank, Robert. *"Don't Call Me Gentle Charles": An Essay on Lamb's Essays of Elia*. Corvallis, OR: Oregon State University Press, 1976.

Friedman, Michael. *The Making of a Tory Humanist: Wordsworth and the Idea of Community*. New York: Columbia University Press, 1979.

Froebel, Friedrich. *The Education of Man*. International Education Series. Trans. W. N. Hailmann. 1885; New York: Augustus N. Kelley, 1970.

Frye, Northrop. *Anatomy of Criticism*. Princeton: Princeton University Press, 1957.

Galbraith, Mary. Handout on Allan Schore's *Affect Regulation and the Origin of the Self* distributed at her talk, "A Childhood Studies Approach to Children's Literature," at the Children's Literature Association Conference, Calgary, Alberta. July 1999.

Garland, Madge. *The Changing Face of Childhood*. London: Hutchinson, 1965.

Garlitz, Barbara. "The Baby's Debut: The Contemporary Reaction to Wordsworth's Poetry of Childhood." *Boston University Studies in English* 5 (1961): 85-94.

———. "The Immortality Ode: Its Cultural Progeny." *SEL* 6 (1966): 639-49.

Gaull, Marilyn. "'Awake in Araby.'" The Mary Moorman Memorial Lecture. 1998.

———. "Wordsworth and the Six Arts of Childhood." *1800: The New Lyrical Ballads*. Ed. Nichola Trott and Seamus Perry. New York: St. Martin's Press, 2000.

Giblin, James Cross. *Chimney Sweeps: Yesterday and Today*. New York: T. Y. Crowell, 1982.

Gill, Stephen. *William Wordsworth: A Life*. Oxford: Clarendon Press, 1989.

Goldberg, Susan, Ro Muir, John Kerr, Eds. *Attachment Theory: Social, Developmental, and Clinical Perspectives*. Hillsdale, NJ and London: Analytic Press, 1995.

Goldman, Albert. *The Mine and the Mint: Sources for the Writings of Thomas De Quincey*. Carbondale, IL: Southern Illinois University Press, 1965.

Goldstein, Laurence. *Ruins and Empire: The Evolution of a Theme in Augustan and Romantic Literature*. Pittsburgh: University of Pittsburgh Press, 1977.

Gosse, Edmund. *Father and Son: A Study of Two Temperaments*. Boston: Houghton Mifflin, 1965.

Greenberg, I. Martin. *The Hamlet Vocation of Coleridge and Wordsworth*. Iowa City: University of Iowa Press, 1986.

Greenwood Ernest. *Aladdin U.S.A.* New York and London: Harpers, 1928.

Grene, David and Richmond Lattimore, ed. *The Complete Greek Tragedies*. 4 vols. Chicago: University of Chicago Press, 1959.

Greven, Philip J., Jr., ed. *Child-Rearing Concepts, 1628-1861*. Itasca, IL: F. E. Peacock, 1973.

Griggs, Earl Leslie, "Coleridge and His Son." *SP* 27 (1930): 635-47.

———. *Hartley Coleridge: His Life and Work*. 1929; Folcroft, PA: Folcroft Library Editions, 1971.

———. "Hartley Coleridge on his Father." *PMLA* 49 (1931): 1246-52.

Hailmann, William. *Law of Childhood, and Other Papers*. Chicago: A. B. Stockham, 1889.

Hall, N. John. *Max Beerbohm's Caricatures.* New Haven and London: Yale University Press, 1997.
Hammond, J. L. and Barbara Hammond. *The Town Labourer: The New Civilization 1760-1832.* New York: Doubleday, 1968.
Hartman, Geoffrey. "Wordsworth and Goethe in Literary History." *The Fate of Reading.* Chicago and London: University of Chicago Press, 1975: 179-200.
Hartman, Herbert. *Hartley Coleridge: Poet's Son and Poet.* London: Oxford University Press, 1931.
Hayter, Alethea. "De Quincey's Smashed Vision." *TLS* August 9, 1985: 871-72.
———. *Opium and the Romantic Imagination.* Berkeley and Los Angeles: University of California Press, 1968.
Hazlitt, William. "Mr. Wordsworth." *The Spirit of the Age, The Complete Works of William Hazlitt.* Ed. P. P. Howe. 1932; New York: AMS Press, 1967: 11: 86-95.
———. "On Wit and Humor." *English Romantic Writers.* Ed. David Perkins. New York: Harcourt, Brace & World, 1967: 642-56.
Heath, William. *Elizabeth Bowen: An Introduction to Her Novels.* Madison: University of Wisconsin Press, 1961.
Heinzelman, Kurt. "Dorothy and William Wordsworth at Grasmere." *Romanticism and Feminism.* Ed. Anne K. Mellor. Bloomington and Indianapolis: Indiana University Press, 1988: 52-78.
Henderson, Arnold. "Some Constants of Charles Lamb's Criticism." *SiR* 7 (1968): 104-16.
Herbert, Christopher. "De Quincey and Dickens." *VS* 18 (1972).
"Hesba Stretton" [Sarah Smith]. *Jessica's First Prayer, Little Meg's Children, Alone in London, Pilgrim Street.* New York and London: Garland, 1976.
Holland, Norman. *The Dynamics of Literary Response.* New York: Oxford University Press, 1968.
Holmes, Jeremy. "'Something There Is That Doesn't Love a Wall': John Bowlby, Attachment Theory and Psychoanalysis." *Attachment Theory: Social, Developmental, and Clinical Perspectives.* Ed. Susan Goldberg, Ro Muir, and John Kerr. Hillsdale, NJ and London: Analytic Press, 1995: 19-44.
Hopkins, Brooke. "Wordsworth, Winnicott, and the Claims of the 'Real.'" *SiR* 37 (Summer 1998): 183-216.
Hopkins, Gerard Manley. *The Later Poetic Manuscripts of Gerard Manley Hopkins in Facsimile.* Ed. Norman H. MacKenzie. New York and London: Garland, 1991.
Howe, H. W. *Greta Hall: Home of Coleridge and Southey.* Rev. Robert Woof. Stoke Ferry, Norfolk: Daedalus Press, 1977.
Hume, Fergus. *Aladdin in London.* Boston and New York: Houghton and Mifflin, 1892.
Hunt, Leigh. "Deaths of Little Children." *Essays of Leigh Hunt.* Ed. Reginald Brimley Johnson. London: Dent, 1891: 1-7.
Huston, Anne Marshall. *Understanding Dyslexia: A Practical Approach for Parents and Teachers.* Lanham, MD: Madison Books, 1992.

Improving the Lot of Chimney Sweepers: One Book and Nine Pamphlets. British Labour Struggles: Contemporary Pamphlets 1727-1850. New York: Arno Press, 1972.

Instructions for the Erection of Your Aladdin Home. Bay City, MI: Aladdin Company of Bay City, Michigan, 1921.

Isham, Frederick. *Aladdin from Broadway.* New York: Bobbs Merrill, 1913.

Ivor-Parry, Edith. ed. *In the Gardens of Childhood. An Anthology in Prose and Verse for All Childlovers.* London: G. Routledge, 1913.

Jacobus, Mary. *Romanticism, Writing and Sexual Difference: Essays on* The Prelude. Oxford: Clarendon Press, 1989.

Jameson, Frederic. *The Political Unconscious.* Ithaca, NY: Cornell University Press, 1981.

Jarrell, Randall. *The Complete Poems.* New York: Farrar, Straus and Giroux, 1969.

Jerrold, Walter, ed. *Bon-Mots of Charles Lamb and Douglas Jerrold.* London: Dent, 1893.

Johnson, Alexandra. "The Drama of Imagination: Marjory Fleming and Her Diaries." *Infant Tongues: The Voice of the Child in Literature.* Ed. Elizabeth Goodenough, Mark Heberle, and Naomi Sokoloff. Detroit: Wayne State University Press, 1994: 80-109.

Johnson, Frances E. and Diana Markowitz, "Do Poverty and Malnutrition Affect Children's Growth and Development: Are the Data There?" *Malnourished Children in the United States: Caught in the Cycle of Poverty.* Ed. Robert Karp. New York: Spring Publishing Co., 1993: 3-12.

Johnston, Kenneth R. *The Hidden Wordsworth: Poet, Lover, Rebel, Spy.* New York: W. W. Norton, 1998.

Jordan, John Emory. *De Quincey to Wordsworth: A Biography of a Relationship.* Berkeley: University of California Press, 1962.

Kagan, Jerome. *The Nature of the Child.* New York: Basic Books, 1984.

Kant, Immanuel. *Critique of Judgment.* Trans. J. H. Bernard. New York: Hafner Pub. Co., 1951.

Keay, John. *The Honourable Company: A History of the English East India Company.* New York: Macmillan, 1991.

Keble, John. *Keble's Lectures on Poetry 1832-1941.* Trans. Edward Kershaw Francis. 2 vols. Oxford: Clarendon Press, 1912. Trans. of *Praelectiones Academicae.* 1844.

———. *Lyra Innocentium: Thoughts in Verse on Christian Children, Their Ways, and Their Privileges.* Oxford: John Henry Parker, 1846.

Key, Ellen. *The Century of the Child.* 1898; London and New York: E. P. Putnam's, 1909.

Kilvert, Francis. *Kilvert's Diary: Selections from the Diary of the Rev. Francis Kilvert.* 3 vols. Ed. William Plomer. 1938; London: Jonathan Cape, 1960.

Kincaid, James R. *Child-Loving: The Erotic Child and Victorian Culture.* New York: Routledge, 1992.

———. *Erotic Innocence: The Culture of Child Molesting.* Durham and London: Duke University Press, 1998.

Kipling, Rudyard. *Stalky & Co.* Ed. Isabel Quigley. Oxford and New York: Oxford University Press, 1987.

Knoepflmacher, U. C. "Mutations of the Wordsworthian Child of Nature." *Nature and the Victorian Imagination.* Ed. U. C. Knoepflmacher and G. B. Tennyson. Berkeley: University of California Press, 1977: 391-425

Kuhn, Reinhard. *Corruption in Paradise: The Child in Western Literature.* Hanover and London: University Press of New England, 1982.

Lamb, Charles and Mary Lamb. *The Letters of Charles and Mary Anne Lamb.* Ed. Edwin W. Marrs. 3 vols. Ithaca, NY and London: Cornell University Press, 1975.

———. *The Letters of Charles Lamb to Which are added those of his sister Mary Lamb.* Ed. E. V. Lucas. 3 vols. London: Dent and Dutton, 1935.

———. *The Works of Charles and Mary Lamb.* Ed. E. V. Lucas. 5 vols. 1903; New York: AMS Press, 1968.

Leask, Nigel. *British Romantic Writers and the East: Anxieties of Empire.* Cambridge: Cambridge University Press, 1992.

Lefebure, Molly. *The Bondage of Love: A Life of Mrs. Samuel Taylor Coleridge.* London: Victor Gollancz, 1986.

———. "The Imagination of Mrs. Coleridge." *Coleridge's Imagination: Essays in Memory of Peter Laver.* Ed. Richard Gravil, Lucy Newlyn, and Nicholas Roe. Cambridge: Cambridge University Press, 1985: 79-87.

———. *Samuel Taylor Coleridge: A Bondage of Opium.* New York: Stein and Day, 1974.

———. "'Toujours Gai': Mrs. Samuel Taylor Coleridge, 'A Most Extraordinary Character,' Reviewed in the Light of Her Letters." *CLB* n.s. 30 (April 1980): 105-20.

Lempriere, J. *Biblioteca Classica; or, Classical Dictionary.* Reedited E. H. Barker with corrections by Charles Anthon. 1797; London: John Bohn, 1828.

Lerner, Laurence. *Angels and Absences: Child Deaths in the Nineteenth Century.* Nashville and London: Vanderbilt University Press, 1997.

Lindop, Grevel. *The Opium-Eater: A Life of Thomas De Quincey.* New York: Taplinger, 1981.

Liu, Alan. *Wordsworth: The Sense of History.* Stanford: Stanford University Press, 1989.

Logan, Eugenia, ed. *A Concordance to the Poetry of Samuel Taylor Coleridge.* Gloucester, MA: Peter Smith, 1966.

Logan, William, ed. *Words of Comfort for Parents Bereaved of Little Children.* 4th ed. London: James Nisbet and Co., 1867.

MacBean, L. *The Story of Pet Marjorie (Marjorie Fleming).* London: Simpkin, Marshall, Hamilton, Kent and Co., 1904.

MacIntyre, Alasdair. *After Virtue: A Study in Moral Theory.* Notre Dame, IN: Notre Dame University Press, 1981.

MacKenzie, John. "Hunting and the Natural World in Juvenile Literature." *Imperialism in Juvenile Literature.* Ed. Jeffrey Richards. Manchester: Manchester University Press, 1989.

Malkin, Benjamin Heath. *A Father's Memoirs of his Child (Thomas W. Malkin)*. With a design by W. Blake. London: Longman, Hurst, Rees, and Orm, 1806.

Malson, Lucien. *Wolf Children and the Problem of Human Nature*. New York: Monthly Review Press, 1972.

Maniquis, Robert M. *Lonely Empires: Personal and Public Visions of Thomas De Quincey*. Literary Monographs 8. Madison: University of Wisconsin Press, 1976.

Marcus, Steven. "Some Representations of Childhood in Wordsworth's Poetry." *Opening Texts: Psychoanalysis and the Culture of the Child*. Ed. Joseph E. Smith and William Kerrigan. Baltimore: Johns Hopkins University Press, 1985: 1-16.

"Margaret Fleming." *National Dictionary of Biography*. Vol. 19. Ed. Leslie Stephen. London, 1889: 19: 28.

Martorelli, Reynaldo, Fernando Mendoza, and Ricardo Castillo. "Poverty and Stature in Children." *Linear Growth Retardation in Less Developed Countries*. Ed. John Waterlow. New York: Raven Press, 1988: 57-73.

Masson, David. *De Quincey*. New York and London: Harper and Brothers, 1901.

Matthews, Gareth B. *Philosophy and the Young Child*. Cambridge, MA and London: Harvard University Press, 1980.

Mayr, Ernst. *The Growth of Biological Thought: Diversity, Evolution, and Inheritance*. Cambridge, MA and London: Belknap Press of Harvard University Press, 1982.

McDonagh, Josephine. *De Quincey's Disciplines*. Oxford: Clarendon Press, 1994.

McFarland, Thomas. *Romantic Cruxes: The English Essayists and the Spirit of the Age*. Oxford: Clarendon Press, 1987.

McGann, Jerome. *The Romantic Ideology: A Critical Investigation*. Chicago and London: University of Chicago Press, 1983.

McGavran, James Holt, Jr. "Catechist and Visionary: Watts and Wordsworth in 'We Are Seven' and 'Anecdote for Fathers.'" *Romanticism and Children's Literature in Nineteenth-Century England*. Ed. James Holt McGavran, Jr. Athens and London: University of Georgia Press, 1991: 54-71.

———. ed. *Literature and the Child: Romantic Continuations, Postmodern Contestations*. Iowa City: University of Iowa Press, 1999.

———. ed. *Romanticism and Children's Literature in Nineteenth-Century England*. Athens and London: University of Georgia Press, 1991.

———. "Wordsworth, Lost Boys, and Romantic Hom(e)phobia." *Literature and the Child*. Ed. James Holt McGavran. Iowa City: University of Iowa Press, 1999: 130-52.

Meynell, Alice. *Childhood*. London: B. F. Batsford, 1913.

———. *The Children*. London and New York: John Lane, 1897.

———. *The Poems of Alice Meynell*. London: Oxford University Press, 1940.

Meynell, Wilfred, ed. *The Child Set in the Midst by Modern Poets*. London: Leadenhall Press, 1892.

Miles, Alfred H., ed. *Charles Kingsley to James Thomson. The Poets and Poetry of the Nineteenth Century*. London and New York: Routledge and Dutton, 1905.

Miles, T. R. and Elaine Miles. *Dyslexia: A Hundred Years On*. Milton Keynes and Philadelphia: Open University Press, 1990.

Miller, J. Hillis. "Thomas De Quincey." *The Disappearance of God: Five Nineteenth-Century Writers*. Cambridge, MA: Harvard University Press, 1963: 17-80.

Miller, Karl. *Doubles: Studies in Literary History*. Oxford: Oxford University Press, 1985.

Mishra, Vijay. *The Gothic Sublime*. Albany: State University of New York Press, 1994.

Monaghan, Patricia. *The Book of Goddesses and Heroines*. New York: Dutton, 1981.

Monsman, Gerald. "Charles Lamb's Elia and the Fallen Angel." *SiR* 38 (Spring 1999): 51-60.

———. *Confessions of a Prosaic Dreamer: Charles Lamb's Art of Autobiography*. Durham, NC: Duke University Press, 1984.

Montgomery, James. *The Chimney-Sweeper's Friend*. 1824. Intro. Donald H. Reiman. A Garland Series. Romantic Context Poetry: Significant Minor Poetry 1789-1830. New York and London: Garland Publishing Inc., 1978.

Moore, Robert L. "Justification Without Joy: Psychohistorical Reflections on John Wesley's Childhood and Conversion." *History of Childhood Quarterly* 2 (1974): 30-52.

Moorman, Mary. *William Wordsworth. The Early Years, 1770-1803*. Oxford: Clarendon Press, 1957.

———. "Wordsworth and His Children." *Bicentenary Wordsworth Studies in Memory of John Alban Finch*. Ithaca and London: Cornell University Press, 1970: 111-41.

Morley, F. V. *Lamb Before Elia*. London: Jonathan Cape, 1932.

Morrison, Arthur. *A Child of the Jago*. 1896; London: Boydell Press, 1982.

Mozley, Thomas. *Reminiscences: Chiefly of Oriel College and the Oxford Movement*. 2 vols. London: Longmans, Green and Co., 1882.

Mudge, Bradford Keyes. *Sara Coleridge, A Victorian Daughter*. New Haven and London: Yale University Press, 1989.

Mulcahy, Daniel J. "Charles Lamb: The Antithetical Manner and the Two Planes." *SEL* 3 (1963): 517-42.

Mulvey-Roberts, Marie., ed. *The Handbook to Gothic Literature*. New York: New York University Press, 1998.

Munson, Gorham. *Aladdin's Lamp: The Wealth of the American People*. New York: Creative Age Press, 1945.

Myers, Mitzi. "Introduction: Here's Looking at You Kid: or, Is Culturing Childhood Colonizing Casablanca?" *Nineteenth-Century Contexts*. 21.2 (1999): 157-67.

———. "Little Girls Lost: Rewriting Romantic Childhood, Righting Gender and Genre." *Teaching Children's Literature: Issues, Pedagogy, Resources*. Ed. Glenn Sadler. New York: The Modern Language Association of America: 1992: 131-42.

———. "Of Mimicry and (Wo)Man: *Infans* or Forked Tongue?" *Children's Literature* 23 (1995): 56-60.

———. "Reading Children and Homeopathic Romanticism: Paradigm Lost, Revisionary Gleam, or 'Plus Ça Change, Plus C'est la Même Chose'?" *Literature and* the Child: Romantic Continuations, Postmodern Contestations. Ed. James Holt McGavran. Iowa City: University of Iowa Press, 1999: 44-84.

Nabholtz, John R. "Drama and Rhetoric in Lamb's Essays of the Imagination." *SEL* 12 (1972): 683-703.

Naddaff, Sandra. *Arabesque: Narrative Structure and the Aesthetics of Repetition in the 1001 Nights.* Evanston: Northwestern University Press, 1991.

Needham, George C. *Street Arabs and Gutter Snipes: The Pathetic Young Vagabond Life in the Great Cities, with Records of Work for their Reclamation.* Boston: D. L. Guernsey, 1884.

Newlyn, Lucy. "The Little Actor in his Mock Apparel." *Wordsworth Circle* 14 (1983): 30-39.

Nodelman, Perry. "The Other: Orientalism, Colonialism, and Children's Literature." *ChLAQ* 17.1 (Spring 1992): 29-35.

Olnick, Stanley. "A Critique of Empathy and Sympathy." *Empathy I*. Ed. Joseph Lictenberg, Melvin Bornstein, and Donald Silver. Hillsdale, NJ and London: Analytic Press, 1989: 137-66.

Onorato, Richard. *The Character of the Poet: Wordsworth in "The Prelude."* Princeton: Princeton University Press, 1971.

The Oriental Moralist, or the Beauties of the Arabian Nights' Entertainment. Trans. Rev. Mr. Cooper. London: E. Newbery, 1800.

Orwell, George. *An Age Like This 1920-1940. The Collected Essays, Journalism and Letters of George Orwell.* Vol. 1. Ed. Sonia Orwell and Ian Angus. New York: HBJ, 1968.

The Oxford Dictionary of English Proverbs. 3rd Ed. Rev. F. P. Wilson. Oxford: Clarendon Press, 1970.

Page, H. A. [Pseudonym for A. H. Japp.] *Thomas De Quincey: His and Writings.* London: John Hogg, 1890.

Parker, Reeve. "Finishing Off 'Michael': Poetic and Critical Enclosures." *Diacritics* (Winter 1987): 53-64.

Parr, Richard B. "Weight Loss: Its Effect on Normal Growth Patterns." *Evaluation and Management of Eating Disorders: Anorexia, Bulimia, and Obesity.* Ed. Kristine L. Clark, Richard B. Parr, and William P. Castelli. Champaign, IL: Life Enhancement Publications, 1988: 91-104

Partridge, Eric. *A Dictionary of Slang and Unconventional English.* 7th ed. New York: Macmillan, l970.

Pasternak, Boris. *Dr. Zhivago.* Trans. Max Hayward and Maya Harari. London: Collins and Harvill Press, 1958.

Pattison, Robert. *The Child Figure in English Literature.* Athens: University of Georgia, 1978.

Percival, Thomas. *A Father's Instructions to His Children.* Dublin: P. Byrne, 1790.

———. *Parental Instructions: or, Guide to Wisdom and Virtue desired for Young Persons of Either Sex.* 1788; New York: Harper Brothers, 1846.

Percy, Thomas. *Reliques of Ancient English Poetry.* Ed. Henry B. Wheatley. 3 vols. London: George Allen and Unwin, 1927.

Perkins, David. *English Romantic Writers.* New York: HBW, 1967.
Philips, C. H. *The East India Company 1784-1806.* Cambridge: Cambridge University Press, 1970.
Phillips, George L. *England's Climbing Boys: A History of the Long Struggle to Abolish Child Labor in Chimney Sweeping.* Publication #5 of the Kress Library of Business and Economics. Boston: Baker Library-Harvard GSBA, 1949.
Piaget, Jean. *Behavior and Evolution.* Trans. Donald Nicholson-Smith. 1976; New York: Pantheon Books, 1978.
———. *The Child's Conception of the World.* Trans. Joan and Andrew Tomlinson. 1929; Frogmore, St. Albans, Herts.: Paladin, 1973.
———. *The Language and Thought of the Child.* 1923; First English ed. 1926; New York and Scarborough, Ontario: Meridien for NAL, 1959.
———. *The Moral Judgment of the Child.* Trans. Marjorie Gabain. 1932; Harmondsworth, Middlesex: Penguin, 1977.
Platzner, Robert. "De Quincey and the Dilemma of Romantic Autobiography." *Dalhousie Review* 61 (1981-82): 605-17.
Playfair, Giles. *The Prodigy: A Study of the Strange Life of Master Betty.* London: Secker and Warburg, 1967.
Plotz, Judith. "The *Annus Mirabilis* and the Lost Boy: Hartley's Case." *SiR* 33 (Summer 1994): 181-200.
———. "Childhood Lost, Childhood Regained: Hartley Coleridge's Fable of Defeat." *Children's Literature* 14 (1986): 133-48.
———. "Imaginary Kingdoms with Real Boys in Them; or, How the Quincey Brothers Built the British Empire." *The Wordsworth Circle* 27.3 (Summer 1996): 131-36.
———. "In the Footsteps of Aladdin: De Quincey's Arabian Nights." *The Wordsworth Circle* 29.2 (Spring 1998): 120-26.
———. "Literary Ways of Killing a Child: The 19th-Century Practice." *Aspects and Issues in the History of Children's Literature.* Ed. Maria Nikolajeva. Westport, CT and London: Greenwood Press, 1995: 1-24.
———. "On Guilt Considered as One of the Fine Arts." *The Wordsworth Circle* 19.2 (Spring 1988): 83-88.
———. "A Modern 'Seer Blest': The Visionary Child in *The Virgin in the Garden.*" *Essays on the Fiction of A. S. Byatt: Imagining the Real.* Ed. Alexa Alfer and Michael Noble. Westport, CT: Greenwood Press, forthcoming.
———. "'The Perpetual Messiah': Romanticism, Childhood, and the Paradoxes of Human Development." *Regulated Children/Liberated Children: Education in Psychohistorical Perspective.* Ed. Barbara Finkelstein. New York: Psychohistory Press, 1979.
———. "The Pet of Letters: Marjorie Fleming's Juvenilia." *ChLAQ* 17. 4 (Winter 1992-93): 4-9.
Pollock, Linda. *Forgotten Children: Parent-Child Relations from 1500 to 1900.* Cambridge and New York: Cambridge University Press, 1983.

Porter, Roger. "The Demon Past: De Quincey and the Autobiographer's Dilemma." *SEL* 20 (1980): 591-609.
Poster, Mark. *The Critical Theory of the Family.* New York: Seabury Press, 1978.
Prime, Samuel Irenaeus, et al. *The Smitten Household; or, Thoughts for the Afflicted.* New York: Anson D. F. Randolph, 1856.
Quick, Herbert. *Aladdin: A Romance of Yankee Magic.* New York: Henry Holt, 1904.
Randel, Fred V. *The World of Elia: Charles Lamb's Essayistic Romanticism.* Port Washington, New York and London: National University Publications-Kennikat Press, 1975.
Rawnsley, H. W. "Reminiscences of Wordsworth among the Peasantry of Westmoreland." *Wordsworthiana: A Selection of Papers Read to the Wordsworth Society.* Ed. William Knight 1889; Folcroft, PA: Folcroft Library Edition, 1979: 78-119.
Rea, John. "Hartley Coleridge and Wordsworth's Lucy." *SP* 28 (1931): 118-35.
Reed, Gail S. "The Antithetical Meaning of the Term 'Empathy' in Psychoanalytic Discourse." *Empathy I.* Ed. Joseph Lichtenberg, Melvin Bornstein, Donald Silver. Hillsdale, NJ and London: Analytic Press, 1984: 7-24.
Rehder, Robert. *Wordsworth and the Beginnings of Modern Poetry.* London and Totowa, NJ: Croom Helm and Barnes and Noble, 1981.
Richards, Jeffrey, Ed. *Imperialism and Juvenile Literature.* Manchester and New York: Manchester University Press, 1989.
Richardson, Alan. *Literature, Education, and Romanticism: Reading as Social Practice, 1780-1831.* Cambridge: Cambridge University Press, 1994.
———. "Romanticism and the End of Childhood." *Literature and the Child.* Ed. James Holt McGavran. Iowa City: University of Iowa Press, 1999: 23-43.
Richter, Jean Paul. *Levana; or, The Doctrine of Education.* 1806; Trans. A. H. London: George Bell and Sons, 1876.
Rieff, Philip. *Freud: The Mind of the Moralist.* 1959; Garden City, NY: Anchor-Doubleday, 1961.
Riehl, Joseph. "Charles Lamb's Essays on Education: Christ's Hospital and the Growth of Elia." *PAPA* 8 (Spring 1982): 42-52.
Robinson, Henry Crabb. *Henry Crabb Robinson on Books and Their Writers.* Ed. Edith J. Morley. 3 vols. 1938; Rpt. New York: AMS Press, 1967.
Roe, Nicholas. *The Politics of Nature: Wordsworth and Some Contemporaries.* New York: St. Martin's Press, 1992.
———. *Wordsworth and Coleridge: The Radical Years.* Oxford: Clarendon Press, 1988.
Roman, Laura E. "Delving into De Quincey's Palimpsest: Myth-Making, Digressions and an Unpublished Text." *The Wordsworth Circle* 26.2 (Spring 1995): 107-12.
Rose, Jacqueline. *The Case of Peter Pan; or The Impossibility of Children's Fiction.* Philadelphia: University of Pennsylvania Press, 1993.
Rosenblum, Robert. *The Romantic Child from Runge to Sendak.* The Walter Neurath Memorial Lecture 1988. New York: Thames and Hudson, 1988.
Rousseau, Jean Jacques. *Emile.* Trans. Barbara Foxley. London and New York: Dent and Dutton, 1976.

Runciman, James. *Side Lights*. London: T. Fisher Unwin, 1893.
Russell, Matthew. *Little Angels: A Book of Comfort for Mourning Mothers*. London: Burns and Oates, 1909.
Russett, Margaret. *De Quincey's Romanticism: Canonical Minority and the Forms of Transmission*. Cambridge: Cambridge University Press, 1997.
———. "Wordsworth's Gothic Interpreter: De Quincey Personifies 'We Are Seven.'" *SiR* 30, no. 3 (Fall 1991): 345-65.
Rzepka, Charles A. *Sacramental Commodities: Gift, Text, and the Sublime in De Quincey*. Amherst: University of Massachusetts Press, 1995.
Sangster, Paul. *Pity My Simplicity: The Evangelical Revival and the Religious Education of Children 1738-1800*. London: Epworth Press, 1963.
Sargent, Helen Child and George Lyman Kittredge. *English and Scottish Popular Ballads*. Boston: Houghton Mifflin, 1932.
Schapiro, Barbara. *The Romantic Mother: Narcissistic Patterns in Romantic Poetry*. Baltimore and London: Johns Hopkins University Press, 1983.
von Schiller, Friedrich. *Naive and Sentimental Poetry and On the Sublime: Two Essays*. Trans. Julius A. Elias. 1795; New York: Frederick Ungar, 1966.
Schorsch, Anita. *Images of Childhood: An Illustrated Social History*. New York: Main Street Press-Mayflower Books, 1979.
Scoggins, James. "Images of Eden in the Essays of Elia." *JEGP* 71 (1972): 198-210.
Scott, Walter. *The Surgeon's Daughter*. 1827; Vol. 25, Centenary Edition of the Waverley Novels. Edinburgh: Adam and Charles Black, 1898.
Scudder, Horace. "Childhood in English Art and Literature. II" *The Atlantic Monthly* Vol. 56, no. 336 (October 1885): 471-84.
———. *Childhood in Literature and Art*. Boston: Houghton Mifflin and Co., 1894.
Shairp, John Campell. *Studies in Poetry and Philosophy*. 1868; Port Washington, NY and London: Kennikat, 1970.
Shlien, John. "Empathy in Psychotherapy: A Vital Mechanism? Yes. Therapist's Conceit? All too Often. By Itself Enough? No." *Empathy Reconsidered: New Directions in Psychotherapy*. Ed. Arthur Bohart and Leslie Greenberg. Washington, DC: American Psychological Association, 1997: 63-80.
Simpson, David. *Wordsworth and the Figuring of the Real*. Atlantic Highlands, NJ: Humanities Press, 1982.
Smyth, Thomas. *Solace for Bereaved Parents; or, Infants Die to Live*. New York: Robert Carter, 1846.
Snyder, Robert Lance. Ed. *Thomas De Quincey: Bicentenary Studies*. Norman, OK: University of Oklahoma Press, 1981.
Sommerville, Charles John. *The Rise and Fall of Childhood*. Beverly Hills, CA: Sage Publications, 1982.
Southey, Robert. *Selections from the Letters of Robert Southey*. Ed. John Wood Warter. 4 vols. London: Longmans, Brown, Green and Longmans, 1856.
Spector, Stephen J. "Thomas De Quincey: Self-Effacing Autobiographer." *VS* 18 (1979): 501-20.

Spignesi, Agnes. *Starving Women: A Psychology of Anorexia Nervosa*. Dallas: Spring Publications, 1983.

Spivak, Gayatri. "Sex and History in *The Prelude* (1805): Books Nine to Thirteen." *In Other Worlds: Essays in Cultural Politics*. New York and London: Routledge, 1999: 46-76.

Steedman, Carolyn. *Strange Dislocations: Childhood and the Idea of Human Interiority 1780-1930*. Cambridge, MA: Harvard University Press, 1995.

Stephen, Leslie. *The English Utilitarians*. Vol. III. *John Stuart Mill*. New York and London: G. P. Putnam's Sons and Duckworth and Co., 1900.

Stern, Daniel. *The First Relationship: Mother and Infant*. Cambridge, MA: Harvard University Press, 1977.

Sterne, Laurence. *The Life and Opinions of Tristram Shandy, Gent*. Ed. Howard Anderson. New York and London: Norton, 1980.

Steward, James Christen. *The New Child: British Art and the Origins of Modern Childhood, 1730-1830*. Berkeley, CA: University Art Museum and Pacific Film Archive in association with University of Washington Press, 1995.

Stewart, David. *Preface to Empathy*. New York: Philosophic Library, 1956.

Strange, K. H. *Climbing Boys: A Study of Sweepers' Apprentices, 1773-1875*. London and New York: Allen and Busby, 1982.

Strickland, Charles. "A Transcendentalist Father: The Child-Rearing Practices of Bronson Alcott." *Perspectives in American History* 3 (1969): 5-73.

Strong, Roy. *And when did you last see your father? The Victorian Painter and British History*. Over Wallop, Hampshire, UK: Thames and Hudson, 1978.

Swinburne, A. C. *Selections from the Poetical Work of A. C. Swinburne*. Ed. R. H. Stoddard. New York: Thomas Crowell, 1884.

Tatchell, Molly. *Leigh Hunt and His Family in Hammersmith*. London: Hammersmith Local History Group, 1969.

Tave, Stuart. Introduction. *New Essays by Thomas De Quincey*. Princeton: Princeton University Press, 1966.

Taylor, Anya. "'A Father's Tale': Coleridge Foretells the Life of Hartley." *SiR* 30 (Spring 1991): 37-56.

Thompson, Denys. "Our Debt to Lamb." *Determinations: Critical Essays*. Intro. F. R. Leavis. 1934; New York: Haskell House, 1970: 199-217.

Thompson, Edward and G. T. Garrett. *The Rise and Fulfillment of British Rule in India*. Allahabad: Central Book Depot, 1962.

Thompson, Francis. *Complete Poetical Works of Francis Thompson*. Ed. Wilfred Meynell. New York: Boni and Liveright, [1918?].

The Thousand and One Nights, commonly called in English The Arabian Nights' Entertainments. Trans. Edward William Lane. 3 vols. London: Charles Knight, 1839-40.

Tillotson, Geoffrey. "The Historical Importance of Certain *Essays of Elia*." *Some British Romantics: A Collection of Essays*. Ed. James V. Logan, John E. Jordan, and Northrop Frye. n.p.: Columbus: Ohio State University Press, 1966: 89-116.

Tirebuck, William, Ed. *The Poetical Works of Bowles, Lamb, and Hartley Coleridge.* London: Walter Scott, 1887.

Twain, Mark. "Marjorie Fleming, The Wonder Child." *Europe and Elsewhere: The Writings of Mark Twain.* The Stormfield Edition. New York and London: Harper Brothers, 1929: 358-76.

Wagner, Gillian. *Barnardo.* London: Weidenfeld and Nicolson, 1979.

Walker, Barbara. *A Woman's Encyclopedia of Myths and Secrets.* San Francisco: Harper and Row, 1983.

Ward, J. P. "'Came from Yon Fountain': Wordsworth's Influence on Victorian Education." *Victorian Studies* 29.3 (Spring 1986): 405-46.

Warner, Marina. *Six Myths of Our Time: Little Angels, Little Monsters, Beautiful Beasts, and More.* New York: Vintage, 1995.

West, Edward Sackville. *Thomas De Quincey: His Life and Work.* New Haven: Yale University Press, 1936.

Wiener, David. "Wordsworth, Books, and the Growth of a Poet's Mind." *JEGP* 74 (1975): 209-20.

Willey, Basil. *The Eighteenth-Century Background: Studies on the Idea of Nature in the Thought of the Period.* Harmondsworth: Penguin, 1962.

Williams, John. *Wordsworth, Romantic Poetry and Revolutionary Politics.* Manchester: Manchester University Press, 1989.

Wilson, John. *Noctes Ambrosiae.* Rev. ed. 5 vols. New York: W. J. Widdleton, 1863.

Wollheim, Richard. *The Thread of Life.* Cambridge: Harvard University Press, 1984.

Woodman, Ross. "The Idiot Boy as Healer." *Romanticism and Children's Literature in Nineteenth-Century England.* Ed. James Holt McGavran. Athens, GA: University of Georgia Press, 1991. 72-95.

Wordsworth, William and Dorothy Wordsworth. *The Letters of William and Dorothy Wordsworth: The Early Years. 1787-1805.* Ed. Ernest de Selincourt; 2nd ed. Ed Alan G. Hill. 5 vols. Oxford: Clarendon Press, 1967.

———. *The Letters of William and Dorothy Wordsworth: The Middle Years, Part 1. 1806-1811.* 2nd ed. Rev. Mary Moorman. Oxford: Clarendon Press. 1970.

———. *The Letters of William and Dorothy Wordsworth: The Middle Years, Part 2. 1812-1820.* 2nd ed. Rev. Mary Moorman and Alan G. Hill. Oxford: Clarendon Press. 1970.

———. *The Letters of William and Dorothy Wordsworth: The Later Years. 1: 1821-1830.* 2nd ed. Ed. Alan H. Hill. 5 vols. Oxford: Clarendon Press, 1978-93.

Wordsworth, William and Mary Wordsworth. *The Love Letters of William and Mary Wordsworth.* Ed. Beth Darlington. Ithaca, NY: Cornell University Press, 1981.

Wordsworth, William. *The Fourteen-Book Prelude.* Ed. W. J. B. Owen. The Cornell Wordsworth. Ithaca and London: Cornell University Press, 1985.

———. *Lyrical Ballads and Other Poems, 1797-1800.* Ed. James Butler and Karen Green. The Cornell Wordsworth. Ithaca and London: Cornell University Press, 1992.

———. *The Poetical Works of William Wordsworth*. Ed. Paul Sheats. Boston: Houghton Mifflin, 1982.

———. *The Prelude 1799, 1805, 1850*. Ed. Jonathan Wordsworth, M. H. Abrams, and Stephen Gill. Norton Critical Edition. New York: Norton, 1979.

———. *The Prelude: A Parallel Text*. Ed. J. C. Maxwell. Harmondsworth, Middlesex, UK: Penguin, 1978.

———. *The Prose Works of William Wordsworth*. Ed. Alexander B. Grosart. 3 vols. 1876; Rpt. New York: AMS Press, 1987.

———. *Wordsworth's Literary Criticism*. Ed. W. J. B. Owen. London and Boston: Routledge and Kegan Paul, 1974.

Wu, Duncan. *Wordsworth's Reading, 1770-1779*. Cambridge: Cambridge University Press, 1993.

———. *Wordsworth's Reading, 1800-1815*. Cambridge: Cambridge University Press, 1995.

The Young Roscius: Biographical Memoirs of William Henry West Betty. New York: Robert M'Dermut, 1806.

Youngquist, Paul. "De Quincey's Crazy Body." *PMLA* 114.3 (May 1999): 346-58.

Index

"Abraham's Bosom," 62–3, 85, 262n.23
Abrams, M. H. *Natural Supernaturalism,* 254n.2
adulthood vs. childhood, 2–3, 18, 29–30
  Piaget on, 26–30, 212
adultist writing, 46
Aesop, as pariah writer, 146
"Aladdin and His Marvellous Lamp," versions of, 147–50
  De Quincey's redaction, 146–52
Alcott, Bronson, child as idol, 3, 254–5n.3
  metaphysical child's mind, 13
Alcott, Louisa May, metaphysical child, 255n.6
  Little Women, 259n.7
Alderson, Brian, 268n.8
"Amiel," child as redeemer, 3
  as power, 9
amphibium, "Child Angel" as, 106–7
  Browne, 266n.7
animism, 18–19
  in Piaget, 19
  in Wordsworth, 19
  in Blake, 19
  Piaget on defects of animist thinking, 28
Ann, 134, 145
anorexia, De Quincey and, 180–90
  gender and, 190
antiquity, childhood and 8–9, 115, 116, 198–9
  nature as, in Schiller, 8
Arabian Nights, 146, 147
  versions: Galland, 148; Grub Street, 147; Lane, 147; *Oriental Moralist,* children's version, 268n.8; Torrens, 147
  Wordsworth's attachment to, 56
"arabs," 37–8, 257n.13
Ariès, Phillipe, 39

arrest, as Romantic motif, xi–xiii, 72, 217, 108–22
  see also isolation, separation, solitude
Ashton, Rosemary, 194
attachment psychology, 220–1
Augustine, *The City of God,* 143

Babenroth, Charles, 258n.3
Balfour, J. H., 269n.16
Barbauld, Anna Letitia, 20, 136–7, 203
  admired "Aladdin," 147–9
  compared to Edgeworth, 136
  developmental view of childhood, xiv
  "Generous Revenge," 146, 147
  mocked by Lamb, Coleridge, De Quincey, xiv, 150
Barnardo, Thomas John, 34, 51, 261n.16
  works: "My First Arab, 36, 37; "Labours of Love among our East End Arabs," 37; "The Arab Children of our Great City," 37
Barrell, John, 157–8, 144, 268n.6
Barton, Barnard, 88, 95, 97
  "On the Death of a Child of Extraordinary Endowments and Piety," 19
Beaumont, George, 192, 196
Beer, John, 52
Beerbohm, Max, "William Wordsworth in the Lake District, at cross-purposes," xi–xii, 3–4
Betty, William ("Young Roscius") 72, 79
Black, Joel, 267n.2
Blake, William, 95, 98, 103
  animism in, 19
  critique of Innocence, xiv
  works: "The Chimney Sweeper" (Innocence), 15, 96, 97; Lamb's redaction of, 98–100; The Chimney Sweeper" (Experience), 98,

Index

Blake, William, works (*continued*)
   99; "London," 98; *Songs of Innocence and Experience,* 98; "The Tyger," 98, 158
Borges, Jorge Luis, 118, 129, 135
Bowen, Elizabeth, interrogation of innocence, 257n.1
   "The Easter Egg Party," 42–3, 44
Bowlby, John, *Attachment and Loss,* 67, 68
   childhood loss, 67–9, 263n.37
Bowles, William Lisle, 91, 95, 103
   "The Little Sweep," 97
"Brenda," *Froggy's Little Brother,* 36
Brinton, D.G., evolution producing childlike adult, 11
Brown, John, 32
Browne, Thomas, 266–6n.7
Browning, Elizabeth Barrett, childhood plenitude, 7
   "Song for the Ragged Schools of London," 34
Bruss, Elizabeth, 139
Burke, Edmund, 152
Bushnell, John, 60
Byatt, A.S., *The Virgin in the Garden,* 50–51
Byron, H. J., *Aladdin* (pantomime), 149

cannibalism, 117, 126–8
Canton, William, children as: anti-depressant, 3; idols, 254–5n.3; different species, 2; "majority," 2; martyrs, 259n.8
   works: "The Legend of Childhood," 2; "An Unknown Child-Poem," 10–11; *WV Her Book,* 32
Carlyle, Jane, 183
Carlyle, Thomas, 73, 129, 183
Chamberlain, Alexander, 5
   evolution: toward childlikeness, 12–13; toward genius, 12–13
   The Child and Childhood, 4
Chapman, Elizabeth, child as idol, 254–4n.3
child, *see* Essential Child and Romantic Child, 4
childhood, protracted: value of, 12
children of the poor, "children of history," 30, 34–38, 95, 100–1, 106
   antithetical to Essential Child, 38
   avoidance of child terms, 34–5
   dehumanizing terms for, 34–8
   enemy of civilization, 38
   erasure by Romantic Discourse, 34–8
   not children, 105–6
   prematurely old, 36
   see also chimney sweepers and non-children
children's literature, 4–5
   by Barbauld, Edgeworth, Wollstonecraft, Hofland, xiv
   by bluestockings, 136–7
   Hartley Coleridge's reading in, 203
   "Infant Literature," 145–52
   pariah genre, 46–52
   produced by Romantic Discourse of Childhood, 5–30
   realistic, 20
   Victorian and Edwardian, 46
chimney sweepers, 51, 91–106
   Lamb on, 97–106
   and Romantic poets, 95
   as slaves, 95–6, 102
Clej, Alina, 130, 267n.2
Coburn, Kathleen, 220, 221
   praises Coleridge's empathy, 240
Coe, Richard, 159, 255n.4
Coleridge, Berkeley, death, 240
Coleridge, David Hartley, 213, 216, 217; *see also* Coleridge, Hartley
Coleridge, Derwent, 88, 180, 214, 220, 222, 244, 245
   compared to Hartley, 240
   "Memoir" of Hartley Coleridge, 191
   on Hartley's genius, 232
Coleridge, Hartley, 87, 88, 151, 191–215
   air spirit, 222–4: Eolian Harp, 217, 222, 229; as nitrous oxide, 223
   "annus mirabilis" (1806–7), 191–213
   child as archaic, 8–9; fungible, 5, 208–9; immutable, 8, 11, 210
   childhood reading, 213
   childhood *vs.* adulthood, 212
   childhood, as subject of poetry, 206–13
   childlike: 199–203; as excuse, 200
   "doted on," 231–2
   Ejuxria, 3, 24, 195
   fixation on childhood, xiii
   idealism, 14, 224–9: father-son dialogues on thinking, 226–8
   idolized father, 191–97, 232–4 ; 248–51
   journals, 202–3
   littleness, 199, 200: as a subject of poetry, 206
   love of children, 51, 201–2
   obliviousness, 246–7
   Oxford, 214–15
   "over-understood," coopted by father, 233–4, 238–45: themes and images from S. T. Coleridge; 171–2n.20
   personae, 204–5
   Romantic Child, prototype of , 213, 216–32, 247–8, 249: child of joy, 229; child of nature, 217–24; and "The Foster Mother's Tale," 217–9; self-sufficient, 223–4; scripted by father as, 234–5

sobriquets: "Mystagogus," 203; "Coleridge the Less," 238
Tristram Shandy, 235–6: Shandyesque style, 271n.19; Uncle Toby, as 206
Wilkie draws, 196
Works
  "Adolf and Annette," 237–8, 272n.21
  "The Anemone," 206
  Biographia Borealis, 215
  "To a Deaf and Dumb Little Girl," 22–3, 208
  "To Dear Little Katy Hill," 5, 209
  "Dedicatory Sonnet to S. T. Coleridge," 216, 244
  "The Dunce's Execration of Latin," 205
  "To Elizabeth Anne Burns," 205–6
  "Fain I would dive to find my infant self," 210
  "The First Birthday," 203
  "Full well I know—my Friends—ye look on me," 238
  Hartley Coleridge Papers, 191–251
  "Hi diddle dides" (Latin "Hey Diddle diddle"), 270n.8
  "In the Manner of a Child of Seven Years Old," 205
  "To an Infant, Written on a Snowy Day," 208
  "To Jeannette, Six Weeks Old," 202, 212
  "To K. H. I.," 210
  "The Lily of the Valley," 206
  "To Little Annie Gibson," 208
  "Lolly pops and nice mint drops," 202
  "Long time a child, and still a child, when years," 212
  "No Doubt 'tis Heresy or Something Worse," 271–2n.20
  Notebooks: "Dry Leaves Dropping on the Surface of Lethe," 203; "Omnium Gatherum," 202; "Another Brick from Babel," 203; "Bricks without Mortar from the Ruins of Babel," 203; Gripes and Grumblings," 203; "Horae Otissime," 203; "The Waste Book and Daily Chronicle," 197, 203
  "Nursery Lecture by an Old Bachelor," 9
  "Of Such is the Kingdom of God," 211
  "To the Old Year," 212–13
  "On an Infant's Hand," 209
  "On Pride," 271–2n.20
  Poems, 215
  "The Sabbath-Day's Child, " 211
  "The Tale," 214
  "Where dwells the soul through all the dateless years," 207

  "Written in a Bible," 212
  "Youth, love, and mirth, what are they but the portion," 304
Coleridge, Joan, 269n.1
Coleridge, Samuel Taylor, 87, 119, 123, 125, 172, 184
  autobiographical letters, 225
  Barbauld, 147
  childhood idealism: as norm, 14; Hartley's, 14, 245
  childhood plentitude, 6
  childhood thought, 13, 16–17
  children as nature: plants, 9; breeze, 9–10
  empathy and self-forgetfulness, 17–18; 240–1
  fairy tales, 20–21
  Greek grammar for Hartley, 194
  Hartley in 1806–7, 191–213
  Hartley's muse, 237–9: as "White Lady," 237–8
  marginalia on Hartley, 272n.23
  "metaphysical" letters to Wedgwood, 226
  over-identification with Hartley, 233–44: "over-understanding", 227; ventriloquizing Hartley, 233–4; relationship with Hartley, 191–251
  sobriquets: "Phosporus," 203; Ho Makarites 192, 193
  works
    The Ancient Mariner, 237–8
    "Christabel," 5, 216, 217, 237
    "Epitaph on an Infant," 128
    "The Foster Mother's Tale," 217–19
    "Frost at Midnight," 73, 78, 208, 216, 219, 220–1, 234, 243
    "Kubla Khan," 116, 237
    "The Nightingale," 216, 217, 221–2, 241
Coleridge, Sara (daughter), guilt toward Coleridge, 242
  Phantasmion, 237
  sadness, 273n.25
Coleridge, Sara (wife), 213
  affectionate mother, 231
  disprized, 246
  fostered filial respect, 232
Corelli, Marie, *Boy,* 20, 260n.9
Coveney, Peter, 255n.4
  dating cult of childhood, 254n.2
Crabb Robinson, Henry, 87, 228
  Hartley Coleridge's idealism, 14
credulity, praise of, 22–3
  by Wordsworth and Coleridge, 20–21
Cunningham, Hugh, 30

Davy, Humphrey, 10, 192
Dawes, John, 214, 215, 232, 246
Day, Thomas, 65–6; *Sandford and Merton,* 66
De Luca, Vincent, 167
De Quincey, Elizabeth Penson (mother of Thomas De Quincey), 133–6, 137, 189
  models dire mother figures, 136–7
De Quincey, Emily (daughter), 182, 185
De Quincey, Florence (daughter), 181
De Quincey, Margaret (wife), size, 185
De Quincey, Thomas, 20, 107, 129–90
  anorexia, 180–90
  childhood in Manchester, 133–5
  "constituents of happiness," 166
  eating habits, 185–90, 268n.18: in diary, 186–7
  fixation on childhood, xiii
  Gombroon, 3, 154–9; list of great poets, 170
  littleness, 166, 180–90
  love of children, 180, 181
  love of Catherine Wordsworth, 130–1, 174
  size, 183–4: mocked by Carlyles, 183; Maginn, 183; Dora Wordsworth, 184; Lamb, 184; bemuses Dorothy Wordsworth, 184; Southey, 184; as willful, 184
  women: intellectual, 136: hostility to women writers, 136–7
  Wordsworth, William: adulation of *Lyrical Ballads,* 175–6; discoverer of childhood, 2, 44–5; fear of, 179–80; hero-worship of, 166–80; memorization of, 169–70; *The Prelude,* borrowed manuscript of, 169–70; symbiotic with, 179–80; surrogate for, 173–5
  Works
    "The Affliction of Childhood," 163
    "Infant Literature," 145–52, 179–80
    "Introduction to the World of Strife," 152
    "Levana and Our Ladies of Sorrow," 143
    The Literature of Knowledge and the Literature of Power," 159, 160
    "The Nursery in the Desert," 268n.7
    "The Revolt of the Tartars," 145
    "The Spanish Military Nun," 145
    "The Theban Sphinx," 145
    "Walking Stewart," 145
    Confessions of an English Opium Eater, 163, 164, 186, 187
    The English Mail Coach, 135, 164
    Recollections of the Lakes and the Lake Poets, 164
    The Stranger's Grave, 169
    Suspiria de Profundis, 143, 164, 169, 176
De Quincey, William (son), death, 181; 184, 189
  post-mortem, 269n.16

De Vere, Aubrey, 200–1
Demos, John, 39
Devlin, D. D., 167
Dickens, Charles, *Our Mutual Friend,* 15
"discovery of childhood," 1–2, 44–5, 254n.2
Douglas, Wallace, 264n.46

Easthope, Antony, 58, 82
Eating, Lamb and, 118–28
  De Quincey, and, 180–90
  see also anorexia
Eaton, Horace, 171
Edax (Lamb character), 119, 121, 126
Edgeworth, Maria, 136–7
  compared to Barbauld, 136
  developmental view of childhood, xiv–xv
  mocked by Lamb, De Quincey, xiv–xv
  The Parent's Assistant, 147
Edgeworth, Richard, 20, 65
Edmundson, Mark, 54, 259n.3
Eilenberg, Susan, 261n.22
Ejuxria (imaginary kingdom), "The History of Saint Malo," 245
Elia (Lamb persona), 87–8, 89, 90–1, 114, 265n.5, n.5
  changeling, 114
Emerson, Ralph Waldo, child as "perpetual Messiah," 3
  child as embodiment of Natural Law, 7
  empathy, and attachment theory, 239–40
  Coleridge's, 240–1
  morally ambiguous, 272–3n.24
  self-forgetfulness, 17–18
Eolian Harp, 271n.14, 272n. 20
Erl-King (Goethe), xii–xiii, xv
eudaemonia, 263n.37
  recalled by De Quincey, 142
  Wordsworth's possible reading of, 263n.36
Essential Child, *see also* Romantic Child
  antiquity, 8–9
  Canton on, 8
  conservative force, 8
  dynamism of, 9–11
  embodied in Hartley Coleridge, 200
  embodiment of Natural Law, 7–8
  essential child vs. actual existing child, 24–5
  fungible, 5
  Hartley Coleridge on, 8–9
  immutable, 8
  mental qualities of, 13–30: animism, 18–19; poet, 18–19; non-specialist, 18–19; idealism, 13–15; vision, 19–22; unitary

thought, holism, imagination, 15–18; autonomy in solitude, 20–21, 22–4
outside institutions of culture, 24–5
redeemer, 3–4, 254–5n.3
timeless, 67
ungendered 107
Evelyn, John, 31
evolution, prefigured in Child, 11–13

fairy tales, 230–21
The Father's Assistant, De Quincey's patriarchal misprision, 147
fathers, non-attachment of, 58
  failure of, in "Michael," 59–61
feral child, 65
fixation on childhood, xi–xiv
Fleming, Dinah, 202, 215
Fleming, Marjory, 18; as Romantic prodigy, 32–3
Fletcher, Eliza, 202
folkloric tradition in Wordsworth, 64–5
food, and Lamb, 118–28
Fox, Caroline, 200
Fox, Sarah, 201, 202
Freud, Sigmund, introjection, 117
Froebel, Friedrich, child as idol, 254–5n.3
  childhood as nature, 255n.4
  children and gardens, 6
  Child Study, 4

gardens, and children, 6, 9
Garlitz, Barbara, 255n.4
Garrett, G. T. 158
Gaull, Marilyn, 64, 260n.11, 262n.26, n.27
  Wordsworth's boyhood, 47, 49
genius, the Child as, 6
gender, 136–7; 265n.5
Gilbert, Ann, "The Stolen Child," 95
Gill, Stephen, 61
Glass, John, 94
Godwin, William, 196, 122–23, 231
Goldman, Albert, 267n.2
Gombroon, 154–59
"Goody Two Shoes," 203, 212
Gosse, Edmund, child's resistance to father, 249–50
Gould, John, 269n.19
Greta Hall, 197, 213, 232
Griggs, Earl Leslie, 196, 202
Grimaldi, Joseph, 150, 193

Hall, Mrs. Samuel, 142
Hall, Samuel, De Quincey's guardian, 137

Hamlet, 79
  Wordsworth and, 49, 72, 82
  Wordsworth's "Hamlet vocation," 82, 84
Hammond, J. L. and Barbara, 93
Hanway, Jonas, 95
Harry Ransom Humanities Research Center, 269n.1
Hartley Coleridge Papers, 269n.1, 191–251
Hartley, David (philosopher), 217
Hartley, David (philosopher), Coleridge rejects, 226, 227
Hartman, Geoffrey, "eudaemonia," xii
Hauser, Caspar, Hartley's response, 247
Hazlitt, William, 102, 258n.3; "Staccanto," 203
Heinzelman, Kurt, 67
Ho Makarites 'Ο Μακαρίτης, 236, 238; Hartley's term for Coleridge, 270n.3
Hofland, Barbara, xiv; "Frank and Will," 95
Hogg, James, 186
Holland, John, 95
Hopkins, Brooke, 82, 259n.3, 262n.28
Hopkins, Gerard Manley, 58
Hudson, J.C., 95–6
Hume, David, Coleridge rejects, 227
Hunt Leigh, 87, 88, 108
  "Deaths of Little Children," 46–7
  fixation on childhood, xiii
  "Skimpole," xiii
Hunt, Thornton, 108–9, 111, 113, 271n.16
  Lamb's "favorite child," 88
Hutchinson (later Wordsworth), Mary, 61
Hutchinson, Sara, 191, 193, 197, 218, 229, 230
  obliquely wooed, 243–4

idealism, normal in children, 13–15
  Hartley Coleridge's boyhood idealism, 14
  Piaget's "realism," 27
  Wordsworth's, 13
idolatry, toward the Child, 38–9, 254–5n.3
  toward Wordsworth, 168–80
imaginary kingdoms: Allestone (Malkin), 3; Ejuxria (Hartley Coleridge), 3; Gombroon (De Quincey), 3; Gombroon and Tigrosylvania, 153–9; Gondal and Gaaldine (Brontes), 3; Never-Never Land (Barrie), 3
innocence, term infrequent in Wordsworth, 56–7
  cant of, 57
involutes, compared with spots of time, 162–4, 168
integration, of childhood and adulthood, in female Romantics, xiv
introjection of child self, 117–28
isolation of child and childhood, 63, 63–85
  experimentally isolated, 65–6
  feral child, 65

isolation of child and childhood (*continued*)
  incommunicability, 72–7
  by rhetorical emphases, 69–71
  self-sufficiency, 77–85

Jackson, William, 231
  Ejuxria, 245
Jacobus, Mary, 57, 71, 72
James (servant), 83
Jameson, Frederic, 162
Jean Paul, *see* Richter
Jekyll, Gertrude, *Children and Gardens,* 6
Johnston, Kenneth, 76
Jordan, John, 167
Jordan, John, 267n.2

Kant, Immanuel, Coleridge affirms his doctrine, 226–7
Keble, John, 26, 46
  innocence of Judas, 56–7
  Lyra Innocentium, 56
  Wordsworth as Primary Poet, 258n.3
Key, Ellen, *The Century of the Child,* 4
Kilvert, Robert Francis, childspotting, 41, 42, 44
  Gipsy Lizzy, 26
  Wordsworth as ideal, 42
Kincaid, James, 130
  childhood memory, 165
  "child-loving," xii
  Essential Child as ungendered, 5
Klein, Melanie, introjection, 117
Knight, Charles, 182
Knoepflmacher, U. C., 45, 255n.4
Kohut, Heinz, 244, 273n.24
  empathy, 239
Kuhn, Reinhard, 255n.4

Lamb, Charles, 87–128, 134, 172, 192
  age-youth link, 114–16
  avoiding term "child," 35
  Blake, 97–101
  boy-man, 87–91
  chimney sweepers, 101–6
  distinction between adulthood and childhood, 2–3
  food, 118–28
  Hartley Coleridge," 225
  oxymorons, 111–13
  racism: 265–5n.6; *Othello,* 265–6n.6
  Thornton Hunt, 108–9, 111, 271n.16
  walled precincts, 101–11
  Works
    "The Adventures of Ulysses," 122–3

"A Bachelor's Complaint of the Behaviour of Married People," 88, 126
"Blakesmoor in H___shire," 110, 111
"The Child Angel," 87, 106–8
"Christ's Hospital Five and Thirty Years Ago," 89
"The Dessert,"127
"A Dissertation upon Roast Pig," 123, 127
"Dream Children," 110, 116–7
Essays of Elia, 97
"The Gipsy's Malison," 88
"Grace before Meat," 126
"*Hospita* on the Immoderate Indulgence of the Pleasures of the Palate," 123, 126
Mrs. Leicester's School, 113
"New Year's Eve," 89
"The Old Benchers of the Inner Temple," 110
"On an Infant Dying as Soon as Born," 112
"Parental Recollections," 113
Poetry for Children, 97
"Popular Fallacies," 105
"The Praise of Chimney Sweepers," 97, 98, 103–5, 121
"Recollections of Christ's Hospital," 110
"The Superannuated Man," 114
"A Sylvan Surprise," 97, 102
"To T.H.L., A Child," 108–9, 112
"That Home is Home though it is Never so Homely," 105–6
"The Witch Aunt," 113
"Witches, and Other Night Fears," 89, 108, 113
Lamb, Elizabeth (mother of Charles Lamb), 89, 90
Lamb, John (brother of Charles Lamb), 89, 122
Lamb, John (father of Charles Lamb), 89, 90
Lamb, Mary, 89, 192
  psychotic break, relapses, 90
  Works: "Breakfast," 125; "The Changeling," 114; "Choosing a Profession," 97, 102; *Mrs. Leicester's School,* 113; *Poetry for Children,* 97; "The Two Boys," 124; "The Young Mahometan," 113
Lamb, Sarah (aunt), 89
Landor, Walter Savage, 2
Laslett, Peter, 67
Lefebure, Molly, 197
Lempriere, J., *Classical Dictionary,* 143
Lepus (Lamb persona), 118, 128
Les Miserables, 259n.8
Levana, 129, 145
  Richter's *Levana* vs. De Quincey's, 142–44
Lewis, Monk, 193, 263n.36

Lindop, Grevel, 130, 182–3, 268n.12
  De Quincey family size, 269n.17
Little Lord Fauntleroy (Burnett), 46
littleness, 264–5n.48
  chimney sweepers', 96–7
  De Quincey's, 180–90
  Hartley Coleridge's, 200
  "L" for little, in Elia, 265n.5
Liu, Alan, 56, 85
  normal orphanhood, 66–7, 71
  panoramic spots of time, 71
Lloyd, Charles, 129, 145, 172–3
Locke, John, Coleridge rejects, 226
Logan, William, child as idol, 254–5n.3
Longfellow, Henry Wadsworth, 9
loss, pathologies of, in Wordsworth's poetry, 67–85
Lucas, E. V., 119, 122

MacIntyre, Alasdair, on narrative, 236
MacKenzie, John, 286n.10
Maginn, William, 183
Malkin, Thomas, 18; Allestone, 3, 24
Malson, Lucien, 65
Marcus, Steven, 75, 80, 264n.44
Maria Edgeworth, 20
Marlowe, Christopher, "The Passionate Shepherd to his Love," 109
Marvell, Andrew, "The Garden," 110
Matthews, Gareth, 226
McDonagh, Josephine, 267n.2
McFarland, Thomas, 265n.5
McGann, Jerome, 24
McGavran, James Holt, 45, 47, 260n.12
meat-eating, 118, 123, 125–7
Meynell, Alice, anti-prodigy, 31
  child as different species, 2
  child as nature, 7
  "Two Boyhoods," 19
Meynell, Wilfred, discovery of childhood, 2
Mill, John Stuart, 31, 32, 156, 215
Miller, J. Hillis, 39, 139, 267n.2
Miller, Karl, 178
Milton, John, 137, 138–9
  De Quincey as Satan, 267n.4
  double of Wordsworth, 177
Mishra, Vijay, 166
Monboddo, Lord, 155
Monsman, Gerald, 115
Montagu, Anna, 194, 195, 196, 232
Montagu, Basil, 52–53, 75
Montgomery, James, 51, 98, 103
  Works: *The Chimney Sweeper's Friend and Climbing Boy's Album*, 91, 95–101; "The Dream," 96; "Easter Monday at Sheffield," 96–7
moon, and Hartley Coleridge, 218, 220, 224
  in Indian poem in Coleridge notebook, 271n.18
  joint attention to, 221
  moon-child axis, 222
  in S. T. Coleridge's poetry, 271n.15
Moore, Thomas, 91
Morrison, Arthur, *A Child of the Jago*, 36
mothers, Wordsworth's mother recalled, 45
  ineffectual, 57–8
Mozley, Thomas, 214–15
Mudge, Bradford, 273n.25
Muloch, Dinah, child as idol, 254–5n.3
Myers, Mitzi, 45, 46, 47, 255n.4
Mysore 157; Mysore Wars, 157–8

Needham, George, 37
Nesbit, E. (Edith Bland), 263n.35
Newlyn, Lucy, 271n.13
Nitrous Oxide, 10, 223, 224
  metaphor for Hartley Coleridge, 9, 243–3
non-children
  canny children, 105–6
  old children, 35–6
  prodigies, 30–4
  street arabs, 34–8
  see also children of the poor

Old age, identified with childhood, 114–16; 198
  see also antiquity
Onorato, Richard, 264n.46
Opium Wars, 154, 152
The Oriental Moralist, 268n.7
orphan, Wordsworth as, 47
  advantages of being, 55–6
orphanhood, as ordinary, 66–7

parent, rejection of and creativity, 73–5
  resistance to, 74–7
parenthood, freedom from, 85
  ineffective institution, 57
  liberation from, 61–63
pariahs, 37, 144–5
  Aesop as, 146
  child-victims as 144–8
  Hobson-Jobson, 267–8n.5
  Opium Eater as, 145
  Ruth as, 176
  Wordsworth, Coleridge, and De Quincey as, 167
Parker, Reeve, 60–1
Parsons, Talcott, 60

Pasternak, Boris, 53, 260–1n.15
Pattison, Robert, 255n.4
Penrose, Thomas, on De Quincey's list of poets, 171
Penson, Thomas, 156
Percival, Thomas, 146
  "A Generous Return for an Injury," 147
  Parental Instructions (a.k.a. *A Father's Instructions to His Children*), 147
Percy's Reliques of Ancient English Poetry, 64
Perrault, Charles (author), 203
Perrault, Claude (architect), 203
Pestalozzi, Johann Heinrich, Child Study, 4
Phaedrus, misquoted, 146
Philips, Ambrose, 112
Philips, C. H., 268n.9
Phillips, George, 94
Piaget, Jean, animism, 28, 256n
  authoritarianism and childhood psychology, 29
  childhood cognition, 26–30
  moral self-regulation in childhood, xiv
  "realism" or "a-dualism," 27
  reinforces and critiques Romantic analysis, 26–30
  syncretist childhoods thinking, 27–8
  see also idealism
Platzner, Robert, 267n.2
Pollack, Linda, 258n.3
Poole, Thomas, 14, 214, 241
  Berkeley Coleridge's death, 229
  Hartley Coleridge's idealism, 228–9
Porter, David, 93
Porter, Roger, 267n.2
power and the child, 25
  Coleridge, 25–6
  Keble, 26
  Kilvert, 26
  in painting, 25–26
Priestley, Joseph, 10
"Princes in the Tower," 62
prodigies, 30–4
  deplored, 31–32: by Meynell, 31; by Mill, 31; by Wordsworth, 31–2; by Canton, 32
"puer aeternus," 39

Quincey (later De Quincey), Elizabeth Penson (mother of Thomas De Quincey). *See* De Quincey, Elizabeth
Quincey, Elizabeth (sister of Thomas De Quincey), 134, 144, 144, 145, 165, 181, 189
  death, 137–41, 162
  and "We are Seven," 176–7
Quincey, Jane (sister of Thomas De Quincey), 134
Quincey, Richard ("Pink," brother), physical vigor, 184

Quincey, Thomas (father of Thomas De Quincey), 133–4, 153
Quincey, William (brother of Thomas De Quincey), 134, 152–9, 184

Randel, Fred, 90, 119–20, 128
Rank, Otto, Family Romance, 142
Rea, John, 271n.13
regression, in Bowen's adults, 43
  in Hartley Coleridge, 198
  in object relations theory, 270n.6
  in "Ruth," 180–1
Rehder, Robert, 82
Richardson, Alan, 30, 77, 255n.4, 258n.3
Richter, Jean Paul, 115, 132; *Levana*, 142–3
Riehl, Joseph, 265n.4
Riewald, J.G., 259n.1
Riley, James Whitcomb, *A Child-World*, 4
Roberts, Samuel, 92, 96, 100
Robinson Crusoe, 193, 213
  isolation in, 65–6
  loved but never completed by Hartley, 246
Roe, Nicholas, 263–4n.41
Rogers, Samuel, 91
Roman, Laura, 155
Romantic Child, Hartley Coleridge stars as, 213, 216–32
  produced by Coleridge and Wordsworth, 216–30
  see also Essential Child
Romantic Discourse of childhood, 5–30
Romantic Ideology, and Essential Child, 24
Rose, Jacqueline, 255n.4
Rousseau, Jean Jacques, 29, 65, 66
  Emile, 80
  praised by Day, 254n.2
Runciman, James, 36–7
  poor children as parasites, 37
  poor children as savages, 38
Russett, Margaret, 167, 277n.2; 268–9n.13; 269n.15
Rzepka, Charles, 157, 160, 2676n.2

Schiller, Friedrich von, 6, 87, 99, 101, 220, 254–5n.3
  On Naïve and Sentimental Poetry, 6
Schleiermacher, Friedrich, 12
Schopenhauer, Arthur, 6
Scoggins, James, 110
Scott, Walter, 32, 74, 91, 97, 192
  The Surgeon's Daughter, 158
Scudder, Horace, career in juvenile literature, 253–4n.1
  discovery of childhood, 1–2

separation, of childhood from adulthood, 106–17
  as continent, 1, 2
  as discipline, 4
  as different species, 2–3
  in imaginary kingdoms, 5
  in oxymoronic utopia, 111–4
  male Romantics on, xiv; 3–4
  in sequestered realm, xv, 3–4, 108–17
Shaftesbury, Anthony Ashley Cooper, Lord, 34–35, 37, 51
Shlien, John, 273n.24
Silverman, Kaja, 156
Simpson, David, 263n.41
Smart, George, 94
solipsism, Wordsworth and, 50
  Piaget and, 27
  see also solitude
solitude, as defining childhood, 22–4, 160–1
  honored: in Hartley Coleridge, 23; in De Quincey, 23; in Wordsworth, 23
  Piaget on, 29
  see also solipsism
Sommerville, C. J, 38, 39
Southey, Cuthbert, 231
Southey, Robert, 172, 214, 197
  deplores De Quincey's carelessness, 182
  Hartley as "Moses," 225
  hears Hartley Coleridge's history of future kings of England
  "philagathos," 232
  The Doctor, 271n.19
Spivak, Gayatri, 58
splitting, in object relations theory, 270n.6
spots of time and involutes, 162–4,168
Stansfield, Richard, 93
Steedman, Carolyn, littleness, 264–5n.48
Stern, Daniel., 239
Sterne, Laurence, discussed by Coleridge in 1807, 193
  Sentimental Journey, 193
  *Tristram Shandy,*193, 235: Shadyesque names at Greta Hall, 235; model of regressive self-reflexive deferral, 236; Uncle Toby, 195, 206, 213
Stevens, Robert, 100–1
Steward, James Christen, *The New Child,* 63–4
Stone, Lawrence, 39
Strickland, Charles, 260n.9
Strong, Roy, 262n.24
suffering, childhood, foregrounded in De Quincey autobiography, 129–34

superfoetation, 115, 128
  see also introjection
Swinburne, Algernon, 20, 206

Tave, Stuart, 167
Taylor, Anya, 271n.11
Tennyson Turner, Charles, "Letty's Globe," 11
Tertullian, *Ad Nationes,* 1439n.8
Thackeray, William Makepeace, 87
Thelwall, John, 76, 77, 263–45n.41
Thompson, Edward, 158
Thompson, Francis, 206
Tigrosylvania, 154–59
  see Mysore, 157
Tipu Sultan, 157–8
"transitional object" (Winnicott), and "Alice Fell," 73
Trivedi Servoru Sarman, 271n.18
Tussaud, Madame, 62, 262n.24
Twain, Mark, 32

Vallon, Annette, 61, 62
Valsamis, Marius, 269n.16
Varro, *Lingua Latina,* 143
Victorian Child Romance, 42, 43
vocation of childhood, xi
  among male Romantics, xiv

"waifs and strays," 37–8, 257n.13
Ward, J. P., 258n.3
Warner, Marina, 45, 255n.4
Wedgwood, Josiah, 226
Wedgwood, Thomas, 65
Whittier, John Greenleaf, 4, 254n.3, 261n.16
Wiener, David, 262n.27
Wiggin, Kate Douglas, 15
Wilkie, David, 192, 232
  academician, 270n.4
  "The Blind Fiddler," 196, 197
Williams, John, 76
Williams, William K., 180
Wilson, John, 185–6, 269n.18
Wilson, Mrs. ("Wilsy," Greta Hall housekeeper), 201, 231–2, 267
Winnicott, D. W., 81–2, 248, 259n.3, 262n.28
  "good enough" parent, 52
  "transitional object," 73
Wollstonecraft, Mary, xiv
Wordsworth, Caroline (illegitimate daughter) 52, 61, 62, 63
Wordsworth, Catherine (daughter), 167, 172, 173, 180, 181; death, 53, 161
  De Quincey's love for, 130–1, 174

Wordsworth, Dora (daughter), 184
Wordsworth, Dorothy, 52, 61, 62, 72, 184, 185, 196, 245–6, 261n.17
  criticizes Sara Coleridge, 231
  on De Quincey, 174, 175–6
  on hopeless Hartley Coleridge, 270n.2
  servants' insults, 83
Wordsworth, John (father), 68
Wordsworth, John (son), bad reader, 52
  De Quincey's understanding of, 173–4, 180
  possible dyslexia, 53, 261n.17
Wordsworth, Mary, 52, 173, 190
Wordsworth, Thomas (son), death, 53
Wordsworth, William, 16, 20, 27, 28, 41–85, 91, 97, 129–30, 214
  Aladdin magician, 179–80
  animism in, 19
  anti-surveillance, 53
  attacks analytic training, 17
  autobiographical memorandum, 47–9
  boyhood idealism, 13
  capitalization, 5
  child labor, 51–2
  childhood anger, 48–9
  chimney sweepers, 51
  dangers of parental presence, 54–5, 56
  De Quincey's devotion to, 166–80: allusions to, 168–9
  educating the gifted child, 54–5
  fixation on childhood, xiii
  "good-enough father," 52
  Hartley Coleridge, compared to, 51
  lost girls, 167
  mother, 48
  not child-lover, 51
  orphan, 47, 66
  as parent and guardian, 52–5
  pariah, 167
  produces Romantic Child, 216
  solipsism, 50
  spots of time, 83–4; and involutes, 168
  tragic childhood personality, 48–9
  Works: "Address to my infant Daughter," 72
  "Address to the Scholars of the Village School of ____," 72
  "Alice Fell,"67, 69, 73
  "Anecdote for Fathers," 17, 75–7
  "Beggars," 74
  "The Blind Highland Boy," 22, 69, 74
  "Catechising," 48
  "Characteristics of a Child Three Years Old," 77, 78
  "Convention of Cintra," 173
  "The Danish Boy," 79
  "An Evening Walk," 57
  The Excursion, 51
  "The Fountain," 58
  "To H. C., Six Years Old," 78, 216, 223, 234
  "Her Eyes are Wild," 79
  "Home at Grasmere," 50
  "The Idiot Boy," 22, 74
  "In Sight of the Town of Cockermouth," 52
  "Infant M____ M____," 77
  "It is a Beauteous Evening, Calm and Free," 61–3, 71
  "The Kitten and the Falling Leaves," 77
  "Lucy Gray," 79
  Lyrical Ballads, 171, 196, 197: De Quincey's enthusiasm for, 175
  "Michael," 46, 59–61
  "The Norman Boy," 70, 77
  "Ode: Intimations of Immortality," 15, 58–9, 69, 216
  "Personal Talk," 77
  "The Pet Lamb," 72
  "The Poet's Dream," 70
  "Preface to *Lyrical Ballads,*" 169
  The Prelude, 15, 17, 19, 21–2, 31–2, 50, 55–6, 57, 69, 71, 77, 82, 84, 163, 166–7: as model for De Quincey, 168: manuscript lent to De Quincey, 169–70
  "Ruth," 79–81, 175, 219
  "Sequel to the Beggars," 74
  "The Solitary Reaper," 69, 70
  "Surprised by Joy," 53
  Theater Child (*Prelude* 7), 71–2, 74
  "There Was a Boy" (Boy of Winander), 23, 69–60, 71, 77, 82, 218
  "Three Years She Grew in Sun and Shower," 78–9
  "Tintern Abbey," 179
  "Two April Mornings, 58, 69
  "Vandracour and Julia," 56
  "We are Seven," xi, 15, 17, 25, 69, 134, 175, 262n.32; and "Ruth" as sibling poems, 174–7; and De Quincey, 170, 175; upper and lower-case in, 262–3n.34
Wordsworth, Willy (son), 88
Wordsworthian rescue narrative, 43–4
Wu, Duncan, 64, 262n.26

Youngquist, Paul, 166

Zizek, Slavoj, 5